Russia

BUSINESS SURVIVAL GUIDE

Third Edition

Russian Information Services
Montpelier, Vermont

Русская Информационная Служба
Москва, Российская Федерация

First edition: October 1990
Second edition: August 1991
Third edition: March 1992

Published by:
Russian Information Services
89 Main Street, #2
Montpelier, VT 05602 USA

in cooperation with:
Russkaya Informatsionnaya Sluzhba
B. Kondratyevskiy per. 4, kor. 2, kv. 168
Moscow, USSR 125056

Cover design by:
Marketing Arts
Bridge Street Marketplace
Waitsfield, VT 05673, USA

Moscow City Street Map by:
Northern Cartographic, Inc.
4050 Williston Rd.
South Burlington, VT 05403

Printed by:
Villanti & Sons, Printers
119 Industrial Ave.
Willison, VT 05495

Russian Information Services, Montpelier, VT USA

Library of Congress Catalog Card Number: 92-081080
ISBN 1-880100-06-1

Russia Business Survival Guide

Russia Business Survival Guide is a cogent, comprehensive briefing for persons traveling on business and/or pleasure to Russia. This publication is in a constant state of update, such that each publication of the guide is much like a snapshot of the state of doing business in Russia. The present snapshot was taken in March 1992.

Much has changed in Russia since the last publication of this guide (previously titled *Moscow Business Survival Guide*) in August of 1991. The failed August coup and its aftermath have torn the USSR into 15 new nation states. The consequent changes in the business atmosphere have been incredible. Those changes are reflected in the present edition, which takes as its focus Russia, rather than simply Moscow or the former Union.

Many significant changes have been introduced with this third publication of the Survival Guide. Not the least significant of these is the excellent new city street map of Moscow, created by Northern Cartographic of Burlington, VT. The Business Yellow Pages and Telephone Directory sections have also been totally reformatted to include even more useful information. Across sections, information and references are more interactive.

Editor-in-Chief of *Russia Business Survival Guide* is Paul Richardson. Associate editors are Stephanie Ratmeyer, S. Todd Weinberg and Bella Gubnitskaya. Contributors and reviewers include, David Kelley, Annemarie Wollam, Kate Moore and Fred Harrison.

Corrections and comments are enthusiastically encouraged. Please contact Russian Information Services at 28 East State, Montpelier, VT, 05602, ph. (802) 223-4955, fax (802) 223-6105 or, in Moscow, at Bolshoy Kondratyevskiy pereulok 4, korpus 2, kv. 168, phone/fax (095) 254-9275.

Russia Business Survival Guide is just one of a series of publications of Russian Information Services on doing business in Russia and the Commonwealth. Other publications include: *Where in Moscow and Where in St. Petersburg* (white and yellow page directories, with full color city maps); *Russian Business Reports*, a weekly newsletter; and *Business Legal Materials*, a compilation of legal acts of Russia on investment and foreign trade. For more information, contact Russian Information Services at the addresses above.

All information in this guide is the most authoritative information available at the time of printing.

The Editor
March 1992

''On entering the country of the Russians, one sees at a glance that the social order as arranged by them can serve only for their use. One must be Russian to live in Russia, although on the surface everything proceeds there as elsewhere. The difference is in fundamentals...''

Marquis de Custine, 1839

CONTENTS

Table of Contents

I. Reference Information 1

II. Preparations 45

III. Travel and Accommodations 63

VII. Doing Business 107

VIII. Russian Business Law 121

I. Reference Information

Time Zones of Russia and the Commonwealth

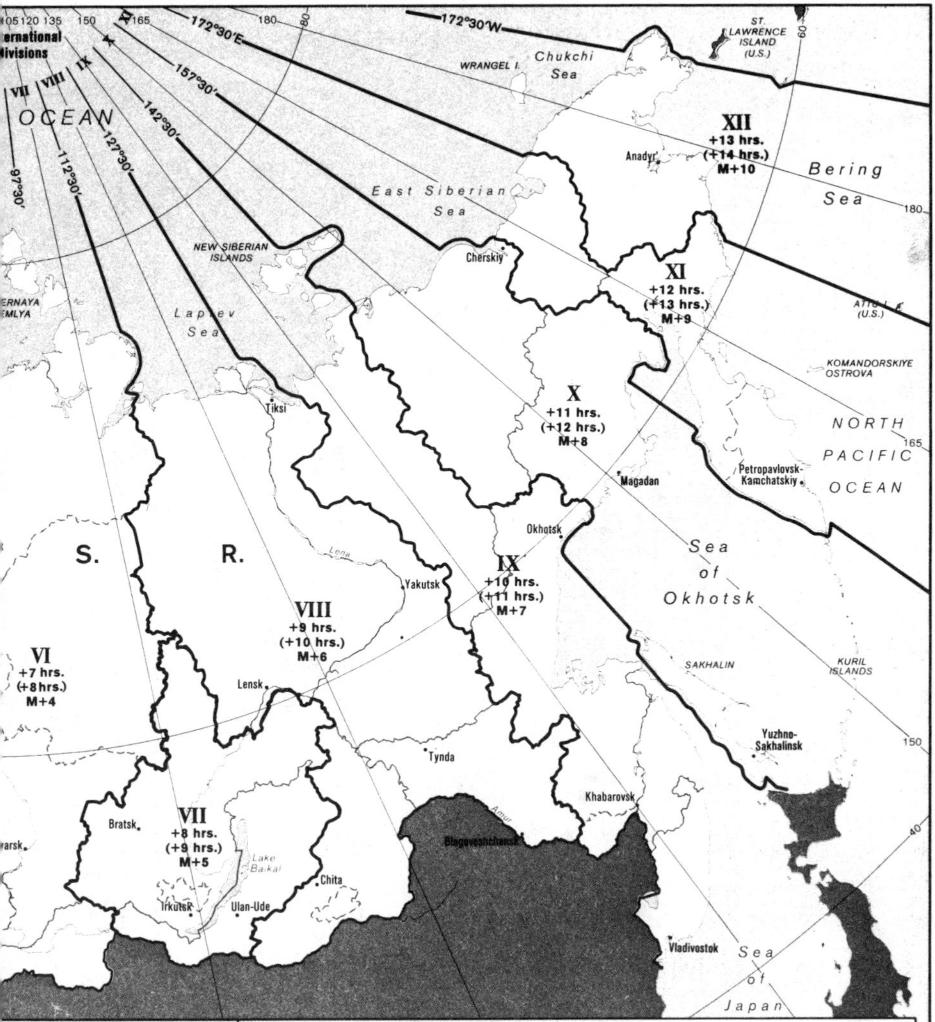

International Time Zone

rs. Number of hours ahead of Greenwich Mean Time (GMT or Z)

rs.) Number of hours ahead of GMT (1 April–1 October)

1 Number of hours ahead of Moscow Time

CIS-USA Time Difference Calculator

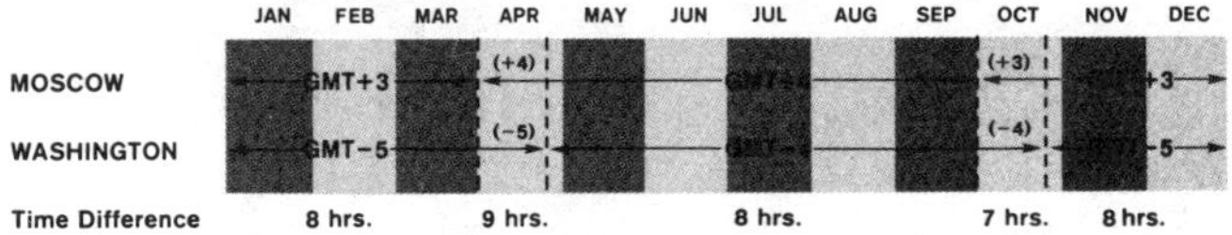

Daylight Savings Time

CIS Standard time plus 1 hour—year-round
Standard time plus 2 hours—1 April to 1 October

USA Standard time plus 1 hour—fourth Sunday in April to fourth Sunday in October

Average High and Low Temperatures, Moscow and St. Petersburg (°C)

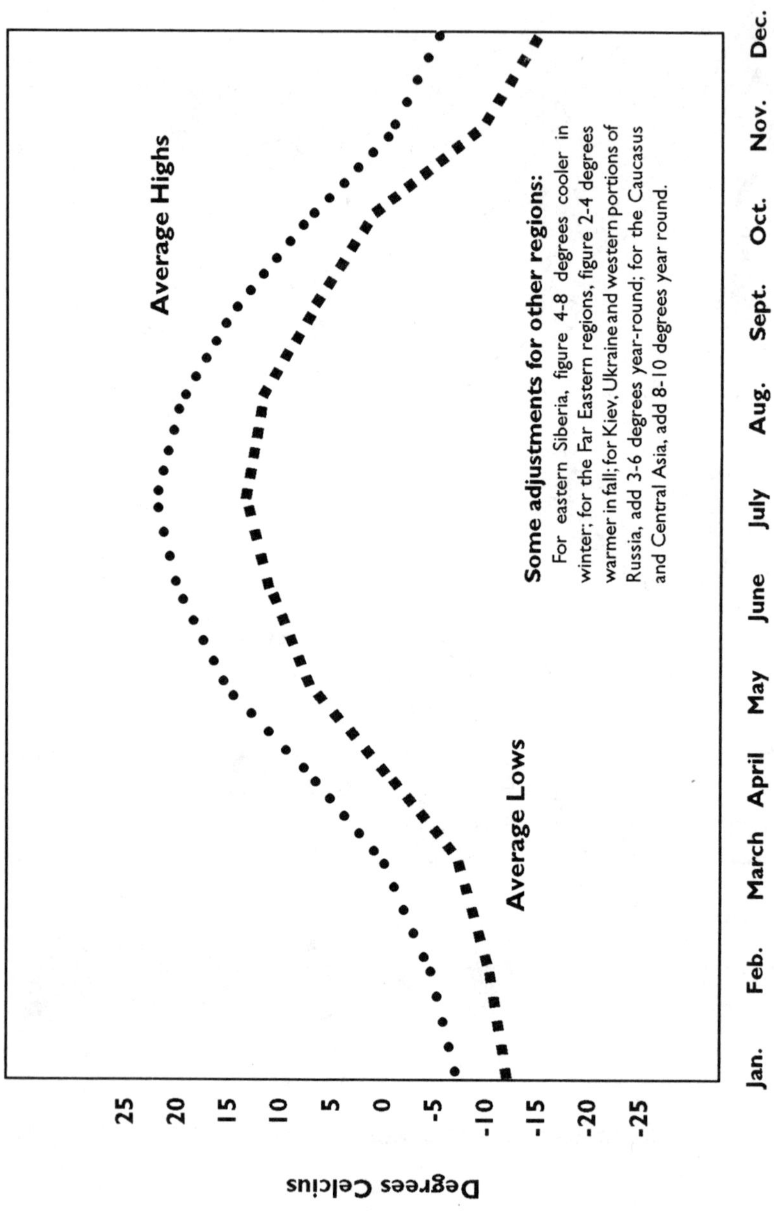

Russia Facts

Population of Russia, in millions: 148.7

Population which is male/female: 47%/53%

Percent of all Russian enterprises headed by women: 6.5%

Percent of all Russian medical doctors who are women: 66%

Number of years Russia was ruled by a communist government: 74

Inhabitants of Russia who are of Russian nationality: 81.5%

Students who are taught in the Russian language: 98.1%

Number of births/deaths per 1000 persons in Moscow: 10.5/12.8

Number of births/deaths per 1000 persons in St. Petersburg: 10.8/12.2

Russians eating under 7 oz. of meat monthly in 1990/1992: 20.9%/32.8%

Rank of Europe, Asia & America as destination for Russian exports: 1,2,3

Percent of Russian schools with a computer lab: 37.1%

Change in housing construction 1990-1991: -22%

Life expectancy of Russian males/females at birth (years): 63.8/74.3

Sales in 2nd hand stores 1985/1990 (mln. rubles): 2,397/6,255

Waste water dumped annually 1985/1990 (mln. m^3): 11,981/27,799

Increase in retail price index, 1991: 92%

Increase in average worker's monthly salary, 1991: 80%

Increase in average collective farmer's salary, 1991: 46%

Change in imports/exports, 1991: -46%/-29%

Percent of all Russian births by unmarried women: 11.2%

Number of abortions per 100 births: 134.2

A Short Chronology of Soviet History

1888 Crowning of Nicholas II, the last Russian Tsar.

1905 Russo-Japanese War and the First Russian Revolution, which results in minor compromises towards more democratic rule and the first Duma, or Parliament.

1914 World War I begins.

1917 The February "bourgeois" revolution deposes the Tsar and places a weak and ineffective Duma "in control". The Bolsheviks, a faction of the Russian Communist Party, seize power in the October "Revolution," a coup which overthrew the Duma after elections threatened to severely limit the Bolsheviks' power in local Soviets. The first act of the new Bolshevik government was to end Russian participation in the World War.

1918 Civil war breaks out between the Reds (Bolsheviks) and the Whites (mainly Monarchists).

1922 The USSR is founded after three years of civil war and the conquest by the Reds of the Ukraine, the Caucasus, and Central Asia.

1924 Vladimir Ilyich Ulyanov (Lenin), father of the Revolution, dies of a stroke.

1928 The first Five Year Plan is inaugurated; the liberal NEP (New Economic Plan) instituted by Lenin after the Civil War is set aside; Josef Stalin begins his rise to power by attacking Leon Trotsky and the left. He uses the post of General Secretary of the Party to engineer control, as this post has control over political appointments.

1936-7 While the purges lasted throughout the 1930s and, indeed, throughout Stalin's reign, they are at their worst in these dark years of Soviet history.

1939 The Molotov-Rippentrop pact divides Poland between the USSR and Germany and Stalin annexes the Baltic republics. Hitler's march into Poland begins WWII days after the pact is signed; Stalin's countermarch into divided Poland commences shortly thereafter.

1941 World War II begins for the USSR in June when Hitler invades the Soviet Union. The USSR will suffer huge casualties and near defeat as the Nazis broach the very outskirts of Moscow and blockade Leningrad for 900 days before the tide turns at the Battle of Stalingrad in 1943.

1945 World War II ends and Eastern Europe is ceded to the Soviet sphere of influence. One after another, Eastern European countries fall under communist rule.

1953 Josef Stalin dies. For three years Georgi Malenkov and Nikita Khrushchev vie for party leadership. The arrest and execution of Beria, Stalin's infamous head of the KGB, is the beginning of the end of the Great Terror of Stalin's reign.

1956 The 20th Party Congress signals Khrushchev's ascendancy as First Secretary of the Communist Party. His "secret speech" inaugurates a Thaw in the socio-political sphere. Meanwhile, Soviet tanks roll into Hungary when the indigenous regime attempts to declare an independent line and pull out of the Warsaw Pact.

1961 The Berlin Wall is erected after years of confrontation over administration rights and the status of Berlin.

1964 The "hair-brained" schemes of Nikita Khrushchev are brought to an end by a bloodless coup engineered while the leader was vacationing on the Black Sea. Leonid Ilyich Brezhnev adopts the post of General Secretary.

1968 Soviet tanks roll into Czechoslovakia and the Brezhnev Doctrine is born: It is the Soviet Union's duty (and right) to protect fraternal socialist regimes from counter-revolutionary threats from without or within.

1972 SALT II is signed, heralding in an era of detente with the West.

1979 Soviet tanks roll into Afghanistan, reinvigorating the cold war. They will stay for 8 years and cost nearly 2 million Afghan and Soviet lives.

1982 Leonid Ilyich Brezhnev dies; he is replaced by Yuri Andropov.

1984 Yuri Andropov dies; he is replaced by Konstantin Chernenko.

1985 Konstantin Chernenko dies in March. Mikhail Sergeevich Gorbachev becomes General Secretary of the Communist Party.

1986 A nuclear power plant at Chernobyl, in the Soviet Ukraine, explodes, irradiating Europe.

1987 January 13, joint ventures between Western firms and Soviet enterprises become possible. Cooperative firms, a form of private enterprise, are allowed.

1988 The last Soviet troops leave Afghanistan.

1989 Eastern European Communist States fall in succession: Hungary, Poland, Czechoslovakia, Romania, East Germany, and Bulgaria. The Berlin Wall comes down. In the USSR the new Congress of People's Deputies and a revamped Supreme Soviet are touted as an enfranchisement of the Soviet people.

1990 The Supreme Soviet slowly asserts more power and authority in society while that of the Party wanes. Laws on land ownership and private ownership of the means of production are passed. A new, stronger Presidency is created; Mikhail Gorbachev is elected to the post by a 59% majority in the Congress of People's Deputies. Lithuania is the first Soviet republic to test the limits of reform by declaring independence; the rest of the republics (excepting Kazakhstan) follow suit. After many aborted attempts at cooperation, jurisdictional and political battles flare between the republics and the central government.

1991 in Review

The year 1991 was the most tumultuous year in Russian and Soviet history at least since the second world war and perhaps since 1917. A union of nations which was bound together for centuries crumbled in the aftermath of a stunningly inept political coup; the Communist party was outlawed, as was the KGB; the Warsaw Pact dissolved and the cold war ended with a wimper; democracy and a market economy, neither having deep roots in Russian tradition or experience, were unequivocally established as the goals of these nations.

The signifiance of these events requires more detailed treatment, thus the chronology below.

January

1 In his New Year's address, USSR President Mikhail Gorbachev states "...the coming year is very important. This year a decision shall be taken about the fate of our multinational state. For all Soviet people, there is no more sacred task than the preservation and renewal of the Union, in which all its people shall live freely and well..."

13 Fourteen persons are killed and more than a hundred wounded in the storming of the Vilnius (Lithuania) press offices and radio tower by special Soviet forces (OMON).

22 A USSR Presidential decree is read on the nightly news program Vremya which calls for the removal from circulation of all 50 and 100 ruble notes in the next 72 hours. Some 8 billion rubles are removed from circulation.

26 Joint army and militia patrols of major cities are announced; a USSR Presidential decree is issued on "struggle with economic sabotage and other economic crimes," giving the militia broad rights to enter companies and enterprises and conduct "economic investigations."

31 A 5% sales tax is set in accordance with a December 29, 1990 decree to that effect. The tax takes effect March 1.

February

9 Lithuanian national referendum approves status of Lithuania as a independent and democratic republic. Two days later Iceland is the first state to recognize Lithuania.

12 Prime Minister Valentin Pavlov warns of secret plot by Western banks to wreck the Soviet economy.

18 Prime Minister Pavlov announces forthcoming price hikes. Hoarding of consumer goods begins.

19 Chairman of the Russian Supreme Soviet, Boris Yeltsin, announces on central television his categorical disagreement with the policies of President Gorbachev and calls for his resignation. A week of demonstrations for and against Yeltsin commences.

25 At an extraordinary meeting, the members of the Warsaw Pact agree to dissolve the military alliance before March 31, 1991.

March

1 A strike of coal miners begins in Kuzbass and quickly spreads throughout the country to include over 200 mines. The miners' main demands are for better pay and working conditions. They also call for Gorbachev's resignation. The strike will last two months.

3 Some 74% of Latvian voters in a national referendum vote for an independent Latvia; 78% of Estonian voters call for an independent Estonian state.

10 The largest public meeting since the advent of *perestroika* is held. Some 500,000 people come out in support of Yeltsin, the miners and Russian sovereignty.

17 A referendum is held on the fate of the Union. A "renewed federation of sovereign republics" is approved by 70% of voters across the USSR. In Russia, 71% vote in favor of a directly elected Russian President. In Ukraine 83% of voters approve sovereignty for that republic.

April

2 The Pavlov price increases are put into effect, raising prices an average of three to four times.

3 Pavlov holds discussions with striking miners and pledges to meet all economic demands, but conveys that President Gorbachev will not resign under pressure. Strikes continue.

23 President Gorbachev meets with leaders of nine republics (touted as 9 + 1 meeting) at Novo Ogareva. The leaders issue a joint communique calling for immediate measures to stabilize the country's political and economic situation. The leaders agree to scale back price increases, work on a Union treaty and hold nationwide elections.

24 Benchmark Communist Party (CPSU) meeting sees Gorbachev under fire as General Secretary, but rumours of his ousting are premature. Plenum announces that some 1.8 million persons quit the party in 1990, while only 108,000 joined.

30 Yeltsin goes to the Kuzbass to meet with miners and breaks the two month old strike with the pledge that Russia will assume jurisdiction over the mines.

May

6 Russian KGB is created through protocol signed between Yeltsin and KGB chief Kryuchkov.

12 The last Soviet SS-20 nuclear ICBM is destroyed in Kapustin Yar.

13 Russian TV begins regular broadcasting.

22 OMON troops attack customs points of Lithuanian republic.

25 Russian Supreme Soviet declares June 12 a Russian holiday, in honor of June 12, 1990, when Russia declared its sovereignty.

26 Presidential elections in Georgia vote in Parliamentary Chairman Zviad Gamsakhurdia with 79.4% of the vote.

June

5 President Gorbachev receives Nobel Peace Prize in Oslo.

12 Some 75% of Russian voters participate in the first popular Presidential election in Russian history and elect Boris Yeltsin with 57% of the vote. His closest rival, former Prime Minister Nikolai Ryzhkov, polls just 17% of the vote. The conservative Zhirinovskiy polls 8% of the vote to place third.

17 At the USSR Supreme Soviet, Prime Minister Pavlov announces the state budget deficit for the year has reached 39 billion rubles. The revenue losses attributable to the anti-alcohol campaign begun in the early eighties is put at 200 billion rubles. Pavlov and a handful of conservatives make a first move, calling for special powers for the government and declaration of a state of emergency.

21 Gorbachev stands up to the conservatives in the parliament, openly breaking with Pavlov and addressing him, saying, "Do not create problems. We must take care of business, not stoke the fires of public hysteria."

July

1 Official registration of the unemployed begins.

3 Former Foreign Minister Eduard Shevardnadze quits the Communist Party; Gorbachev meets again at Novo Ogarevo with republican leaders (9 + 1).

4 RSFSR law is passed, On Privatization of Municipal and State Enterprises and Housing.

10 Boris Yeltsin is sworn in as Russian President.

20 President Yeltsin issues a decree calling for removal of party organizations within institutions and organizations located on the territory of the RSFSR.

25 Routine plenum of the CPSU Central Committee. As it turns out this will be the last such plenum.

29 Gorbachev meets with Yeltsin and Nazarbaev (President of Kazakhstan), whereat the latter two urge him to make fundamental changes in the Union government, including removal of [future coup plotters] Yanaev, Pugo, Kryuchkov and others.

31 During US President Bush's visit to Moscow, he and Gorbachev sign the long-negotiated START treaty to reduce strategic nuclear weaponry; meanwhile 6 persons are killed in brutal attacks on Lithuanian customs points.

August

4 President Gorbachev departs for a vacation in the Crimea.

15 Aleksander Yakovlev, an architect of perestroika is first kicked out, then quits the Communist Party. In a document published on the 17th, he warns of "a party leadership preparing for social revanchism, for a party and state coup."

16 Draft of the Union treaty, to be signed on the 20th, is published in the press.

19 Beginning at 6 am, a declaration of a state of emergency, issued by the coup plotters, is announced over the various news channels. By 10 am, troops and tanks have taken up positions at key points in and leading to Moscow. Thousands of Muscovites surround the "White House" [Russian parliament and government building] to protect it from advancing tanks. At 12:30 Yeltsin mounts a tank and reads his message to the Russian people in which he calls formation of the State of Emergency Committee a coup.

20 Huge meetings take place in Leningrad and in front of the White House. An evening curfew is announced to begin at 11 pm.

21 Around 1 am in a skirmish with some tanks, three young Muscovites are killed. By morning, it is clear a storming of the White House will not occur, and at 11 am a special session of the RSFSR Supreme Soviet is convened. By evening, the coup plotters begin to back off and the coup falls apart.

22 Gorbachev returns to Moscow from Foros with a family noticeably shaken. The coup plotters are arrested. Interior Minister Pugo commits suicide. A huge public rally takes place before the White House. The Moscow mayor confiscates all CPSU property in Moscow. This also occurs in Leningrad.

24 Gorbachev quits as General Secretary of the CPSU and calls for its Central Committee to dissolve itself.

25 President Yeltsin issues a decree confiscating all CPSU property in Russia and abroad.

26 A special session of the USSR Supreme Soviet halts the activity of the CPSU and begins an investigation into the coup. Parliament Chairman Anatoly Lukyanov is implicated in the coup and is ousted from that post.

September

2 The special USSR Supreme Soviet session reopens with a proposal by Gorbachev and the leaders of 10 republics for a Confederation of Sovereign States. The dying central government and parliament set about erecting temporary governing bodies for a "transitional period." The US recognizes the independence of the three baltic states.

6 RSFSR Supreme Soviet resolves to return Leningrad its prior name of St. Petersburg. In its first act of the transitional period USSR State Council recognizes the independence of the baltic states.

8 Ayaz Mutalibov is elected in an uncontested election as first President of Azerbaidjan.

19 Belorussian republican Supreme Soviet declares the republic to be called Republic of Belarus.

21 Ninety-nine percent of residents of Armenia vote in favor of Armenian independence.

October

1 Alma Ata is the site for a meeting of delegations representing 13 of the former republics and independent states.

18 Leaders of eight sovereign states (Armenia, Belarus, Kazakhstan, Kirgyzistan, Tadzhikistan, Turkmenistan, Uzbekistan and Russia) and President Gorbachev sign a Treaty on Economic Cooperation.

23 By a Resolution of the USSR State Council, the KGB is abolished.

26 A referendum in Turkmenistan shows 94% favor independence.

28 At the Fifth Congress of People's Deputies of the RSFSR, Yeltsin comes out strongly in favor of radical economic reform. Ruslan Khasbulatov is elected Chairman of Parliament by 559 votes to 331.

30 USSR Gosbank issues 200 ruble notes.

31 RSFSR Congress of People's Deputies approves the new flag for Russia. Figures are released to show a poor harvest in comparison to 1990.

November

1 Russian President receives new powers under the Russian constitution, specifically, the right to halt the activity of legal acts of executive organs and any other bodies' decisions if they should contradict the Constitution or laws of the RSFSR.

6 Yeltsin issues a decree halting all activity of the CPSU on Russian territory and nationalizing all of its property.

8 Yeltsin declares a state of emergency in Chechen-Ingush where the new president, Dzhokhar Dudaev, was to be inaugurated.

11 Georgian President Gamsakhurdia declares that all USSR military forces located on Georgian territory are Georgian national property. Moldavian president Snegur follows suit.

14 In Novo Ogarevo leaders of seven republics agree on the formation of a Union of Sovereign States.

25 Yeltsin issues a decree calling for the "commercialization" of state retail enterprises before January 1, 1992.

December

1 A referendum in Ukraine sees 90% of voters cast votes in favor of national independence. Some 62% of voters also vote in favor of the state's first popularly elected president, Leonid Kravchuk. The first national direct presidential election in Kazakhstan sees the singular candidate, Nursultan Nazarbaev receive 98.6% of the vote.

3 Vnesheconombank institutes free sale of hard currency to citizens. The bank buys dollars for 90 rubles and sells them for 99.

4 Russian President Yeltsin issues a decree recognizing Ukraine.

8 In a swift turn of events, the leaders of Ukraine, Belarus and Russia meet outside Brest and sign a pact to create a Commonwealth of Independent States (SNG in Russian, CIS in English) to be headquartered in Minsk. Presidential elections in Moldova give the only candidate, Mircea Snegur, over 98% of the vote.

20 RSFSR Supreme Soviet enacts a decree abolishing the USSR Gosbank.

22 Anti-Gamsakhurdia rebels lay seige to the presidential palace in Tbilisi, Georgia. The seige will end with Gamsakhurdia's ousting and departure from Georgia.

24 USSR ceases to be a UN member, and its seat passes to the Russian Federation, to include its seat on the Security Council. New 500 ruble notes are issued.

25 RSFSR Supreme Soviet adopts for the new state the name of Russian Federation (Russia). Mikhail Gorbachev resigns as President of the USSR and Commander in Chief of the USSR Military, handing over control for nuclear weapons to Boris Yeltsin. The USSR flag is lowered from over the Kremlin. US President George Bush recognizes the independence of Russia, Ukraine, Belarus, Armenia, Kazakhstan and Kyrgizistan.

26 At a final meeting of the USSR Supreme Soviet, the body votes itself out of existence and formally declares that the USSR no longer exists.

29 Islam Karimov wins in Presidential Elections in Uzbekistan and some 98% of voters come out in favor of independence.

1992 The year begins with painful price increases of 300-400%. With inflation raging at 10-20% per week, the government pledges to stabilize it to 10% a month. Georgian President Gamsakhurdia is finally forced out of power by armed rebels and flees to neighboring Armenia. Conflict between Russia and Ukraine heats up over the issue of control over military forces. Ukraine introduces a coupon system which is just a first step to creation of an independent Ukrainian currency, the hryvnia.

Russian Place Name Changes

Few things signify the changing of the guard in Russia more than the casting off of the names imposed on Russian cities under communism, and reversion to the pre-communist designation. Below is a list of Russian cities whose names have been changed back, followed by street name changes in Moscow and St. Petersburg.

CITY NAME CHANGES

Communist **(former)** name	Original **(present)** name
Andropov	Rybinsk
Brezhnev	Naberezhnie Chelny
Chernenko	Sharypovo
Georgiu-Dej	Liski
Gorkiy	Nizhniy Novgorod
Kalinin	Tver
Kaspiyskiy	Lagan
Kuybyshev (Tatar SSR)	Bolgar
Kuybyshev (Samara oblast)	Samara
Leningrad	Sankt-Peterburg
Ordzhonokidze	Vladikavkaz
Partizanskiy	Gashun-Burgista
Ustinov	Izhevsk
Sovetskoe	Shatoy
Sovetskoe village	Kashkhatau village
Sverdlovsk	Ekaterinenburg
Svetogorsk	Shamilkala
Teuchezhesk	Adygeysk
Zagorsk	Sergiev-Posad

MOSCOW NAME CHANGES

Below is a list of most Moscow street names (and squares, regions and bridges) which were changed between 1917-1989 to "communist" designations. **Those indicated in bold type have been changed back** to their "pre-communist" names. The others remain to be changed.

Streets, Bridges and Squares

Alekseya Tolstovo, ul.	Spiridonovka ul.
Barrikadnaya ul.	Kudrinskaya ul.
Bogdana Khmelnitskovo, ul.	**Maroseyka ul.**
Bolshaya & Malaya Kolkhoznaya Ploschad	**Sukharevskaya ploshchad**

Communist **(former)** name	Original **(present)** name
Chaikovskovo, ul.	**Novinskiy bulvar**
Chekhova, ul.	Malaya Dmitrovka
Chernyshevskovo, ul.	**Pokrovka ul.**
Chkalova, ul.	**Zemlyanoy val**
Dmitrova, ul.	**Yakimanka, ul.**
Dobryninskaya ploshchad	Serpukhovskaya ploshchad
Dobryninskaya ul.	**Korovy val, ul.**
Dzerzhinskovo, ul.	**Bolshaya Lubyanka ul.**
Frunze, ul.	**Znamenka ul.**
Georgiu-Deja, ul.	**2-aya Peschanaya ul.**
Gertsena, ul.	Bolshaya Nikitskaya ul.
Gogolevskiy bulvar	Prechistenskiy bulvar
Gorkovo, ul.	**Tverskaya ul.** (out to Garden Ring) **1-aya Tverskaya-Yamskaya** (to Tverskaya zastava)
Kachalova, ul.	Malaya Nikitskaya ul.
Karla Marksa, ul.	**Staraya Basmannaya ul.**
Kazakova, ul.	Gorokhovaya ul.
Kirova, ul.	**Myasnitskaya ul.**
Krasnaya Presnya ul.	Bolshaya Presnenskaya ul.
Kropotkinskaya ul.	**Prechistenka ul.**
Kuybysheva, ul.	**Ilyinka ul.**
Komsomolskaya Ploshchad	Kalanchovskaya Ploshchad
Leninsky Prospekt	Bolshaya Kaluzhskaya ul. Kaluzhskoe shosse
Lermontovskaya ploschad	Krasnovorotskaya ploshchad
Maly Pionerskiy pereulok	**Maly Patriarshiy pereulok**
Metrostroyevskaya ul.	**Ostozhenka ul.**
Oktyabrskaya ploshchad	Kaluzhskaya ploshchad
Pionerskiy prud	**Patriarshiy prud**
Ploshchad Belorusskovo Vokzala	**Tverskaya Zastava**
Ploshchad Dzerzhinskovo	**Lubyanskaya ploshchad**
Ploshchad Gagarina	Ploshchad Kaluzhskoy Zastavy
Ploshchad Ilyicha	Rogozhskaya Zastava
Ploshchad Kommuny	Yekaterininskaya ploshchad
Ploshchad Mayakovskovo	Staraya Triumfalnaya ploshchad
Ploshchad Nogina	Varvarskaya ploshchad
Ploshchad Repina	Bolotnaya ploshchad
Ploshchad Revolyutsii	Voskresenskaya ploshchad
Ploshchad Sverdlova	Teatralnaya ploshchad
Ploshchad Vosstaniya	Kudrinskaya ploshchad
Ploshchad 50-letiya Oktyabrya	**Manezhnaya ploshchad**
Prospekt Kalinina	Vozdvizhenka ul.
Pushkinskaya ploshchad	Strastnaya ploshchad
Pushkinskaya ul.	Bolshaya Dmitrovka ul.

Communist **(former)** name	Original **(present)** name
Prospekt Kalinina	**Novy Arbat, ul.** (from the Moscow river to the boulevard ring)
	Vozdvizhenka, ul. (from boulevard ring to ul. Mokhovaya)
Prospekt Mira	1st Meshchanskaya ul.
Prospekt Marksa	**Mokhovaya ul.** (Borovitskaya ploshchad to Manezhnaya ploshchad)
	Okhotny Ryad (Manezhnaya ploshchad to Teatralnaya ploshchad)
	Teatralny proezd (Teatralnaya ploshchad to Lybyanskaya ploshchad)
Razina, ul.	**Varvarka, ul.**
Shosse Entuziastov	Vladimirskoe shosse
Sovetskaya ploshchad	Skobelevskaya ploschad
Spartakovskaya ul.	Yelokhovskaya ul.
Suslova, ul.	**Aminyevskoe shosse**
Suvorovskiy bulvar	Nikitskiy bulvar
Ustinova, ul.	**Oseniy bulvar**
Valtera Ulbrichta, ul.	**Novopeschanaya ul.**
Volgogradskiy prospekt	Novoryazanskoe shosse
Vorovskovo, ul.	Povarskaya ul.
Zhdanova, ul.	**Rozhdestvenka ul.**
25 Oktyabrya, ul.	**Nikolskaya ul.**

Moscow Regions

Voroshilovskiy	**Khoroshevskiy**
Zhdanovskiy	**Taganskiy**

Moscow Metros

Dzerzhinskaya	**Lubyanka**
Gorkovskaya	**Tverskaya**
Kalininskaya	**Aleksandrovskiy sad**
Kirovskaya	**Chistye prudy**
Kolkhoznaya	**Sukharevskaya**
Lenino	**Tsaritsino**
Ploshchad Nogina	**Kitai-gorod**
Ploshchad Sverdlova	**Teatralnaya**
Prospekt Marksa	**Okhotny ryad**
Shcherbakovskaya	**Alekseevskaya**
Zhdanovskaya	**Vykhino**

ST. PETERSBURG NAME CHANGES

Communist **(former)** name	Original **(present)** name
Streets, Bridges, Canals, Parks and Squares	
Anny Ulyanovoy, ul.	**Polozova, ul.**
Bratskvo. ul.	**Maly Sampsonievskiy prospekt**
Brodskovo, ul.	**Mikhailovskaya ul.**
Bulvar Profsoyuzov	**Konnogvardeyskiy bulvar**
Chaikovskovo, ul.	Sergievskaya ul.
Dekabristov, ul.	Ofitserskaya ul.
Detskiy part Oktyabrskovo raiona	**Yucupovskiy sad**
Dzerzhinskovo, ul.	**Gorokhovaya ul.**
Fofanovoy, ul.	**Enotaevskaya ul.**
Fotievoy, ul.	**Eletskaya ul.**
Gertsena, ul.	Bolshaya Morskaya ul.
Gogolya, ul.	Malaya Morskaya, ul.
Kalyaeva, ul.	**Zakharyevskaya ul.**
Kanal Groboyedova	Yekaterinskiy kanal
Kanal Krushteyna	**Admiralteyskiy kanal**
Khalturina, ul.	**Millionnaya ul.**
Kirovskiy most	**Troitskiy most**
Kirovskiy prospekt	**Kamennoostrovsky prospekt**
Komsomolsky most	**Kharlamov most**
Krasnaya ul.	**Galernaya ul.**
Krasnoy Konnitsy, ul.	**Kavalergardskaya ul.**
Lesnoy prospekt	Nyustadtskaya ul.
Liteyny most	Aleksandrovsky most
Marata, ul.	Nikolaevskaya ul.
Marii Ulyanovoy, ul.	**Grafskiy pereulok**
Mayakovskaya, ul.	Nadezhdinskaya ul.
Mendeleevskaya liniya	Universitetskaya liniya
Moskovskiy prospekt	Zabalkanskiy prospekt
Most Leytenanta Shmidta	Nikolaevskiy most
Most Pestelya	**Panteleymonovskiy most**
Most Stroiteley	Birzhevoy most
Most Svobody	**Sampsonievsky most**
Nab. Krasnovo Flota	Angliyskaya nab.
Nab. Leytenanta Shmidta	Nikolaevskaya nab.
Nab. Robespyera	Voskresenskaya nab.
Narodny most	Politseyskiy most
Nekrasova, ul.	Basseynaya ul.
Olega Koshevovo, ul.	**Vvedenskaya ul.**
Park Chelyuskintsev	**Udelny park**
Petra Lavrova, ul.	**Furshtadtskaya ul.**

Communist **(former)** name	Original **(present)** name
Pionerskiy most	**Silin most**
Ploshchad Aleksandra Nevskovo	Krasnaya ploshchad
Ploshchad Dekabristov	Senatskaya ploshchad
Ploshchad Kommunarov	**Nikolskaya ploshchad**
Ploshchad Iskusstv	Mikhailovskaya ploshchad
Ploshchad Mira	**Sennaya ploshchad**
Ploshchad Ostrovskovo	Aleksandrinskaya ploshchad
Ploshchad Radishcheva	Preobrazhenskaya ploshchad
Ploshchad Revolutsii	**Troitskaya ploshchad**
Ploshchad Stachek	Narvskaya ploshchad
Ploshchad Truda	Blagoveshchenskaya ploshchad
Ploshchad Vosstaniya	Znamenskaya ploshchad
Podbelskovo, pereulok	**Pochtamptskiy pereulok**
Prospekt Gaza	**Staro-Petergofskiy prospekt**
Prospekt Karla Marksa	**Bol. Sampsoniyevskiy prospekt**
Prospekt Mayorova	**Voznesensksya prospekt**
Prospekt Maksima Gorkovo	**Kronverkskiy prospekt**
Prospekt N.I. Smirnova	**Lanskoe shosse**
Prospekt Obukhovskoy Oborony	Shlisselburgskiy prospekt
Prospekt Ogorodnikova	**Rizhskiy prospekt**
Prospekt Stachek	Narvskoye shosse Petergofskoe shosse
Prospekt Shchorsa	**Maly Prospekt**
Pushkinskaya ploshchad	Birzhevaya ploshchad
Rakova, ul.	**Italyanskaya ul.**
Sad im. F.E. Dzerzhinskovo	**Lopukhinskiy sad**
Saltykova-Shchedrina, ul.	Kirochnaya ul.
Shosse Revolyutsii	Porokhovskoe shosse
Skorokhodova, ul.	**Bolshaya Monetnaya ul.**
Sofi Perovskoy, ul.	**Malaya Konyushennaya ul.**
Soyuza Svyazi, ul.	Pochtamtskaya ul.
Sverdlovskaya nab.	Poluostrovskaya nab.
Square at Ploshchad Ostrovskovo	**Ekaterininskiy skver**
Tolmacheva, ul.	**Karavannaya ul.**
Voinovo, ul.	**Shpalernaya ul.**
Voitika, ul.	**Vitebskaya ul.**
Zhelyabova, ul.	**Bolshaya Konyushennaya ul.**
Zodchevo Rossi, ul.	Teatralnaya ul.

Russian Business Information Resources

Commercial interest in Russia and the Commonwealth has, in recent years, grown in direct proportion to the opening of those countries' economies. Concomitant with this surge in interest has been a growth in the number and types of information resources available. The flood of potentially useful information is often overwhelming and confusing. This section strives to provide a concise and reasonably comprehensive survey of the various types of information resources available in printed, electronic and other formats.

PERIODICALS

This section is restricted to periodicals which mainly or exclusively focus on the former Soviet Union, with particular reference to business issues. Thus, unless they have a particular bearing on business and trade activity, academic, literary, and social action journals are excluded.

Publications are divided into general interest publications and special interest publications. Each listing tells the frequency of the publication, its average length, and the price for an annual subscription, unless otherwise stated.

For books and other information materials of use to business persons, frequent travelers or companies, refer to the section following.

General Interest Periodicals

ASBI Soviet Index, ASBI, Inc., c/o Gadsby and Hannah, 125 Summer St., Boston, MA 02110-1620, phone (617) 345-7005, fax (617) 345-7050. *A weekly collection of abstracts from periodicals and newspapers from around the Commonwealth. Abstracts are usually a single sentence long and are arranged by subject matter.* (Weekly; $560)

Business America Magazine, Public Affairs, Superintendent of Documents, U.S. Government Printing Office, Washington, DC 20302, phone (202) 783-3238. *General interest publication which frequently provides useful information on US trade policies as well as contact information and listings of conferences and trade shows. Frequently covers Russia.(Monthly; $42)*

Business Eastern Europe, Business International, 40 Duke Street, London, W1A 1DW, phone (71) 493-6711, fax (71) 491-2107. *A pricey weekly publication which focuses on the entire region, utilizing the broad resources available to Business International and the Economist Intelligence Unit. Includes spotlights on certain industries, profiles, consideration of legal, taxation and economic issues and even some business travel.(Weekly; 12 pp.; $1,100)*

Commersant, c/o Refco Publishing, 111 West Jackson Blvd., Chicago, IL 60604, ph. (312) 930-6500. *The English version of Russia's home-grown business weekly newspaper is available in the West with a delay of usually 2-3 weeks. The Western* *version is a "stripped-down" translation of the Russian original, but retains the original's distinct editorial style and most of the Russian weekly's content. (Weekly; 16 pp.; $150)*

Countertrade Outlook, DP Publications, Box 7188, Fairfax Station, VA 22039, phone (703) 425-1322, fax (703) 425-7911. *Focuses on countertrade, barter and other non-monetary centered trade transactions worldwide. Good deal of focus is on former USSR. As much oriented at following legal and organizational developments in international countertrade as in citing deals done. (48 issues/yr.; 4 pp; $488)*

Country Report: Commonwealth of Independent States, The Economist Intelligence Unit, 40 Duke Street, London W1A 1DW, phone 71-493-6711, fax 71-499-9767; in the US: Business International, 215 Park Ave. South, New York NY 10003, phone (212) 460-0600, fax (212) 995-8837. *An excellent quarterly round-up of political, foreign policy and economic developments in the Commonwealth. Astute and cogent analyses, with clear presentations of economic information. More space given to larger economic and political issues, less to business developments. Subscription also includes a country profile. (Quarterly; 60-100 pp.; $255)*

Current Digest of the Soviet Press, 3857 N. High St., Columbus, OH, 43214, phone (614) 292-4234. *A weekly publication which translates articles from the Russian and Commonwealth press and/or abstracts them. The translations are specifically intended for teaching and research, and although translations typically appear about 6 weeks after publication in Russia, this is an excellent source of background reading on politics and economics. Indexed quarterly. (Weekly; 30-40 pp.; $160, $80 for academics)*

Delovie Lyudi: Business in the Ex-USSR, SCII, 4 rue Brunel, 75017, Paris, France, phone 33-1-43-809-000, fax 33-1-42-677-548, in the US: 330 West 42nd St., Suite 2600, New York, NY 10036, phone (212) 629-4460, fax (212) 629-4463. *This monthly magazine is the product of a Russo-French joint venture and the publication is put out simultaneously in English and Russian. The writing is done almost entirely by Russian staff (thus the English is a translation) and is oriented as much at its Russian as its Western audience. In addition to monthly special reports on sectors of the economy, it features usually insightful portraits of prominent business people. It has a unique Opportunities feature where everything from job to trade opportunities are offered. (Monthly; 100-120 pp.; $85)*

East-West Business Analyst, Debos Oxford Publications, Ltd., Kennett House, Suite 2, 108/110 London Road, Oxford, England OX3 9AW. *As the title indicates, this monthly publication focuses on all of Eastern Europe. Typically an issue focuses on a single country and is very "econometric" in approach, relying on presentation of tables and graphs, as well as several pages of news. (Monthly; 8-10 pp.; $125)*

Eastern Europe Finance, DP Publications, Box 7188, Fairfax Station, VA, 22039, phone (703) 425-1322; fax (703) 425-7911. *A very good bi-weekly publication which* *focuses on Eastern Europe and the CIS, with particular emphasis on trade, finance, banking, insurance and any money-related issues. (Bi-weekly; $387)*

Eastern Europe Reporter, Bureau of National Affairs, 1231 25th Street NW, Washington, DC, 20037, phone (202) 452-4200. *A very comprehensive and high-quality bi-weekly publication, EER features much in-country reporting and a unique and useful governmental perspective. Reporting often features input and reactions from government officials and private practitioners. A "deals concluded" section covers the whole region and the publication features full texts of important legislation. While the publication is a newcomer to the market, when it comes to coverage of both Eastern Europe and the former USSR, this publication is unquestionably one of the two or three best. (Bi-monthly, indexed; 30-50 pp.; $775)*

Economist Intelligence Unit, 40 Duke Street, London, W1A 1DW, phone (71) 493-6711, fax (71) 491-2107. *A wide range of quality information products are published periodicallyby EIU and its American partner, Business International. These include* ***Global Forecasting Service, Country Risk Service, Regional Reference: USSR,*** *and* ***Offices and Agencies in Eastern Europe***. *They also publish one-off research studies of certain sectors of the Russian/USSR economy and/or analyses of investment options. On the whole the quality of the analyses is quite high, with prices to match.*

Ecotass, Pergamon Press, Maxwell House, Fairview Park, Elmsford, NY 10523, phone (914) 592-7700. *A weekly bulletin surveying economic news collected by the former Soviet Tass (not ITAR) news agency and published out of the UK. Often includes texts of short decrees and other legal acts. Format is akin to a news wire release. (Weekly; 16 pp; $335)*

Eye on the East, Pacific-Sierra Research Corp., 1401 Wilson Blvd., Suite 1100, Arlington, VA 22209, phone (703) 527-4975. *This bi-weekly publication covers all of Eastern Europe and the former USSR, with demonstrably more time spent on the former. Clearly on the current-news (vs. cerebral analysis) end of the newsletter spectrum, it covers the news on a country-by-country basis. The broad scope of the newsletter makes for mainly short pieces on selected topics but does feature some direct reportage from in-country.(Bi-weekly; 8 pp.; $225)*

FBIS Daily Reports: Central Eurasia, NTIS, US Department of Commerce, 5285 Port Royal Road, Springfield, VA 22161, phone (703) 487-4630. *This daily compendium of translations from the Russian and Commonwealth press and media provides a wealth of useful information for the specialist, but will drown you in information if you do not have the time to get through it all (**Interflo**, abstracted below, reviews the contents of this for its subscribers). Also ask about JPRS translations, which come out less frequently but cover longer articles and documents, including some legislation. Also available is a publication called simply **Central Eurasia**, which is published twice weekly and costs $335/yr. (Daily; $525)*

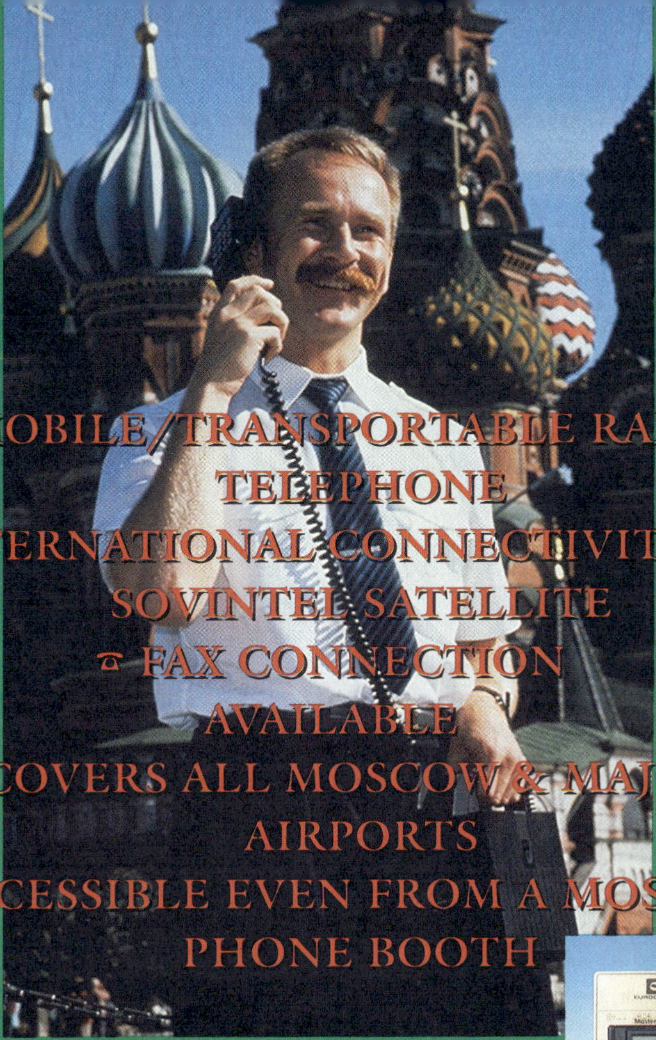

EUROCARD
MasterCard
NOKIA

A new standard for business reporting on the new Russia

RUSSIAN BUSINESS REPORTS

Volume 1, Number 9 — 14-20 March 1992

A joint publication of East-West Information Consortium and Russian Information Services, Inc.

Waiting for a bond market

By Fred Harrison
Editor in Chief

See Bonds, page 2

In Brief...

Kuzbass on the verge of strikes

Minister calls the shots

Timely Information

Published weekly, *Russian Business Reports* provides you with up-to-the-minute reporting on key business, economic, trade and legal developments, direct from Moscow and other Commonwealth republics. It's the information you need, when you need it, to make important investment and other business decisions.

Complete Information

Early each week, *Russian Business Reports* gives you:

- **Four pages of the week's top business and economic news,** plus a commentary that puts recent developments in perspective.
- **News abstracts** summarizing the most important business and economic developments from around the Commonwealth, sifted from over 50 of the most relevant national and republican publications.
- **Databank,** key economic and investment data presented in tables, charts and graphs, highlighting the most important trends.
- **Special features,** including guest columns by business professionals working in-country and exclusive interviews with top government and business people, with particular focus on **the practical side** of doing business in the Commonwealth.

Concise Information

Russian Business Reports gets to the point. It's eight pages weekly of the most essential business and economic news, presented in an efficient, highly readable format. It filters out the noise, and gives you only what you need to know.

Reliable Information

Russian Business Reports is the only independent, Western business weekly on Russia and the Commonwealth. It's written and edited by a highly experienced, Moscow-based staff headed by Fred Harrison, former Washington bureau chief of the Canadian *Financial Post*. This is quality reporting that you can rely on.

RUSSIAN INFORMATION SERVICES

89 Main Street, #2
Montpelier, VT 05602 USA
phone (802) 223-4955
fax (802) 223-6105

Bolshoy Kondratyevskiy per. 4
korpus 2, kv. 168
Moscow 123056, Russia
phone/fax (095) 254-9275

Geonomics Newsletter, Geonomics Institute, 14 Hillcrest Ave., Middlebury, VT 05753, phone (802) 388-9619, fax (802) 388-9627. *This newsletter and other periodic publications of the Geonomics institute are included in the annual fee for membership, which also entitles one to discounts on books and seminars. The newsletter most often features very readable seminar transcripts on current topics, book reviews and summaries of Geonomics activity, which is heavily, but not exclusively focused on the former USSR and Eastern Europe. (Bi-monthly; 16 pp.; $85 as membership fee)*

Harriman Institute Forum, Harriman Institute, Columbia University, 420 West 118 Street, 12th floor, New York NY 10027. *This publication treats contemporary issues with an analytical/academic bent. Published by one of the leading Russian studies institutes in the United States, the Forum can be counted on to be thought provoking and of a high caliber. (Monthly; 10-20 pp.; $30)*

International Information Report, 2612 P Street, NW, Washington DC 20007, phone (202) 333-3533. *A monthly compendium of reports, information and sources of information available in and through the US Government, foreign governments and some private sources. Is accesible on-line through NewsNet (see On-line information resources section below). (Monthly; 8 pp; $120)*

Interflo, Paul Surovell, P.O. Box 42, Maplewood, NJ 07040, phone (201) 763-9493. *A monthly overview of usually 200+ articles from both the Western and Commonwealth press dealing with trade and investment. Usually also includes excerpts or full reprints of short legal acts or US government compiled economic data of interest. An excellent shortcut to surveying the US government's periodical publications (i.e. FBIS, JPRS) on Russia, and one of the best periodical values. (Monthly; 30-40 pp.; $142)*

Journal of US-USSR Trade and Economic Council, 805 Third Ave, New York, NY 10022, phone (212) 644-4550; fax (212) 752-0889. *A newsletter for US-Soviet Trade and Economic Council members only. Features good wrap-up of deals done. (Monthly; free with membership)*

Mars (Metro Area Russian Services), P.O. Box 53305, Washington, DC 20009. *With a specific focus on Russophiles in the DC area, this monthly is gossipy and light. Sometimes has job opportunities listed. Its "Beets and Pieces" section features useful tidbits for persons living in the DC area. (Monthly; 8 pp.; $20)*

Moscow Magazine, PO Box 6805, 2001 JH Haarlem, The Netherlands, phone (023) 319-423, fax (023) 323-589. *This monthly magazine is the best English language mass circulation publication on Moscow and the Commonwealth. It covers business, the arts, political life and current topics and is well written and edited. Includes restaraunt reviews and an annotated alphabetical listing of professional services and retail outlets known as the Moscow Handbook. Particularly oriented at resident expatriate community in Moscow. (Monthly; 70-100 pp.; $60)*

New Outlook, American Committee on US-Soviet Relations, 109 11th Street, SE, Washington DC 20003, phone (202) 546-1700. *This quarterly publication features a variety or articles on Russian life, economy and reforms. The tone of articles is varied and translations of Russian materials is often a feature. (Quarterly; 100-120 pp.; members only)*

PlanEcon, 1111 4th Street, NW, Suite 801, Washington, DC 20005-5603, phone (202) 898-0471, fax (202) 898-0445.

In addition to the two periodical publications listed below, PlanEcon publishes two specialized quarterly publications, ***PlanEcon Energy Report*** *and* ***PlanEcon Chemical Report****, which are 60-80 pages in length and sell for $800/yr, and a semiannual publication,* ***PlanEcon Review and Outlook****, which summarizes economic performance and forecasts for the future on a country by country basis, typically devoting 20-40 pages to each country and selling for $500 per country.*

PlanEcon Business Report*. This bi-monthly newsletter focuses on the entire Eastern Europe and Commonwealth region with sections on privatization, legislation, the economy and foreign trade. Industry by industry reportage of developments and deals is the report's stongest suit. Includes a modicum of economic data. (Bi-monthly; 20 pp.; $760)*

PlanEcon Report*. This pricey publication focuses on major macroeconomic and trade developments throughout Eastern Europe and the Commonwealth and is of most interest to academics. Typically, issues will focus on particular countries or sectors and treat them in great detail both descriptively and in graphs and tables. (25-30 issues/yr; 30-40 pp.; $1,400)*

Problems of Communism, US Information Agency, 301 4th Street SW, Washington DC 20547, phone (202) 619-4230, fax (202) 619-4173. *This bi-monthly collection of analytical essays, book reviews and more academic-type writing is perhaps the best value in providing quality background information to the business person. Leading academics and analysts are its main contributors and most pieces are 10-20 pages in length. It covers all former and remaining communist states. (Bi-monthly; 120-160 pp.; $11)*

RFE/RL Daily Report, RFE/RL, Inc., 1775 Broadway, New York, NY 10019, phone (212) 397-5300, fax (212) 397-5374. *A very extensive (usually eight page) review of mainly political events and news from around the Commonwealth and Eastern Europe. Is available by mail (price below) or by fax ($1000/yr), or on-line via Sovset' (see On-line information resources section below). Also available is* ***RFE/RL Research Report****, a weekly publication which provides some detailed analysis of the week's events (price: $150). (Daily; 8 pp; $350)*

Russian and East European Finance and Trade, M.E. Sharpe, Inc., 80 Business Park Drive, Armonk NY 10504, phone 800-541-6563. *Compendiums of academic-style articles, mainly translated from Russian and East European journals, covering issues related to international trade, finance and reform. (Quarterly; 100-120 pp.; $223)*

Russian Business Reports, Russian Information Services, 28 East State, Montpelier, VT 05602, phone (802) 223-4955, fax (802) 223-6105. *This eight-page publication is the only weekly business newsletter of its type published in the West. It features four pages of business news stories independently reported direct from Russia and the Commonwealth by highly experienced Western and Russian reporters, two pages of 50-100 word abstracts of important business, trade and economics articles published in papers and journals throughout the Commonwealth, an overview of important economic and business data, and a weekly editorial to put the news into perspective. It is published by the people who bring you* ***Russia Business Survival Guide, Where in Moscow*** *and* ***Where in St. Petersburg****. (Weekly; 8 pp.; $495)*

Russia Express, International Industrial Information, PO Box 12, Monmouth, Gwent NP5 3YL, UK, phone 600-890-274, fax 600-890-774. *This bi-weekly includes a few in-depth articles, but the majority of the publication focuses on short blurbs about "deals done". Included is a subscription to Russia Express Contracts, a monthly listing of opportunities available to Western investors in the former Soviet Union, grouped by 100 projects classifications under eleven major headings. (Bi-weekly; 20 pp.; $420)*

Soviet Business and Trade, Welt Publishing, 1413 K Street, NW, Suite 800, Washington, DC 20005, phone (202) 371-0555. *One of the oldest periodicals in the field, this bi-weekly has a distinctive "deals concluded" format. Concise and very eclectic in the news items it covers, a subscription to this publication includes a complimentary subscription to the monthly* ***East/West Technology Digest****. (Bi-weekly; 4 pp.; $249)*

Soviet Observer, The, ASBI, Gadsby & Hannah, 125 Summer Street, Boston, MA 02100-1620, phone (617) 345-7050, fax (617) 345-7050. *A monthly general interest newsletter that treats 4-6 news stories in depth, building on re-reporting of Commonwealth news items with additional interviews and analysis. (Monthly; 8 pp.; $270)*

Surviving Together, ISAR, 1601 Connecticut Avenue, NW, Washington, DC 20009, phone (202) 387-3034. *Ostensibly oriented at exchange and educational programs, this is a good general information publication for the business person as well. It is a valuable resource for picking up on important events, deals and happenings occuring outside "the mainstream" -- things many business newsletters gloss over. (Tri-annually; 80-100 pp.; $25)*

Hi-Technology/Computers

East/West Technology Digest, Welt Publishing Company, 1413 K Street, NW, Suite 800, Washington, DC 20005, phone (202) 371-0555. *This two-to-four page xeroxed monthly consists mainly of equipment sales offers to Western companies by Russian counterparts. (Monthly; 2-4 pp.; $99)*

Eastern European & Soviet Telecom Report, International Technology Constultants, 2940 28th Street NW, Washington, DC 20008, phone (202) 234-2138. *This monthly is exactly what the title suggests. It provides a comprehensive country by country shake* *down of developments and trends in the telecom, media and high-tech sectors. Highly informative, very comprehensive and well organized. (Monthly; 20 pp.; $479)*

Rel-EAST East-West High Tech Information Service, EDventure Holdings Inc., 375 Park Avenue, Suite 2503, New York NY 10152, phone 212-758-3434, fax 212-832-1720. *This publication is targetted at the hi-tech, computer hardware and software markets and provides insightful analyses of developments in these markets in Eastern Europe and the Commonwealth. A subscription includes other special publications and "ad hoc telephone time" with the publisher, Esther Dyson, who is also publisher of Release 1.0, a newsletter for the Western computer industry. (Quarterly; $995)*

Soviet Aerospace and Technology, Phillips Publishing, Inc., 7811 Montrose Rd., Potomac, MD 20854, phone (800) 777-5006, fax (301) 309-3847. *A bi-weekly publication covering the most recent developments in primarily the aerospace sphere. (Bi-weekly; 8 pp; $595)*

Legal/Accounting

Butterworth Central Eastern European Law Bulletin, Butterworth Legal Publishers, 90 Stiles Road, Salem, NH 03079, phone (800) 548-4001. *This quarterly publication looks at doing business in the region from a strictly legal point of view, with equal emphasis on theoretical examinations of legal issues and developments and the practice of doing business in light of these same issues. (Quarterly; 16-20 pp.; $385)*

East-West Executive Guide, World Trade Executive,PO Box 761, Concord, MA 01742, phone (401) 454-2000, fax (401) 454-2005. *Features longer, more in-depth analyses of current issues than most competitive publications. Has a distinctly juridical bent and features articles contributed mainly by practicing legal professionals, yet serves as a bridge between specialized legal literature and the general interest publications by focusing on case studies and the "how-tos" of doing business in Russia and Eastern Europe. One of the best. (Monthly; 28-32 pp.; $576)*

East European Business Law, Financial Times Business Information Ltd., Tower House, Southampton St., London WC2E 7HA, phone 71-240-9391, fax 71-240-7946 [in the US, PO Box 891, Darien, CN 06820, phone (203) 656-2701, fax (203) 655-8332]. *This monthly features extracts from recent business and trade legislation passed throughout Eastern Europe and the Commonwealth and a modicum of commentary to illuminate the texts. With a country by country treatment, commentaries of recent developments are concise and useful. (Monthly; 24-30 pp.; $722)*

Parker School Bulletin on Soviet and East European Law, Transnational Juris Publications, Inc., PO Box 7282, Ardsley-On-Hudson, NY 10503, phone (915) 693-0089, fax (914) 693-8776. *A concise and readable monthly overview of legislative changes in the region. Includes commentaries by practicing professionals and leading academics. (10 issues/yr; 16-20 pp.; $255)*

Russian Commonwealth Law Report, Buraff Publications, 1350 Connecticut Ave., NW, Suite 1000, Washington, DC 20036, phone (202) 862-0990, fax (202) 862-0999. *A pricey alternative which features mainly translations of important legislation, and two or three commentary articles per issue. Its best feature is its 50-100 word briefs on legal activity throughout the Commonwealth. (Bi-monthly; 12 pp.; $970)*

Soviet Law: The Bottom Line, Chadbourne and Park, 30 Rockefeller Plaza, New York, NY 10112, phone (212) 408-5100. *This quarterly publication is written and edited by practicing lawyers of Chadbourne and Parke and its Russian joint venture partners and can provide a useful practitioners view. (Quarterly; 8 pp.; Free upon request)*

Regional Focus

Russian Far East Update, PO Box 22126, Seattle, WA 98122, phone (206) 447-2668. *Carves out its niche by its exclusive focus on the Far Eastern regions of Russia. Thoroughly surveys the Russian press for related articles, and is unquestionably the most up-to-date and comprehensive resource for persones and companies with a specific interest in this region. (Monthly; 12 pp.; $190)*

Ukrainian Business Digest, 21 Bridge Square, Westport CT 06880, phone (203) 221-7450. *A thorough information resource on business developments in Ukraine. Features good in-country reporting. Each month's issue contains 8-10 300-500 word articles on current developments, tables and occasional listings of companies active in Ukraine. (Monthly; 12 pp.; $495 -- companies, $245 -- individuals)*

Travel

Travel Manual to Russia, 12 South Dixie Highway, Lake Worth, FL 33460, ph. (407) 585-5305, fax (407) 582-1353. *Published at irregular intervals for travel agents arranging group travel to Russia and the Commonwealth. Contains useful travel information and recommendations. (Irreg.; 4-8 pp.; free)*

Soviet Travel Newsletter, International Intertrade Index, Box 636, Federal Square, Newark, NJ 07101. *A monthly publication with a target audience of travel professionals, this can also be a useful newsletter for frequent travelers to Russia and the Commonwealth. (Monthly; 4 pp.; $62)*

BOOKS

There are tens of thousands of books in print on hundreds of topics relating to Russia, the former Soviet Union and the new Commonwealth. The books listed below are merely an introductory sampling of this broad literature. Each book has different qualities to recommend it, and each is considered by the editors of this publication to be among the best and/or most interesting in its sphere of concentration. Many of the books listed will not be "standard issue" to most bookstores or libraries and may require a special order or inter-library loan. The extra effort is guaranteed to be worthwile. Books highly recommended are marked with an asterisk (*).

General Interest

John Bushnell, ***Moscow Grafitti: Language and Subculture***. Unwin Hyman, 1990. *Contemporary treatment of the current issues and forces shaping Russian society, with particular focus on life in Moscow.*

*Craig Copetas, ***Bear Hunting with the Politburo***, Simon & Schuster, 1991. *An insightful analysis of the "early" days (1988-89) of capitalism in the Soviet Union, with particular emphasis on the first capitalists, the "cooperativshiki". Very well written and required reading for anyone who wishes a realistic view of what private enterprise is up against in Russia.*

Moshe Lewin, ***The Gorbachev Phenomenon: A Historical Interpretation***. University of California Press, 1991. *One of the many recent interpretations of the tumultuous events begun in 1985, written by a respected political scientist.*

Richard Lourie, ***Russia Speaks: An Oral History from the Revolution to the Present***. Harper Collins. *An insightful use of oral history to provide insights into Russian life in the 20th century.*

David McKenzie and Michael W. Curran, ***A History of the Soviet Union***. Wadsworth Publishers, 1991. *A recently revised edition of one of the better textbook-style treatments of Soviet history.*

*Susan Massie, ***Land of the Firebird: The Beauty of Old Russia***. Touchstone Books, 1982. *One of the best easier reading historical tomes, this by the co-author of* Nicholas and Alexandra.

*Yale Richmond, ***From Nyet to Da: Understanding the Russians***, Intercultural Press, PO Box 700, Yarmouth, ME 04096, phone (207) 846-5168. *An insightful look at the Russian character with very useful reflections on Russian national character and how it impinges on more effective negotiation and interaction. By a veteran foreign service officer. ($15.95)*

Charles A. Ward, ***Moscow and Leningrad: Buildings and Builders*** (vol. 1); ***A Topographical Guide to Russian Cultural History*** (vol. 2). K.G. Saur Publishers, 1989/90. *For those in search of architectural and cultural detail on the two capitals of Russia, these cannot be beat.*

Business Reference

CIS Datafile, Central and East European Trade and Technology Assistance Center, International Division, US Chamber of Commerce, 1615 H St. NW, Washington, DC 20062, phone (202) 463-5460, fax (202) 463-3114. *Lists key contacts in selected sectors of the economy; investment related legislation and information on trade and investment facilitation services. ($47.50)*

Euro-Soviet Trade Directory, Industrial Information Ltd., PO Box 12, Monmouth, Gwent NP5 3YL, UK. *A listing of some 1000 West European companies directly involved in trade with the former Soviet Union. ($125)*

Major Business Organizations of Eastern Europe and the Soviet Union, 1991, Kluwer Academic Publishers, PO Box 358, Accord Station, Hingham, MA 02018-0358. *A listing of 3000 major governmental and business organizations, with address and contact information. ($599)*

Soviet Independent Business Directory, c/o FYI Information Resources, 735 8th Street, SE, Washington, DC 20003, phone (202) 544-2394, fax (202) 543-9385. *A Catalogue of over 2000 independent Soviet businesses, with registration information, contacts, address, and business activities. With indexes. (1991 ed. $110, a 1992 version is in the works.) The company also publishes* ***Ukraine Top 100 Exporters*** *($75).*

USSR Exporters Directory, Dun's Marketing Services, 3 Sylvan Way, Parsippany NJ, 07054-3896, phone (800) 526-0651. *Listing of 2500 companies which import and export actively, with address, product, and financial information, indexed and with SIC codes. ($345) A joint ventures directory and Import/Export Trade Statistics directory are both forthcoming.*

Language

The Pocket Oxford Russian Dictionary, Oxford University Press (Oxford), 1981. *The best of the compact dictionaries.*

Jill Norman and Pamela Davidson, ***Penguin Russian Phrasebook***. Penguin Books (London), 1989. *The best phrase dictionary.*

*Siegfried Kohls, ***Business Russian***. Passport Books, 1990. *The only good business vocabulary-oriented book, albeit a bit dry. Full of useful sample documents, correspondence and exercises.*

Travel Essay

*Marquis de Custine, ***Journey for Our Time: The Russian Journals of the Marquis de Custine.*** Regney Gateway Publishers, 1987. *A must read for any serious student of Russia. An extremely insightful and realistic, albeit hardly positive, description of Russia, much of which, the reader soon realizes, still applies some 150 years later.*

W.O. Gerrare, ***The Story of Moscow***. Kraus Reprint. *Another fine book for persons seeking greater detail.*

Laurence Kelley, ed., ***Moscow, A Traveller's Companion***, and ***St. Petersburg, A Traveller's Companion***. Atheneum, 1983. *Life in the two cities through the eyes of people who have lived there, relying heavily on citations from literature.*

*Elizabeth Pond, ***From Yaroslavsky Station***. Universe Books, 1988. *A description of the author's ride on the Trans-Siberian express, with interesting digressions into all the major issues and topics of Russian life.*

Laurens van der Post, ***Journey into Russia***. Island Press, 1984 (originally published 1964). *An excellent chronical of a monumental trip to all corners of the then Soviet Union.*

Travel Guides

*Victor and Jennifer Louis, ***The Complete Guide to the Soviet Union***, Third Edition, St. Martin's Press, 1991. *Excellent city by city tourist guide to the former Soviet Union, with maps of over 140 cities. A useful reference guide.*

Evan and Margaret Mawdsley, ***Blue Guide: Moscow and Leningrad***. A.C. Black (London), 1989. The most detailed, yet compact tourist type guide, organized in a "walks through the cities with narration" format.

*Paul Richardson, ed., ***Where in Moscow*** and ***Where in St. Petersburg,*** Russian Information Services, 1992. *Taking up where the standard travel guides leave off, these guides offer a combination of directory information and maps that is invaluable for the new age of independent travel to Russia's two capitals.*

*Martin Walker, ***The Harper Independent Traveler: Soviet Union***. Harper and Row, 1990. *Written by the former London* Guardian *Moscow Correspondent, this volume features some of the best writing of this genre and is full of useful insights and observations.*

ON-LINE INFORMATION RESOURCES

Currently, very good resources are available from a variety of electronic channels which provide information on on developments in Russia and the CIS. And because of the ever-expanding reach of electronic information resource networks like Compuserve, Telenet and Internet, in most cases you simply call a local phone number and pay $15-20 an hour for usage, or about the cost of a long distance phone call.

There are two services which are dedicated to the Russian and Slavic areas. Other, more mass-user networks provide additional, useful resources. Electronic mail services for communicating with partners in Russia are treated in some detail in Section VI.

Dedicated On-Line Services

• ***SovAm Teleport,*** 3278 Sacramento Street, San Francisco, CA 94115, phone (415) 931-8500, fax (415) 931-2885 (access via Telenet). Cost $15 per hour.

This San Francisco based company, utilizing its joint venture in Moscow (with nodes in other cities) has established what is arguably the best, most cost-effective Email system between the US and Russia (see Section VI). The company has expanded its services to offer subscribers a number of database and information services. Among those already on-line or in the works are:

Russian Business Legal Materials: *On-line database of all Russian and other former republics' legal acts relating to foreign trade and investment, in English. Searchable by law title, date, keyword, or text within laws or titles.*

Newsbytes Files: *A comprehensive reporting of developments in the Russian and Commonwealth telecom and computer industries.*

Russian Far East Update: *An on-line version of the printed newsletter (see Periodicals section above).*

Daily News: *A clipping file set up by SovAm to rope in national news stories related to Russia and the Commonwealth. Some 20-30 articles are posted daily.*

Classifieds: *A new service on SovAm to allow for posting of announcements, items for sale.and employment search announcements.*

• ***Sovset,*** Center for Strategic and International Studies, 1800 K Street, NW, Suite 400, Washington, DC 20006, phone (202) 887-0200 (accessible via Compuserve, Telenet and Internet). Cost, $15/hr.

Founded mainly for Slavic studies academics, this is a sleeper resource, not used to its maximum potential. In addition to email capabilities accesible from Russia via Compuserve, Sovset' provides several unique information services. It also has a number of on-line conferences, on topics ranging from Arms Control to Law to the Economy to Anecdotes. In the Sovset Data Library section are a number of useful information resources:

Radio Liberty Daily Report: *Also available in a weekly version, this is the most easily accessible and most comprehensive daily news source on the Commonwealth you will find electronically. In a 5-10 minute download you can get detailed and useful back-*

ground information and up-to-date news from around the Commonwealth and Eastern Europe.

Eastern Europe Newsletter*: Summaries of recent issues of the newsletter. Focus is on Eastern Europe, but also frequently on Russia.*

Express Chronicle: *an independent weekly newspaper published and edited in Moscow by Alexander Podrabinek since August 1987. Some of the best political reportage available from reporters around the Commonwealth.*

Postfactum Analytical Reports: *With some considerable delay, offers excerpts from reports by Postfactum (Moscow based news agency which is affiliated with publisher of Commersant).*

Perspective Reports: *Briefing papers issued by Brown University's Center for Foreign Policy Development, these are reports on current issues of importance to foreign policy and business communities. Only summaries and tables of contents are placed on-line; the papers themselves are made available upon request and free of charge to Sovset' members.*

Soviet Prospects: *Bulletin on events in the USSR and Eastern Europe edited by Gabriel Schoenfeld, a Senior Fellow at the Center for Strategic and International Studies (CSIS). It is published eight times a year by the CSIS Soviet and East European Studies program. Only published in part on-line. Instructions given on-line for receiving the full bulletin.*

Parker School SEEL Bulletin: *Another print publication placed on line after some delay (see review above in Periodicals section).*

Kennan Institute: *In addition to a schedule of the institute's speakers and activities, records of past meetings and reports are also available on-line. Some excellent reports can often be found here on the import and directions of Russian political and economic change.*

Sovset News: *Transcripts of US Congressional hearings bearing on events in Russia and the Commonwealth.*

Non-Dedicated On-Line Systems

• ***Compuserve,*** Customer Services, P.O. Box 20212, Columbus, OH 43220, phone (800) 848-8990.

This popular information service instituted, in the wake of the August 1991 coup, a forum for monitoring events in the former Soviet Union. You get there by typing GO USSR (when logged on to Compuserve). The forum gives access to the following services:

Soviet Crisis Newsclips: *A special clipping service continually updated with reports from the Washington Post and major international wire services, including Reuters, UPI, and ITAR.*

Any user who signs up for Executive Option service on Compuserve can create a similar type of clipping file oriented to their particular interests (i.e. using keywords such as "Russia" and "oil").

Investors Forum: *Designed for investors of all stripes and with interests not limited to the former Soviet Union, you can nevertheless search for relevant messages, files and discussions taking place in this forum.*

The Journalism Forum: *A similarly broad usage forum for discussion of the media coverage and the availabilty of news from the former Soviet Union.*

U.S. Department of State Travel Advisories: *Accesses travel advisories on any country, including the former Soviet Union (still listed under Soviet Union at the time of printing).*

Issues Forum: *Access to an on-line conference entailing discussion of the situation in Russia, in Message Section 9, "Russian Turmoil."*

• ***MCI Mail,*** 1150 17th Street, NW, Suite 800, Washington, DC 20036, phone (800) 444-6245.

This email provider (see Section VI below) can also provide access to the Dow Jones News Service (//NEWS), which has daily news and which can conduct customized searches for users (//QUEST). A clipping file can also be created (//CLIP). News of the former USSR is also available on the Dow Jones service (.R/UR). In all cases, the services are a bit pricey ($2-3 per minute during prime time and $0.50 to $2 for non-prime time), but user-friendly and mainly efficient. For users of ***Prodigy*** *and* ***PC Telemail*** *or* ***SprintNet,*** *these services offer similarly configured access to news and news clipping services.*

• ***NewsNet,*** 945 Haverford Road, Bryn Mawr, PA 19010, phone (800) 345-1301 or (215) 527-8030.

Access to a number of useful news and information services, for a premium price. In addition to International Information Report, Russia Express and Russia Express Contracts (profiled in the periodicals section above), it also allows access to USSR Business, Soviet Perspectives and Federal News Service (speeches and transcripts of press conferences from Russia). The cost is $15 per month, plus $1.50 per minute for usage time. A special starter kit is available for $79.95.

US GOVERNMENT OFFICES AND SERVICES

For the sake of brevity, the addresses of government organizations which provide various kinds of information are listed immediately below, with any specific phone numbers or offices noted within references:

[DoS] Department of State, 2201 C St. NW, Washington, DC 20520

[DoC] Department of Commerce, 14th St. and Constitution Ave., Washington, DC 20230

[E/IB] Export/Import Bank, 811 Vermont Avenue NW, Washington, DC 20571, phone (202) 566-4490; fax (202) 566-7524; or 11000 Wilshire Blvd., Los Angeles, CA 90024, phone (213) 575-7425; fax (213) 575-7428

[ITC] International Trade Commission, 701 E St. NW, Washington, DC 20436

[OPIC] Overseas Private Investment Corporation, 1129 20th Street NW, Washington, DC 20527, phone (202) 457-7162; fax (202) 331-4234

Export Licensing

Electronic Application Filing: Electronic communication is speeding export control processes. The Department of Commerce's ELISA system allows for electronic filing of license applications. Within the ELISA system there is also a system known as EXPERT, which helps exporters determine if a given technology is export controlled. Finally, exporters can communicate directly with Department of Defense licensing officers through ELISA II.

For more information on Electronic Filing of Export License Applications, contact IBEK Corporation, (202) 463-0904 or OCR International, (301) 881-0532. Both are officially licensed with DoC.

Export Administration Regulations: This publication is published by the Department of Commerce, and may be ordered from Superintendent of Documents, U.S. Government Printing Office, Washington, DC 20402, ph. (202) 783-3238. The price is $87 per year (stock # 903-017-00000-7).

Other useful numbers:
Bureau of Export Administration, DoC, ph. (202) 377-2721
Export License Voice Information System: (714) 660-0144 or (603) 598-4300
Tracking Export License Applications: (202) 377-2752

Exporting, Export Financing and Insurance

Guide: The book *Financing Exports and US Direct Investments Abroad*, can be obtained (April, 1992 publication date) from the Government Printing Office Bookstore at (202) 783-3238.

Hotline: The Export/Import Bank operates a Small Business Hotline at (202) 566-8860.

The International Trade Administration operates a US Export/Import Bank Automated Information System at (800) 424-5201.

Information: Finance and Countertrade Division, DoC, Room 144006, phone (202) 377-4434.

US Trade and Development Program, SA-16, Room 309, Washington DC, 20523, phone (703) 875-4357; fax (703) 875-4009. Funds feasibility studies, training programs, etc. which have priority status in the CIS and relate to US Export potential and have untied financing.

Insurance: Foreign Credit Insurance Association, Suite 1622, 40 REctor St. New York, NY 10006, phone (212) 227-7020; fax (212) 513-4704 (with other offices in Chicago, Houston, Miami and Los Angeles). Export credit insurance against commercial and political losses.

Geographical Information

Maps: Declassified CIA maps on the former USSR can be ordered through the NTIS order desk at (703) 487-4650 or (800) 836-8080. But first get a copy of the catalogue by calling the Public Affairs office of the CIA at (703) 351-2053.

Information, General

Department of Commerce, Russia and Independent States: (202) 377-4655, fax (202) 377-8042.

Department of State Russia Desk: (202) 647-8640

Economics Division (aid to CIS): (202) 647-9370

Commercial Visas/Exchange Department: (202) 647-8956

Eastern European Business Information Center (EEBIC): (202) 377-2645

European Bank for Reconstruction and Development, c/o International Trade Administration DoC, ph. (202) 377-1246, fax (202) 377-3954.

CIA Publications: To subscribe to all CIA declassified publications, the annual subscription fee is just $375. To order, call (202) 707-9527 or write to DOCEX, Exchange and Gifts Division, Library of Congress, Washington, DC 20540. Among these are directories of leaders, maps, economic data resource and reference publications.

Market Studies and General Reports

Country Market Studies: A market study of Russia ("Industry Sector Analysis") or any of the other Commonwealth states, based on research by the International Trade Administration, is available through DoC district offices. Call (202) 377-3363 for the closest district office.

Statistics

East-West Trade: The Department of Commerce can provide some statistics on trade and investment for a fee. Contact DoC at (202) 377-5291 to get connected with your district office Trade Specialist.

Travel Information

Passport information: For information on what is necessary to get a passport, call (202) 647-0518.

Travel Advisory Information: For the latest travel advisories, call (202) 647-5225, or write to Overseas Citizens Services, Bureau of Consular Affairs, DoS, Room 4800. This is also valid for emergency information, such as the death of a US relative while that person is abroad. Advisories are also accesible on Compuserve (GO USSR or GO STATE).

US-Soviet Trade and Economic Council

While not a US Government agency, this private association is the closest thing to a US-CIS Chamber of Commerce. It offers its support, research and other services only to members, and membership fees are based on a graduated scale depending upon the type and size of a company. For more information, contact:

US-Soviet Trade and Economic Council, 208 805 Third Ave., 14th Floor, New York, NY 10022 phone, (212) 644-4550.

Other Resources

Further assistance may also be obtained from the following Russian organizations:

Amtorg, 1755 Broadway, New York, NY 10019, ph. (212) 956-3010

Trade Representation of the Russian Federation, 2001 Connecticut Ave., NW, Washington DC 20008, ph. (202) 232-5988; fax (202) 232-2917

BRITISH GOVERNMENT OFFICES AND SERVICES

Two government offices can offer assistance in issues of trade and investment in Russia and the Commonwealth.

Department of Trade and Industry, Ninth Floor, Kingsgate House, 66-74 Victoria Street, London SW1E 6SW, phone (071) 215-5000, fax (071) 828-3258, telex 8813148 DIHQ G.

Foreign and Commonwealth Office, King Charles Street, London SW1A 2AH, phone (071) 270-3832, fax (071) 270-3282.

Also located in the UK is:

European Bank for Reconstruction and Development, 122 Leaden Hall St., London EC3V 4QL, phone (71) 338-6000, fax (71) 338-6100

For more in-depth assistance, you will want to contact the British-Soviet Chamber of Commerce. They maintain a Moscow office (see Telephone Directory) which supports members in their visits to Russia, and organize seminars and group visits to Russia. Members receive a monthly internal newsletter and the BSCC Journal. Members are also entitled to discounts on individual accomodations while in Moscow. For more information, contact:

British-Soviet Chamber of Commerce, 60a Pembroke Road, London W8 6NX, phone (071) 602-7692, fax (071) 371-4788.

CANADIAN GOVERNMENT OFFICES AND SERVICES

The first stop for information/assistance when doing business in Russia is:

Canada-USSR Business Council, 2 First Canadian Place, Suite 2125, P.O. Box 11, Toronto, M5X 1A9, phone (416) 862-2821, fax (416) 862-2820. Provides full trade and consulting support to members, both in Canada and Russia, with substantial capability in Ukraine as well. Publishes bi-monthly newsletter. Office in Moscow (see Telephone Directory).

The only government office which can be of assistance is:

Department of External Affairs and International Trade, East European Trade Division (RBT), 125 Essex Drive, Ottawa, K1A OG2, ph. (613) 996-6835.

EUROPEAN AND JAPANESE CHAMBERS OF COMMERCE

All of the following are very active agents for their members, liasoning with both Russian and home governments. All, except the German, have offices in Moscow.

French-Soviet Chamber of Commerce, 22 Avenue Franklin Roosevelt, 75008 Paris, phone 422-59-710, fax 435-97-473, telex 651909

Italian-Soviet Chamber of Commerce, via S. Tomaso 5, 20121 Milano, phone 720-04-008, fax 805-2009, telex 333821.

Japan-USSR Trade Association, Sanko Building 6-4-3, Kojimachi Chiyodaku, Tokyo, phone (03) 3262-8401, fax (03) 3262-8403, telex J 27213

Finnish-Soviet Chamber of Commerce, Annankatu 32A, 00100 Helsinki, phone (90) 693-1066, fax (90) 693-1442, telex 121589 FISOP.

Germany

Ost-Ausschuss der Deutschen Wirtshaft, Gustav Heinemann Ufer 84-88, 5000 Koeln 51, phone (221) 3708-417, fax (221) 3708-730.

Bundesstelle fuer Ausenhandles Information, Blaubach 13, 5000 Koeln 1, phone (221) 20571, fax (221) 2057-212.

Russian Embassies in Foreign Countries

AUSTRALIA

Embassy: 78 Canberra Avenue, Griffith A.C.T. 2603, Canberra, phone (62) 95-90-33; (Consular Dept.) 95-94-74, telex 61365 SOVPOSOL AA, (Consular Dept.) 62602 SOVPOSOL AA..

Consulate: 7-9 Fullerton Street, Wolluhra, Sydney, N.S.W. 2025, phone (612) 326-11-88, 326-18-66, 326-17-02, telex 73606 SOVCON AA.

AUSTRIA

Embassy: Reisnerstrasse 45-47, 1030 Wien, phone (222) 713-12-15, 712-12-29, (Consular Dept.) 712-32-33, telex 47136278.

Consulate: Burgelsteinstrasse 2, 5020 Salzburg, phone (6212) 241-84, telex 47632655.

BELGIUM

Embassy: 66 Avenue De Fre, 1180 Bruxelles, phone (2) 374-68-86, 374-34-06, telex (Consular Dept.) 4665272.

Consulate: Della Faililaan 20, 2020 Antwerpen, phone (3) 829-16-11, telex 4435779.

CANADA

Embassy: 285 Charlotte Street, Ottawa, Ontario, KIN 8L5, phone (613) 235-4341, 236-1413, telex 26(21)0533332, (21)0533514.

Consulate: 3655 Avenue de Musee, Montreal, P.Q., HIW ISI, phone (514) 843-5901, 288-0932, telex 26(21)05560071, 26(21)05560469.

DENMARK

Embassy: Kristianiagade 5, 2100 Kobenhaven, phone (31) 42-55-85, 42-55-86, (Consular Dept.) 38-23-70, telex 5516943.

FINLAND

Embassy: SNTL: Suurlahetysto, Tehtaankatu 1 B, 00140 Helsinki, phone (0) 66-18-76, 66-18-77, 60-70-50, (Consular Dept.) 66-14-49, telex 57125577.

FRANCE

Embassy: 40-50 Boulevard Lannes, 75016 Paris, phone (1) 45-04-05-50, 45-04-71-71, (Consular Dept.) 45-03-06-56, telex: 4211761, (Consular Dept.) 42642830.

Consulate: 3 avenue Ambroise-Pare, 13008 Marseille, phone (91) 77-15-25, telex 42440272.

GERMANY

Embassy: Waldstrasse 42, 5300 Bonn 2, phone (49-228) 31-20-85, 31-20-87, 31-20-74, (Consular Dept.) 31-20-89, telex (Consular Dept.) 41885615 VISAD.

Consulate: Unter-den-Linden 63-65, Berlin 1080, phone (372) 229-1129, telex 69114024 BERLIN DD.

GREAT BRITAIN

Embassy: 13 Kensington Palace Garden, London W8, phone (71) 229-3628, 229-3620, 229-3629, (Consular Dept.) 229-3215, telex (Consular Dept.) 51261420.

GREECE

Embassy: Palais Psychico, 28 Nikiforou Litra, Athens, phone (1) 672-5235, 672-6130, (Consular Dept.) 647-1395, 647-2949, telex 601223553 LOTO GR.

ICELAND

Embassy: 33 Gardastraeti, Reykjavik, phone (1) 1-51-56, 2-85-64, telex (Consular Dept.) 5012200.

INDIA

Embassy: Shantipath, Chanakyapuri, New-Delhi 110021, phone (11) 60-60-26, 60-61-37, 60-58-75, telex: 813161791 USSR IN.

Consulate: 42 Jamogandas Marg (Old Nepean Sea Road), Bombay: 40006, phone (22) 822-36-27, 822-36-28, telex: 811175939 SOVK IN.

Consulate: 31 Shakespeare Sarani, Calcutta 700017, phone (33) 44-20-06, 44-49-82, telex 81217774 SUSG IN.

Consulate: 14 Santhome High Road, Madras 600004, phone (44) 7-11-12, 7-13-00, telex 81417515 SOCV IN.

IRELAND

Embassy: 186 Orwell Road, Rathgar, Dublin 6, phone (1) 97-75-25, 97-57-48, 97-47-92, 69-38-12, telex (Consular Dept.) 50033622.

ITALY

Embassy: via Gaeta 5, 00185 Roma, phone (6) 494-1681, 494-1683, 494-1680, 494-1649, (Consular Dept.) 86-71-23, telex (Consular Dept.) 43622310.

Consulate: via Sant'Aquilino, 20148, Milano, phone (2) 404-6741, 404-6742, telex 43326571.

Consulate: via Ghirardelli Perscetto 16, Genova, phone (10) 31-54-10, telex: 43222899.

JAPAN

Embassy: 1-1 Azabudai, 2-chome, Minato-ku, Tokyo, 106, phone (3) 583-4224, 583-5982, 583-4297, (Consular Dept.) 583-4445, telex (Consular Dept.) 7224231 SOVPOSOL J.

Consulate: Osaka-fu Toyonakashi Nishi Midorigaoka 1-2-2, phone (6) 848-3452, telex 7265908.

Consulate: 826 Nishi 12-chome, Minami 14-jo, Chuo-ku, Sapporo, 064, phone (11) 561-3171, telex: 720932305.

LUXEMBURG

Embassy: Luxemburg-ville, Chateau de Beggen, phone (1) 422-333, 422-334, telex 40260445.

MEXICO

Embassy: Jose Vasconselos 204 (Condesa), Delegacion Cuanthema, 06140, phone (5) 515-6155, 515-6055, telex (Consular Dept.) 221772516 URSS ME.

Consulate: Avenida Vicitimas, 5 y 6 de Julia N 1045, Veracruz, phone (9) 35-25-60.

NETHERLANDS

Embassy: Andries Bickerweg 2, 2517 JP Den Haag, Holland, phone (70) 345-1300, (Consular Dept.) 345-1301, telex 4434585.

NEW ZEALAND

Embassy: 57 Messines Road, Karori, Wellington, phone (4) 76-61-13, (Consular Dept.) 76-67-42, telex (Consular Dept.) 7431727 SOVPOSOL NZ.

NORWAY

Embassy: 0271 Oslo 2, Drammensveien 74, phone (2) 55-32-78, 55-32-79, (Consular Dept.) 44-91-77, telex 5674110.

SPAIN

Embassy: Madrid-6, c/Maestro Ripoll, 14, phone (1) 262-2264, 411-0706, 411-2524, (Consular Dept.) 411-2957, telex 5245632 URSS E, (Consular Dept.) 5247677 KOSU E.

SWEDEN

Embassy: Gjorwellsgatan 31, 11260 Stockholm, phone (3) 13-04-40, 13-04-41, 13-04-44, (Consular Dept.) 20-86-52, 53-37-32, telex (Consular Dept.) 5414830.

Consulate: St. Sigfridsgatan 1, Box 5093, 40222 Goteborg, phone (31) 40-80-84, 40-84-00, 20-60-93, telex 5427637.

SWITZERLAND

Embassy: Brunnadernrain 37, 3006 Berne, phone (31) 44-05-66, (Consular Dept.) 44-05-67, telex (Consular Dept.) 45911297.

Consulate: Rue Schaub 24, 1202 Geneve, phone (22) 34-79-55, 34-90-83.

TURKEY

Embassy: SSCB Buyukelciligi, Karyagdi Sok, 5 Cankaya, Ankara, phone 139-2122, 139-2123, telex (Consular Dept.) 60746151.

Consulate: Istaklal Caddesi, 443 Beyoglu, Istanbul, P.K. 529-Betaglu, phone (1) 144-26-10, 144-16-93.

UNITED STATES

Embassy: 1125 16th Street, N.W., Washington, D.C. 20036, phone (202) 628-6412, 628-7551, 628-7554, (Consular Dept.) 332-0737, telex 232248400, (Consular Dept.) 232248708.

Consulate: 2790 Green Street, San Francisco, CA 94123, phone (415) 922-6644, 922-6642, 922-6643, telex 236034755.

Consulate: 9 East 91st St., Manhattan, NY 10128, phone (212) 472-4732.

Travel Agents/Visa Services

While any travel agent can arrange travel to Russia, some companies have built a specialty on, or have specific experience with, travel to Russia. Many also can provide visa expediting services.

AUSTRALIA

Intourist, Underwood House, 34-49 Pitt Street, Sydney NSW 2000, phone (02) 277-652, telex INTAUS AA 176604

AUSTRIA

Intourist, Scwedenplatz 3-4, 1010 Wien, Osterreich, phone 63-95-47; telex 114524 INTOUR

CANADA

Canadian Gateway, 7000 Bathurst, Unit C-8, Toronto, Ontario L4J 7L1, phone (800) 668-8401; fax (416) 660-7004,; telex 06-964737. (visa expediting and both group and individual travel arrangements)

Intours, 1013 Bloor St. West, Toronto, Ontario MCH 1M1, phone (416) 537-2165; fax (416) 537-1627; telex 06-218557

P. Lawson, 1st Canadien Place, Toronto, Ontario, M5X 1B9, phone (416) 862-8020; fax (416) 862-2390.

ENGLAND

Barry Martin Travel, Suite 343 Linen Hall, 162 Regent Street, London W1X 1RA, phone (71) 439-1271, fax (71) 434-0813

East-West Travel Limited, 15 Kensington High Street, London W8 5NP

Intourist, Intourist House, 219 Marsh Wall, Isle of Dogs, London E14 9FG, phone (01) 538-3202, telex 27232 INTMOS

Intravel Ltd., World Trade Centre, International House, 1 St. Catherine's Way, London E1 9UN

Overseas Business Travel, Ltd., 117-119 Leman Street, London E1 8EX

FRANCE

Intourist, 7 Boulevard des Capucines, 75002 Paris, France, phone (47) 42-47-40; telex 680180 INTOUR.

FINLAND

Area, Pohjoisesplanadi 2, Helsinki, phone (90) 7661-491

Intourist, Etela Esplanaadi, 14, 00130 Helsinki 13, Finland, phone (90) 631, telex 124654 INTOUR.

GERMANY

Intourist, Friedrichstrasse 153A, 1080 Berlin, phone 229-1948, 228-1492, telex 115173 INTOUR • 1000 Berlin, Kurfurstendamm 63, phone (030) 88-00-70, telex 185392 INTOUR • Stephanstrasse 1, 6000 Frankfurt am Main 1, phone (069) 28-57-76, telex 414232 INTOUR.

ITALY

Intourist, Piazza Buenos Aires 6/7, 00198 Roma, Italia, phone 86-38-92; telex 626367 INURSS.

JAPAN

Intourist, Roppongi Heights, 1-16, 4-chome Roppongi, Minato-ku, Tokyo, Japan, phone (03) 584-6617, (03) 584-6618, telex 27645.

SWITZERLAND

Intourist, Usteristrasse, 9 Lowenplatz, 8001 Zurich; phone (01) 211-3335; telex 813005 TOSU CH.

UNITED STATES

Barry Martin Travel, 19 West Street, Suite 3401, New York, NY 10004, phone (212) 422-0091, fax (212)344-1997.

Capital Visa, 13113 Ideal Drive, Silver Springs, MD 20906, phone (800) 727-VISA, fax (301) 933-0024.

Duke Travel Services, 2033A 38th St. SE, Washington, DC 20020, phone (202) 582-0280, fax (202) 582-0674.

East West Ventures, Inc., P.O. Box 14391, Tucson, AZ 85732, phone (800) 833-4398.

Express Visa Service, Inc., 2150 Wisconsin Ave., Suite 20, Washington, DC 20007, phone (202) 337-2442, fax (202) 337-2253.

Intourist, 630 Fifth Ave. #868, New York, NY 10111, phone (212) 757-3884, 757-3885, telex REP INTUR 62614 UW.

Rahim Travel, 12 South Dixie Highway, Lake Worth FL 33460, phone (800) 556-5305, fax (407) 582-1353, telex 362788.

Russia Travel Bureau, 225 East 44th Street, New York, NY 10017, phone (212) 986-1500, fax (212) 490-1650.

Tour Designs, Inc., 616 G Street, SW, Washington, DC 20024, phone (202) 554-5820, fax (202) 479-0472, telex 904266.

Visa Advisors, 1930 18th St., NW, Washington, DC 20009, (202) 797-7976.

METRIC CONVERSION

Russia uses only metric measurements. The table below may therefore be of some help.

LENGTH

1 centimeter	0.394 inches
1 inch	2.540 centimeters
1 foot	0.35 meters
1 meter	3.281 feet
1 yard	0.9144 meters
1 kilometer	0.6214 mile
1 mile	1.6094 kilometers

WEIGHT

1 gram	0.03527 ounce
1 ounce	28.35 grams
1 pound	0.4536 kilos
1 kilogram	2.2046 pounds
1 met. ton	0.9842 Eng. ton
1 Eng. ton	1.016 metric ton

SQUARES

1 sq. centimeter	0.1550 sq. inch
1 sq. inch	6.452 sq. centimeters
1 sq. meter	10.764 sq. feet
1 sq. foot	0.09290 sq. meters
1 sq. meter	1.196 sq. yards
1 sq. yard	0.8361 sq. meters
1 sq. kilometer	0.386 sq. mile
1 sq. mile	2.59 sq. kilometers

VOLUME

1 tsp.	5 ml
1 cup	0.24 liter
1 liter (dry)	0.908 quart
1 quart (dry)	1.101 liters
1 liter (liquid)	1.0567 quarts
1 quart (liquid)	0.9463 liters
1 US gal. (liquid)	3.785 liters
1 Imp. gal. (lqd)	4.546 liters
1 liter (liquid)	0.264 US gal.
1 liter (liquid)	0.220 Imp. gal.

CLOTHING SIZES

WOMEN

Suits and Dresses						
American	8	10	12	14	16	18
British	10	12	14	16	18	20
Russian	36	38	40	42	44	46
Stockings						
American & British	8	8½	9	9½	10	10½
Russian	0	1	2	3	4	5
Shoes						
American	6	7	8	9		
British	4½	5½	6½	7½		
Russian	36	37	38	40		

MEN

Suits/Coats							
American	36	38	40	42	44	46	
Russian	46	48	50	52	54	56	
Shirts							
American & British	15	16	17	18			
Russian	38	41	43	45			
Shoes							
American & British	5	6	7	8	9	10	11
Russian	38	39	41	42	43	44	45

TEMPERATURE

(°F - 32) x 5/9 = °C

(°C x 5/9) + 32 = °F

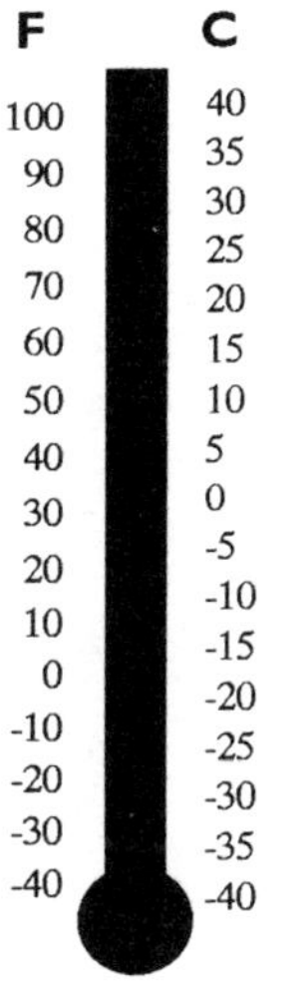

II. Preparations

Russian National Holidays

January 7	Russian Orthodox Christmas
March 8	International Women's Day
May 8-9	Victory Day (WWII)
June 12	Independence Day
December 30-January 2	New Year's

What to Do Before You Leave

The most important thing to do is to gather information. The previous section of this book details the sources and types of information available. Since the direct costs and opportunity costs of a business trip to Russia are quite great, you should do everything you can to make your trip as worthwhile as possible. You cannot over prepare.

To summarize the advised preparation in terms of information gathering:

- Talk to people who have made the same type of trip -- find out what went right and what went wrong, and why.
- Study up on the state of development of the area of the economy you are interested in. This is relatively easy to do if you have access to a major university or city library. Review the types and source of information surveyed in Section I to select those of most use to you.
- Check if your local of city chamber of commerce has resources it can provide. State commercial and development offices can also often be of assistance.

In addition to gathering information, there are some other advised preparatory measures to take:

- Apply early for a visa (see section below on Visas and Visa Support).
- Be certain your contacts will be in Moscow when you are there. July to September is vacation time in Moscow. Late December is also slow, as is the first week of May (check the table on the page opposite for a list of Russian holidays).
- Use government agencies (where applicable and possible -- see the previous section), and private Russian companies (see Yellow Pages), to help arrange meetings with Russians in advance. Western law and consulting firms with offices in Moscow or St. Petersburg can also be of assistance in this regard (see the Yellow Pages under Legal Advice). It is best to arrange at least a few meetings before you leave, but not too many, as this will not leave you with enough flexibility.
- Similarly, arrange for transport support and translation services before you leave, if either is something you will need. Accommodation must likewise be reserved ahead of time, often long in advance (see Section III, Accomodation and Travel, for information on hotels and other accomodation and travel alternatives. See also the list of Travel Agents in Section I).
- If you plan to work toward a joint venture agreement or contract of some type, prepare a draft agreement (both on paper and on computer disc) before you leave, and have it translated into Russian.

Things to Take Along

If you have not left already, you should consider including some or all of the following items to make your trip more pleasurable, successful, comfortable, etc.:

- One bottle of Pepto-Bismol and a few rolls of antacids;
- One bottle of aspirin;
- Small box or bag of laundry soap -- the hall ladies in your hotel will often agree to do your laundry, but frequently they do not have detergent;
- Spare roll of toilet paper;
- An umbrella if you are going between March and October;
- Galoshes or shoes you do not mind soiling (city sidewalks are grimy in summer, icy, salty and slushy in winter, and otherwise very wet and messy);
- *Very* warm clothes if traveling October-April (including a hat and overcoat); a warm trench coat for May and September;
- Business cards, preferably with Russian on one side;
- Small, business-type gifts, i.e. pocket calculator, pens, pocket flashlight, lighter or other gadgets with your firm name on them (or even without);
- 10 blank business letterheads for typing an unexpected letter to a Ministry or an invitation to visit your home country;
- Pocket dictionary of Russian-English (or relevant first language);
- Power converter for hair dryer, shaver, etc. **Russia is on 220 volts, 50 Hz**, the plug is a two-pin, European plug;
- Extra pens;
- Alarm clock (do not count on being able to get a wake-up call);
- Universal flat bathtub stopper for doing laundry in your sink;
- Extra pair of glasses or contact lenses;
- Two copies of all relevant phone numbers;
- Photocopy of your passport and visa, kept separately from the originals in case of loss or theft;
- Prescription medication -- if you suffer from dry skin, bring some lotion in winter, indoors it will be very warm and dry;
- Chewing gum;
- ***Russia Business Survival Guide***

Visas and Visa Support

FOREIGNERS TRAVELING TO RUSSIA

All foreigners must have a visa to enter and exit Russia. Your visa, along with your passport, will be carefully inspected each time you enter and leave the country.

A visa is a sheet of paper which lists information about you, including your name, year of birth, passport number, etc., and indicates the dates during which you may be in Russia, which cities you may visit, the purpose of your visit, and which organization has sponsored your visa. **Three different types of visas exist for non-diplomats: business visas, tourist visas, and private individual visas.** Each type can be valid for various lengths of time.

A **tourist visa** is arranged through a tourist agency when booking travel to Russia. A **private individual visa** is based on an invitation issued on your behalf by a Russian citizen, through their local UVIR (visa registration) office. This latter is a comparatively long and tortuous process and not recommended. Since this is a business guide, the following, more detailed discussion relates only to business visas.

It should be noted at the outset that existing USSR visas are still honored in Russia (and most of the Commonwealth), if their term has not expired.

Persons visiting Russia on business are granted **business visas** by the Ministry of Foreign Affairs. In order to obtain a business visa, you must be sponsored by a Russian organization that can "support" your visa, i.e. demonstrate to the Ministry of Foreign Affairs that it is necessary for you to visit Russia and that it is in a position to be responsible for helping to facilitate your stay in the country. Only ministries, state organizations, joint ventures and or enterprises which are officially registered in the city soviet (city council) can support visas.

Single Entry Business Visa

This is the predominant, recommended and simplest type of visa to obtain. And until you have an established reason for a long term business relationship (be it a joint venture or otherwise), this is the type of visa you will receive. What follows is a description of the process you and your Russian contacts must go through each time you need a single-entry business visa.

Inform your business contacts or partners that you wish to visit Russia. It is best to give at least one month's notice of your desire to visit, if this is possible. The major difficulty in getting a visa is that the process can be very slow. When you and your Russian contacts have agreed on a date for your visit, add a couple of days onto each end of the time period to allow for slow arrival of the visa and possible extensions of your visit.

Send your contacts a copy of the first pages of your passport, the dates of your visit, a list of the cities you will need to visit, and the name of the city from which you will be departing immediately before entering Russia. If, for example, you are flying to Moscow via Helsinki, you will list Helsinki as the departure city, even if your travels originated somewhere else. Your departure city is the last stop before landing in Russia. Your passport must be valid at least three months beyond the date of your planned departure from Russia.

After your sponsoring organization has received all the required information from you, it should send you a written invitation via telex, fax or letter, inviting you for a business visit for the time period specified. ***When you receive this letter, you must send it, two passport-size photos, and a photocopy of the first pages of your passport to the Russian embassy or consulate in your home country, along with a visa application form (which you can get from the larger travel agencies or the embassy or consulate -- a sample is printed on the page opposite, this is only a sample, not for submission), and a processing fee of $20.***

You now wait until this embassy or consulate issues your visa. This may end up being the most time consuming part of the process. The turn-around time of visa applications has gotten much shorter and more predictable in the last couple of years. Processing typically should take about 10 working days.

It does happen that permission for a visa is denied. This can be because the invitation was issued by a non-registered Russian organization or company (registration must be with the local city soviet, i.e. it must be a legally functioning enterprise or organization). But it can also be because the Russian government has identified a problem of some sort in your record.

While it is rare that an explanation accompanies a specific visa refusal, in the past, illegal currency exchange and/or other types of interaction with the black market during previous visits to Russia were grounds for refusal. Other possible reasons for refusal are previous violation of visa rules, violations of customs regulations and/or criminal behavior. Refusals on political grounds have, to the best of our knowledge, ceased.

Multiple Entry Business Visa

If you foresee travelling frequently to Russia over the next several months, you may seek to get issued to you a multiple entry (in Russian: многократная) visa. These visas are now issued for a one-year or two-year period and allow the bearer to enter and exit at will, without getting a new visa for each visit.

This visa, however, is a bit more difficult and time consuming to obtain. Your contact in Russia, instead of sending you the invitation letter directly, must make application at the Ministry of Foreign Relations, and the latter must send a telex to the embassy in your home country for that embassy to clear a multiple entry visa request.

Sample Visa Application Form

Форма № 95

КОНСУЛЬСТВО (консульский отдел посольства) СССР в ______________________
страна

Place for photograph

QUESTIONNAIRE

ATTENTION! Please type, or print using ball-point pen. Incorrect information may cause denial of visa, denial of permission to cross the USSR border, or annulment of visa on the USSR territory.

ВИЗОВАЯ АНКЕТА

ВНИМАНИЕ! Писать четко, обязательно шариковой ручкой или на машинке. Неправильные данные могут повлечь за собой отказ в визе, в пересечении границы СССР или аннулирование визы на территории СССР.

1	Nationality	Национальность
2	Present citizenship (if you had USSR citizenship when and why you lost it)	Гражданство (если Вы имели гражданство СССР, то когда и в связи с чем его утратили)
3	Surname (in capital letters)	Фамилия
4	First name, patronymic (names)	Имя, отчество (имена)
5	(If changed, your surname, name (names) and patronymic before the change)	(Если изменяли, то Ваша фамилия, имя и отчество (имена) до изменения)
6	Day, month, year of birth / 7. Sex	Дата рождения / Пол
8	Object of journey to the USSR	Цель поездки в СССР
9	USSR department, organizations proposed to be visited	В какое учреждение
10	Route of journey (points of destination)	Маршрут следования (в пункты)
11	Date of entry / 12. Date of departure	Дата начала действия визы / Дата окончания действия визы
13	Passport N°	14. Категория, вид и кратность визы
15	Index and name of the tourist group Индекс, наименование туристской группы	
16	Place of work or study, position its address, telephone number Место работы или учебы, должность, адрес, номер телефона	
17	Permanent address, telephone number Адрес постоянного местожительства, номер телефона	
18	Place of birth (if born in the USSR, when and where to emigrated) Место рождения (если Вы родились в СССР, то куда и когда эмигрировали)	
19	Number of previous trips to the USSR Сколько раз были в СССР	Date of the latest trip Дата Вашей последней поездки

	Surname Фамилия	First name, patronymic Имя, отчество (имена)	Date of birth Дата рождения	Permanent address Адрес местожительства
20. Children under 16 years travelling with you Дети до 16 лет, следующие с вами				
21. Relatives in the USSR Ваши родственники в СССР				

I declare that the data given in the Questionnaire are correct

Я заявляю, что все данные, указанные в анкете, являются правильными

Date ______________
Дата

Personal signature ______________
Личная подпись

1639

If permission from the Ministry of Foreign Relations is so granted, your contact/sponsoring organization should send you a copy of the visa support letter, which you can then forward with your application to the Russian embassy.

If you are just beginning to develop a business relationship with people in Russia, you will find it much easier to simply get a single-entry business visa, as described above, for each trip to the country. If you find later that a multiple entry visa is necessary, it is suggested you seek to have one issued while you are in Moscow for a business trip. With a bit of pushing and savvy on the part of your Russian partner, this is a much easier task to manage while you are in-country.

Employees of joint ventures and members of their families, as well as persons who are working on contract with state organizations or ministries, will want to obtain (and have an easier time obtaining) multiple entry visas. Having one means many fewer hassles overall.

Registration Upon Arrival

You are required to register with UVIR within 72 hours of your arrival in Russia. If you are staying in a hotel, the hotel will hold your passport for 1-2 days and take care of the registration for you. If you are not staying in a hotel, make sure that someone in your sponsoring organization takes your passport to UVIR and registers you. Each time you travel to a different city, you must technically be registered with the local authorities before departing or within 72 hours. Foreigners staying in Russia long-term are no longer required to register with the militia.

Avoiding Visa Headaches

There are two things you can do to avoid the headache and worry over a late issue of a visa.

(1) As suggested above, request that your visa be valid from a few days prior to your scheduled departure date.

(2) After receiving your visa support letter from your Russian contacts, send all your materials to a company that specializes in expediting visas. These companies deliver your documents to the correct offices, make follow-up calls to check on the status of your visa, and will express mail it to you the day it is issued. See Section I under Travel and Visa Agencies for a short list of such organizations.

Alternatively, by enclosing a $30 fee instead of the standard $20, you can receive "rush service" from the Russian embassy itself, whereby your application is processed in five (instead of 10) working days.

Traveling to Other Cities in Russia

It used to be that, by law, foreigners could only travel to those cities which were indicated on their visa. This is ending. The official line of UVIR in Moscow is that visas are not required for any cities, and that foreigners can travel to any city which is not "closed" (for security reasons). But the requirement is still being enforced sporadically, and it pays to cover all bases for the time being. To get any city listed on your visa, simply make sure that travel to such city is clearly indicated by your Russian partners in their invitation.

There is no longer a restriction on foreigners forbidding travel outside a 40 kilometer limit from the city which they are visiting.

The visa requirements for travelling to cities in other states of the Commonwealth (i.e outside Russia) can be confusing and are expected to fluctuate for the coming year. Presently, visas are being issued at the border for Ukraine and the Baltics (for a small fee). Holding a Russian visa usually makes entering contiguous states easier (all former republics, excepting Georgia, are currently honoring Russian visas). If you are outside Russia, check with the Russian embassy (see Section I) for visa rules. If you are in Moscow, contact the embassy of the state you wish to visit (see Telephone Directory under "Embassy of...").

Length of Visa

It is unwise to stay in Russia past the expiration date on your visa. It is simple enough to have your partners extend your visa dates (or do it yourself with a visit to UVIR -- see the Yellow Pages for hours and location in Moscow). If your visa does expire before you leave the country and you have not extended it, you may be required to pay a fine. You will not be detained in Russia. However, the next time you try to get a visa to enter the country, you could face difficulties and long delays. It could also place your sponsoring organization in a difficult position.

RUSSIANS TRAVELING ABROAD

If you decide that it is necessary to meet with your Russian partners or contacts in your home country, they will have to get international passports and exit visas before they can leave Russia. While an emigration and freedom of travel law has been passed (albeit by the former Soviet parliament), it will not go into full effect until January 1993.

The first thing you need to do is invite your associates by means of an official "Letter of Invitation" on your company letterhead. This letter must include the following information in your own language (Russian is optional):

- The full name, address and passport number of the person being invited;
- The full name of your company;
- The full address and phone numbers of your company inside the country your guests will visit, plus a short description of the nature of your business (your

company address cannot be in Canada if your guests will be going to the United States);

- An outline of planned meetings or conferences, with as exact an itinerary as possible and an exact statement of the purpose of the trip;
- Dates of the trip.

The letter must be notarized. This is very important. The easiest way to do this is at your embassy in Moscow or St. Petersburg. Go letter in hand (call ahead to find out when you can get such a letter notarized) and have it notarized on the spot. If you are in your home country, you should call the Russian embassy or consulate nearest you and find out what the current notarial requirements are (see Section I for addresses of Russian embassies); they differ from country to country and can be quite strict.

When your contacts receive this letter, they must take this letter (and some passport photos) to the city UVIR headquarters to obtain an exit visa. Then an UVIR officer takes the person's passport and exit visa to the proper embassy to get the entry visa, if required. You should encourage them to contact the embassy or consulate ahead of time to get full instructions and get an estimate of the time it will take to process their request.

The US Commercial Office (USCO) has introduced a special service enabling easier processing of exit visas for Russians invited on business to the US by American companies. Your contact must take the invitation letter, his or her passport, two photographs, and a typed, completed visa application to the USCO office between 4:30 and 5:30 Monday, Wednesday or Friday. For more information, contact the USCO office at the number listed in the Telephone Directory (under Embassy of the United States).

The process for individuals (non-business visas) is much the same, only that the Russian takes the invitation to their local UVIR office, not the city UVIR headquarters.

Customs Regulations

ARRIVING BY PLANE

You will know you are in Russia when you begin the process of passport control, baggage collection, and customs. The process is slow (but improving), has long lines, and can be arbitrary and chaotic, particularly at Sheremetevo Airport in Moscow.

At passport control your visa and passport will be scrutinized by young border guards. If your visa is in order and you have not arrived outside the effective dates of your visa, you should have no problems and be through in about 15-30 minutes, depending upon lines.

The arrival of your bags on the conveyer belts can take anywhere from 10 minutes to an hour. While you are waiting for your bags to come, you can track down a customs declaration form if you were not given one on the plane, and fill it in. You may not be able to locate one in your native language. For this reason, and to let you know what to look for, a sample form is printed in this section. You will be asked to declare all money, jewelry, videotapes, electronic items, and other objects of value. Write down everything of this sort. In theory, if you do not declare it coming in and you have it on the way out and do not have a receipt for having bought it into Russia, you cannot take it with you. Better safe than sorry.

If your luggage is lost *en route*, report immediately to the lost luggage office off to the side of the baggage claim area. This is a frequent enough occurrence anywhere in the world, much less Moscow, to suggest that the traveler have in a carry-on what is needed to survive for two days. In fact, recently problems with baggage theft and "pillaging" have been on the rise. Valuables should therefore be in a carry-on, and a hard sided suitcase that can be locked is recommended.

Upon collecting your baggage you proceed to customs. There are now green (nothing to declare) and red (something to declare) channels. The lines for the red channel are always long. If you want to be able to progress through the green channel you should not have more than $50 worth of hard currency (including cash and travelers' checks) with you. There is no limit to the amount of money a foreigner can bring into the country (for Russians there is a $200 limit without bank documentation), and there are no longer any limits on "luxury items" such as cigarrettes, perfume or alcohol (although there are limits on taking them out).

The obvious implication of the declaration procedure is that, upon leaving, you should not be taking anything out with you that you cannot prove to have brought in with you or purchased in a hard currency shop, nor should you have more currency than you came in with.

There is a duty free shop before you go through customs at Sheremetevo (Moscow) or Pulkovo (St. Petersburg) and you can buy some luxury items there if you want to bring them in as gifts or for personal consumption.

If you are traveling on a business visa, you are probably less likely to have your baggage searched, particularly if you travel light. Those who look suspicious (unfortunately this is often judged by skin color) or who travel heavy seem to have their bags checked more closely. On the way out of Russia, the same general rules apply, but with recent customs crackdowns it is more often that an outgoing passenger's bags are checked, at least cursorily.

The customs officer will verify your customs declaration (if you go through the red channel) and make some marks on it. Your customs declaration will then be given back to you. ***Your customs declaration is a very important document. Do not lose it.*** Keep your declaration slip with you and/or your passport at all times. If you change hard currency for rubles in a bank and wish to be able to change it back before you go, you will need to have the initial operation marked on this declaration. You will have to fill in another declaration upon leaving the country. If you lose your incoming declaration you, theoretically, will not be allowed to take out any of the money or goods on your export declaration, because you would not be able to prove you came in with them.

If you lose your customs declaration, you should request that your embassy write a letter to that effect addressed to Central Customs, Komsomolskaya ploshchad 1a, Moscow, requesting issuance of a duplicate declaration. Most often replacement declarations are not granted, especially if you have entered Russia more than several weeks ago, or at a point other than Moscow. If the traveler cannot get a replacement declaration, he should be advised to tell the Customs inspector upon departure that he has lost his old declaration, fill in a new declaration, and be sure that he is carrying an absolute minimum of cash (as opposed to traveller's checks or other non-negotiable instruments).

It does happen that customs officials ask to see the wallets of travelers in order to verify the amount of money being brought in or out. In other words, lying about this figure is not in your interest. It will only cost you grief and probably bring you little gain.

For departure from Russia, allow 30-45 minutes for customs before check-in time at your airline.

ARRIVING BY TRAIN

If you come into Russia from Helsinki or elsewhere by train, you will want to be very mindful of the customs regulations just mentioned and those discussed below. Whether arriving in or departing from Russia by train, it is logical and true that the customs officers will have more time and opportunity for customs inspection. Expect more customs difficulties when traveling by train. Expect to have your papers and belongings subjected to much closer scrutiny.

RESTRICTIONS AND LIMITATIONS

Recent legal acts have drastically limited the number of items subject to import duties. Still, there are certain items subject to different types of restrictions and limitations. These are summarized below.

Art, icons and precious metals: Objects of art, gold, precious stones, icons, and the like are all being monitored tightly at exit customs control. Be sure that anything of this sort which you buy can be taken out of the country duty free.

Anything which may be deemed of historical or cultural value is forbidden from export. Items of historical or cultural value are (for example): sculpture, graphics and paintings by outstanding artists of any period or country, icons and other religious items, Russian and foreign manuscripts, books dating before 1977, porcelain and crystal, rugs and tapestries, coins and jewelry, restored

Sample Customs Declaration Form

Keep for the duration of your stay in the USSR or abroad. Not renewable in case of loss.

Persons giving false information in the Customs Declaration, or to Customs officers shall render themselves liable under laws of the USSR.

CUSTOMS DECLARATION

Full name ____________________

Citizenship ____________________

Arriving from ____________________

Country of destination ____________________

Purpose of visit ____________________
(business, tourism, private, etc.)

My luggage (including hand luggage) submitted for Customs inspection consists of ____________________ pieces.

With me and my luggage I have:

I. Weapons of all descriptions and ammunition ____________________

II. Narcotics and appliances for the use thereof ____________________

III. Antiques and objects of art (paintings, drawings, icons, sculptures, etc.) ____________________

IV. Soviet roubles, Soviet government bones and lottery tickets, as well as V/O «Vneshposyltorg» cheques and Venshtorgbank rouble cheques series A ____________________

V. Currency other than USSR roubles (bank notes, exchequer bills, coins), payment voucher (cheques, bills, letters of credit, etc.), securities (shares, bonds, etc.) in foreign currencies, precious metals (gold, silver, platinum, metals of platinum group) in any form or condition, crude and processed natural precious stones (diamonds, brilliants, rubies, emeralds, sapphires and pearls), jewelry and other articles made of precious metals and precious stones, and scrap thereof, as well as property papers:

Description	Amount / quantity		For official use
	in figures	in words	
US dollars			
Pounds sterling			
French francs			
Deutschemarks			

VI. USSR roubles, other currency, payment vouchers, valuables and any objects belonging to other persons ____________________

I am aware that, in addition to the objects listed in the Customs Declaration, I must submit for inspection: printed matter, manuscripts, films, video- and sound recordings, postage stamps, pictorial matter, etc., as well as items not for personal use.

I also declare that my luggage sent separately consists of __________ pieces.

(Date)__________ 198__

Owner of luggage __________
(signed)

A. Cleared on entry to (exit from) the U.S.S.R:

No.	Description of objects	Quantity (in words)

B. Cleared Rbls. ________________ with/without authorization to spend or change abroad
Customs clearance

BANK RECORDS

Purchase of foreign currency							
Date	Foreign currency	Rubles	Name of bank	Date	Foreign curency	Rubles	Name of bank

Re-exchange of unexpended rubles

furniture. If you are in doubt about a specific purchase, Russian customs authorities can be consulted at Komsomolskaya ploshchad 1a, ph. 975-4460.

Objects of art can be exported if you go through the proper procedures. This requires registration of the object with the Ministry of Culture to obtain a *spravka*, which can take up to a month. If the Ministry of Culture determines that the object may be exported, a letter is prepared for customs with the tax to be charged (100 percent of the value of the item). To have the object evaluated and obtain a *spravka*, take the object to the Ministry of Culture at ul. Chekhova 29 (open Tuesdays 10-14:00) in Moscow. The Ministry of Culture requires three photographs of the object. Get them done ahead of time.

Do not worry about declaring souvenirs (but be sure they are souvenirs and not valuable works of art) you have picked up on the Arbat, Izmailovo Park or other open-air markets. But do not try taking out a suitcase-full of Palekh lacquered boxes. Items purchased at hard currency stores can be taken out without limit, so long as you retain the receipt.

Caviar and consumer goods: Russian customs regulations state that the export of sturgeon and salmon caviar by foreign citizens is permitted without limitation on condition of presentation of a receipt that the caviar was purchased for hard currency "according to established procedures." Caviar obtained through other channels (i.e. for rubles) is not permitted for export.

Regulations also limit the export of other consumer items. The value of consumer goods (and presumably gifts, but this is not so strictly enforced) purchased for rubles which may be taken out of the country may not exceeed 300 rubles. Among this category is foodstuffs and cameras, watches, perfume, etc.

No more than 1.5 liters of vodka, 100 cigarettes and 2 liters of wine may be taken out (this can be overridden by considerations of what you may have brought in and stated on your declaration, or by goods you can prove to have purchased at hard currency stores).

Computers and electronics: There is some confusion as to whether computers and other consumer electronics can be brought in duty free. As with many things, the law is being inconsistently applied. There is a law which requires you to pay a deposit upon entry with such items, and the deposit is refunded to you if you leave with the items. This is to discourage speculation. You should resist this in the case of a personal laptop computer or shortwave radio, etc. (see Personal Use Doctrine below) But if you are bringing in consumer electronics to sell at a commission store (which is legal) you should be prepared to pay the duty.

If you wish to bring a computer to Russia from a Western country subscribing to CoCom restrictions, there are still come CoCom restrictions on exporting computers into Russia. For the most part, any off-the-shelf type computer may be exported under General License. Only larger, mainframe-type or super-mini type computers require special licensing procedures.

By way of guidelines, you may export 286 and 386 machines with up to 32 megabytes of RAM, with a processing speed of up to 35 mhz (a 32 bit bus cannot be exported under General License). An internal hard disk of up to 2 gigabytes is allowed (with up to 5 additional hard disks and a total storage space of 10.3 gigabytes) and LAN support but no wide area networking is allowed. Finally, the system cannot exceed a data signalling rate of 20 million bits and cannot have an internetwork gateway. If any of these limits are exceeded, a Validated License is necessary.

CoCom is presently revising its specifications to simplify classification procedures. You may wish to contact your Department of Commerce or Foreign Trade (or relevant chamber of commerce -- see Section I) for the most up to date information. In the United States call the Office of Technology and Policy Analysis at (202) 377-0899.

Currency and monetary instruments: A limited number of rubles (1000) can be taken into or out of Russia. You cannot take more hard currency out of Russia than you brought in. Technically you are required to write down on your customs declarations (in and out) all travelers' checks and any monetary instruments made payable to you, but many people do not.

Narcotics and firearms: Narcotics and firearms may not be imported into or exported from Russia. Many Western over-the-counter drugs theoretically require permission from the Ministry of Health to be brought into the country, but allowance for personal use is given.

Printed and recorded material: Pornography and defamatory material may not be brought into (or out of) Russia. Russian standards of pornographic material are still much stricter than in the West. Sexually explicit photographs constitute pornography.

Written material must, theoretically, be declared, but do not sweat this one. In theory "sensitive" items can be confiscated and have been in the past. Just use common sense. Don't bring in original manuscripts or documents without leaving a copy at home. If you are carrying into or out of the country internal (Russian) government documents which might be deemed of a sensitive nature, you should have a letter from the appropriate ministry or department which gave you the documents, vouchsafing the fact that you have proper authority to be carrying these papers on your person.

Video tapes are the focus of current crackdowns. Current regulations allow five cassettes for personal use. Leave these sealed if you can for entry, so there will be no chance they will be seen as recorded material. Customs regulations forbid import into Russia of recorded video cassettes (meaning commercial movies, not personal recordings).

Trade samples: You can take trade samples both into and out of Russia without much problem, provided you have the proper documentation and provided the samples do not infringe any of the restrictions mentioned above. To exit with trade samples, have the company which has given you the samples prepare a letter in Russian, with the appropriate stamps, attesting to the fact that these are samples and should not be subject to export restrictions. If you feel the need, you can prepare a similar letter for samples which you are importing.

A final consideration: A guiding principle for what you should or can bring in with you without any difficulty or duty could be called the **Personal Use Doctrine**. If you can reasonably claim that the items you are bringing in with you are for your personal use, whether they be cosmetics, film, a laptop computer, or books, then you should have no problem. If you are bringing in 10 pairs of new jeans or 40 blank video cassettes, it will be very difficult to claim these are for personal use (unless perhaps you are staying for an extended period).

Confiscation: In the event you have something confiscated upon entry, you will normally be issued a receipt for the item. This receipt, or *kvitantsiya* allows you to reclaim the item on your way out (in theory). Undeclared currency or undeclared valuable property may be subject to permanent confiscation. If the items confiscated are considered "contraband", a protocol detailing the reasons for the seizure will also be made out. Contraband and items confiscated upon exit will not likely be returned to you.

III. Accommodations and Travel

Accommodations

The situation with travel accommodations in Russia is improving. First, the growth of private enterprise has led to a flourishing of private tour agencies and bed and breakfast operations. Second, the activity of joint ventures and Western investment has led to renovation of a handful of landmark Moscow and St. Petersburg hotels. While space is often still hard to come by, if you know where and how to look, you will find that, as opposed to even a year or two ago, accommodation choices have become better and more numerous.

If you or your host have not already arranged for accommodation, it is suggested you begin settling this issue well in advance of any travel to Russia. And even if you have traveled to Russia frequently, you will want to survey some of the newer alternatives now open to you. Whereas in years past all bookings for independent travel had to go through Intourist, now booking a room can be as easy as sending a fax or telex to a joint venture hotel, or contacting a Western representative of a Russian hotel or bed and breakfast service. Of course, you can still arrange for a room through a local travel agent or Intourist (see Section I for addresses).

At present there are basically two accommodation choices for the individual traveler: hotels, of which there are joint venture hotels and Russian state-owned hotels, and accommodation in private homes.

HOTELS

Joint venture hotels are former state-owned hotels that have been renovated and/or are being operated under the aegis of a Western-Russian joint venture. The level of service tends to be very high, as do the prices. State-owned hotels usually offer a much lower quality of service for a not much lower price.

Despite the inroads being made by large Western hotel chains, such as Radisson, Novotel and Intercontinental, there remains a certain characteristic Russian (some would say Soviet) quality to major hotels in Moscow and St. Petersburg. This said, it is noteworthy that service personnel in some of the new joint venture hotels are better paid and thus more motivated than their counterparts in state-run hotels, and are more responsive to the usual expectations of the Western business traveler. This is gradually leading to a "warming" of the atmosphere at such landmark hotels, and away from the unaccommodating service and poor facilities characteristic of hotels in the Soviet period.

In state-owned hotels, Soviet habits unfortunately still cling to deep roots. The staff remains under-paid and under-motivated and thus generally unaccommodating. The front desk is more often a place of dread and red tape rather than for problem solving and services. Room service is difficult to come by and staff can be intrusive (expect maids to come into your room without knocking). Support and business services, as well as hotel sundries stores are on the rise, but generally still not adequate.

In the two-tiered (ruble/dollar) economy which now exists in Russia, you can expect that hotels where foreigners stay will continue to attract people hawking souvenirs and trinkets. These merchants used to be known as "black marketeers" but can now operate freely and openly (assuming they have paid off the right people). While it is no longer "illegal" to deal with these merchants, it still pays to be very cautious and wary. Shams, scams and cons are on the rise. Gypsy beggars, secret rendevous' and cab rides without known destination are to be avoided at all costs (see Crime in Section IV). The fact is that there is little available through this sort of trading that cannot now be obtained through commercial shops or at places like Izmailovo Park and the Arbat (in Moscow) or Catherine's Park (in St. Petersburg).

Most major tourist hotels, especially the state-owned ones, still retain some variation of the hall lady (lt;ehyfz - dezhurnaya) system, whereby a woman monitors your hotel floor around the clock. You exchange your key for your hotel entrance pass (ghjgecr -- propusk) with her (or with someone at a more centralized location) when you are leaving the hotel, and do the reverse when you return. She is the first person to turn to when you need a shirt ironed, when you want bottled water, a taxi, room service, when something does not work in your room, etc. A tasteful gift to one of these ladies upon arrival may help to make most any ensuing accommodation problems melt away.

Along with the generally better level of business and support services which the newly refurbished joint venture hotels offer, quite often they also offer an easier access to money changing. The day when all major tourist hotels had exchange points is past and these newer hotels often maintain exchange point services exclusively for their clientele.

The next three pages contain a table summarizing the relative quality, size and prices of major Moscow and St. Petersburg hotels. If you are in the process of deciding on a place to stay, this may offer some guidance. The main phone, fax and telex numbers of hotels now open are listed in the Yellow Pages under Hotels and in the Telephone Directory under the name of the Hotel. If you don't find a hotel listed in the following table, it is either because foreigners very rarely stay there or because it does not register on the rating scale.

By way of information, a deluxe room is the Russian terminology for accomodation *en suite*; a luxe or semi-luxe room is a partial suite (includes a small seating or dining area).

Moscow Hotels

	JV or State Hotel	Class of Hotel	No. Rooms	Cost Single	Cost Double	Other rooms
Aerostar	JV	★★★	200	$135	$185	$195-230 luxe, $205-255 deluxe
Arbat (Oktyabrskaya II)	State	★★	107	$200-235	$200-235	$380 semi-luxe, $470 deluxe
Belgrade (II)	State	★	806	$120	$140	$210 semi-luxe, $290 deluxe
Budapest	State	★	16	$95	$100-110	
Inflotel (Aleksandr Blok)	JV	★★	71	$115	$138	$200 deluxe
Intourist	State	★★	458	$211	$300	$341 suite
Kosmos	State	★★	1767	--	$96	$133 semi-luxe, $207 apartment
Leningradskaya	State	★	346	$100	$145-190	$215 semi-luxe, $270 deluxe
Marco Polo	JV	★★★	64	$180	$215	$290 semi-luxe, $360 luxe
Metropol	JV	★★★★	403	$300-360	$390-450	$420-510, semi-luxe, $710 exec. suite, $810 deluxe, $1250 Pres. suite
Mezhdunarodnaya	State	★★★	250	$219	$228	$437 semi-luxe, $850 Pres. suite
Minsk	State	★	300	$130	$180	
Molodyozhnaya	State	★	630	--	$65	$90 semi-luxe

NOTE:

The information in this table was gathered just prior to publication. Room rates are subject to change without notice. The ratings for hotels are based on a polling of travel agents and business people who travel frequently to Russia and use the following parameters:

★★★★ **Highest class hotel.** Would be a first class hotel in any world capital. Unsurpassed restaurants, customer service and business services.

★★★ **Very good to excellent hotel.** Fine restaurants. Good to excellent customer service and business services. Very comfortable, but there is one step higher.

★★ **Average to good hotel.** Restaurants OK but not consistent. Customer service standards low; few or no business services.

★ **Passable hotel.** Restaurants not suggested. Customer service is poor to non-existent. No business services.

Moscow Hotels, cont.

	JV or State Hotel	Class of Hotel	No. Rooms	Cost Single	Cost Double	Other rooms
Moskva	State	★★	700	$110	$145	$180-233 semi-luxe, $285 deluxe
Novotel	JV	★★★	510	$149	$149	$199 triple, $280 adj. rooms or room with view
Olympic Penta	JV	★★★	300	$336	$400	$840 deluxe single, $844 deluxe double
Pekin	State	★★	50	$100	$102-140	$200-250 semi-luxe, $270-400 deluxe
President (Oktyabrskaya I)	State	★★★	200	$200	$240	$350 semi-luxe, $470 deluxe
Pullman-Iris	JV	★★★	211	$220	$250	$141 living room, $330 suite, $670 Pres. suite
Rossia	State	★	3091	$100	$120	$240-300 semi-luxe
Savoy	JV	★★★	86	$255	$320	$410 semi-luxe, $810 deluxe
Sheremetevo	State	★	120	--	$120	
Slavyanskaya-Radisson	JV	★★★	430	$210	$263	$420-630 deluxe
Sovietskaya	State	★★	100	$169	$169	$216 alcove, $295 semi-luxe, $391 deluxe, $494 apartment
Spros	JV	★★	32	$200		$330 luxe
Tsentralny Dom Turista	State	★	500	$65	$80	$146 semi-luxe, $260 deluxe
Ukraine	State	★	1500	$125	$155	$250 semi-luxe, $300 deluxe
Zolotoe Koltso (Belgrade I)	State	★	460	$120	$140	$210 semi-luxe, $290 deluxe

St. Petersburg Hotels

	JV or State Hotel	Class of Hotel	No. Rooms	Cost Single	Cost Double	Other rooms
Astoria	JV	★★★	800	$170	$210	$400 deluxe, $600 suite
Dvorets Molodyozhy	State	★	400	--	560R	800R luxe
Evropeyskaya (Grand Europe)	JV	★★★★	301	$175-285	$205-315	$285-340 luxe, $340-375 deluxe, $440-550 suite, $820 deluxe suite
Helen (in Sovietskaya)	JV	★★	--	$90	$136	$120 triple
Karelia	State	★	995	--	$40	
Sankt Peterburg	State	★★	700	$110	$125	$190 luxe, $265 deluxe
Morskaya	State	★★	300	$40	$50	$100 deluxe
Moskva	State	★★	777	$111	$120	$200 luxe, $280 deluxe
Okhtinskaya	JV	★★	300	$65	$140	$140 deluxe
Oktyabrskaya	State	★	--	640R	770R	1400R luxe, 1900R deluxe
Pribaltiyskaya	State	★★★	1200	--	$168	$246 deluxe, $374 suite
Pulkovskaya	State	★★★	540	$164	$186	$266 deluxe
Rossiya	State	★★	600	650R	900R	1100R luxe
Sovetskaya	State	★	1110	$90	$136	$150 deluxe
Sputnik	State	★	--	620R	820R	530R luxe/pp
Vyborgskaya	State	★★	410	576R	768R	480R luxe/pp

ACCOMMODATION IN PRIVATE HOMES

Accommodation in private homes (apartments) has the advantage over hotels in being somewhat more flexible and inexpensive. And the educational aspect should not be overlooked. This option runs the gamut from bed and breakfast arrangements to staying with friends and acquaintances, which up until a few years ago was not legal.

When staying with friends, you will be responsible for dealing with visa registration yourself; read up on this in Section II under Visa Support.

The new bed and breakfast alternative offers an entirely different experience from accommodation in hotels, and can be particularly desireable for longer stays. A number of Western companies have solid Russian counterparts they work with to arrange this type of accommodation. As well, Moscow or St. Petersburg based travel companies (see Yellow Pages under Travel Agencies) or apartment leasing companies (see Yellow Pages under Apartments) can also offer such services. The terms, prices and procedures of each varies. Generally, it is recommended to work through a Western partner of a bed and breakfast venture. Often they can also arrange for your visa support, thus taking care of two problems at once (in fact it only makes sense to work through a company that can handle visa support as well). To that end, some such companies are listed below. Where possible, available cities and pricing information have also been included.

American International Homestays, Route 1, Box 68, Iowa City, IA 52240, phone (319) 626-2125, fax (319) 626-2129. [Moscow, St. Petersburg, Irkutsk and major capitals].

Cultural Access Network, Box 4410, Laguna Beach, CA 92652, phone (714) 497-6773, fax (714) 497-6809. [Moscow, St. Petersburg; $75 per night].

East-West Ventures, Inc., P.O. Box 14391, Tucson, AZ 85732, phone (800) 833-4398. [Moscow, St. Petersburg, Kiev, Sochi; $42-64 per night; also offer visa support, driver and translator services]

I.B.V. Bed and Breakfast Systems, 13113 Ideal Drive, Silver Spring, MD 20906, phone (301) 942-3770, fax (301) 933-0024.

International Bed and Breakfast, P.O. Box 823, Huntington Valley, PA 19006, phone (800) 422-5283, fax (215) 663-8580.

Pioneer East/West Initiatives, 88 Brooks Ave., Arlington, MA 02174, phone (617) 648-2020, fax (617) 648-7304.

Progressive Tours, 12 Porchester Pl., Marble Arch, London W2 2B5, phone (071) 262-1676.

Travel

One of the first problems to be faced when arriving in Moscow or St. Petersburg is arrangement of transport while you are in the city. If this is not something a host organization is looking after, then you should bone up on the range of options open to you. But first, you should get the lay of the land.

GETTING ORIENTED IN MOSCOW

It always helps to get an understanding of the geography of a city before trying to get around it. It also makes the place seem a bit less foreign.

You will notice in looking at the map in the back of the book that Moscow is a city founded on a river. Actually, it is founded on three rivers, but two have been put largely underground. The Moscow (Москва) river is the most important geographical feature in the city, but it can also provide the greatest source of confusion in navigation. This is because it does not flow in a straight line through the city, but snakes its way north and south, forming something of a tongue and groove feature in the city center (where the Kremlin lies in the center of the tongue).

Your best bet is not to use the river as a source of orientation, except in the city center. You are better off orienting to the fact that the major city roadways are a series of concentric rings with major arteries intersecting them and stretching outward. The two major rings are the Boulevard Ring and the Garden Ring. Navigating with respect to these two rings (and sometimes the outer Ring Road) and a major cross road will help you remember which end is up. It is helpful to remember that the metro system is similarly organized about a main ring line (see Metro Map inside front cover).

GETTING ORIENTED IN ST. PETERSBURG

St. Petersburg, for over 200 years Russia's capital, is a city founded on a river delta with the specific purpose of being a maritime city. The river Neva is therefore the most important geographic feature of this "Venice of the North."

The plethora of bridges and canals between the city's 44 islands in the Neva's delta are enough to create significant confusion for the first time visitor.

Your best bet is to focus on the "half-circle" of the city center which is bordered by the river Fontanki on its round edges and the river Neva along its "straight" edge. This half-circle can then be seen as divided into wedges by the three major avenues, Nevsky Prospekt, ul. Dzerzhinskovo, and Prospekt Mayorovo. Certainly Nevsky Prospekt is the most important area of commercial activity in the city.

There are then two major islands which form the other half of the circle, on the other side of the Neva. These are Vasilevsky island, where the University is located, and Petrogradsky island, to which Peter-Paul Fortress is attached. Both are mainly residential, and most industrial activity is in the southern regions of the city near the airport, or on the "Vyborg side," also across the river from the main commercial center.

Two key points for orientation in St. Petersburg are the spires of Peter-Paul Fortress and the Admiralty, which can both be seen from most places near the center. The Admiralty spire, Golden with a silhouette of a sailing ship at its peak, is the true center of the city and is the apex of the three main avenues in the "half-circle." The taller spire of Peter-Paul Fortress is topped with a cross.

The metro is not as central a part of public transport in St. Petersburg as is the case in Moscow, particularly in navigating the city center. Many points are easily accessible by trolley buses. If you have a lot of ground to cover, rent a car or stick to cabs. For maps and the most up-to-date directory information on St. Petersburg, pick up a copy of *Where in St. Petersburg* (see the order form in the back of the book).

PUBLIC TRANSPORT

In general, given the loads it must carry, public transport in both Moscow and St. Petersburg is good. And because it is ridiculously inexpensive, it is crowded and not always your best bet for getting places in a hurry. As well, bus and tram routes are not easily understandable to the non-Russian speaker or non-resident. The metro, however, can be a good way to get around on your own if you can read some Cyrillic (or simply count stops).

The metro system dates from the 1930s in Moscow and from the 1950s in St. Petersburg. Trains run, during daytime hours, about every 2-3 minutes (usually more frequently). The metro is to be avoided at all costs during rush hours, between 7-10 a.m. and 4-7 p.m., unless you have a deep yearning to "get close" to Russia.

All public transport costs 50 kopeks per ride. One pays for the metro ride by depositing a metro token (which you can buy at a change window, sometimes only two at a time when supplies are short) in automated entry gates inside metro stations. Buses and trams require you to purchase *talony* (талоны) or tickets at metro stations, kiosks, or on the buses and trams themselves, and to validate them by stamping them in punches hanging on the inside of the cabin. Prices for public transport have risen over 300% in the past year. More increases are expected over 1992.

You can also buy a monthly pass good for unlimited travel on all public transport for 60 rubles. If you plan on riding public transport a lot, have your Russian contact buy one of these *ediny bilet* (единый билет) for you before your arrival as they are only on sale at selected metro stations beginning the middle of a month for the coming month. They can save a lot of hassle fumbling for coins (or even getting them when supplies are low).

Metro, Buses and Trolleybuses operate from 6 a.m. to 1 a.m.; Trams 05:30 to 01:30. Metro transfer stations (переходы -- *perekhodi*) close at 00:30.

TAXIS

If you need to get somewhere fairly quickly, and want to do it above ground and without being crushed by fellow travelers, this is the way to go.

Taxis in Moscow and St. Petersburg are notoriously dirty and dangerous. Courtesy is not a watchword in the Russian hack's lexicon. While there are certainly excellent, good, and poor taxi drivers everywhere, your average Russian taxi driver is ruder to others on the road, more lead-footed, and less concerned with your personal comfort and safety than his counterpart in, say London, Rome, or New York. Every stop light is a drag strip opportunity, and every pedestrian is an open target (making *babushkas* run seems a favorite pastime of most all Russian drivers, who have very different notions of pedestrian right-of-way than you might be accustomed to).

Some of this is changing as price rises have caused taxi drivers to have to meet higher daily revenue quotas and to compete for a scarcer consumer ruble. It has gotten much easier since the beginning of 1992 to catch a cab and to get where you want to go. And whereas in times past passengers had to "beseech" the driver to go where they wanted to go, these changing times are seeing drivers become much more accomodating, quoting the full price of the ride before it begins, and much more frequently charging according to the standard tariffs. The little green light in the passenger side of the taxi's windshield, which announces that the taxi is available, is also now a more accurate indicator of the cab's availability.

It should be said that, when speaking of taxi drivers, also included are "gypsy cab" drivers, which means both self-employed drivers, and your average Russian who is just looking for a few extra rubles to meet petrol bills, and is willing to drive you somewhere if it is not too far out of his way (the masculine is accurate usage when speaking about driving, as very few women in Russia drive -- rumor has it there are less than a dozen female taxi drivers in Moscow, a city of 9 million). If you ride in cabs regularly, you can count on riding 40-50% of the time in gypsy cabs (where, unlike in official cabs, you are required to wear a seatbelt, or at least drape it across your shoulder; putting on a seatbelt in an official cab, by contrast, is not required and, in fact often viewed by the driver as an insult). In fact, you may occasionally be offered rides in some quite unusual and interesting vehicles. Given the recent rise in crime against foreigners, you are advised to be somewhat wary about riding "gypsy-style".

As stated above, meters are more often than in the past the basis for cab fares, which are now levied at ten times that which ticks off on the meters (two rubles initial fee, plus two rubles per kilometer during the day [06:00 - 20:00] and three rubles per kilometer at night [20:00- 06:00] -- there are extra charges for baggage). As a foreigner, you can expect to pay a "negotiated" rate as often as not (more often if you don't speak the language). If you have a taxi ordered for you by the hall lady in your hotel (or if you do it yourself), which you must usually do at least half a day in advance, but theoretically can be done an hour in advance (see Yellow Pages under Taxis), then you will pay the metered rate. The additional cost for booking a cab in advance is 20 rubles for daytime hours, 25 rubles for evening hours.

Being recognizable as a foreigner also opens you to demands of hard-currency payment for rides, particularly late at night, and particularly around foreign tourist hotels and from the airport (from where it is now nearly impossible to get a ride for rubles; in fact, it is ***highly*** recommended to use a private "limo" service from the airport to your hotel -- just go up to one of the taxi counters at the airport or call or fax ahead of your arrival -- see Yellow Pages). If you have to pay with hard currency, it is usually a safe thing to do and a more certain way to get where you want to go. A couple dollars should get you a very long distance in the present cab market. To know how much to offer, consider that it is not that difficult to rent a cab for the day for $20. In any case, be cautious about flashing lots of dollars or being too "free" with them. See the section on Crime, in Section IV for some consideration of this issue.

The shrewder (and often more patient) traveler gets rides for rubles by knowing how much above the official price to negotiate ("tip"). The closer you are to major foreign tourist hotels, the farther away from the center you are asking to be driven, and the later it is in the evening (particularly on weekends), will drive up the price accordingly. A 10-15 minute daytime ride around town is worth about 30-50 rubles and you can get most places you need to go by offering 100 rubles (for gypsy cabs you can count on lower prices). In general, prices for cabs are somewhat lower in St. Petersburg than in Moscow.

You may also want to consider unofficially hiring a cab for the day, the going rate being about 150-200 rubles per hour. If you think you are doing pretty well getting cabs for rubles, remember that even when you can pay rubles, you will generally end up paying much more than a Russian would (although you may have an easier time getting a cab to stop). You can also hire a cab for the day through one of the private cab companies listed in the Yellow Pages under Taxis.

In the event you get a taxi driver who goes by the meter, it is advisable and courteous to tip about 10%. In general, taxis are a good way to get around, if you are willing to brave excessive speeds and exhaust fumes. It is cheap, and faster and more direct than public transport.

CAR RENTAL

The spread of private enterprise to Russia has widened the alternatives for car rental services. Some good deals can be found, but some real rip-offs also need to be avoided. See the Yellow Pages under Car Rental for a list of some alternatives. Most offer cars either with or without drivers.

Two points (warnings?) ought to be to kept in mind when choosing to rent a car to drive yourself. First is the large number of half-crazed taxi and bus drivers you'll be driving among (particularly in Moscow). Second is that neither Moscow nor St. Petersburg are, in any sense, easy cities to navigate. Street signs are sparse and well-hidden, making it very easy to commit traffic violations. Left turns and right turns are often prohibited by an obscure, unlit sign. And your inevitable transgressions of traffic laws are, particularly at intersections, closely monitored by the ubiquitous GAI traffic officers (ГАИ -- pronounced "guy-ee").

In sum, if you know your way around Moscow or St. Petersburg already, read Russian, and do not mind a bit of added tension on your trip, car rental may be the way for you. Otherwise, stick to taxis or rental cars furnished with driver. If you do decide to rent a car, here is what you need to know.

License: You must have an International Drivers License (obtained from AAA in the United States) to drive in Russia, and your home country license as well, although GAI rarely get beyond your International License. You can, of course, also drive with a Russian license.

If you do not have an International license, you can get a Russian one by taking your valid license from your home country (along with two passport photos and 5 rubles) to the GlavUPDK Spetsavtotsentr in Moscow at ul. Kievskaya 8, ph. 240-2092. You may have to pass a written test and simulation (complete with model cars), plus a driving test.

Traffic violations: In the event you are pulled over for a traffic violation, the usual fee is 30 rubles, which can be paid on the spot. More serious violations, such as driving under the influence of alcohol (which is very strictly punished), or inflicting serious human or property damage in an accident can bring fines of up to 800 rubles and land you in jail. Middle range violations, such as driving without a license or not stopping when signalled to by a militia (GAI) officer (this consists of a flick of the baton and signalling you over toward the curb), can bring fines of 30-80 rubles. There have been sporadic incidents of harrassment of foreign drivers during the last year, yet this has been on the decline of late. (See the notes on Crime, Section IV.)

Accidents: If you should get in an accident, the law is that none of the vehicles in the accident may be moved until a GAI officer comes around and takes measurements and writes up a report. This policy is the cause of most Moscow traffic jams. An accident ensures an unhappy and bureaucrat-filled visit, so drive carefully. If you do get in an accident, you will be instructed by the GAI officer where you will need to go to fill in necessary accident report papers. This will depend upon where your vehicle is registered. Take all potentially relevant paperwork (license, registration, insurance papers) and a translator if you need one.

Street signs: Street names are in Russian (Cyrillic) and are usually posted on the corners of buildings. Road signs are mainly in keeping with internationally accepted graphical signage, but there are enough important signs in Russian that you should have a reading knowledge of Russian if you want to drive safely.

Rules of the road: Some important driving rules should be noted. Always wear your seatbelt (you will be stopped if you don't). Horns are for emergencies only. Headlights are never used in city limits except in dimmed position, *even at night*. The speed limit in the city limits is 60 kph (37 mph); outside the city it is 90 kph (56 mph). Turning right on red lights is prohibited. Even in the daytime, headlights must be turned on (in dimmed intensity) when entering tunnels and turned off when exiting. If there isn't a street sign saying you can turn right or left at an intersection, technically you cannot. Left turns are almost never possible on major roads; you drive on to a U-turn lane, then come back and make a right turn. Drinking and driving is a very serious offence.

Gas Stations: Three types of gasoline are available: 76 octane, 93 octane, and 95 octane. Most stations have the former two. Do not use 76 octane unless you are told the car has been adapted for this, and in this event use only 76 octane. To be allowed to fill up with 95 octane, one theoretically must have ration cards, but usually if you drive up in a foreign car no one asks any questions. Alternatively, you can try offering twice the price, which meets with mixed results.

In the Yellow Pages you will find, under Gas Stations, a list of Moscow city gas stations by region and a list of stores that sell oil and grease for Russian cars. For St. Petersburg gas stations, consult the guide, *Where in St. Petersburg*.

SIGHTSEEING

Moscow

Should your trip allow sightseeing time, your best bet is to have a native (either one of your hosts or even a taxi driver) give you a drive through the center of Moscow. There are more than enough attractions to see in and around Red Square and the Kremlin. For further points of interest, check your more conventional tourist guide books (see the notes on Books in Section I) or ask the service bureau at your hotel for some help (be prepared in the latter case to pay hard currency). See Tourism in the Yellow Pages.

A further interesting way of sightseeing can be via trams. More frequently than buses they allow you to sit down and see out (except in winter when the windows are usually fogged up). Their routes can take you through some of the more interesting, older neighborhoods of Moscow (as this was the first form of public transport in Moscow), and they offer the advantage of being able to get off at virtually any stop, cross the tracks and take the same numbered tram back to where you started.

Boat rides on the Moscow river in summer are also a relaxing way to see the city and the outlying areas. Boats stop at many landings along the river and run fairly frequently during daytime hours. For a good half-day trip, start at the Kievsky Train Station stop and ride around the peninsula to get off at Gorkiy Park and go for a stroll there.

The view from Lenin Hills (formerly Sparrow Hill) on a clear day is also not to be missed. For a quiet afternoon in a park atmosphere, try a stroll around Novodevichy or Danilovsky monastery, Kolomenskoe, Sokolniki, the Botanical Gardens, Tsaritsyno or Izmailovo Park.

If you are interested in hitting the pavement and stopping in shops, we recommend Pyatnitskaya, Tverskaya (Gorkiy) and Petrovka Streets, and the Arbat, for their high shop density and uniqueness. The old section of town known as Kitai Gorod (Chinese City), where foreigners lived under the Czars, was a major commercial center and may pose some interest for that reason. Likewise, the section near and around Novokuznetskiy metro station has much charm.

For serious shopping for souvenirs, there are two popular places to go: the Arbat and the Vernisage at Izmailova (weekends only, go to Izmailovo Park metro station). Over time, the wares for sale have gotten progressively "kitschier", but there are still always deals to be had. See also the shops listed under Souvenirs in the Yellow Pages.

If you are looking for a day trip outside the city, there are a number of places in close driving range to visit. Most notable are Sergeyev Posad (formerly Zagorsk), Arkhangelskoe, and Gorkiy Leninskie. A bit farther off are Klin, Abramtsevo, and Borodino.

St. Petersburg

St. Petersburg is more compact than Moscow and easier to navigate on foot. Aside from that, you cannot get the flavor of the canals or the beautifully decorated facades from driving around in cars or trams, so sightseeing on foot is a necessity.

Be sure to see St. Isaac's Cathedral, Peter-Paul Fortress and Palace Square (Dvortsovy ploshchad). If you have a spare day in the city, spend it at the Hermitage, with a side trip to the restored Menshikov Palace across the river. But these are just some highlights; St. Petersburg is filled with points of artistic, architechtural and historical interest, all of which are detailed in conventional tourist guides (see the notes on Books in Section I).

Boat rides on the canals (except in winter) are an inexpensive and interesting way to see the city. Boats depart every 15 minutes from Anichkov bridge (where Nevsky Prospekt meets Fontanka embankment) or opposite the entrance to the Hermitage.

If you are interested in shopping, a walk up and down Nevsky Prospekt is the recommended itinerary. Start at Palace Square and walk up one side at least to Gostiny Dvor, then cross and walk back. You'll get your fill.

For a quiet afternoon in a park, try Kirov Park on Yelagin island. It has walking paths, boating, a bathing beach as well as an exhibition hall and theaters. Boating is also possible at Park Pobedy (Victory Park). Lenin Park and the Botanical Gardens, on opposite sides of Petrogradskiy ostrov (island), are also nice.

If you want to get outside the city, visit the former Imperial palaces in Petrodvorets, Pushkin or Pavlovsk, all in close range. Boats and trains service these palaces, or you can rent a car and drive.

TRAVEL BEYOND MOSCOW AND ST. PETERSBURG

The same guidelines that apply in Moscow and St. Petersburg are also true for other major cities in Russia. Usually, however, the quality of accommodation and availability of goods and services is better in the two capitals than in other cities. Especially if you are traveling east, it can be much more difficult to make an international phone call or find a competent translator.

With the exception of a few direct international flights to major Commonwealth cities like Tallinn, Vilnius , Riga and Kiev (and Magadan from Anchorage), it is necessary to travel via Moscow to most points within Russia and the Commonwealth. Before leaving Moscow, be sure that you have a visa(s) for the city(ies) you plan to visit (see Visas and Visa Support in Section II). The official word is that visas are no longer necessary for travel to other cities, with travel permitted to all cities which are not "closed." Even so, it will take a while for this official line to "filter down."

Time was, all foreigners were subject to a 40 kilometer travel limit outside the city they were visiting. Like the visa requirements this is no longer imposed, but not communicated unequivocally to all points of the former empire.

It is advised to have your accommodation reserved in advance. The travel agents listed in the Yellow Pages can arrange this. Regarding travel to cities in other states of the Commonwealth, see the notes on Visas in Section II.

As a final general note about traveling within Russia and the Commonwealth, it is highly advisable not to bring with you items that you cannot bear to lose, or that are irreplaceable. Remember, you and your luggage will stand out as being clearly "foreign" and will be a more tempting target for thieves. Keep your passport and all valuable documents with you (and not in your luggage) at all times.

Getting Tickets

If the organization that is sponsoring your visit does not arrange the booking and purchase of your air/train tickets, and you have not done so from your home country, you can book your internal travel through travel agencies listed in the Yellow Pages or through the travel desk of a major hotel. You can also deal directly with Aeroflot to book a flight, but if you do not speak Russian and do not enjoy waiting in long lines, it is simpler to avoid this.

It is ***very*** difficult to get tickets for internal travel with less than 72 hours advance booking, so the earlier you submit your request, the better your chances are of traveling. In general, you will have a better chance of getting the flight or train you want if you book through a travel agency than if you book directly with Intourist or Intourtrans. Travel agencies usually have direct contacts that help speed up the process of confirming bookings. If your internal flights were booked before you arrived in Moscow, it is recommended that you reconfirm them at the travel desk in your hotel or directly through Intourist or a travel agent (again, see the Yellow Pages).

Aeroflot is still the only airline which makes internal flights in the Commonwealth and Russia. This will change in the next few years. But until it does, you must face the difficulty of dealing with a transportation monopoly in great disarray.

As of February 1990, all foreigners were required to pay in hard currency for their internal Aeroflot tickets (when checking in for flight and boarding, all passengers are asked to present a passport). An exception may be if you are buying a ticket in a city in the provinces. Often they will not have the ability to accept hard currency and you will be "required" to pay in rubles. Rail tickets can still be purchased for rubles, although a special ruble conversion rate for foreigners is expected. Rail tickets to Helsinki must (at least from the Russian border) be paid for in hard currency. Prices for internal flights (and rail tickets) have sky-rocketed with recent price hikes. Likewise, Aeroflot must now pay much higher prices for fuel. This, combined with the disintegration of the Soviet Union, is causing interminable delays with air travel. Aeroflot jets are often having difficulty re-fueling in the provinces, making return to Moscow or St. Petersburg somewhat difficult.

It is wise to make a note of the reference number you will be given for your travel reservations, and to keep this with your tickets when they have been issued. This is especially true for flights. There is a chance that when you arrive at the airport with tickets in hand, you will be informed that your name is not on the passenger list and you therefore will not be allowed to board the plane. This occurs because flights are regularly over-booked (especially as fuel shortages have restricted their number). If this happens to you, it is best to simply remain at the counter, present your reference number, and point out that you paid in hard currency for your ticket. A bit of obstinacy may be required on your part, but in the end "hard currency passengers" are rarely bumped off of flights.

It used to be that for air and rail travel within the former USSR, arrival and departure times were given in Moscow time. This convention has shattered with the assertion of the former republics' independence. Some places are still using the Moscow time standard (i.e. within most of Russia), but other places are certainly not (i.e in the Baltics and Ukraine). Check the time differences chart on the map printed on page 2-3 to calculate local arrival and departure times vis-a-vis Moscow time. Check locally to see which standard is being used.

Air Travel

Moscow has four airports, Sheremetevo I and II, Domodedovo and Vnukovo, so it is very important to find out from which airport your flight is scheduled to leave. Sheremetevo I is for flights to the North and West, including St. Petersburg; Sheremetevo II is for international flights; Domodedovo (Russia's largest airport) is for Eastern destinations; Vnukovo is for southern destinations. All of the airports are quite a distance outside the city; allow one hour traveling time to get to the airport by car or taxi; allow one and a half hours to get to Domodedovo (a 46 km drive).

St. Petersburg has two airports, Pulkovo and Rzhevka. Pulkovo has two terminals. Pulkovo I services domestic flights, Pulkovo II services international flights. Rzhevka handles short distance domestic flights.

Be sure to arrive at the airport at least one hour before your flight is scheduled to depart, and be warned that if you do not allow yourself that much time you stand a chance of not getting on the flight. Check-in and boarding take longer in Moscow or St. Petersburg than in most Western cities.

When you arrive at the airport, keep in mind that foreigners often must go to a separate check-in desk, usually located somewhat apart from the main check-in hall. You locate this desk by looking for a blue and white "Intourist" sign. Your taxi driver or your Russian hosts will almost certainly know where it is located. After you have presented your ticket and checked your baggage (weight limit is 44 lbs.), you will be directed to a waiting room until it is time to board the plane.

When the plane is ready for boarding, an Aeroflot/Intourist representative will escort you to the plane. Usually foreigners are driven out to the plane and seated in the front of the forward cabin before the other passengers come aboard -- this is considered First Class. Do not expect to be extremely comfortable during the flight. "First class" and "club class" as you may know them do not exist for internal flights. All of the seats are very close together and there is little room for carry-on luggage. The cabins are also generally not as clean or well-maintained as they are on other airlines.

Unless the flight is more than several hours long, food and drink may not be served. If you suspect that you will be hungry or thirsty during the flight, it is best to bring your own provisions (bottled water is highly advised). Unless you enjoy being very conspicuous, however, it is advisable not to bring cans of Western beverages, and easily identifiable Western foods.

When the plane lands at your destination, an Aeroflot/Intourist representative will usually be on hand to escort foreigners to the luggage claim area reserved for them.

It is essential to reconfirm the next flight on your itinerary as soon as possible at the Intourist or other travel desk of your hotel.

Train Travel

Many foreigners find that travel by train is easier, more comfortable and more convenient than air-travel if the destination is relatively close to Moscow or St. Petersburg. For example, a common way for a business person to travel between Moscow and St. Petersburg is by the night train which usually leaves either city at just before midnight and arrives in the other city between 8:00 and 9:00 am. In the summer months, it is even light enough early enough to allow for a view of the country-side.

One of the advantages of traveling by train is that you depart and arrive in the center of a city, instead of 30-40 minutes outside of it. And, unless you have more than 77 lbs. of luggage with you, you do not need to wait to collect it when you arrive at your destination. Train travel can also be more relaxing because you have more room to move around and stretch out than you have on a plane. In the winter months, when airports are often closed due to bad weather conditions, train travel is also more reliable. And with recent fuel shortages causing huge delays with air travel, train travel, while slower, is a more certain mode of transport.

If you plan to eat on the train, it is advisable to bring your own food and lots of it. Dining cars are not always available, especially on night-trains, but are available on longer rides. Definitely bring your own supply of water (bottled water can now be bought in most major Moscow and St. Petersburg hotels), even for brushing your teeth. It is advisable to bring your own toilet paper or tissues. If you travel "soft class" (see below), sheets, blankets and towels will be provided, but you will be asked to pay a small ruble fee for these when you board the train or when you buy your ticket.

Several different classes are available for train travel, and you must specify what you want when you request your reservation. By all means travel first class. There are two types of cabins available. A *coupé* cabin has four berths, two up, two down. A soft class cabin has two berths and is a hair bigger. If you do not buy the whole compartment for yourself (which you can do, but which is getting more expensive), you will share it with others. Be forewarned that it is not a convention to assign persons of the same sex to a compartment, so if you do not already have a traveling companion, be prepared to share a compartment with either males or females. A first class compartment usually has cushioned berths, a small table, reading lamps and a radio. Restroom facilities are located at the end of the car. In no case should you agree to ride by *platzcar*, which is an open bunk car. There are also sitting (*sideniye*) cars. It is preferable to have a cabin in the middle of the train car as they are less noisy.

You can buy train tickets through Intourist or other travel agencies if you want to pay hard currency. You can also simply go to the train station where the train will leave from (or to the Advance Ticket Sales office -- or Intourtrans office in Moscow at ul. Petrovka 15 and nab. Kanala Griboyedova in St. Petersburg) and buy a ticket, if it is more than 48 hours or less than 24 hours before the train leaves. See the Yellow Pages under Train Information for a telephone number you can call to order tickets from home and have them delivered to you there. Usually if you order tickets 3-4 days in advance you will not have trouble with availability.

Both Moscow and St. Petersburg have more than one train station, so be sure to find out from which station your train will leave. As a general guide:

In Moscow: Byelorusskiy Station serves Byelorussia and Poland and the West; Kiev Station is for the Ukraine; Leningrad Station is for the North and Leningrad and Helsinki; Riga Station is for the Baltics; Yaroslavl Station serves the East and North Russia; Kursk Station serves the Caucausus and the Crimea, Pavelets Station serves Southeastern Russia, Kazan Station serves the Urals, Central Asia, and Western Siberia.

In St. Petersburg: Finland Station serves trains to Vyborg, Repino, Razliv and to and from Finland; Warsaw Station is for trains to Tallin and Riga; Baltic Station is for trains to the southern outskirts of the city and Petrodvorets; Moscow Station serves Moscow, the North East and South of Russia; and Vitebsk Station handles trains to Pushkin, Pavlovsk and Belarus and Ukraine.

It is best to be at your train at least 30 minutes before departure time -- trains tend to leave more promptly than planes. The conductor will ask for your ticket before you will be allowed to board the train. Be sure you get the ticket booklet, including the cover, back if you have other tickets in it. Once the train is underway, the conductor will usually serve hot tea before you leave and in the morning on overnight trains.

IV. Money

THE RUBLE(S)

The two things subject to the most radical change in the last half of 1991 and the first half of 1992 have been rubles and the law. Despite these changes, however, the ruble is still not a freely convertible currency. Steps are finally being taken in this direction, but real convertibility is still some time off.

The basic thrust of recent changes has been a radical devaluation of the ruble and allowing a measure of its free exchange internally. This decentralizing trend, which began in late 1991, is slowly being reversed by the Bank of Russia, as it begins to assert some control over currency and banking.

In previous editions of this publication, we have attempted to clarify the different ways which the ruble can be valuated by explaining that there were really three different types of rubles. For all intents and purposes, there are now four different rubles. By way of explanation:

Commercial Ruble

This is also called the gold ruble or invalutny ruble. This ruble was "established" by Stalin in the 1950s and has existed for accounting purposes only ever since then.

For some time, there were just two rubles, this one and the paper ruble (see below). It was worth $1.60 and was the only rate at which you could legally buy rubles at when traveling. It was also the official rate of exchange for trade operations and for valuation of purchases in hard currency stores. This ruble was devalued in late 1990 by three times, then again in 1991 by ten times. The value of the commercial ruble now fluctuates in relation to the tourist ruble (see below), ranging at about one-half its value and set by the Russian State Bank. This is the ruble exchange rate at which "mandatory" sales (taxation) of hard currency earnings take place. It is also the rate at which state enterprises purchase goods from ministries, which the latter have purchased abroad for hard currency.

Tourist Ruble

On November 1, 1989, this ruble was "created" by a ten-fold devaluation of the old ("official") commercial ruble. The intent was to wipe out black market trading in currency. The black market continued to flourish, however, and on April 1, 1991 the Soviet government devalued this ruble again -- four-fold. At that time, 27.6 rubles = 1 dollar US. Subsequent minor devaluations (prompted by a legal act which forced a change in the exchange rate when a certain amount of dollars were sold for rubles in currency auctions) pushed the rate to 32:1 (to the dollar) and 47:1. In late 1991, all restrictions were taken off individual exchanging of rubles for hard currency and commercial banks were allowed to set their own rates of exchange, which peaked at around 150-170:1 and dropped, in February of 1992 to around 75:1.

This is the rate at which tourists (and private Russians) may buy rubles at designated offices or banks (see Yellow Pages under Money Changing). These institutions are allowed to set their rates of exchange independently, but the difference between buy and sell rates cannot be more than 10%. At the time of printing, the rate of exchange was hovering around 110R:1$

Private exchange between individuals outside such institutions (which may also be taken literaly, since these change points have become a magnet for private money changers) is still a black market, illegal operation.

You can change hard currency for rubles at this rate freely, without a declaration, by merely presentling identification. But if you plan on changing your rubles back into dollars, you should have the operation noted on your customs declaration.

Paper Ruble

This is the ruble which is obtained from labor and from internal commercial operations. It can still be seen as distinct from the tourist ruble because the latter is obtained only through sale of dollars (or other hard currency). If a Russian cannot obtain dollars, he or she must work for rubles, thus the true value of the paper ruble is somewhat higher than the tourist (individual) exchange rate would suggest. It represents the value of work performed on the internal market. The paper ruble (also often called the "wooden" ruble) can be turned into dollars by individuals at the tourist (individual) rate, and by enterprises, for foreign trade purposes, at the interbank currency exchange. As regards individuals, this is a very new development.

The Russian minimum wage is (at the time of printing) 550 rubles per month (about five dollars at the tourist ruble rate) and the average monthly wage is around 1500-2000 rubles per month, or an average hourly wage of about 10 rubles. Rampant inflation is making it tougher to keep up for the average Russian who earns only paper rubles (vs., say, a cab driver who can earn a few dollars and turn them into rubles at the highly devalued tourist rate). This is even more true of pensioners and students, who often receive less than the minimum wage.

Still, it is also true that there are a lot of rubles floating around, ready to be soaked up by any worthy consumer commodity that becomes available. This will continue to be the case until serious privatization occurs, at which point the ruble will also be somewhat strengthened against hard currencies.

Inflation has led the Soviet, and now Russian government to introduce higher and higher ruble notes. First 200 ruble notes and then 500 ruble notes were introduced. And there is a chance that old 50 and 100 ruble notes "confiscated" by the Soviet government in January of 1991 to soak up excess liquidity will be reintroduced into the money supply. Until that occurs, the foreign traveler should beware of being given old, non-valid 50 and 100 ruble notes by cab drivers or street vendors. Check the date of issue of the bill (it should be 1991 or later).

Auction Ruble

This is a ruble bought and sold first through the now halted currency auctions and now through the Interbank Currency Exchange which is being strictly overseen by the Russian State Bank (and in which foreign companies still cannot directly participate). The rate is usually a bit higher than the tourist rate and, when auctions were being held throughout the former Soviet Union, rates varied greatly from city to city. At auctions in some non-Russian cities where dollars are scarcer, such as Tallinn, auction rates have topped 300:1. In effect this is a ruble accessible only to banks and enterprises. It is more than an accounting tool, in the sense that these rubles are very tangible, insofar as the deals struck auctions occur and money is exchanged.

Denominations

The ruble comes in denominations of 1, 3, 5, 10, 25, 50, 100, 200 and 500 rubles. The larger denominations (50-1000) are often of little use at kiosks and newsstands, etc., as they will often not have change.

The ruble consists of 100 kopeks. Kopek coins are denominated in 1, 2, 3, 5, 10, 15, 20, and 50. There is also a series of ruble, two ruble and five ruble coins, but these are infrequently used. Certain kopek coins are necessary for certain things and you may want to try and have a few on hand: you will need two 1k coins, a 2k or 10k piece to make local calls from a phone booth (it only costs 2k, but a 10k fools the phones, as sometimes does, interestingly enough, an American dime) -- it is anticipated that payphones will shortly be changed over to 15k, however; metro tokens are the same size as 5k pieces, but the latter haven't worked to ride the metro for almost a year now; small change is always useful in that vendors are very protective of the coins they have and usually ask if you have exact change.

Changing Money

To change hard currency into rubles (paper rubles), you will need to present some form of identification, i.e your passport or driver's license. You can change money at certain commercial banks or at appointed exchange bureaus in certain hotels (see Yellow Pages under Money Changing). If you are changing hard currency into rubles and desire to change them back later, you will need to have your exchange operation noted on the declaration you filled out upon entering the country. You can exchange with hard cash, travelers checks, or sometimes with your credit card. In current conditions, the tourist exchange rate is changing weekly, and sometimes daily. And different banks and exchange points will offer different rates.

You are advised not to change rubles through "unofficial" channels. This is still a crime. If you get caught, the best you could hope for is detainment for several hours, the worst that could happen is a three to five year prison sentence. In any case, you will not be welcomed back to Russia.

If you have a good contact in Moscow or St. Petersburg, you may want to tell them to change some rubles for you ahead of your arrival. With the devalued tourist ruble exchange rate, exchange points are often out of cash early in the day and, paradoxically, the cheaper the ruble gets, the harder is it to exchange for them.

Purchasing

In stores, cooperative restaurants, and state restaurants you should always pay in rubles (paper rubles) rather than with credit card. The price to you will be many times less. With restaurants you may often have to pay hard currency to get in, and that is a choice you must make. Rarely will Russian stores accept credit cards and never should you use them there. When buying souvenirs in the Arbat or outside "usual" trading networks, try never to pay with hard currency.

In hard special currency stores you can pay only with hard currency, be it cash, credit card, and rarely travelers checks. In general, travelers checks are a hassle in Russia and are only readily accepted without objections when exchanging money. Cash and credit cards are the best form of hard currency to carry -- in fact credit cards rank above cash insofar as come July 1, 1992 a new law is expected to take effect which will bar the use of dollars on Russian soil for hard currency purchases. If you do bring cash, small bills are preferable because making change will be easier and it will be convenient for tipping, cab rides, etc.

Purchases made in hard currency grocery and other stores with a credit card are now typically charged (on your card slip) in dollars, Finnmarks or DM. In St. Petersburg the latter two are more common than in Moscow, where the dollar holds sway. Most often prices are marked in dollars. Some stores are now starting to institute arbitrary minimum and/or maximums on credit card usage, so it is adviseable to have two types of cards (i.e. AMEX and VISA) for any eventuality.

CRIME

The "golden days" when Russia was about the safest place in the world to travel to (with respect to crime) are gone. As a foreigner in Moscow or St. Petersburg (more so in Moscow) you stand out as a person with hard currency. And as inflation leads to more marked differences between the paper ruble and the tourist ruble (see above), the likelihood of a tourist or business traveler being a crime victim increases. This is not to say that Moscow and St. Petersburg have become dangerous, just that they are no longer as safe as they used to be and some precautions are in order.

Stay away from parks at night.

Avoid black marketeers and beggars (especially the bands of gypsies). These people are often pickpockets as well. Do not give donations to "suspicious looking" beggars. In particular, be wary of black marketeers and gypsies in front of tourist hotels, and, in Moscow, in front of the Bolshoi Theater, on Red Square, on the Arbat, and on Kalininskiy Bridge (leading to the Ukraine hotel). In St. Petersburg, avoid the square in front of Gostiny Dvor and be wary in Catherine's Park. Do not leave money in your hotel room, and carry it with you in a secure place.

Be careful who you visit and what cars you get into. The incidence of foreigners being slipped a "mickey" has reached anecdotal levels, but is not yet widespread. Be cautious about accepting invitations to first-time acquaintances' apartments. Only use an official "limo" service from the airport. And at night, stick to official taxis, versus gypsy cab rides.

Don't be flashy. Showing lots of dollars around in restaurants and other semi-public or fully public places is not adviseable. There have been cases of harrassment of foreign motorists by militia officers, but this is very rare and declining. If you suspect this is about to happen to you, be polite, do not speak Russian, and be "accommodating." Look for a badge number.

Use the buddy system. If you want to walk the streets at night, stick to main avenues and, when possible, take along a friend.

If you are mugged or assaulted, which is unlikely but possible, get in touch with the militia or service bureau in your hotel, and or with your embassy, which is interested in keeping track of these types of occurrences and may be able to provide some assistance.

V. Food

Food

OPTIONS

If you are called upon to fend for yourself at mealtime in Russia, you are likely to go wrong. This is simply because good restaurants are hard to find, hard to get into, and perhaps hard to order at (particularly if you do not speak Russian). Offer to buy a Russian friend or business associate lunch and have them pick the place. If you go on your own, you are likely to cop out and go to a hotel restaurant or state restaurant, and certainly in some of the newly refurbished joint venture hotels you can get an excellent meal. But fine national cuisine and many interesting dining opportunities exist in places only locals know of.

It has gotten increasingly more expensive to dine out in Moscow and St. Petersburg (considerably more so in Moscow) with the devaluation of the ruble and price increases. Foreigners are less often able to eat better and more for the equivalent of a few dollars changed into rubles, and more and more of the finer restaurants are accepting credit card payment only. Certainly very few still offer liquor or wine for rubles.

Your best bet is to learn the ground rules before ordering your meal. Find out what currency you will be paying in (and who is paying), and if it is in dollars converted from ruble prices, at what rate. This is where your local guide can be of considerable assistance.

Below is a list of types of restaurants to try, in order of preference:

Private and Cooperative Restaurants

Cooperative restaurants (or just coops) were the Soviet Union's first foray into capitalism begun back in 1986. Since then, they have helped set a standard for decently prepared and costly meals, two things for which standard fare state-owned restaurants were rarely noted. In the past six months to a year prices have skyrocketed in coops, primarily because of price increases in food and because the Russian *nouveau riche* has been willing to pay these prices for a readily accessible, quality meal. When coops first began operating, it was scandalous for a meal to cost 5 rubles. Now prices for dinner can range from a couple of hundred to a thousand rubles per person for a meal. Lunches are somewhat less costly than dinners.

Reservations are recommended for evening meals, particularly at popular coops. Popular state restaurants and some cooperatives require a week's advance notice for reservations, but at most places calling in the morning or the day before assures you a table. When making your reservation (best to have a Russian speaker do this), ask about the availability of liquor. Most coops offer liquor or wine only for hard currency (credit card). If they do not offer liquor or wine, they usually will not frown on you bringing your own bottle of wine (but may charge a corking fee).

If, when you arrive, your table full of *zakuski* (appetizers) laid out to greet you, it is wise to check into the cost of this welcome, as this is where many places will try to fill out your bill (about 50-100 rubles per dish). You might also want to find out ahead of time if the coop has live music or a floor show, which can mean an extra charge on your bill and very loud music. Avoid coops with floor shows if you want to converse with your dinner companions (This goes for all types of restaurants). See the list of restaurants in the Yellow Pages.

Joint Venture Restaurants

These figure below coops because their prices are invariably in hard currency (a notable exception being McDonalds Moscow and Pizza Hut on Kutuzovskiy prospekt in Moscow), and quite high by American or European standards. The majority of these are in the newly refurbished hotels like the Metropol, Savoy, Olympia, Alexander Blok and Pullman in Moscow and the Astoria and Evropeyskaya in St. Petersburg. As noted above, the food at these restaurants (and at some of the non-hotel based joint venture restaurants) is generally of a consistently high quality, and you usually can't go wrong. Still, as with restaurants the world over, check into the reputation for quality and pricey-ness to avoid surprises. Again, see Restaurants in the Yellow Pages; joint ventures are duly marked as such.

State Restaurants and State-owned Hotel restaurants

Your most difficult problem here may be getting in. The employees of these restaurants just do not get paid enough to really care about customers, so you can bet on encountering obstacles to getting a table in these establishments. But these entities will soon be privatizing, so look for changes on this front (when these restaurants will shift over to the private restaurant category in terms of price and services).

The food is generally fair to lackluster, and the service abysmal. But the prices are very low. Here you can sometimes get alcohol for rubles, and quite a bit of food for your money. Always ask the waiter for his/her recommendations, and always order with an eye to freshness. Pates can be dangerous, and beef is usually a safer bet than pork or chicken. Chicken Kiev is usually a safe bet anywhere you go, however, and a good *kapusta* (marinated cabbage salad) or Stolichny Salad (potato and meat salad) are usually on the menu, as is fresh cheese, herring and caviar.

Your waiter will likely warm up to you if you order plenty of alcohol and caviar, as there is then the prospect of something like a real tip in it for him. Even if a service charge is included in the bill, tip generously but not ostentatiously, i.e. about 10%.

Stolovayas (Cafeterias) in State Enterprises

Your visit may offer you the opportunity to eat in the cafeteria of your host organization. Depending upon the priorities and influence of the enterprise, you could see cafeteria cooking in Russia at its worst or best.

Almost every state enterprise has its own *stolovaya* to counteract the lack of eating establishments in Moscow, and prices are heavily subsidized (a lunch rarely runs more than 10-15 rubles). Some of these stolovaya can be very good (jump at the opportunity to eat at a government *stolovaya*). Again, follow the recommendations of those you are eating with. Prior to recent price hikes and the removal of state subsidies, there were often good, inexpensive meals to be had at these establishments. Increasingly the food is worse and the prices higher.

Other Stolovayas and Restaurants

Public *stolovayas* are available for your patronage throughout Russia, but without a strong recommendation and/or a staggering hunger, these places are to be avoided. The prices are low, as are generally the health standards. They have long depended on subsidies and most will be soon going out of business or privatizing.

The food and service are generally not worth mentioning, but there are a few places that offer pleasant surprises in both categories. Many of these places are stand-up affairs, and many are, in fact, not a bad place to go for tea and a pastry (*pirozhnoe*) if they offer that. Meats are best to avoid in these establishments. You can consider your visit well-rounded if, upon the recommendation of a trusted Russian, you try the *pelmeni* (a Siberian meat dumpling) or *blini* (pancakes) offered in some of these stolovaya. Prices, again, are very low.

SOME GENERAL TIPS FOR DINING OUT

• Do not drink the water. Moscow water is fairly harmless, but not if your system is not used to it. St. Petersburg water should not be drunk on any condition; it harbors the *giardia* bacterium, which is harmless if your system is used to it, debilitating if not. Tea and coffee are always safe. Water in the provinces is generally unpredicatable. Bring bottled water.

If you get desperate, the safest water is probably that in the newest hotels. What goes under the name of mineral water in Russia is very salty and carbonated. *Mors*, *sok* and *napitok*, the ubiquitous (and usually quite tasty) fruit beverages of infinite variety are made from water, but few people have problems with them (in Moscow). Bottled water is available in most major hotels and in hard currency grocery stores (see the Yellow Pages).

• Always make reservations. Larger state-owned hotel restaurants cater to groups and reservations only. Thus, individuals are not welcomed without reservations, and even in that event do not expect red carpet treatment.

• Tipping is increasingly expected. 10-15% is adequate.

• When you go out for lunch in a Russian restaurant, expect it to take at least an hour to hour and a half. When you go out to dinner, it is a night-long engagement. Most Russian restaurants do not try to turn tables every 45 minutes as Western restaurants do. You will not be hurried along; sit back and relax. When a Russian goes out to dinner, it is for a night of entertainment.

• When dining with Russian guests or hosts, the rule is usually that the host pays for the meal. If you are eating out with persons whose organization will probably not pay for the meal, insist on paying or at least going dutch. While you can joke about the low value of the ruble over dinner, do not ever be ostentatious or throw a lot of rubles around when it comes time to pay the check. Remember, most Russians do not eat out that often. The prices have just gotten too high.

• Always carry a cotton handkerchief for dining out, as Russian cities are dirty, and you will probably want to wash your hands before eating, and often restaurant rest rooms lack clean towels (although hot air dryers are often available). The handkerchief will also come in handy for wiping off silverware in some of the greasier of greasy spoons.

• If it is on the menu, it is not necessarily available, particularly where state restaurants are concerned. Russian restaurants are subject to radical fluctuations in food supplies. The items that are available will have prices next to them or be indicated in some way. Some items may, at first request (in state restaurants) be unavailable. But often a little "encouragement" helps uncover forgotten stashes.

VI. Communication

City codes within the CIS

Page 2 of the Telephone Directory

International country and city dialing codes

Page 2 of the Yellow Pages

Phones

The Russian phone system is still arguably the worst in any industrialized country. Line quality is poor to abysmal. Cut-offs and crossed-lines are frequent. International phone lines are difficult if not impossible to access. In general, be prepared to be frustrated by your contact with the Russian phone system.

This said, it bears noting that some huge strides have been made by Russo-Western joint ventures to, in effect, leap-frog the limitations of the antiquated Russian phone system, parts of which date to before the 1917 revolution. Cellular overlays, microwave transmitters and innovative satellite patches are providing some temporary and valuable solutions for direct international dialing. Mobile phones can be leased for car or home. And AT&T will soon introduce its USA Direct service to Moscow (US Government loosening of Cocom-related restrictions are also allowing the addition of more international satellite channels, which also makes getting a call *into* Russia much easier).

Still, the domestic phone system remains founded on a decaying copper wire system (some Moscow phone lines laid in 1905 are still in use) which, along with mechnical switching is noisy and ennervating. The aim of this section, therefore, is to help you make the best of this situation and to take advantage of the new high-tech solutions.

PLACING A CALL

Phoning from a phone booth on the street costs 2 kopeks (expect this to rise in the near future to 15k). You can also use a 10 kopek piece or occasionally an American dime. Intercity calls cost from 30k to 2.10R for a unit of time, depending upon the distance.

For directory assistance in getting a local phone number, dial 09.

Long Distance Dialing within Russia and the Commonwealth

To dial long distance direct within Russia and the Commonwealth, you must first dial 8, wait for the dial tone, then dial the city code (see the table on page two of the Telephone Directory), then the local phone number. For example, if you needed to dial the Nizhny Novgorod number 78652, you would dial 8-8312-78652.

From some cities you will need to order inter-city calls with the operator, depending upon the capabilities of the local network. But in major cities you can direct dial to most other major cities. From Moscow you can dial most anywhere. From some provincial cities, however, you cannot direct dial Moscow.

Connection times can be very long, due to the fact that Russia still relies on mechanical telephone switching systems. If your call has not connected within one minute, hang up and try again.

Other problems: You will often need to add zeroes to the local portion of a phone number to make a total of 7 digits, but not always. From some phones you will need to dial the number of the phone you are calling from after dialing the number you are calling. In Moscow, to find out your line's ability to dial inter-city calls and what extra numbers you may need to add, call 271-9118. This is also the number to dial if you have any problems with intercity dialing.

To get the city codes for cities not listed in the table on the first page of this section, find out the local directory assistance phone number from your hotel desk. It differs from city to city; in Moscow it is 07.

Dialing Internationally

To dial internationally, if you have a direct line, you must dial 8, wait for the dial tone, then 10, then the country code, then the city or area code (without the zero which may often precede it), then the number within the country you are dialing. See the table on page two of the Yellow Pages for a full listing of international country and city codes.

If your phone does not have a direct dial capability, you have several choices. First, you can book a call with an international operator. To book an international call while in Moscow or St. Petersburg, dial 8, wait for a dial tone, then dial 194 or 196. From a hotel, dial (in Moscow) 333-4101. There are operators who speak English; when the operator answers the phone, say clearly and slowly: "Pah angleesky." They ought to understand and hook you up with the right operator. Tell the operator what you want. If you want the next possible available line, be prepared to wait several hours to get a call back from the operator. You can set a specific time for the operator to call you back with the call connected, but do not be surprised if you do not get called back or get called back later than requested. It happens.

To save costs, the Moscow phone company has layed off operators which normally serviced international calls from midnight to 9 am. Thus it is now theoretically possible to dial directly from any Moscow phone between these times according to the procedures above. But there are 9 million other potential competitors for a *very* limited number of outgoing lines.

The present costs for calling Europe are 27 rubles per minute, for the US 54 rubles per minute, for Australia 63 rubles, and for Japan 36 rubles per minute. If you are staying in a hotel, be sure to ask ahead of time what the per minute rates are. If you are quoted a ruble price, be sure to get the exchange rate at which you will be paying. If you wish, you can connect up and have your party call you back (find out your hotel's switchboard number, or your room's direct number -- the caller may also have to give your hotel room number). But remember, it can be very difficult to get through to Russia from some countries.

Second, you can, from some apartment phone numbers in Moscow, dial directly to some Scandinavian countries. Thus, you can call AT&T USA Direct in Oslo, pay 27 rubles a minute for connect time, plus AT&T charges from Oslo to the US. Access to this channel has been "limited" and may be sporadically available until AT&T USA Direct gets instituted in Moscow and St. Petersburg. MCI is also working on a similar service.

The Finnish company AMT offers cellular car phones, which now can hook into international direct dial lines through the firm's partnership with Sovintel. See the Yellow Pages under Car Phone.

Many hotels have installed expensive hard currency direct dial debit card booths. See the Yellow Pages under International Phone for locations and prices.

For persons setting up offices, there are a number of joint ventures offering different technological fixes to leap-frog the bottleneck in international dialing. Check the Yellow Pages under Telecom for a listing of these companies and the general focus of their activities. Everything from installation of local and international direct lines, to cellular phones, to independent Inmarsat direct links via satellite from any location in Russia.

Calling Russia Direct from the West

Since the Fall of 1989, it has been possible to direct dial Moscow from the United States. It has long been possible to do this from most European countries. Other cities can be dialed from the US and European countries via an international operator, but you must most often contend with low capacity lines.

To dial Moscow, dial 011-7-095, then the Moscow number.

The best time to call Moscow from the US is during non-business hours (i.e. nights and weekends), and at any time your ability to dial successfully will depend upon where in the US you are calling from. New York and Washington are best placed on the US network and western cities like Houston and San Diego are much farther down on the electronic totem pole and will, irregardless of the time, find direct dialing much more difficult.

FAX

Sending faxes to and from Russia is usually guaranteed to end in frustration. Rarely is line quality sufficient to sustain a quality transmission, and business hours are the most difficult time to get through. And at $2-3 per minute, the costs can be astronomical. From Europe, the situation is, of course, somewhat better.

Still, a growing number of Russian businesses now have fax machines (vs. the old telex standby), and it is becoming as much a mainstay of business activity there as in the West. A fact is worth noting in this context. A fax machine in Russia must be registered with the local authorities (in this instance the local telephone network), and its hook-up inspected by them. There is an initial hookup fee and an annual "service charge." Of late, there have been campaigns to catch unregistered fax machines, with "offenders" paying fines which basically amount to the hookup and annual fees, plus a factoring.

For places in Moscow to send a fax to or from (service bureaus), see the Yellow Pages, under Fax.

Electronic Mail

One way any business or individual can circumvent communications difficulties (i.e. relying on phone and fax communications with Moscow or outlying areas) is to tap into an electronic mail (email) service. Because this requires only local calls at either end of a communication channel and not a direct link between communicating parties, it is a much simpler, more flexible, and usually less expensive means of communication.

Several companies operate email services which are primarily Russian-Western services. And most of the major email services that can be accessed in the West can be accessed from Moscow, St. Petersburg and from anywhere else in the former Soviet Union from where a call can be placed directly to one of these cities.

Most email systems are inexpensive to use on the Western side (i.e. sending from the US to Russia or receiving in the US from Russia). The most expensive part of the equation in any case is sending and receiving on the Russian end. Prices between services vary, as do the services and features each provides.

Another advantage of email is that you can very easily send and receive telexes right from your computer. This is particularly important since most Russian businesses and factories still use telex (not fax) as a primary means of communication. This puts you in easy touch with all points of Russia and the Commonwealth with a simple keystroke.

For offices in Moscow where you or your Russian partner can sign up for an email account, see the Yellow Pages under email. To use email in Russia, the user *must* have either a modem with error correction capability (to compensate for the bad lines), often known as **MNP5 Error Correction**, or telecommunications software which can effect the same type of correction.

To get started in the West, you can contact any of the offices below to set up an email account. You will also need a modem and communications software to fit your computer system. If you are already using an email service, chances are, if a Russian partner can get hooked up on a system there, they can communicate with you via Internet addressing (ask your email service's customer service department about this).

Electronic Mail Services to Communicate with Russia

Compuserve, PO Box 20212, Columbus, OH 43220, phone (800) 848-8990

This well-known electronic mail and bulletin board system can be accessed from Moscow via the VNIIPAS host (contact SovAm Teleport JV for a host account -- see the Telephone Directory) and offers the best alternative for speedy transfer of binary files, because it supports transfer protocols aside from Kermit. While reasonably priced on the Western end, a bit pricey in Russia. Accessible from Moscow, St. Petersburg and Kiev.

Glasnet, 437 Mundel Way, Los Altos, CA 95072, phone (415) 948-5753; fax (415) 948-1474

This system cuts costs to users by using packet sending, whereby messages are stored up and sent every couple or hours in batches. The ruble costs in Moscow are somewhat high and often negotiated on contract. For a Russian account, contact Glasnet in Moscow (see Telephone Directory).

Infocom, in the US, phone (800) 441-0926

This Russo-Finnish joint venture has been much lower profile than Sprint or SovAm and a bit pricier as well. It links you into the large Infonet network. Not as widespread a service in North America; in Europe, call directory assistance for the local affiliate company. For a Russian account, contact Infocom JV (see the Telephone Directory).

MCI Mail, 1150 17th Street NW, Suite 800, Washington, DC 20036, phone (800) 444-6245

A very user-friendly atmosphere and cost-effective on the US or European side, but a bit pricey on the Russian end, since traffic goes through the VNIIPAS host. For a Russian account, contact SovAm Teleport in Moscow (see the Telephone Directory).

SovAm Teleport, 3278 Sacramento St., San Francisco, CA 94115, phone (415) 931-8500, fax (415) 931-2885

The email provider which provides the best service value. Your Russian partner can access the system and pay in rubles, and you pay a reasonable fee for access in the US. Delivery is nearly immediate and the system also supports fax, telex capabilities and binary file transfer. The company is also developing a range of database services which users can access on-line. For a Russian account (access numbers in Moscow, St. Petersburg, Kiev), see the address for SovAm Teleport in the Telephone Directory.

Sovset, CSIS, 1800 K St. NW, Suite 400, Washington, DC 20006, phone (202) 887-0200.

Primarily a network for academics, this is nonetheless the network for slavophiles. Accessible worldwide through Bitnet, Internet and Telenet, this is also accessible from Moscow by using the VNIIPAS host (contact SovAm Teleport, see Telephone Directory) to access the Compuserve host, which can then hook you into Sovset. Very cost effective, but a bit less user-friendly interface.

Sprint Telemail, 12490 Sunrise Valley Drive, Reston, VA 22096, ph. (800) 736-1130; in Norther Europe: Norton House, Kingsland Business PArk, Basingstoke RG24 OPL, England; in France: Z.A. De Courtaboeuf, Miniparc Du Verger, 1 Rue De Terre Neuve, 91967 Les Ulis Cedex B

Sprint offers a nice user interface for an additional fee which will help you keep your email organized (Compuserve also now offers a similar system). Prices are reasonable on the US and European end, but high on the Russian end. Best selling point is that this system, which also has the usual fax, telex and database/news service access capabilities, is run by Telenet, which is the world's largest email network, making international access easier. For a Russian account (access numbers in Moscow, St. Petersburg and soon other cities), see the address for Sprint Networks in the Telephone Directory.

Telex

As noted above, one of the main ways to communicate from all points of Russia and the Commonwealth is by telex. Sending telexes can be inexpensive and simple. You can send telexes from almost any post office in any city or town in Russia. And if you have email back at your home office, this may be the most viable way to communicate quickly.

The present rates (expect these to rise) for sending telexes are (denoted in rubles per minute (100-200 words) of send time; the telex operator will usually give you a price quote before sending):

To the United States	24.70R
To Australia	36.40R
To Japan	28.30R
To the UK	8.86R
To France, Germany, Norway	8.05R
To Finland	6.43R
To Sweden	7.24R

Mail

The Russian mail system is slow, unrealiable and not very safe. It's ok for personal letters, but don't send anything of value by the post. Use one of the alternatives listed under Express Mail below.

The cost of a domestic letter is 55 kopeks, for an international letter 5.25R, and for an international postcard 3.50R (these are considerable increases over past rates; expect this trend to continue).

Express Mail

A number of Western companies, either independently or through joint ventures, now provide express letter and package service to and from Russia. Typical delivery time (to Moscow or St. Petersburg) is 3-4 days to and from the US and 2-3 days to and from Europe. Delivery to outlying cities takes somewhat longer. For Moscow pick up or contact numbers, see the Yellow Pages under Express Mail. For St. Petersburg, see *Where in St. Petersburg*.

The following companies are currently serving the major CIS and Baltic cities (subject to change without notice, this information is correct at the time of printing). Prices fluctuate greatly according to the city being delivered to. The basic price for a one pound package to Moscow (from the US) is indicated, where available. Other cities often carry a surcharge. Call the carrier for more information.:

Federal Express:(800) 247-4747; UK: (203) 637-637, $69.

DHL:(800) 225-5345; UK: (081) 890-9393, $71.

Emery Worldwide: (800) 443-6379, $90

Prompt International Couriers: UK: (081) 571-1709

TNT Skypack: (800) 558-5555; UK: (081) 848-1111, $58.50

UPS: see local phone directories for local and regional 800 numbers, $55-65.

National mail services, such as US Postal Service and Royal Mail also provide express mail services to Moscow and some major cities, usually using the Russian mail service for outlying cities.

Most all air carriers serving Russia also offer air cargo or air freight services. See Yellow Pages under Airlines for a list of such carriers. See also Shipping Agents.

VII. Doing Business

Doing Business

By Paul Richardson

This new period in Russian history offers unique opportunities and certain risks for investors. The Russian investment frontier has been open for just over five years. Thousands of firms and individuals have ventured east in that time. Some have been wildly successful; most have been sobered; many have failed. This section considers some of the lessons of the past five years and, at the same time, summarizes some of the unique aspects of the Russian market.

THE RUSSIAN STYLE OF BUSINESS

When in comes to understanding the Russian business culture, it is prudent to remember that an imprint of 70 years of communist administrative style and practice lays heavy on Russian industry and trade. It is also worth remembing that, while Russia lived some 74 years under communist rule, it has lived over a thousand years (the last 74 included) under authoritarian and autocratic rule. There are only remote pockets of democratic or free market experience in the whole of Russian and Soviet history.

At times it may be difficult to discern which elements of the present Russian style of business are "Russian" and which are "Soviet." Irregardless, there are certainly some distinctive characteristics of the Russian business "style" which are unique.

It should be noted that this is a necessarily cursory review of some of the characteristics of Russian business culture. While there are certainly risks in such generalization, there must be a starting point for understanding potential cultural differences which are bound to arise when doing business in Russia.

Red Tape

In 1839, the Marquis de Custine, while waiting to enter Russia through St. Petersburg, unnerved by the customs bureaucracy, was consoled by a Russian customs agent who commented that "Russia is the land of useless formalities." In this respect at least, Russia has not changed much in 150 years.

Doing business in Russia means daily taking on a bureaucracy with few equals. Be it in customs clearing, taxation or enterprise registration, red tape binds the economy and society to the point of strangulation. Notaries, auditors, bookkeepers and inspectors hold the businessperson hostage to an endless procession of stamps, forms and signatures.

But, as in Custine's case, the bureaucrat himself is also long-suffering and will often beat you to the punch in decrying the bureaucracy's injustices and intractibility. This rebellion against the system, while working complacently within it, often leads to a frustrated bureaucrat finding himself able to overlook minor infractions for personal gain (in fact, one could argue the system is supported by such outlets for personal gain). But short of bribery there is the opportunity to use the latent sympathy of individual bureaucrats to ease a difficult situation. This should not be taken to the extreme, however. Crying outrage most often begets stonewalling.

Formalism

The bureaucracy's useless formalities belie a more general formalism in the business sphere which is in stark contrast to the more casual Western business style, in particular the American.

Paper communications are very formulaic and formal (see Siegfried Kohl's *Business Russian*, reviewed in Section I, for samples).

Business is rarely conducted over the phone, and face to face negotiations are the only real forum for decision-making. For this, the Soviet KGB carries much of the blame. But it is also that Russians very much feel that any matter of import should be discussed by looking one another in the eyes.

Even the simplest meetings are termed negotiations *(peregovori)* and include a certain protocol all their own. There is the ceremonial exchange of business cards, the rambling speeches, the tea and cookies, and the ever serious tone implying that issues of great import are being negotiated.

The problem with such meetings, which certainly hearken back to the pre-1987 period, is that they take time, too much time. They are rarely productive in a practical sense. But certainly the older management personnel, raised in the communist form of economic management, are more prone to this type of formalism. The younger and newer entrepreneurs tend to eschew such formalism and rightly place a higher value on their time and energies.

Sense of Time

Even the younger, more impatient Russians, however, share with their counterparts among the older management a sense of time and timeliness which differs somewhat from Western business practice.

Being late for business meetings is far from taboo in Russia. In fact it is almost the rule. Punctuality is very rare. Given that, expect meetings to drag on into overtime.

The flip side of this more casual relationship to time is that Russian business people generally have a greater reserve for patience than their Western counterparts. They are likewise more conservative (pessimistic?) about change and schedules for change. Therefore, expect new ideas to be met with a brick wall of skepticism. Expect change to meet with great delays. Conversely, expect decisions made and commitments believed in to be pursued with incomparable vigor and effort.

Maneuvering

Every negotiation is an occasion for Machiavellian intrigues, maneuvering and posturing. Rest assured that there is nothing personal in this and great malice is not usually intended. This is just part of the game as they see it. Not unlike a round of chess.

Whereas Americans and other Western business persons tend to work from the assumption that the result of any negotiation should be a win-win situation, all too often Russian business people are zero-sum thinkers: our side cannot win without putting the other side at a disadvantage.

This is reinforced by a general political and business ethos that implies that, in order to get by, you must deceive the authorities and find loopholes in laws. So far there has been little in Russian business legislation to show such behavior to be unjustified. For now, the sphere of business is a sphere of intrigues and mirrors.

"Svyazi"

For seven decades, the binding force which held the Soviet economy together was the Communist Party. It was an institutionalized "old boy" network. Doing anything of consequence under the old system required Party approval and patronage. If you didn't have connections (*svyazi*), you stood little chance of getting anywhere or getting anything done.

While the edifice of both the Soviet Union and the Party has crumbled, the importance of connections in this highly bureaucratic society has not waned. It has just become less institutionalized.

Rare is the occasion when a business meeting will not be a venue for name dropping and claims of uncommon influence (at the highest levels). It is often difficult, if not impossible, to test the veracity of these claims, but the importance of "friends in high places" is not to be overlooked.

The importance of connections and access is heightened by deeply ingrained traditions of patronage and cooptation. Connections and the ability to take care of your friends are real indicators of status, still even more so than the new status symbols of incipient capitalism. But this is not surprising in a society where the economy has always been highly politicized and statist (and founded on scarcity).

Cult of Largesse

Russians are lovers of grand designs and largesse. It is often said that, much as with Texans, this has to do with their geographic disposition, that huge open spaces give rise to expansive thinking. Irregardless of the reasons, Russians, like Americans, love to do things in a big way. You only need to look at the Stalinist architecture of Moscow or the feat of St. Petersburg for examples.

The positive connotations of this are ambition and vision (i.e the Virgin Lands program and the Soviet Space Program). The negative connotations are hastiness and inability to build a proper foundation (Stalin's sinking Palace of Soviets and the poor quality of St. Petersburg water come to mind). And unfortunately, too many of the "first wave" of Russian entrepreneurs are after the fast buck and the big score, erecting empires on sand. Too few recognize the value of building lasting value and doing one thing and doing it very well. This is merely a matter of channeling innate ambition and vision, which, some have postulated, will be the manner of the coming "second wave" of Russian entrepreneurs.

Egalitarianism

Any Western investor who begins an enterprise in Russia and takes on a significant number of employees will soon notice some real differences between Russian workplace mentality and that in the West. Russian workers (particularly the older ones) typically expect a much higher level of support and non-wage compensation. This is very much a result of a scarcity economy and of uncertainty (and of course of the big-brother socialism which gave birth to such an economy).

As well, Russian workers seek higher levels of workplace democracy. This is a legacy of socialist trade unions (which are yet a force to be reckoned with in Russia) and of the Russian *mir* or village, where decisions were made consensually and supported unanimously.

Stretching from these same roots, Russian workers are much more sensitive than their Western counterparts to wage differentials. From childhood, collectivism has been stressed over individualism and even individual bonuses for individual achievement are much less preferred than group bonuses based on group efforts.

CHOOSING A PARTNER

The present somewhat uncertain times, along with the lessons of the last five years, recommend a more circumspect and cautious approach to the selection of a partner and the cementing of business relationships.

The process of choosing a partner can be either passive or proactive. The passive approach means working with the first person who comes along who claims expertise and capabilities in your area of interest. A proactive stance means you and the goals and needs you identify drive your search. Only a proactive stance is in your best interests.

If you think that there is an opportunity for your business in Russia, try to step back far enough from the project idea to identify all of the components. What needs to be put in place--from your point of view--for the project to succeed? Identify what you need for real estate, equipment, supplies, personnel and so forth. Ask yourself, when considering a partner, how effectively the Russian organization can provide what is necessary.

Do not choose a partner before you know exactly what your needs are. Do not choose a partner unless they have a proven ability to satisfy those precise needs. Beware the prospective partner who claims to be capable of everything. Doing any *one* thing in Russia is difficult.

Keeping these points in mind, there are some questions you should ask yourself before getting too closely tied with any partner.

What to Ask About a Partner

- Do your potential partners have any experience in foreign trade or business management? Are they registered to conduct foreign trade?
- Does your potential partner have any valuable political affiliation? And in these uncertain times, what does this mean?
- Does your prospective partner want to build General Motors overnight or are they willing to focus, to start slowly and carefully?
- Does your partner measure business/organizational success in the number of bodies employed or by the bottom line? Can they construct a realistic business plan?
- Do the people that work with your prospective partner have good educational backgrounds? Did they achieve their current position by virtue of skill and intelligence or was there some other, less valuable reason? How do they go about selecting and hiring personnel?
- Does your prospective partner have an abundance of young, energetic personnel?
- Does your partner have access to a valuable section of the market you are targeting, or the supplies you will need to provide your service or product?
- Will your partner have a ***real ownership*** interest? That is, will the partner be making a commitment or investment and getting a return in a fashion that will motivate people -- will there be individual motivation as opposed to merely institutional motivation?
- Would you be working with this partner because you like him/her or because you have so far found no one else to work with? Too many people have been unwilling to admit the latter when it is the case and have thus contributed to the high failure rate of joint ventures. Would you work with these people in your home country?

Getting Started

If you have found a partner you feel you can work with, it is most adviseable to begin working with your partner on a contract basis, if your type of venture would allow this. You need to develop a framework within which you can test one another's abilities, strengths and weaknesses, while not committing blindly to a long term engagement. If the Western partner is contributing technology, it can be provided on a lease or license basis, as opposed to contributing to the equity or authorized capital or a new joint venture.

Such an arrangement also allows you to get to know the market, the environment, your partner and the problems you will face. When you are fully informed, you can always form a more lasting structure. The joint venture mechanism has often shown itself to be a too-inflexible mode of investment in Russia, but it does have its place, particularly where large investments are concerned, and those oriented at export production.

The key is to go slowly and not commit more resources than your familiarity with the Russian market can bear. The Russian market is significantly different from any other that it bears emphasizing the importance of this. The thousands of unexecuted Letters of Intent, and the hundreds of inactive joint ventures are a testimony to the unrealistic expectations and misplaced efforts of thousands of Western and Russian firms.

BUSINESS ETIQUETTE

Good etiquette is, in most cases, a matter of simple common sense. The following guidelines for the business traveler to Russia should help you adjust to some of the cultural difficulties you may encounter.

Dress: Most Russian business people have high expectations of Western business people. You will be judged immediately by the way you dress. Dress conservatively and well. Shoes are especially important, as is a nice hat in winter.

Discretion: Few people are as critical of Russia as Russians. But do not mistake their remarks as an invitation for your criticisms. Russians are also very proud, and justly so, of their country. It may at times be easy to criticize Russia for its innefficiency. But it is a mistake to focus on the present problems and suffering while overlooking the achievements of Russian and non-Russian cultures and the economic and social potential of these peoples.

Meetings: Allow extra time to be on time. Getting places takes a long time (and is subject to innumerable mishaps). While being on time may often not seem too important to your Russian contacts, it should always be very important to you.

Shake everyone's hand firmly when you greet them.

Defer to the senior official to lead the meeting, and wait to be given the floor. Be firm and polite at all times; don't be pushy and don't be pushed. Try to get an agenda worked out before the meeting gets started or too far along.

Accept cookies and tea when offered. Tolerate smoking in meetings if you don't smoke (if you are completely intolerant of smoking, doing business in Russia is not for you). Ask first before lighting up to smoke and share your cigarettes generously.

A good translator avoids a thousand headaches. Do all you can to test your translator out in informal situations before you enter into formal situations. A simultaneous translator can be more efficient, but distracting.

Background: When preparing for meetings, know who you are meeting with, how important this person is, what his/her background is, etc. Remember, this is a culture which is based on patronage and status. Before a meeting starts, know who everyone in the room is and why they are there -- you will thus avoid stepping on egos. And be sure they know who you are and why you are there (and not someone else).

Know something about the company, association or department these people work in/for. As anywhere in the world, you will flatter people by showing them that what they do is known about by someone they previously did not know. You will also impress your hosts with your seriousness about working with them.

Communication: Never underestimate the importance of written communications in Russia. The country runs on paper (and rubber stamps). Do not commit something to writing lightly, and retain any written records. When in doubt, notarize.

Written communication is formulaic and formal. Be sure you address the addressee formally. For letters in English, follow good Western business correspondence etiquette. Always type letters. Consult a knowledgeable Russian on writing any letter in Russian.

Fax your letters if your contact has a fax (which is now becoming more common), or send by telex, which is ubiquitous in the former USSR. Use these as your main means of communication. Don't rely solely on the mail. Faxes and telexes will get the most reliable and timely responses -- but also send copies through the mail. You can set up telex capability (and fax for that matter) on your PC with a modem (see Section VI, Communications).

Gifts: There are three types of gifts. The first is the token gifts you should bring along to hand out to business contacts. These souvenirs (lighters, pens, solar calculators with your logo on them) are essential and may be part of what is expected.

The second type of gift is favors. There are things you will be able to provide that no one else can, that are either unavailable or unobtainable in Russia. These run the whole gamut and you should try whenever you feel it is right to do all you can to help -- you will rarely regret it.

The final type of gift is "the sucker gift." It is more of a bargain for exchange: computers for apartments, VCRs for cars, etc. Often you can get a good bargain. But you can also get taken to the cleaners. The best slogan for doing business in Russia is: Believe it when you see it. Receiving before giving is also a good policy. Understand that you are engaged in trade *(torgovlya)*, and if you do not get what was promised, you probably have no recourse.

Business cards: There is a ritual exchange of business cards at any business meeting or negotiation. Do not underestimate the importance of this event. Your business card may be all the information your Russian partner has on you. Make sure your cards say what you want to say about you and your firm -- try to have them in Russian.

Money: You are bound to find yourself, while in Russia, in situations which involve significant hard currency outlays and yet your Russian counterpart will not have a hard currency expense account. What starts out as generosity can easily turn into exploitation. Think this issue out ahead of time and do not be extravagant unless this is the image you want to convey. Know where you are going, know what it costs (what currency), and know who is going to pay.

This is part of a larger issue. The imbalance of hard currency resources can easily corrupt a business relationship. A main reason some Russians desire to do business with Western companies is to have access to the resources and privileges hard currency brings in Russia. Extravagant spending on partners may impress them, but it will not encourage financial responsibility and is not a healthy give and take. Similarly, beware of extravagant ruble spending by potential partners as an attempt to impress you. It should be a red flag of potential financial imprudence.

After work: While it is sometimes frowned upon to conduct business outside normal working hours, your host will often feel the need to take you out on the town, have receptions, etc. Feel free to discuss business insofar as your host takes the lead. But be better prepared at these times to show an interest in and knowledge of Russia, its history, politics, arts, and culture. Show yourself not to be all business.

Many foreign business people are not accustomed to consuming hard liquor (i.e vodka and cognac) in the quantities and frequency which is accepted at dinners and receptions in Moscow. Don't go overboard in your desire to fit in. Russian hospitality has a well-deserved reputation around the world. But know how and when to say no.

Customs and Superstitions: Russian culture is steeped in superstition. Some aspects apply, quite seriously, to business. Russians will joke about these superstitions, but deep down they will also take these things very seriously. As well, there are some customs and points of etiquette which you should adhere to. Both customs and superstitions are listed below. Judge for yourself which they are:

- Never shake hands over a threshhold: it will lead to an argument.
- Don't whistle indoors: you will blow your money away.
- Take off your shoes when visiting a home and your hat when indoors. Take off your suit coat in meetings only after asking if it is alright.
- Russia is still a very male-chauvinist society. Women in business should always dress conservatively or will end up being thought below their position. Women are not expected to pay for themselves or to be assertive in social situations.
- Always bring flowers or wine when invited to a Russian's home. Always bring an odd number of flowers; even numbers are for funerals.
- Be careful when refusing food or drink when visiting friends; they will likely take it as a slight.
- Never pour wine back-handed. It is considered an insult to the person for whom you are pouring.
- Never put your feet up on furniture; it is considered very rude.
- If you call someone on the phone and they don't recognize your voice, it means you will soon be rich.
- "Rough" language is frowned upon in "educated society."
- A black cat crossing your path is a bad omen taken very seriously.
- Before going on a long trip, sit down for a few minutes to collect your thoughts: you trip will go better.
- Be careful complementing something in a host's home; they may try to give it to you.
- Do not sit at the corner of a table; you will end up single.
- If you leave something behind when departing Russia, it is a good sign; it means you will be back.

Tolerance: You will probably meet with many situations in Russia which you would normally consider "intolerable". Tolerate them. Be flexible. If you want to be doing business in a comfortable atmosphere, your way, you should be doing business elsewhere.

--Paul Richardson is President of Russian Information Services, Inc., has consulted on and operated a number of ventures in Russia, and is Editor of ***Russia Business Survival Guide, Where in Moscow and Where in St. Petersburg****.*

The New Enterpreneurs

By Fred Harrison

The bizarre bazaar which is the commercial side of post-Soviet Russia includes thousands of little wooden kiosks scattered about in shantytown-style "shopping centers," important-sounding commercial banks which in fact do business out of cellars and old warehouses, and literally hundreds of commodity exchanges which are 19th century trading halls in all but name.

THE EXCHANGES

Flip on your hotelroom TV set in Russia and you will immediately be struck by the "birzha" phenomenon: The thousand or so commodity exchanges which have sprouted in the C.I.S. in the past two years are now the principal buyers of television advertising time, popping up as sponsors of anything from game shows to kids' cartoons.

Why a thousand exchanges? Well, the number is excessive, of course. But initially, the absence of a commercial wholesale market -- and the collapse of the State's supply system -- made the so-called "exchange movement" extraordinarily profitable, so much so that anyone with access to a large room and a couple of computers could make a ruble fortune as an exchange founder. A bit like cellular phone firms did in the west during the Eighties.

In fact, apart from the absence of electronic tickers and natty blue suits, the big difference between a conventional western exchange and those which have developed here is this question of profitability. Paradoxically, western exchanges are not designed to make profits.

In a sense, they are co-operatives or mutual societies meant to facilitate trading, so that the traders make the profits. But in post-Communist Russia and the other ex-republics, the exchanges are overwhelmingly proprietary. In fact, within the infant securities market just now starting to develop, 70% of all corporate shares on offer were issued by exchanges themselves.

Intriguingly though, by early 1992, these securities were starting to hit tough times. The market for the stocks -- and, probably, the market for exchanges -- appeared to have peaked, and a wave of what western securities analysts might call consolidation was in order. In other words, a lot of the thousand exchanges, perhaps most of them, are now not expected to survive the year.

Why? In part, just because they are not all necessary. Improving communications facilities mean that, increasingly, pricing information and trading are starting to occur between regions, putting small local exchanges out of business.

But also, price reform is removing at least some of the profitability. Let's take a real example. Late last year, a broker dealing through the Russian Commodity & Raw Materials Exchange, the largest of these institutions, came across a huge consignment of state-produced butter. He was able to put a lock on this consignment at appallingly low state prices. Then, he put the butter on offer at

DELOVIE LYUDI

BUSINESS IN THE EX-USSR

the new business dimension

DELOVIE LYUDI, launched under the title of BUSINESS IN THE USSR two years ago, is published first and foremost for the market of the republics of the former Soviet Union. It enables Russian decision-makers, influential figures and the new entrepreneurs to follow the efforts being made to modernize and liberalize the internal economic structure.

DELOVIE LYUDI also offers Western businessmen a precious and unique source of information.

It provides an exceptional medium for communicating details concerning their companies, products and services.

DELOVIE LYUDI is available in two editions with identical contents: 120,000 copies in Russian and 40,000 copies in English for the international edition.

Written in Moscow by a team of local high-level journalists, well-connected in top economic and social circles, DELOVIE LYUDI is independent, objective and thorough.

Subscription/ Advertising:

SCII
4, rue Brunel
75017 - Paris - France
Tel: (1) 43.80.90.00
Fax: (1) 42.67.75.48

Ul. Profsoyuznaya 73
117342 Moscow,
USSR
Tel: (7-095) 333 33 40
Fax: (7-095) 330 15 68
Telex: 414 741
PREMO SU

THE INDEPENDENT ECONOMIC MONTHLY

the exchange at "real" commercial prices. It was immediately grabbed, no doubt for the private restaurant trade, and the broker made an overnight commission of 500,000 rubles. Broker's fees are negotiable but range from 1.5% to 10%.

Even in western terms, $5,000 (the approximate value at the time) is pretty good money for a day's work. But the exchange also made its cut on the deal, a trading fee measuring 0.175% of the value.

But on January 2 in Russia, state prices on a great many products were either decontrolled or raised. The "arbitrage value" of buying from the state and selling commercially was greatly lowered. Obviously, the commissions available were the same, but the opportunities became fewer as state-employed sellers were given the freedom to secure their own higher prices. And as volumes of trading through the exchanges plummeted, the exchange trading fees started to decline.

There were other factors eroding exchange movement profitability. Taxes, for one. Under International Monetary Fund and western-country tutellage, the new Russian government was trying to put its fiscal house in order, and wipe out the huge budget deficit it inherited from the collapsed Soviet government. That meant huge new taxes at all levels, put particularly applicable to the profits of the emerging commercial sector.

And one more factor: the banks.

One very good justification for the truly enormous profits available to brokers and the exchanges during their earliest days -- well, last year actually -- was the stupendous array of commercial risks they faced. The decrepid and totally unreliable old Soviet bank clearing system meant that payments by bank transfer could take up to six months. So brokers scoured the countryside looking for saleable goods carrying suitcases filled with millions of rubles. Then there was the question of delivery: Who could guarantee that a contract for delivery on such-and-such a date would be fulfilled? After all, this is a country notorious for its shortage of boxcars and hijackings of entire freight trains.

But late in 1991, another of the rising new elites of post-Communism, the commercial bankers, started to get interested in the brokers' profits.

THE BANKS

The new Russian banks are hardly what westerners would call banks at all. They are, most commonly, venture capitalists, providing (by Soviet standards) high-interest loans and even some equity financing to startup businesses. According to Mikhail Hodorkovski, chairman of Menatep Financial Group, one of the biggest of these institutions, they provide these funds not in any conventional western way, with business plans or five-year forecasts, but "by touch and feel." At this, a form of investment banking, he maintains his bank and a handful of others are more skilled than anyone on Wall Street.

And this relationship with the new entrepreneurial class is now leading the bankers to look at the profits available from trade finance. Theoretically, this is risk assessment, something any banker worth his pinstripes knows is his line of work.

Example: Assuming no new, modern clearing system is established -- though in fact the independent bankers were busy trying to establish their own early in 1992 -- it should be possible to lend against receivables. This is called factoring, and it can be hugely profitable, as long as the clearing delays are at least statistically predictable. Maybe one wire transfer out of 10 will take six months but if, on average, most transfers only take a month, the banks could then set a loan rate high enough to cover the inflation-driven cost of that one really bad delay.

In other words, the banks are starting to provide the brokers and their suppliers with a new financial service that matches their needs, but in doing so they are starting to absorb some of the profits of each deal. Piece by piece, commercial risks -- and commercial profits -- are being spread around, as the evolving business culture starts to take root.

So take it seriously, this new class of "commersants," with all its strange attachments to flashy cars, trashy "pop" culture and armies of private body-guards. And remember this: Mikhail Hodorkovski, one of the czars of modern Russia and head of an 800-employee financial organization which now even boasts overseas affiliates, is only 27 years old. Have the *nouveau riche* ever, anywhere been quite as *nouveau* as this?

*-- Fred Harrison resides in Moscow, is Editor-in-Chief of **Russian Business Reports,** a weekly business news publication reported from Moscow, and is a principal in East-West Information Consortium, a consulting and information services company.*

VIII. Russian Business Law

Knowing the Law

The two recent benchmarks which define the legal atmosphere for doing business in Russia are January 1987 and July 1991. In January 1987, legislation was passed which allowed direct foreign investment in the Soviet Union for the first time since the 1920s. Over the next four years, some 3000 joint ventures were registered in the USSR.

In July of 1991, Russia passed the law *On Foreign Investment Activity in the RSFSR*. For the first time broad ownership rights and benefits were granted to investors and, along with a similar union level law passed a day later (and a USSR Presidential Decree issued six months prior), this law placed foreign investors on an equal, and in some ways better, footing with Russian companies.

There is reason for optimism in the opportunities made available by these and other legal changes. But this optimism should be tempered with a recognition of the fact that there are some serious legal issues to be resolved before Russia will have created a reasonably stable and predictable investment climate. Among these issues are:

- resolution of complex inter- and intra-state jurisdictional and ownership issues: Who owns the assets of the dead Soviet state?;
- rationalization and simplification of tax legislation, to include a general lowering of tax rates to less onerous levels;
- granting citizens and investors land ownership rights;
- conducting serious and broad privatization of housing and enterprises;
- simplifying the enterprise registration process; and
- making the ruble internally, and then internationally convertible.

Each of these are massive problems unto themselves; together they represent the challenges the Russian economy faces and thereby reflect the large reserve of patience and optimism any investor must have.

With these realities noted, the following pages summarize the more important Russian legal acts relating to foreign investment, and review the types of and avenues for such investment.

RUSSIAN FOREIGN INVESTMENT LAW

On July 4, 1991, the Russian Law, *On Foreign Investment Activity in the RSFSR*, was passed. More liberal and inviting than its all-Union counterpart, it now stands as a cornerstone of legal norms regulating investment activity in Russia. While generally deferring resolution of lesser and tangential issues to later legislation and regulations, the law is nevertheless specific on several important points.

The key statement is in Article 6: "The legal regime of foreign investments and investment activity may not be less favorable than the regime for the property, proprietary rights, and investment activity of legal entities and citizens of the RSFSR, with the exceptions stipulated by the present Law."

The Law puts foreign investors on an even footing with Russian business persons, granting the right to purchase shares in existing joint stock companies and privatizing state and municipal enterprises, to acquire various types of property and rights, including land and mineral use rights. It asserts, as is the case with all related Russian legislation, the primacy of the ruble for such transactions.

Three types of equity investment are open to foreign investors as regards the establishment of enterprises: joint ventures, fully owned subsidiaries, and affiliates. The procedures for establishing each are enumerated (see the relevant sections below).

The law explicitly allows investors to maintain ruble accounts in Russia (along with a law passed in November 1990). Such monies, provided they are obtained from earnings within the RSFSR, may be used to buy hard currency at auctions, to reinvest in the economy, and to buy shares in Russian companies, although foreign investors cannot use rubles to buy shares or securities if those rubles are acquired at rates lower than the State Banks' s commercial rate (See Section IV on the ruble).

Certain activities (insurance, banking, brokering) require licenses. Otherwise, foreign investors can engage in any activity stated in their enterprise's statute, or which is not disallowed by existing legislation.

If a foreign investor's share in an enterprise is greater than 30% in an enterprise in which it was a founder, or greater than 50% in a previously existing enterprise whose shares it purchased, then that enterprise shall pay no import or export duties. In any case, equipment and supplies which are imported as the foreign investor's investment in an enterprise are duty free. The law allows for various advantageous circumstances for investment in Free Economic Zones.

JOINT VENTURES

Russia does not have a law on joint ventures. Thus, the union level law (of January 13, 1987, with subsequent ammendments) continues to operate, with consideration of changes introduced by the Russian law, *On Foreign Investment Activity in the RSFSR* and *On Enterprises and Enterprise Activity*.

Increasingly, foreign investors are looking at the option of direct investment through joint stock companies or small enterprises, or through wholly-owned subsdiaries or affiliates (each of these investment options is treated below). Still, the joint venture investment mechanism remains the most tested and widespread vehicle for foreign investment. The following pages summarize the status of current legal acts and regulations regarding the establishment and operation of joint ventures in Russia.

Registration

If the establishment capital fund of the joint venture is to exceeed 100 million rubles, the venture's registration must have the prior approval of the Russian Council of Ministers. In all cases, a joint venture is registered with the Ministry of Finance.

The documents required for registration are:

(1) written request by the founders for registration of the joint venture;
(2) properly notarized copies of the joint venture's charter and agreement;
(3) conclusion of required "expertiz" (examination) in cases where required;
(4) from the Russian side, a notarized decision (letter of consent) from the owner(s) of any assets or property being contributed to the joint venture, as well as notarized copies of each Russian partner's establishment documents;
(5) documents attesting to the liquidity of the foreign investor (ability to make the specific capital contributions) issued by the investor's bank or another financial institution (with a certified translations of said documentation into Russian);
(6) an extract from the trade register from the country of the foreign investor's origin, proving the legal status of the investor's company according to local law (with certified translation into Russian).

Documentation

Joint ventures are created with four separate documents. These documents are the letter of intent, the feasibility study, the joint venture agreement, and the joint venture charter.

The ***letter of intent*** can be a very simple one or two page document. It merely evidences both sides' good faith intentions to enter into serious contractual negotiations to create a joint venture. It can serve a very useful purpose by setting forth the goals and interests of the potential partners and by putting their objectives on paper prior to the expenditure of any significant amounts for negotiations, travel, attorneys' or accountants' fees. There is no particular form that the letter of intent should comply with. It is not registered with any ministry. It serves to establish a basic understanding between the partners and it should be written in a manner they think will best serve their interests or best clarify the threshold questions that appear at the outset to be most crucial. It is not binding.

The ***feasibility study*** or -- to be more precise -- the technical and economic substantiation (TEO in Russian) of the joint venture is intended to establish the financial viability and basis for the project. It typically takes on a business plan form that many Western businesses are already familiar with.

Essentially the TEO is a market study and financial plan. It serves the same purpose it would serve anywhere else. It is a mechanism for getting a handle on the prospect of the enterprise -- both for the participants and for lenders and superior management bodies in Russia.

The **agreement** is the essential contract between the partners and is usually the heart of the documentation. The **charter** is the organizational framework of the enterprise. It is the joint venture's most important document. Both of these documents now follow a fairly standard "boiler-plate" format and can be easily tailored to your needs by your lawyer. This said, some general caveats to the process of drafting these documents should be noted:

- The doctrine of *ultra vires* is enforced with some strictness in Russia. The joint venture should have a very carefully worded statement of purpose. It should be broad and clear. Explicitly assert your purposes and your rights in the foundation documents.
- Ownership protection and property rights regarding any inventions or new technology developed by the enterprise should be carefully circumscribed in the documents. You should also set out a clear procedure for obtaining access to enterprise finances including clear, regular procedures for supplying partners with information on profits and losses.
- Be very explicit in allocating responsibility, financial and otherwise, between the parties.
- The reserve funds created by Russian law are the equivalent of costs and taxes that get careful consideration in the West. At a minimum, you should specify the amount of annual appropriations to these funds for each partner so that the cost is precise and predictable.
- Draft a clause that limits inspections or audits to specific circumstances or at least regular intervals.
- Set out the exact dates for distribution of profits and the procedures for making those distributions.
- Be sure all real estate and property issues (payment for facilities, utilities, pace of renovation, etc.) are explicitly enumerated.
- Retain significant Western partner input into and/or veto power over hiring and firing management personnel and spending beyond certain threshholds.
- Any employee profit-sharing programs should be included in the charter, with consideration of relevant tax and currency issues.
- Draft a clear and unequivocal liquidation clause that allows each partner, at a minimum, to walk away with the equivalent of capital and equipment invested.

Accounting and Taxation

- The joint venture must maintain its books on model forms prepared by the Ministry of Finance, have its bookkeeping done by accountants directed by the Accountant General and file statistical reports in accordance with "established procedure." The good news is that Russian accounting standards are approaching internationally accepted accounting standards, which means keeping only one set of books to satisfy both partners.

- Russian joint ventures with foreign firms are tax exempt for two years from the date at which they first declare a profit. This means for the year in which profits are declared and for one additional year.
- Joint ventures, in the absence of a tax treaty to the contrary, and after expiration of the period of exemption, are required to pay a 35% profits tax and a possible 15% additional transfer tax upon transfer of any profit to the foreign partners' domicile. For joint ventures where the Western partner's share of the establishment fund is less than 30%, a 45% profits tax applies.
- Independent of the level of foreign participation, joint ventures whose profitability (net margin) exceeds 50% must pay a 75% tax on all profits earned above the 50% profitability level.
- Equipment and supplies are exempt from customs, tariffs or taxation.
- There are strong tax incentives for joint ventures that can be developed in the Far Eastern Economic Region. Likewise, newly developing Free Trade Zones (FTZs) are able in independently set tax incentives for foreign investment.
- There are special tax exemptions available in industries the Russians are particularly anxious to develop (i.e. medicine and agriculture).
- There is a 10% tax on all hard currency earnings, which is payable to the Currency Stabilization Fund for the Bank of Russia.
- Enterprises are directed to pay 5% of their foreign currency earnings to their city council or local governments. Enterprises that are a part of the state agricultural system may be required to pay a 70% deduction from foreign currency earnings as a result of export operations.
- Joint ventures are subject to a value added tax (VAT). This tax is presently set at 28% of the added value and is passed entirely on to the consumer, insofar as the tax must be included in a product's selling price.
- A number of profits tax breaks apply to joint ventures. Specifically, joint ventures will enjoy a deduction from taxable profits of: 30% of total monies spent on environmental protection measures; 100% of the sum invested in health care centers, retirement homes, pre-schools, pioneer camps, cultural and sports centers, educational institutions and housing projects; 100% of the sum donated to certain charities; 100% of the sum devoted to agricultural improvements.
- Taxes are payable in rubles with the following exceptions: goods and services which are imported into Russia for sale in hard currency pay hard currency taxes; the transfer tax on joint venture profits is payable in the currency of transfer; the VAT tax is payable in hard currency for goods sold in hard currency.
- The joint venture must pay taxes on income derived outside as well as inside Russia (except in cases overridden by foreign tax treaties).

• While there are no "taxes" on items which a joint venture produces and exports, there are customs duties which apply to a broad range of good. The duties are evaluated in ECUs and payable in rubles at the market rate of exchange.

• Estimated taxes are to be paid quarterly with a final return due March 15.

• Transfer tax refunds based on exemptions negotiated by the joint venture must be applied for -- the application must be filed within one year of when the tax was due.

• Year end accounting procedures in Russia are very different from in the West. And while this is changing, it is advised to seek the counsel of an accountancy firm in Moscow to make proper filings (see Yellow Pages under Accounting).

Structure

• Joint ventures are legal entities with the right to acquire property, sue, contract and so forth.

• The foreign partner is entitled to own any percentage of the venture, as agreed to by the partners, although there are strong tax incentives for the foreign party to own more than 30%.

• The management of the venture can be foreign or Russian or a combination of either.

• The venture is intended to have the same limited liability as a Western corporation.

• Fundamental business issues require unanimous consent of the board (joint ventures should spell out in their documentation what issues will require unanimous consent--a number are set out in the law itself).

Labor Management

• The venture must deduct reserve funds from its profits for the social development of its personnel until the reserve fund equals 25% of the establishment fund. The amount deducted annually is decided by the board of directors.

• Pay, working conditions, social security and so forth are all regulated by Russian law (see section on Labor Law below).

• Employees who are foreign nationals work under the same labor laws as Russian employees and must pay the same income tax rates. All income taxes on all forms or income (rubles or hard currency) are payable in rubles. Given recent devaluations of the ruble, these taxes can be as high as 60% (see the section on taxation below).

Sale/Property Rights

• Shares in the venture are freely transferrable, subject to the terms of the agreement between the parties.

- The venture may be liquidated by the Council of Ministers or according to the terms of the agreement between the parties. Liquidation occurs automatically within one year from registration (unless a longer term is specified in the founding documents) if the parties have not made their respective capital contributions to the venture.
- The joint venture's "industrial property rights" are intended to be protected by Russian law, but patent issues are complex and require competent legal advice.

Financial and Banking

- Insurance can be purchased on world markets.
- Joint ventures can take out credits and loans in Russian and foreign banks. No explicit right to hold deposits in such banks is stated in legislation, nor is such a right denied. Joint ventures may hold ruble and hard currency current accounts in any properly registered Russian commercial bank.
- The enterprise's accounting shall not be submitted to foreign governments; however, information necessary for tax returns, Security and Exchange Commission filings and so forth may be released.
- A joint venture is a Russian enterprise and thus, according to the foreign trade liberalization decree, is forbidden from making hard currency settlements with other Russian enterprises, except as regards currency purchase and sale transactions.
- Joint ventures may participate in currency auctions, and may pool hard currency earnings with other joint ventures.

Sales and Production

The foreign currency needs of joint ventures must be met by sales "on foreign markets." On this basis, many joint ventures have, in the past, sold goods and/or services to the extensive foreign community resident in Russia. As of July 1, 1992, barring any further ammendment of the decree liberalizing foreign trade, such sales will be forbidden. Most hard currency stores are thus expected to shift to a credit card only strategy.

Supplies for Production

At present, joint ventures dependent on a regular flow of supplies from within the Commonwealth must design their own system of supply as part of negotiations -- perhaps by identifying essential suppliers and giving them an equity position in the enterprise. Western businesses might also consider "escape clauses" similar to those used in contracts with the US government when supplies are unavailable.

WHOLLY-OWNED SUBSIDIARIES AND AFFILIATES

The Russian law, *On Foreign Investment Activity in the RSFSR* and some Soviet legislation which preceded it, laid a groundwork for legalizing registration and operation of 100% foreign owned companies in Russia. On the surface, organization and registration of such companies is made to appear no more difficult than for Russian enterprises (which is, in fact, far from simple). But so far the path is not very well worn and some "smoothing" has yet to occur in the registration process.

Creation and Registration

• For 100% foreign owned companies, the following documentation must be submitted to the Ministry of Finance (via the registration chamber -- *palata* -- representing it):

(1) application from the Western investor for registration;

(2) two notarized and certified copies of the founding documents (type and contents dependent upon the type of enterprise being founded);

(3) documents attesting to the liquidity of the foreign investor, issued by the investor's bank or other financial/credit institution (with certified translations into Russian);

(4) an extract from the trade register from the country of the foreign investor's origin, proving the legal status of the investor's company according to local law (with a certified translation into Russian);

(5) an "expertiz" (examination) of the project in those cases required by law (when the investment targets certain "sensitive" areas and when investments are of a significant size).

• For creation of an affiliate of an enterprise with foreign investment and affiliates of foreign juridical persons, the following documentation must be submitted to the registration chamber (*palata*):

(1) a declaration, signed by the director of the enterprise which seeks to create the affiliate, with a request to carry out its registration;

(2) a notarized and certified copy of the decision of the competent management organ of the enterprise to create the affiliate;

(3) two notarized and certified copies of the regulations of the affiliate;

(4) notarized and certified copy of the establishment documents of the enterprise creating the affiliate;

(5) an extract from the trade register from the country of the foreign investor's origin, proving the legal status of the investor's company according to local law (with a certified translation into Russian);

(6) an "expertiz" (examination) of the project in those cases required by law.

Typically, temporary registration of such an enterprise can be achieved within one week from submission of the above documents. To achieve permanent registration, the enterprise must, within 30 days, open a bank account, deposit 50% of the charter capital therein, obtain a company seal (stamp), and register at the regional taxation inspectorate (and for import/export codes at the State Statistics Committee if desired). Proof of these actions is submitted to the registration chamber, which will then issue a permanent registration certificate, which is then submitted to the State Committee on Foreign Investment.

The tortuous nature of this process (which is similar to that which any Russian enterprise must go through) has led many private Russian companies (and Western law firms) to offer registration services for foreign companies. Typical fees for these services, at the time of publication, are approximately 100,000 rubles or $10,000.

Taxation

Under the Russian law, *On Foreign Investment Activity in the RSFSR*, wholly-owned subsidiaries and affiliates are subject to a 30% profits tax from the date of their founding. There is also a 10% tax on all hard currency earned, which is earmarked for the State Bank's currency stabilization fund. Other taxes also apply. See the section below on Enterprise Taxation.

Other Considerations

In all other respects, a wholly-owned subsidiary or affiliate operates according to Russian law and is a Russian enterprise. It therefore is subject to the same restrictions and rights with regard to property ownership, labor laws, etc. as Russian enterprises. Certain advantages may be available for creation of such enterprises in Free Economic Zones.

JOINT STOCK COMPANIES

At the end of 1990 the Russian republic passed a joint stock company law that was much more advantageous to the creators of such businesses than the all-Union counterpart passed less than six months previous. This joint stock company legislation made it possible for the first time to found companies whose ownership was divided into transferable shares and which had liability limited to the extent of their assets.

These new companies are of particular importance to foreign investors because they offer new partnership alternatives versus state enterprises, cooperatives or joint ventures. They also offer a more flexible investment option, insofar as there is the opportunity to purchase shares in an enterprise, be it a newly founded one or a privatizing state enterprise. This allows for ownership without the organizational encumbrances of joint ventures. And the relative ease of share transferability (especially in comparison to joint ventures) makes such investment somewhat less risky.

The law allows for "open" and "closed" joint stock companies. For all intents and purposes, both types are treated identically under the legislation. Two important distinctions set the two types of entities apart, however.

First, shares in an open stock company can be sold or ceded to third persons with few restrictions. In a closed joint stock company, the founders retain preeminent right over the disposition of shares; a shareholder may not sell or transfer his/her shares in the enterprise to a third person without the permission of other shareholders.

Second, the minimum statutory capital of the two types of companies is different. Open joint stock companies must have a minimum statutory capital of 50,000 rubles; for closed joint stock companies it is 10,000 rubles.

Persons interested in investing in, forming or doing business with companies of this type are advised to acquaint themselves with the full text of the law. Some of the more important points are covered below.

Creation and Registration

• Companies may be founded by one or more participants, be they enterprises, establishments and organizations, state authorities or individual citizens. Foreign citizens and companies can also be founders (Article 11). Companies are established and operate on the basis of Articles of Association, which are approved at the company's organizational meeting. These Articles

> "shall contain all major characteristics of the Company: the type of the Company; the goals and objectives of its activity; the composition of its founders; the company name and location; the amount of the statutory capital; information on the categories of shares issued...; the consequences of the nonfulfilment of an obligation with regard to share redemption; the procedures for the distrubution of profits and recovery of damages; the structure and competence of the management bodies of the Company and the procedures for their decision making, including a list of items on which unanimity or a qualified majority of votes shall be required." (Article 19)

• Registration requires submission of the following documents to the registration chamber within 30 days of the founding meeting:

(1) a notarized and certified application for the company's registration, which includes the company name, location, its objectives and the main types of activity of the company, the liability of the shareholders, the amount of statutory capital, the names and legal addresses of the founders and their citizenship, and the number of shares acquired by them.

(2) a notarized and certified copy of the Articles of Association of the company;

(3) a notarized and certified minutes of the founding meeting (unless the company has just one founder).

No further documents may be demanded. (Article 24) Registration procedures are basically the same as those for wholly owned subsidiaries, as described above.

- A joint stock company may be established by the conversion of a state enterprise, but this requires a joint decision of the employees and the appropriately empowered state authority.
- In addition to the right to found a joint stock company, foreign investors have the right, as explicitly stated in this law (Articles 3, 4 and 35) and the law *On Foreign Investment*, to purchase shares in existing joint stock companies.

Spheres of Activity

- No limits are placed on the areas of economic activity open to joint stock companies, with the exception that such activity not contravene the laws of Russia or its constitution. Certain types of activity are allowed only to the government (i.e weapon production, tobacco and spirits production, processing of ores and precious metals -- see the Russian law, *On Enterprises and Enterprise Activity*). Certain other areas of activity require approval of the Council of Ministers (e.g. mining, fur, raw materials, timber).

Activity must technically be within the scope of activity defined in the Articles of Association, yet transactions conducted beyond the scope of the Articles are legal insofar as they do not contravene existing Russian law.

- Joint stock companies have the right to establish subsidiaries in Russia or abroad.

Liability

- The resolution invokes limited liability of the partners or founders of the company in the following manner (Article 8): "Shareholders shall be liable for the Company's obligations within the limits of their personal capital contribution." Yet, "wrongful acts" by company executives may require them to pay compensation for damage caused the company.
- A joint stock company created from the conversion of a state enterprise assumes the rights, responsibilities and liabilities of the state enterprise.

Shares and Ownership

- Unless specifically stated in the Articles, the sale or transfer of shares in a joint stock company does not require the consent of the company. Joint stock companies can issue registered, bearer, and preference (dividend) shares (up to

10% of total shares in the case of the latter). The minimum value of a share is 10 rubles. Joint stock companies can also issue bonds.

- In closed joint stock companies, participants enjoy priority right to acquisition of shares which another participant wishes to sell or transfer. Further, the participant may concede a share or a part thereof to a third party or to other participants only with the consent of the other participants, unless stated otherwise in the Charter. Shares can be transferred to third parties only if the participant transferring the shares has paid their contribution in full.
- Sales of over 15% of shares of the company to a legal or natural person (who is not a founder) requires the consent of the Ministry of Finance. Sales of more than 50% of shares requires the consent of both the Ministry of Finance and the State Anti-Monopoly Committee.

Management

Russian joint stock companies are to have a management structure not unlike that of Western corporations. Shareholders elect directors, who in turn elect/hire and oversee management. In addition, the company is to form an auditing commission to oversee and audit financial activities of the company.

Taxation

Joint stock companies are currently subject to a minimum 18% profits tax. Other taxes also apply (see the section below on Enterprise Taxation).

Labor Laws

Under current Russian legislation, all labor issues of import in joint stock companies are to be decided in the process of negotiation of collective and/or individual labor contracts. But the legacy of Soviet labor law still imbues this process with certain expectations and realities. See the section on Labor Law below.

SMALL ENTERPRISES

The legislation on small enterprises builds on the legislation creating joint stock companies. The legislation on small enterprises sought to fill two voids in the economy. First, small enterprises were designed to expand the realm for private enterprise by allowing unrelated private individuals, businesses or organizations to create an enterprise which can hire employees and operate much like a small business. Further, they are not burdened with the statutory capital limits imposed on joint stock and limited liability companies, and their organizational structure is much simpler. Second, small enterprises provide a simple means whereby huge state enterprises, institutes and organizations can be broken up into smaller business entities.

For the most part, small enterprises are governed by the law, *On Enterprises and Enterprise Activity* and legislation affecting the types of enterprises which found the small enterprise. Yet the law does place specific restrictions and norms on the organization and operation of small enterprises. Again, persons interested in investing in or doing business with small enterprises are advised to read the entire text of the law. Some of the more important points are touched on below.

Creation and Registration

- A small enterprise is created on the basis of a charter or set of rules adopted by its founders and registered with the appropriate local Council of People's Deputies. The Council must register the enterprise within two weeks or the founders of a small enterprise can take the matter to court.
- A small enterprise may be created by any combination of individuals (Russian citizens), state, leasing or collective enterprises, joint ventures, social organizations and their enterprises, cooperatives, auction societies, business societies and fraternities, business associations, other enterprises which are legal entities, and state organs which are authorized to manage certain state property. Small enterprises can be based upon any types of property, including mixed types.
- The rules agreed to by the partners specify the organization and operational rules of the enterprise. Therefore, the rules must include information about the type of enterprise, its name and location, the subject and purpose of its activities, its organs of management and control and their competence, the procedure whereby the property of the enterprise and its redemption are determined, how income and/or profit are distributed and the conditions for reorganizing and ceasing enterprise activity. The relations between the founders of the enterprise and the enterprise itself must also be specified in the rules.
- If a small enterprise is founded on the basis of mixed forms of property (i.e. collectively and privately owned), then the type of enterprise is defined according to which type of property makes up the predominant share of total enterprise property. Any obligations or agreements previously entered into by an enterprise, association, or organization from which a small enterprise has been detached are assumed by the latter insofar as the former is a founder of the small enterprise.
- A foreign legal entity may be a founder of a small enterprise but the enterprise must be registered and operated in accordance with the law, *On Foreign Investment Activity in the RSFSR.*

Size

- Depending upon the sphere of economic activity in which the small enterprise engages, restrictions are placed on the number of employees which may be employed by the small enterprise. If the enterprise engages in several activities, that activity which is responsible for the largest volume of goods or services provided is the operative sphere of activity. These limits are: Industry and construction -- up to 200 people; Science and scientific activities -- up to 100 people; Other branches of industry -- up to 50 people; Non-manufacturing -- up to 25 people; Retail sales -- up to 15 people.

- Autonomous republics and localities may also place limits on the amount of total revenue which small enterprises of various sectors may earn and still be classified as small enterprises. Similarly, they may designate minimum numbers of employees for small enterprises.

Area of Activity

Small enterprises are allowed to engage in any type of economic activity in any area of the economy provided: (a) such activity is not forbidden by legislative acts of Russia; (b) such activity corresponds to the purposes specified in the small enterprise's charter or rules.

Labor Laws

Small enterprises are subject to the legislative acts of Russia regarding systems and amounts of payments for labor. The workers in small enterprises are accorded social and medical insurance and social security in keeping with the conditions specified for workers in state enterprises. The small enterprise must pay the fees for these social services in accordance with legislation. See the section below on Labor Laws.

Taxation

- Under recently passed tax legislation, certain types of small enterprises are exempt from taxation during their first two years of operation. This applies to small enterprises engaged in agricultural production and processing of farm produce, consumer goods production, construction, maintenance/construction, building materials production, and to small innovation enterprises. Small enterprises engaged in other activities must pay only 25% of their normal tax rate in their first year of operation and 50% in the second year. Thus, the main reason for founding a small enterprise is to gain the tax benefits of this type of enterprise.
- Profits which are allocated to construction, modernization, retooling and renovation of fixed assets or training and retraining of personnel are tax exempt.
- All enterprises must pay the full tax rate after two full years of operation. If a small enterprise ceases operations before it has been in existence for three years, it is liable for the full measure of taxes for the entire period of its operation.
- Other taxes also apply, including a minimum 18% tax on profits. See the section below on Enterprise Taxation.

COOPERATIVES

For all intents and purposes, cooperatives are now being treated under registration, taxation and other legislation as small enterprises. Consequently, most cooperatives are changing, or in the process of changing into joint stock companies or small enterprises.

PRIVATIZATION

The future of market-oriented reforms in Russia relies on few things as much as on the success and speed of privatization. Some 95% of enterprises and nearly that much of the housing stock is still in the hands of the state. To the extent the Russian government is able to sell off and transfer these assets into private or corporate hands, it will have made huge strides toward establishing real private ownership in the economy.

Present plans are ambitious to say the least. The Russian government seeks to complete most privatization by the end of 1993. In 1992 alone it plans for near total privatization of retailing, catering and welfare amenities, as well as most light and food processing industries. Larger enterprises and those in vital spheres such as mining, banking, power production, communications, and the media, will be privatized more slowly.

The basic mechanism for privatization will be auctions. However, enterprise employees are granted something akin to a right of first refusal on taking over enterprises. All Russian citizens are to receive non-interest bearing privatization bank accounts, into which a fixed amount will be "paid" annually, the balance of which can be applied only to the purchase of stock in privatizing enterprises. When established, it is expected that, as in Eastern Europe, such accounts shall be the basis of a private capital market for enterprise buy-outs. Yet, stock in privatizing enterprises which is bought publicly cannot be resold for three years.

The two government bodies overseeing the privatization effort are the State Committee for Management of State Property (subordinate to the Council of Ministers), whose job it is to inventory all enterprise assets, and the Russian Republic Property Fund (subordinate to the Supreme Soviet), which is to initially be the major shareholder and seller of shares in enterprises.

Enterprises being privatized are protected from "monopolies" in that they cannot be purchased by entities which are more than 25% owned by the state. Take-over artists are also to be discouraged by the provision in legislation that enterprises whose purchase is more than 50% financed by privatization funds cannot be resold for three years.

Privatization of housing is also expected to get underway in 1992, although most of the administrative mechanisms remain to be put in place. The plan forsees granting free to all Russian citizens a specified amount of housing space. Space above this norm (and which is part of the housing a person already occupies) will be purchased at an established rate; similarly, citizens will receive compensation from the state for any unused portion of their quotas. At present, the state plans to allot 18m^2 of space to each individual, plus an additional 9m^2 to each family (the average amount of living space for all Russians is 16.5m^2).

Local councils are to set up privatization commissions to inspect and valuate privatized property. All of this, of course, does not exclude the conduct of housing auctions, which have already begun, with two and three room apartments in distant Moscow suburbs selling for over a million rubles.

The Russian law *On Foreign Investment Activity in the RSFSR* potentially opens up the privatization process to foreign investors by allowing shares in privatizing companies to be bought by foreign companies. Similarly, foreigners will also be able to be buy, lease or rent privatized apartments, offices and buildings directly from their Russian owners. But for now this remains a bit theoretical, since the real processes of privatization have yet to get underway, despite ambitious government plans.

FOREIGN TRADE

The rules and regulations governing foreign trade activity by Russian enterprises (including joint ventures) were changed dramatically by a November 10, 1991, Russian Presidential decree, *On the Liberalization of Foreign Economic Activity in the Russian Federation.* The decree, which took effect January 1, 1992, lifted nearly all previous restrictions on foreign trade activity, while at the same time banned the use of foreign currency on Russian territory (this latter has since been delayed to July 1, 1992). The decree is central to the Russian government's aim of internal ruble convertibility and embodies the following important precepts:

- all types of foreign trade activity, including barter, are permitted;
- all enterprises registered in accordance with the Russian law, *On Enterprises and Enterprise Activity* and the law *On Foreign Investment Activity in the RSFSR*, may conduct import/export activity directly. Further, no special authorization or registration documents need to be submitted to the Ministry of Foreign Economic Relations or any State Licensing Committee (although there is still the need to show a customs official proof of valid registration of the enterprise;
- all taxes on import and export activity are lifted, as are all import duties. Export duties remain on many goods (including those produced by joint ventures), however, and, from January 1, 1992 (Resolution #91), are evaluated in ECUs, and payable in rubles at the market rate of exchange as set by the Russian Central Bank;
- licensing of and quotas on imports and exports are almost wholly abolished; now just some 5% of export items and 3% of import items are subject to licensing or quotas;

• all fixed currency ↔ ruble exchange rates are abolished in the Russian Federation. Banks may buy and sell rubles from citizens at independently set rates; citizens are not required to prove the sources of any hard currency and have unlimited right of purchase and sale of rubles;

• hard currency settlements between Russian enterprises is forbidden, except those involving currency ↔ ruble exchanges;

• the USSR law, *On Currency Operations* is abolished in Russia, as is the USSR Customs Tariff and Customs Code. However, the mandatory sale of 40% of hard currency earnings by Russian enterprises still exists; foreign owned companies and joint ventures (with >30% foreign ownership), pay a tax on hard currency earnings of 10%.

While the decree does greatly simplify and open up foreign trade, it does not obviate certain customs formalities. These are outlined below.

Documentation and Registration

• To receive goods and property at customs and to officially register a shipment, the following documents are required (either the official recipient or a fully empowered representative may present them):

(1) customs shipping declaration;

(2) permission of specified government organs, if the goods or property falls under the control of these organs;

(3) documents affirming payment for the customs procedure and, where necessary, for customs duties and taxes;

(4) other documents indicated in the declaration;

(5) a copy of the enterprise's establishment documents as proof of registration, if not already on file.

• Customs institutions may, as an exception, allow customs registration without a declaration. This is with the understanding that such a declaration will be presented within 15 days after customs registration. In such an instance, the declarant must affirm in written form that the declaration will be presented in the specified time period.

Where to Receive Imported Goods

• Two main customs points are used in Moscow. Items shipped into Russia by air transit Sheremetevo II customs terminal. Goods arriving by truck typically transit Butovo customs point (on the southern outskirts of the city). Goods arriving by train can be claimed at the train station. There are customs agents at all stations where goods can arrive from abroad. Declarations for train arrivals must be processed at Oktyabrskaya Tovarnaya Stantsiya, located at Komsomolskaya ploshchad (see Yellow Pages under Customs). In recent months, private customs clearing houses have been springing up as well, and these may prove more efficient means of receiving goods (again, see Customs in the Yellow Pages).

• In St. Petersburg, goods arriving by air transit Pulkovo customs terminal, those arriving by boat or truck transit Central Customs. For more detailed information see *Where in St. Petersburg.*

• Under current rules, goods and property can also be declared and cleared through customs:

(1) at the declarant's place of business, under the condition that the declarant assumes the costs of bringing the customs official to the site. The declarant may also request the assistance of the customs office in setting up an inspection committee (expert) or designation of a customs representative (see section below on *akt*);

(2) at the location of the customs office, whereby goods or property should be shipped to/received at that office;

(3) at other locations agreed upon with the customs office having jurisdiction for the declarant's region, provided other options are not possible.

The akt *of Receipt*

• When equipment arrives in Russia on contract, the opening of the shipment should be witnessed by an expert (or inspection committee) from customs or the Russian Chamber of Commerce. If the equipment arrives in unsatisfactory condition, the recipient will thereby be protected by a certified statement (*akt*) which will be jointly signed by the expert and the recipient, who will be able to take recourse for compensation with the party sending and/or shipping the equipment. A similar procedure is to be followed in the event damaged goods are received.

• For accounting and inventory purposes in a joint venture or other enterprise registered on Russian soil, any shipment received must be certified by an *akt*. This means drawing up a list of the items received, their quantity, and their value, and having the person who received the goods sign the list.

Processing Fees

• Processing fees for customs clearing vary by organization and type of good being imported or exported. For government organizations the fee is 0.15% of the total price of the contract (one third of this must be paid in the currency of the contract), but not less than 30 rubles. State enterprise property requires no payment in hard currency and the same fee levels apply. Temporarily imported or exported property is subject to a flat 30 ruble fee.

• All other types of enterprises, including joint ventures, cooperatives, joint stock companies and small enterprises, must pay 20 rubles for processing a declaration and 5 rubles for each sheet of paperwork attached to it. In addition, such enterprises must pay the hard currency equivalent of 10 rubles for each declaration and 5 rubles for each additional sheet. Temporarily imported or exported property requires payment of a 30 ruble processing fee (expect these rates to increase).

- No payment for processing is required if:

(1) the total price of declared goods and property is less than 2000 rubles;

(2) property previously imported or exported on a temporary basis is being returned from whence it came;

(3) the goods or property are to be used for the official purposes of diplomatic or consulate representations of foreign states resident in Russia, of international intergovernmental organizations and the representatives of foreign governments which work in them, or of other international organizations which enjoy duty free treatment on Russian territory;

(4) a preliminary declaration is presented for shipments made upon a State writ;

(5) the goods are part of equipment under assembly and if a general declaration covering such goods has been previously filed. If such property subsequently becomes the object of a purchase, sale or barter and is re-declared as such, payment for customs processing follows the procedures specified above.

How to Pay for Processing Fees, Taxes and Duties

- Payment can be made in advance or at the time of customs clearing (if at a customs point such as Sheremetevo II or Butovo). If made in advance, payment should be made by bank transfer to the account of the Russian State Customs Committee. Ruble payments for duties and taxes can be paid to the account of the customs office through which goods are being cleared. The document which, for the bank's purposes, serves as the basis for payment, is the filled-in customs declaration. Proof of payment should accompany the declaration when it is presented at customs.
- Payment can also be made at the customs point, in cash. In general, payment should be made before customs will release the goods or property. Yet an organization or enterprise can present a guarantee letter (*garantiynoe pismo*) with the proper certification as proof that proper payment will be made.

FREE TRADE ZONES (FTZS)

As a mechanism for encouraging foreign investment in targetted regions and industries, Russia has established Free Trade Zones (FTZs) in certain cities, regions and oblasts. Among these are St. Petersburg, Vyborg, Nakhodka, Kemerovo, Novgorod and Nakhodka. The specific "privileged terms" for foreign investment and foreign trade are different for each FTZ, but all have certain elements in common.

• Taxation is reduced. In some cases joint venture tax holidays are lengthened; in others, caps are placed on the tax burden enterprises will have to bear (thus limiting some uncertainty). Generally, profits invested back into the FEZ's development are not taxed.

• Import and export duties and taxes are reduced or eliminated. In general, there are promises of "easing" the process of foreign trade, and quotas and licensing requirements are removed.

• Local authorities are vested with greater authority to register enterprises, set tax rates and terms of lease.

LABOR LAWS

The Russian law *On Enterprises and Enterprise Activity* significantly loosens state control over enterprise labor policy. It recognizes that the impending break-up of state enterprises creates new imperatives to allow private companies to set their own labor policies, within certain parameters. The collective and/or individual labor contracts are the primary basis for regulating labor-management relations, workers' rights, vacation time, etc.

This said, it bears reviewing what may be considered the norms or expectations of Russian workers as developed in the Soviet period, some of which are embodied in still active Soviet labor legislation.

• It is illegal to discriminate against employees or applicants on the basis of sex, race, nationality, or religious beliefs.

• The right to strike is not forbidden, nor is it allowed.

• Employees are expected, for the most part, to work a 41 hour, five or six day week. There are exceptions for teenagers and people employed at hazardous jobs.

• There are eight holidays recognized as Russian national holidays when no one is expected to work. (These are December 30 - January 2, March 8, May 8 and 9, and June 12. If a holiday falls on Tuesday, Monday is also a holiday and the previous Saturday is a workday. In addition, industrial, office and professional workers are entitled to at least 24 working days of leave (*otpusk*) per year with pay based on average salary for the past year.

• Jobs are typically classified according to skill grades and wage categories. Workers can be employed hourly or on a piece work basis. Time and a half is paid for overtime and double time for holidays.

• Management is expected to ensure occupational safety and health. It must satisfy the requirements of building codes. The facilities must meet with the approval of the state sanitary and technical supervisor, the trade union "technical inspectorate," the fire marshal, the trade union committee of the enterprise and any ministry or organization that may oversee the enterprise.

• Special clothing, instruction and safety equipment, as well as medical exams, are required in certain job categories. The enterprise is financially liable for disabilities to employees "arising from the performance of their duties."

• Female workers are afforded somewhat greater protection than males. For example, pregnant women and women with children under the age of one may not work at night (unless it is especially necessary). Pregnant women are guaranteed 112 days maternity leave with pay (140 days in the event of an abnormal birth). They may take up to a year with partial pay for child care.

• At least 2-3 days are to be given to workers getting married; 1-2 days for paternity leave; 2-3 days for a death in the family. There are, similarly, added protections for teenage labor. Special incentives often exist, such as a shortened work day, to encourage employees to continue with their education.

• Labor disputes are resolved, generally, before one of three tribunals:

(1) Labor dispute commissions are set up at the enterprise to hammer out differences internally.

(2) If the commission fails, the dispute is taken to a trade union committee with authority to overrule the commission.

(3) Either management or labor may appeal the trade union committee decision to district (or town) court.

• Cases of theft or property damage go straight to district court. Regarding theft, it should be noted that a doctrine similar to *respondeat superior* carries a special significance. Lost supplies or illegal use of equipment such as photocopiers may be the responsibility of the employer. Theft is very common. One way to avoid it is through adequate compensation and benefits. In some cases employees' contracts can include a clause whereby they are individually or collectively liable for lost supplies. Joint ventures may also want to investigate insurance coverage for this problem or consider some sort of hold back provision such as in construction contracts to cover losses.

• A labor contract, often, cannot be cancelled unilaterally by management. Cancellation is done only with the consent of the employees' trade union. If management wrongfully dismisses or transfers an employee, the management is personally liable for the damage sustained. Generally, employees cannot be transferred to different jobs or different locations.

• While labor law says a place of work can keep an employee from leaving for two months in order to find a replacement, a worker is, in reality, free to leave at will. Likewise, the limits on a manager's ability to fire employees are much less strict than the written laws lead one to believe. One source on labor codes says that one acceptable reason for letting a worker go is "discrepancies of a worker in fulfilling his duties." The worker must be given one month's written notice.

• A percentage of the income of every state enterprise is earmarked for the cultural and sports activities of the trade union. The enterprise also sets aside funds for all employees' "social insurance." These funds are used for disability, maternity leave, pensions, as well as medical treatment and diet supplements.

LEGAL STATUS OF FOREIGN NATIONALS

No new Russian legislation has been passed to date regulating the status of foreign nationals in Russia. Therefore, until this happens, by default Soviet legislation still applies. Yet even Soviet law on the status of foreign nationals is not a monument to precision.

- Foreign nationals in Russia are supposed to "enjoy the same rights and bear the same duties as citizens of the USSR [Russia] unless otherwise laid down in acts of Soviet [Russian] legislation." (Part 1 of Article 3, law *On Foreign Nationals*). All of the labor laws are fully applicable to foreigners. This includes wages, taxation, contracts, leisure time and so forth. Likewise, the provision for maternity leave and other benefits are applicable.
- Foreign nationals who are permanent residents have the right, on the basis of and in the manner prescribed for Russian citizens, to receive accommodation in state and socially owned houses and in cooperative houses. Foreigners (excepting diplomatic personnel) further have the right to pay for accomodation in rubles.
- Resident foreigners must register with the local UVIR (visa registration) office (and, in some localities still, with the militia) within 72 hours of arrival.
- Foreign nationals who are permanent residents are entitled to the same free medical care as Russian citizens. Temporary residents are entitled to medical care as may be prescribed from time to time.
- Foreign nationals, temporary and permanent, must pay taxes, but are likewise entitled to pensions and other forms of social security.
- Foreign nationals have the same educational rights as Russian citizens. And, of course, they face similar obligations. They cannot vote, join political parties, and are not required to serve in the military.
- Foreign nationals may have their period of stay reduced if there are "no longer any grounds" for the stay. The period of stay may also be reduced for a violation of the law. It goes without saying that if the offense is serious enough, the period of stay can be extended. A foreign national's departure from Russia may be postponed until the fulfillment by him or her of property obligations to Russian citizens, organizations or the state.
- Foreign businesses in Russia should become familiar with the basic provisions of visa, customs and currency regulations (see Section II on Visa and Customs), and should be certain their employees do the same. Employees in Russia should be briefed on criminal law (for example illegal currency operations can bring a 15 year prison sentence; "profiteering" is still illegal), housing law, and the court system.

• When travelling in Russia, a foreign national should always have his passport with himself/herself. For instance it is illegal to board a domestic flight without a passport.

PERSONAL TAXATION

Businesses that are considering an investment in Russia need to consider a myriad of personal and enterprises tax issues and absolutely must have legal advice on these questions. This section on personal taxation, and the following one on enterprise taxation, can serve as an introduction to these issues but cannot replace the advice of a competent lawyer or accountant.

• On December 7, 1991, the Russian law *On Income Taxes on Natural Persons* was passed, with significant consequences for the individual taxpayer. Tax rates are based on annual income and go into full effect with income received on or after January 1, 1992. Beginning in 1992, every citizen who receives income outside of enterprises which deduct taxes from salaries shall be required, prior to April 1 of each year, to make a declaration at their local tax organ of revenues actually received and to provide adequate documentation of same.

• The main changes wrought by the new tax law are that there are fewer types of individuals free of the income tax, and, of particular note to foreign workers being paid by joint ventures in hard currency, the highest marginal tax rate has been doubled, from 30% to 60%.

• Salaries earned in hard currency must be valuated in rubles at the commercial rate (currently 55R:1$). Taxes are payable in rubles. Thus, at the current commerical ruble rate, a foreigner earning greater than $7600 per year must pay a 60% tax on all marginal income above that amount. Effectively, this burden can be reduced to around 30%, assuming the free market ruble exchange rate remains equal to about twice the commercial rate. Still, it makes sense for any jont venture or subsidiary or representation to work out a mechanism whereby the foreign national is paid his or her salary in the home country.

• The base tax rate is 12% for salaries of up to 42,000 rubles per year, with all other rates applyied according to the table on the page following.

• A foreigner expecting to earn income in Russia and who will be resident in Russia more than 183 days in a calendar year, must submit a declaration within one month of entering Russia of the amount he/she anticipates earning. Taxes for the year are thus estimated and made payable in three equal parts of 25% of the estimated sum, on May 15, August 15, and November 15. A final declaration (and payment), with any changes, is to be made by March 1 of the following year.

Personal Income Tax Rates

An annual salary of (rubles)	Pays a base tax of... (rubles)	Plus this percent of the amount exceeding the lower threshhold
0- 42,000	0	12%
42,001 - 84,000	5,040	15%
84,001 - 120,000	11,340	20%
120,001 - 180,000	18,540	30%
180,001 - 300,000	36,540	40%
300,001 - 420,000	84,540	50%
420,001 and higher	144,540	60%

• Non-permanent residents (less than 183 days) earning income based on business (i.e. rental income, royalties, licenses) occuring in Russia are subject to a 20% income tax.

• Income for a private company is considered to be income of the individual owning the company and is taxed as such. This requires a separate declaration from the one mentioned above.

• Taxable income is defined in the law as: wages and salaries, *per diem* and other compensations for living in Russia, compensation for education of children, for food, and for family members brought on vacation. Not included as part of taxable income are: payments for social insurance and pensions (made by the employer), compensation for rental of living quarters and a car necessary for business purposes, compensation for business trips.

• All Soviet international tax agreements are still in effect until renegotiation with the separate republics. All reflect similar treatment. Wages and other personal income that are earned by a person in one contracting state are not subject to taxation in the other state as long as the person is not present in the other state for more than 183 days in any given calendar year.

The USSR [Russian] treaties with Sweden, Cyprus, Finland and the United Kingdom provide that technical specialists resident in one contracting state will not be taxed in the other so long as they are not present in the other for more than 365 days in any two year period. It should be noted that in some treaties the tax treatment depends on the residency of the employer. To avoid double taxation the taxpayer must declare tax payments made in other countries.

ENTERPRISE TAXATION

There are potentially 26 different types of federal and local taxes to which an enterprise may be subject, from customs taxes to property taxes to profits and VAT taxes. Only the most general and significant taxes are reviewed below. For a full understanding of tax oblications, consult a competent tax attorney or accountant (see Yellow Pages under Legal Firms or Accountants).

Profits Tax (Business Income Tax)

Joint Ventures: As noted above (See section on Joint Ventures), joint venture profits are subject to a 35% tax, which may be reduced to 10% for joint ventures that are established in the Far Eastern Economic Region, and increased to as much as 45% for joint ventures with less than 30% capital participation by the Western partner (this is as of July 1, 1990). This tax is imposed on the joint venture's net profits and is payable in rubles. The statutes and regulations spell out in only the most general fashion the deductions from gross profits that are permitted to determine net profits (see the section above on Joint Venture Law for a list of these).

Additionally, there is no tax imposed on a joint venture's profits for two years from the point at which the enterprise first shows a profit (based on annual accounting, with the first year in which profits are shown counting as year number one). In the Far Eastern economic region there is a three year tax holiday. For joint ventures in the fishing and mining industries, there is no tax holiday. Free Trade Zones may establish additional tax incentives for investment, as may localities.

The Ministry of Finance may exempt a joint venture from this profits tax completely, or reduce the rate of taxation, or extend the holiday. Since there is considerable latitude in the final determination of the exact level of taxation imposed on the joint venture, the Western partner should give careful thought to the tax package it designs and tries to achieve.

Wholly-owned Subsidiaries and Affiliates: 100% foreign owned enterprises and affiliates are subject to a 30% tax on profits earned, with no exemption period. Certain Free Trade Zones, however, may provide limited exemptions and incentives.

Other Enterprises: Joint stock companies, small enterprises, partnerships, individual enterprises and all registered Russian enterprises are subject to a business income tax of 18%. This is calculated based on total revenues, minus expenses, excepting wages. This rate jumps to 25% for auditing and consulting agencies, 45% for brokerage firms, trading services and investment institutions, 70% for auctions, casinos, video/audio rental companies and companies offering video games.

Value Added Tax

On December 6, 1991, the Russian Parliament passed a value added tax law which set the tax rate at 28% (21.88% for goods with regulated prices). The amount of the tax is to be included in the price of goods sold, and the enterprise is to pay the government the amount of tax collected from goods sold, minus the amount it payed to suppliers (who also include the tax in their sales price). This rate is expected to be lowered soon to around 15-20% and, in fact, is already being lowered to those levels on some goods (i.e. produce) and in some localities.

Excise Tax

Also on December 6, 1991, the Russian Parliament passed a law taxing the sale of liquor, beer, caviar, luxury seafoods, chocolate, tobacco, cars, tires, jewelry, diamonds, furs, high-quality procelain and cut glass, rugs and carpets and natural leather garments. The tax does not apply to goods sold outside the Commonwealth (i.e. exported abroad). The rates are set by the Russian government and vary by the type of product (e.g. furs are taxed at 10-35%, leather 35%, chocolate 40%, beer 25%).

Excess Profitability Tax

Enterprises, including joint ventures, which have a profitability ratio (net margin) in excess of 50% must pay an additional marginal tax on revenues received above the 50% level of profitability. The tax rate for such incomes is presently set at 75%, but is expected to come down.

Currency Earnings Tax

Russian enterprises are required to sell to the Russian State Bank a set amount of all hard currency earnings from exporting. These earnings will be sold at the commercial ruble exchange rate. Presently Russian enterprises must sell 40% of such earnings. Foreign owned companies and joint ventures with greater than 30% foreign ownership are taxed at 10%.

Other Miscellaneous Taxes

- Banking and securities companies are subjct to a 0.5% tax on issuance of securities; the buyer of such securities must also pay a 0.1% tax on the value of said securities.
- Resale of some items, such as cars and computers, is subject to a resale tax of 10% or higher.
- A tax on advertising is being put into effect, which can be levied at up to 5% of the value of advertising services.
- A property tax on enterprise assets is widely expected, with the rate to be set at around 0.5% of the assessed value of those assets.

• Local governments (i.e the Moscow City Government) impose taxes on buildings, motor vehicles, and land.

• There is an investment tax credit law which can take some of the sting out of the above-mentioned laws, allowing a 10% tax deferrment for 5 years on the total value of certain capital investments, with a ceiling of 50% of the total taxable amount.

Withholding (Transfer) Taxes

Joint venture legislation imposes a 15% transfer tax on the profits a foreign partner repatriates. This withholding tax will not be imposed if it conflicts with one of the Soviet Union's [Russia's] double taxation treaties. In the absence of an applicable treaty, the Ministry of Finance has the authority to waive this tax for a specific period of time or to reduce the rate. The Ministry of Finance is supposed to use this authority to encourage particular industries (medical equipment, high technology, consumer goods).

The 1973 US-USSR [Russia] Double Taxation Agreement includes no provisions relating to the distribution of profits or dividends. An American partner is subject to a 15% tax.

There are at least two ways to avoid this tax. First, it is possible to take advantage of the more favorable provisions of other double taxation treaties. Several of these treaties (Austria, Cyprus and Finland, for example) provide that a distribution of profits and dividends are exempt from taxation in the country from which the dividends are remitted. Thus, dividends remitted by a Russian joint venture to a Finnish company would be free of the 15% transfer tax.

Of course, the big problem is whether or not these dividends can be remitted without incurring similar or even larger taxes in the other country. It obviously does not do any good to avoid a 15% transfer tax in Russia only to discover a 25% corporate tax in Austria.

Under the Cyprus-USSR [Russia] Tax Treaty, dividends paid to a resident of Cyprus by a resident of Russia are not subject to taxation in Russia. Furthermore, it appears that under Cypriot law the income of companies that derive their income exclusively from sources outside Cyprus are subject to an income tax of only 4.25% and shareholders receiving a dividend from such a company are not subject to any tax.

Below is a brief table summarizing tax rates in various Western countries which apply to profits repatriated from a joint venture.

Withholding (Transfer) Tax Rates

The rates stipulated in the Income Tax Treaties with major countries are shown in the following table.

Country	Tax Treaty Effective	Percent tax on: Dividends	Interest	Royalties
Austria	1979	0	0	0
Canada	1987	15%	15%	10%
Cyprus	1983	0	0	0
Finland	1987	0	0	0
France	1988	15%	10% (1)	0
FRG	1979	15% (2)	5% (3)	0
Japan	1986	15%	10%	10%
Netherlands		15%	0	0
Norway	1981	20%	0	0
Spain	1987	18%	0	5%
Sweden	1982	15%	0	0
UK	1986	0	0	0
United States	1976	N/A	0	0

(1) Nil for bank loans and commercial credit
(2) 25% for silent partnerships
(3) 25% for profit participating loans

Index

A

B

C

D

E

F

G

H

I

J

K

R

U

V

W

Y

Z

Пицца Хат™

Now you can try our world famous Pan Pizza and enjoy our friendly service right in the center of Moscow — two Pizza Hut restaurants open daily at 12 Tverskaya Street and at 17 Kutuzovsky Prospekt.

There is a range of different specialty Pizzas to choose from when you "eat in", "take away" or make a delivery order.

17 Kutuzovsky		12 Tverskaya
243-1727 243-7978 243-7960	Dine in (both) Slice Bar (12 Tverskaya) Take-Away (17 Kutuzovsky) Delivery Service (both)	229-2013 229-7840

- Hard currency service available at both locations
- Delivery of beverages and wine is available
- Delivery time depends on your address

Pizza Hut®

Пицца Хат™

Moscow Business Yellow Pages

International Country and City Codes

To dial an international call from Russia, first dial 8, wait for a dial tone, then 10, then the country code, followed by the city code and number as listed below. For example, to call Barcelona, Spain, you would dial 8-10-24-3 and the local number.

Algeria	**213**
Argentina	**54**
Buenos Aires	1
Australia	**61**
Melbourne	3
Sydney	2
Austria	**43**
Vienna	1
Bahrain	973
Belgium	32
Brussels	**2**
Bolivia	**591**
Santa Cruz	33
Canada	**1**
Montreal	514
Toronto	416
Vancouver	604
Cameroon	**237**
Chile	**56**
Santiago	2
China	**86**
Peking	1
Shanghai	21
Columbia	**57**
Bogota	1
C.I.S.	**7**
Moscow	095
St. Petersburg	812
Costa Rica	**506**
Cyprus	**357**
Czechoslovakia	**42**
Prague	2
Denmark	**45**
Copenhagen	1 or 2
Ecuador	**593**
Egypt	**20**
El Salvador	**503**
Ethiopia	**251**
Finland	**358**
Helsinki	0
France	**33**
Paris	1
Germany	**49 (W)** **37 (E)**
Berlin	30 (W) 2 (E)
Bonn	228
Dusseldorf	211
Frankfurt	69
Munich	89
Greece	**30**
Athens	1
Guatemala	**502**
Haiti	**509**
Honduras	**504**
Hong Kong	**852**
Hong Kong	5
Hungary	**36**
Budapest	1
Iceland	**354**
India	**91**
Bombay	22
New Delhi	11
Indonesia	**62**
Jakarta	21
Iran	**98**
Teheran	21
Iraq	**964**
Baghdad	1
Ireland	**353**
Dublin	1
Israel	**972**
Jerusalem	2
Tel Aviv	3
Italy	**39**
Florence	55
Milan	2
Rome	6
Venice	41
Ivory Coast	**225**
Japan	**81**
Tokyo	3
Yokohama	45
Jordan	**962**
Amman	6
Kenya	**254**
Korea, South	**82**
Seoul	2
Kuwait	**965**
Liberia	**231**
Libya	**218**
Liechtenstein	**4175**
Luxembourg	**352**
Malawi	**265**
Malaysia	**60**
Mexico	**52**
Mexico City	5
Monaco	**3393**
Morocco	**212**
Namibia	**264**
Nepal	**977**
Netherlands	**31**
Amsterdam	20
The Hague	70
New Zealand	**64**
Nicaragua	**505**
Nigeria	**234**
Norway	**47**
Narvik	82
Oslo	2
Oman	**968**
Pakistan	**92**
Islamabad	51
Panama	**507**
Peru	**51**
Phillipines	**63**
Manila	2
Poland	**48**
Warsaw	22
Portugal	**351**
Lisbon	1
Qatar	**974**
Romania	**40**
Bucharest	0
Russia (See C.I.S.)	
Saudi Arabia	**966**
Senegal	**221**
Singapore	**65**
South Africa	**27**
Spain	**34**
Barcelona	3
Madrid	1
Sri Lanka	**94**
Suriname	**597**
Sweden	**46**
Stockholm	8
Switzerland	**41**
Geneva	22
Zurich	1
Taiwan	**886**
Thailand	**66**
Bangkok	2
Tunisia	**216**
Turkey	**90**
Istanbul	1
United Arab Emirates	**971**
United Kingdom	**44**
Belfast	232
Cardiff	222
Glasgow	41
London	71 (inner) 81 (outer)
United States	**1**
Boston	617
Chicago	312
Dallas	214
Detroit	313
Houston	713
Los Angeles	213
Montpelier	802
New York	212
San Francisco	415
Seattle	206
Washington	202
Uruguay	**598**
Vatican City	**396**
Venezuela	**58**
Yemen Arab Republic	**967**
Yugoslavia	**38**
Belgrade	11

Cross-reference Guide

The following is a list of cross-reference topics for use with the Moscow Business Yellow Pages. Those subheadings shown in bold appear in the Yellow Pages.

Accounting
Advertising
Aerobics, see Gym
Airlines
Airports
Ambulance
American Express office
Apartments
Automobile service see Car service
Automobile sales see Car sales
Automobile rental see Car rental
Art galleries
Art museums see Museums
Bakeries
Banks, Domestic
Banks, Foreign
Ballet see Theater/ Ballet
Bars
Beauty salon see Hair cutting
Bodyguards, see Security
Books
Bowling
Business cards, see Printing
Business publications see Newspapers/ Magazines
Brunch
Calling home see International phone
Car rental
Car phone
Car sales
Car service
Casinos/ Gambling
Changing money see Money changing
Chambers of Commerce
Church see Religious services
Clothing
Coffee shops
Commercial department
Communication see International phone, Fax, Telegram/Telex, Telecom
Computer Sales
Computer Service
Conference rooms
Consulates see Embassies
Contact lenses, see Optical
Consulting firms
Courier services see Express mail
Copiers
Copying
Cosmetics
Credit card loss
Customs
Dentists
Desktop publishing see Printing
Dinner see Restaurants
Doctors see Medical care
Drug stores
Dry cleaning
Electronics
Electronic mail
Embassies
Eye care, see Optical
Exercise see Swimming, Tennis, Gym, Horseback Riding, Golf
Exchanges
Express mail
Farmer's markets see Markets
Fax
Film
Films see Movies
Fire
Flowers
Food
Food delivery
Forwarding agents see Shipping agents
Furs
Furniture
Gambling, see Casinos
Glasses, see Optical
Gas stations
Golf
Government
Gym
Hair cutting
Hardware
Health care see Dentist, Medical care, Drug stores
Horseback riding
Hotels
Ice Cream
Information
International phone
Intourist
Jazz
Language courses
Laundry see Dry cleaning
Legal advice
Libraries
Limos
Liquor
Locks, see Security
Lodging see Hotels
Lost property
Lunch
Mail see Postal
Maps
Magazines see Newspapers/ Magazines
Markets
Massage
Medical care

Key to Abbreviations

Abbrev.	Full word	English
bul.	bulvar	boulevard
kor.	korpus	building
kv.	kvartira	apartment
	most	bridge
nab.	naberezhnaya	embankment
p.	pereulok	lane
pl.	ploshchad	square
pod.	podyezd	entrance
prosp.	prospekt	avenue
pr.	proyezd	passage
sh.	shosse	highway
str.	stroenie	building
	tupik	cul-de-sac
ul.	ulitsa	street
	val	rampart

A

ACCOUNTING

Both Western and Russian accounting and auditing companies can provide the full range of financial services a business in Moscow requires. Only the major Western firms and/or joint ventures are listed below.

Arthur Andersen JV (FRG), ul. Novoryazanskaya 40, ph. 298-6456
Cooper and Lybrand, Pokrovskiy bulvar 4/17, kv. 33, ph. 318-5754
DRT Inaudit, 2nd Samotechnaya per. 1/23, ph. 281-6646
Ernst & Young, Koroviy val 7, office 10, 2nd flr., ph. 237-1250
Price Waterhouse, Bolshoy Strochenovskiy per. 22/25, ph. 276-5902

ADVERTISING

There are only two Western advertising firms in Moscow, but a plethora of Russian firms. A selection of the latter are included below.

Western firms:
BBDO Marketing, VDNKh, Gidrometerologia pavilion, ph. 181-9997
Young and Rubicam/Sovero JV (US), ul. Druzhinnikovskaya 11a, ph. 253-1357

Russian firms:
Informlitsenzreklama JV (FRG), Leninskiy prospekt 146, office 1901, ph. 438-8100
Kamir Advertising Agency, ul. Goncharova 17a, ph. 219-0101
Liniya-Poligraf Advertising Firm, ul. Sovkhoznaya 2, ph. 351-6173
MMM (Moscow Magazine) Design Bureau, Suvorovskiy bulvar 8a, ph. 7083
Metapress Agency, 4th Tverskaya-Yamskaya ul. 4, ph. 972-6453
Metroreklama JV (FRG), Prospekt Mira 41, ph. 288-0309
News-Burda Advertising-Information Service JV, Pushkinskaya ploshchad 5, ph. 209-3674
Planeta-Centre, ul. Tverskaya 6, ph. 292-6927, fax 292-6732
Promita JV (Sweden), Chermyanskiy proyezd 5a, ph. 200-2285
Solidarnost Advertising Firm, ph. 222-0961

AIRLINES

Most airlines have offices in Sheremetevo II airport and if not listed here can be contacted with the help of a hotel service bureau or, in any case, by calling one of these numbers. For addresses or fax or telex numbers, see the Telephone Directory ***(numbers in bold are the airline's office phone number at Sheremetevo)****:*

Aeroflot, Leningradskiy prospekt 37, ph. 155-6647, 156-8019
Air Algerie, Koroviy val 7, section 11, ph. 237-5257; **578-3386**
Air China, ul. Druzhby 6, ph. 292-3387; **578-2725**
Air France, Koroviy val 7, ph. 237-2325; **578-2757**
Air India, Koroviy val 7, section 4, ph. 237-7494; **578-2747**
Alitalia, ul. Pushechnaya 7, ph. 923-9840; **578-2767**
All Nippon Airways, Mezhdunarodnaya II, room 825, ph. 253-1546; **578-5744**
Ariana Afghan Airlines, Koroviy val 7, flr 2, kv. 8a, ph. 238-9779; **578-2719**
Austrian Airlines, Krasnopresnenskaya nab. 12, Office 1805, ph. 253-1670; **578-2734**
Balkan Air, Kuznetskiy Most 3, ph. 921-0267; **578-2712**
Bering Air, ph. 373-9664
British Airways, Krasnopresnenskaya nab. 12, Office 1905, ph. 253-2492; **578-2936**
Chosonminhang (North Korean Airways), ul. Mosfilmovskaya 72, ph. 143-6307; **578-7580**
Continental Airlines, Kolokolnikov per. 11, ph. 924-9050
Cubana de Avacion, Koroviy val 7, sect. 5, ph. 238-0223; **578-2704**
Czechoslovak Airlines, 2nd Brestskaya 21/27, ph. 250-4571; **578-2704**
Delta Airlines, Krasnopresnenskaya nab. 12, Office 1102a, ph. 253-2660; **578-2717**
Finnair, Proyezd Khudozhestvennovo Teatra 6, ph. 292-8788; **578-2718**
Iberia, Kuznetskiy most 3, ph. 921-9293; **578-2791**

Iraqi Airways, ul. Pyatnitskaya 37, ph. 231-2974; **578-2707**

Japan Air Lines, Kuznetskiy Most 3, ph. 921-6448; **578-2942**

JAT (Yugoslav Airlines), Kuznetskiy Most 3, ph. 921-2846

KLM Royal Dutch Airlines, Krasnopresnenskaya nab. 12, Office 1307, ph. 253-2150; **578-2762**

Korean Air (South Korea), Hotel Kosmos, room 1629, ph. 217-1627; **578-2728**

Libyan Arab Airlines, Koroviy val 7, ent. 2, ph. 237-2976; **578-2730**

Linhas Aereas de Angola (Angolan Airlines), Koroviy val 7, Office 8, ph. 237-0010; **578-2773**

LOT Polish Airlines, Koroviy val 7, Office 5, ph. 238-0003; **578-2706**

Lufthansa Airlines, Olympic Penta, ph. 975-2501; **578-3151;** cargo: **578-6758**

Malev Hungarian Airlines, Proyezd Khudozhestvennovo Teatra 6, ph. 292-0434; **578-2710**

MIAT Mongolian Airlines, Spasopeskovskiy per. 7/1, ph. 241-0754; **578-2759**

Romanian Air Transport, ul. Mosfilmovskaya 64, ph. 143-2640

Royal Jordanian Air, , ph. 299-4344

Sabena Belgian World Airlines, Belgrade Hotel, room 721, ph. 248-1214; **578-2713**

Scandinavian Airlines, Kuznetskiy Most 3, ph. 925-4747; **578-2727**

Swissair, Krasnopresnenskaya nab. 12, Office 2005, ph. 253-8988; **578-2740**

Syrian Arab Airlines, Koroviy val 7, ph. 237-1727

THY Turkish Airlines, Kuznetskiy Most 1/8, ph. 292-5121; **578-2728**

Trans World Airlines, Slavyanskaya-Radisson Hotel, room 5028, ph. 941-8146

Yemenia (Yemen Airlines), Sheremetevo 2, Office 646, ph. **578-2708**

AIRPORTS

Airline Ticket Booking, ph. 155-5003

Aeroflot info on all flights: 155-0922

Aerovokzal, Leningradskiy prospekt 37a, ph. 155-0922

Domodedovo Airport: 234-8656; 234-8655 (also a fax)

Sheremetevo II Airport: 578-9101
International: 578-5633; 5614; 5634
Domestic Arrivals: 578-5975; 578-5973
Domestic Departures: 578-5971
Freight booking office: 578-9069
Lost and Found: 578-5612; 578-8248

Vnukovo Airport: 234-8656; 234-8655

AMBULANCE DIAL 03

AMERICAN EXPRESS

You can obtain travelers checks or rubles with your AMEX card at an ATM machine at the main AMEX office and at the Mezhdunarodnaya hotel. As well, this is a sure place for changing AMEX travelers checks into cash (for a 5% commission).

American Express, 21a Sadovo Kudrinskaya, ph. 254-4505; 254-2111; 254-4503

APARTMENTS

A number of private companies operate to help foreigners find apartments, either on long- or short-term basis (Remember that all foreigners must be registered with UVIR). A few of these are:

Chillinger Vika, Uglovoy per. 2/120, ph. 227-4466, 972-4231

Inbiser, ul. Byelomorskaya, ph. 455-9210

Jupiter, Butyrskiy val 7, ph. 250-2300

Nest International Ltd., ph. 921-5100

Nikkonor, ph. 383-7553

Offis, ph. 120-5017

Orgkomitet Joint Stock Company, ul. Ogareva 1/12, str. 2, ph. 203-2655

Pullman Hotel, ph. 485-3287

Real Estate, Suvorovskiy bulvar 5/1, ph. 290-1457

Technopark, VDNKh, ph. 181-9926

Vremya, Pyatnitskaya ul. 62, ph. 233-5081, 229-9089, fax 229-3511

ART GALLERIES

Academy of the Arts, ul. Prechistenka 21, ph. 201-4031

Aktsia Art Gallery, ul. Gertsena 19, ph. 291-7509

Antique Store, ul. Verkhne-Radishchevskaya 9a, ph. 227-0550

Armoury Palace, Kremlin, ph. 221-4720

Art Moderne Gallery, ul. Bolshaya Ordynka 39, ph. 242-0175
Church of Saint George, ul. Varvarka 12, ph. 298-3872
Contemporary Art Center, ul. Dimitrova 6, ph. 238-9666
Guelman Gallery, ul. Dimitrova 2/6, ph. 238-8492
Mars Gallery, Malaya Filevskaya ul. 32, ph. 146-2029
Neo-Shag Gallery, Petrovskiye liniye 1, ph. 200-0562
Oriental Art Museum, Suvorovskiy bulvar 12a, ph. 202-4555
Ostankino Museum (Museum of Serf Art), 1st Ostankinskaya ul. 5, ph. 283-4575
Peresvetov 4 Gallery, Peresvetov per. 4, ph. 275-2228
Pushkin Museum of Fine Art, Volkhonka ul. 12, ph. 203-7998
Rubens Gallery of Modern Art, Verkhnaya Krasnoselskaya ul. 34, ph. 264-8292
Sadovniki Gallery, ul. Akademika Millionshchikova 35, ph. 112-1161
Solyanka Art Gallery, Solyanka 1/2, ph. 921-6332
Taganskaya 31/22 Gallery, Taganskaya ul. 31/22, ph. 278-5578
Theater Salon Gallery, Tverskoy bulvar 11, ph. 290-0215
Tretyakov Gallery (Old), Lavrushinskiy per. 10, ph. 231-1362
Tverskaya 25 Gallery, ul. Tverskaya 25, ph. 299-1844
Andrei Rublyov Museum (Museum of Early Russian Art), Ploshchad Pryamikova 10 (Andronnikov Monastery), ph. 278-1429
Central Exhibition Hall (Manezh), Manezhnaya ploshchad 1, ph. 202-9304
Exhibition Hall of Moscow Artists' Trade Union, ul. Malaya Gruzinskaya 28, ph. 253-7355
Exhibition Hall of the Academy of Arts, ul. Prechistenka 21, ph. 201-3052
Exhibition Hall of the Union of Artists of RSFSR
1st Tverskaya-Yamskaya 46b, ph. 250-1412
Begovaya ul. 7-9, ph. 213-8314
Kuznetskiy Most 20, ph. 928-1844
Tverskaya, ul. 25/9, ph. 299-2289
Moscow Artists' House Hall, Kuznetskiy Most 11, ph. 925-4264
State Tretyakov Art Gallery, ul. Krymskiy val 10, ph. 230-1116

B

BAKERIES

Australian-Soviet Bakery, 29/8 Pyatnitskaya ul. (great bread for rubles with long lines)
Baku-Livan Bakery: (cakes, baklava, and other baked goods) Tverskaya ul. 24, open 11-22
Diana, ul. Mytnaya 74, ph. 230-3614
Slastyona Bakery, Krasnokazarmennaya 3, ph. 261-8626
Lavash Bakery, Bolshaya Sadovaya 3, korpus 6, ph. 251-7888
Olympic Penta Hotel, Olympiyskiy prospekt 18/1, ph. 971-6101

BANKS, DOMESTIC

Aeroflot Bank
Leningradskiy prospekt 37a, ph. 292-5822
ul. Pushkinskaya 4/2, ph. 292-0759
Agrica Commercial Bank, Ulyanovskaya ul. 34, ph. 277-1041
Agrokhimbank, ul. Gritsevitskaya 2/16, ph. 202-3847
Agroprombank, ul. Neglinnaya 12, ph. 928-0084
All Russian Exchange Bank, Bolshoy Matrosskiy per. 1/1, ph. 268-8203
Artibank, ph. 248-3188
Atlant Commercial Bank, Prospekt Mira 50, ph. 280-1302
Aviabank, Ulanskiy per. 16, ph. 207-5856
Avtobank, ul. Lesnaya 41, ph. 258-9090
Bank for the Development of Auto. Industry, Lesnaya ul. 41, ph. 258-4893
Central Bank of Russia, ul. Zhitnaya 12, ph. 237-5145
Centrobank Commercial Bank, ul. Narodnaya 7, ph. 272-0612
Centrocredit Commercial Bank, 2nd Kolobovskiy per. 9/2, ph. 299-6090
Cobra Bank, Maly Gnezdnikovskiy per. 9, ph. 229-0028
Commercial Bank of International Integration, Olympiyskiy prospekt 32, ph. 284-4987

Conversbank Commercial Bank, Bolshaya Ordynka ul. 24/26, ph. 239-2620
Credobank, ul. Osipenko 15/2, ph. 220-3435
Delovaya Rossiya, Klenovy bulvar 3, ph. 112-1310.
Dialog Bank
Radisson-Slavyanskaya Business Center, ph. 941-8434
Staropanskiy per. 4, ph. 921-9104
East-European Investment Bank, Nagornaya ul. 22, korpus 5, ph. 166-1383
Ecorambus Corporation, Petrovsko-Razumovskiy prospekt 27, ph. 212-5679
Elektrobank, ul. Trubnaya 19/12, str. 2, ph. 208-1211
Elektronika Research Institute, Prospekt Vernadskovo 39, ph. 432-9223
Finistbank, Khamovnicheskiy val, ph. 242-0282
Garanti Bank, Mezhdunarodnaya II, room 1425, ph. 253-1589
Gazprombank, ul. Stroiteley 8, ph. 131-0971
Inkom Bank
Sibirskiy proyezd 2, korpus 2, ph. 270-9290
ul. Nametkina 14, korpus 1, ph. 332-0699
Innovation Land Bank, ul. Krasikova 32, room 605, ph. 129-1211
International Bank of Economic Cooperation, Kuznetskiy Most 15, ph. 928-9906; ul. Mashi Poryvayevoy, ph. 975-3861
International Investment Bank, ul. Mashi Poryvayevoy, ph. 975-4008
Izdatbank, , ph.
Khimbank, ul. Myasnitskaya 20, ph. 927-7701
Komtorgbank, ul. Myasnitskaya 47, ph. 207-7096
Kontinent Bank, ul. Gostinichnaya 9, korpus 4, ph. 485-1654
Konversbank, ul. Bolshaya Ordynka 24/26, ph. 239-2093
Koopbank Tsentrpotrebsoyuza, Bolshoy Cherkasskiy per. 15, ph. 923-2790
Menatep Commercial Investment Bank, ul. Dubininskaya 17a, ph. 235-5925
Molodyozhny Commercial Bank, Khamovnicheskiy val 34, ph. 242-0282
Morbank, Bolshoy Koptevskiy prospekt 6, ph. 151-5674
Mosbiznessbank, Kuznetskiy Most 15, ph. 921-8582
Moscow Industrial Bank, ul. Zhitnaya 12, ph. 230-7962
Moscow Interregional Bank, Leningradskiy prospekt 9, ph. 251-5777
Moscow International Bank, ul. Pushkinskaya 5/6, ph. 292-8341; Proyezd Khudozhestvennovo Teatra 6, ph. 292-0709
Mosstroybank, ul. Chekhova 21/18, ph. 299-5860
Mosstroyeconombank, ul. Vavilova 81, ph. 132-2897
Neftegazstroybank, ul. Zhitnaya 14, ph. 238-6474
Neftekhimbank, ul. Myasnitskaya 20, ph. 928-9580
North-Eastern Joint Stock Commercial Bank - Moscow Filial, Prospekt Mira 9/18, ph. 207-7783
Optimum Commercial Bank, Krymskiy val 9, ph. 238-0000
Orbita Bank, 2nd Spasonalivkovskiy per. 6, ph. 238-8720
Promstroybank of the USSR, Tverskoy bulvar 13, ph. 200-7910
Rosbiznessbank, Tokmakov per. 14, ph. 261-1911
Rosinterbank, Orlikov per. 3, ph. 204-4350
Rospromstroybank, Prospekt Mira 84, ph. 281-8936
Rosselkhozbank, ph. 923-1032
Rosskommunbank, ul. Myasnitskaya 13, ph. 921-3950
Rosvneshtorgbank, Kuznetskiy Most 16, ph. 925-5231
Russian Commercial Bank, Leningradskoye shosse 84, ph. 452-1143
Russian Insurance Bank, Studeny proyezd 1, ph. 476-9471
Sberegatelny Bank,
Sredne-Pervomayskaya ul. 38/7, ph. 463-9770; Nemanskiy prospekt 9, ph. 942-3624; Olympiyskiy prospekt 10, korpus 2, ph. 288-4678; ul. Neglinnaya 12, ph. 928-0094; ul. Aviamotornaya 51, ph. 273-5248; ul. Gvozdeva 7/4, ph. 272-2110; ul. Obrucheva 28, korpus 5, ph. 434-6605; ul. Chertanovskaya 32, korpus 1, ph. 314-6111; ul. Svobody 65, ph. 497-6609; ul. Stromynka 19, ph. 269-4433; Volgogradskiy prospekt 1, ph. 276-3301
Sovfintrade Joint Stock Society, ul. Bolshaya Yushunskaya 1a, kv. 3, ph. 318-5787
Soyuzprofbank, Leninskiy prospekt 24, ph. 930-8420
Stankinbank, ul. Tverskaya 20, ph. 209-2857
Status Credit Bank, ul. Krylatskaya 32, kor. 2, ph. 413-7115

Stolichny Bank, ul. Pyatnitskaya 72, ph. 233-5892

Technopolis Innovation Bank, Novopeschanaya ul. 20, ph. 943-4102

Tempbank Commercial Bank, Krutitskiy val 26, ph. 276-3502

Tokobank, ul. Mashi Poryvayevoy 15, ph. 972-9496

Tsentrsoyuzbank, B. Cherkasskiy per. 15, ph. 928-7683

Twenty-First Century Development Commercial Bank, 1st Krasnogvardeyskiy prospekt 12/2, ph. 205-3900

Unikombank, Khrustalny per. 1, ph. 925-3462

VIZA Bank, Gogolevskiy bulvar 3/2, ph. 291-9514

Vnesheconombank

Krasnopresnenskaya nab. 12, ph. 253-1799
Serpukhovskiy val 8, ph. 292-8292
ul. Plyushchikha 37, ph. 246-6788

Vneshtorgbank, Kuznetskiy Most 16, ph. 928-7116

Vostok Bank, ul. Yaroslavskaya 8, korpus 3, ph. 217-6165

Vozrozhdenie Bank, Khrustalny per. 1, ph. 921-6172

Yelbimbank, ul. 2nd Tverskaya-Yamskaya 15, ph. 251-0334

Zheldorbank, ul. Krasnoprudnaya 26/1, ph. 262-8880

BANKS, FOREIGN

Amro Bank, Krasnopresnenskaya nab. 12, Office 1707, ph. 253-1476

Banca Commerciale Italiana, Pereulok Sadovskikh 6, kv. 9, ph. 209-6518

Banca CRT Sovitcom JV (Italy), Kuznetskiy Most 16, ph. 921-3525

Banca Nazionale Del Lavoro, Krasnopresnenskaya nab. 12, Office 1602, ph. 253-1802

Banco Central - Madrid, ul. Mytnaya 1, Office 4, ph. 230-0388

Banco di Napoli, Krasnopresnenskaya nab. 12, Office 1008, ph. 253-2590

Banco di Roma, Pereulok Sadovskikh 4, kv. 8, ph. 209-6625

Banco do Estado de Sao Paulo, Koroviy Val 7, kv. 220, ph. 238-9724

Banco Exterior de Espana, Krasnopresnenskaya nab. 12, Office 1408, ph. 253-2263

Banco Hispano Americano, Krasnopresnenskaya nab. 12, Office 1301, ph. 253-8176

Bank fur Gemeinwirtschaft AG, Proyezd Khudozhestvennovo Teatra 6/5, kv. 35, ph. 292-4839

Bank of America NT & SA, Krasnopresnenskaya nab. 12, Office 1605, ph. 253-7054

Bank of Scotland, Pokrovskiy bulvar 4/17, kv. 34, ph. 207-5998

Bank-Melli-Iran, Smolenskiy bulvar 22/14, kv. 3, ph. 248-2153

Banque Nationale de Paris, Pokrovskiy bulvar 4/17, kv. 19, ph. 207-5888

Banque Paribas, Pokrovskiy bulvar 4/17, kv, 31, ph. 297-5511

Barclays Bank PLC, Pereulok Sadovskikh 4, kv. 14, ph. 209-6452

Cariplo, Bolshoy Gnezdnikovskiy per. 7, 4th flr, ph. 200-4191

Chase Manhattan Bank N.A., Krasnopresnenskaya nab. 12, Office 1709, ph. 253-2865

CIC-Union Europeenne, I'ntl ET CIE., Krasnopresnenskaya nab. 12, Office 609, ph. 253-1182

Commerzbank Aktiengesellschaft, Pereulok Sadovskikh 4, kv. 9, ph. 209-6440

Credit Lyonnais, Pokrovskiy bulvar 4/17, kv. 18, ph. 207-6489

Creditanstalt, Krasnopresnenskaya nab. 12, Office 1108, ph. 253-2752

Credito Italiano, Pokrovskiy bulvar 4/17, kv. 40, ph. 207-0389

Den norske Bank, ul. Pushkinskaya 5/6, kv. 34, ph. 292-0338

Deutsche Bank AG, ul. Ostozhenka 23, ph. 201-2988

Deutsche Genossenschaftsbank, Hotel Intourist, ul. Tverskaya 3/5, room 2009, ph. 203-1621

Donau-Bank AG, Wien, 1st Krasnogvardeyskiy proyezd, Exh. Complex, Pav. 2, ph. 256-7444

Dresdner Bank AG, Krasnopresnenskaya nab. 12, Office 1708, ph. 253-2681

Generale Bank, Krasnopresnenskaya nab. 12, Office 1705-1706, ph. 253-7572

Gotabanken, Pokrovskiy bulvar 4/17, kv. 4, ph. 207-3429

Hypo Bank, Bolshoy Gnezdnikovskiy per. 7, 4th flr, ph. 200-4627

Instituto Bancario San Paolo di Torino, 1st Krasnogvardeyskiy Proyezd, Exh. Complex, Pav. 2, ph. 256-7444

Lloyds Bank PLC, Krasnopresnenskaya nab. 12, Office 1808, ph. 253-8174

Midland Montagu, Krasnopresnenskaya nab. 12, Office 1305, ph. 253-2144

Monte Dei Paschi di Siena, Krasnopresnenskaya nab. 12, #1105-1106a, ph. 253-2677

Morgan Grenfell & Co. Ltd, Pokrovskiy bulvar 4/17, kv. 34, ph. 207-5998

Moscow Narodny Bank LTD, Pokrovskiy bulvar 4/17, kv. 34, ph. 207-5998

National Westminster Bank PLC, Pokrovskiy bulvar 4/17, kv. 33, ph. 207-5739

Nordbanken, Molochny per. 9/14, korpus 3, ph. 201-3714

Okobank, Koroviy val 7, Office 13a, ph. 230-1387

Ost-West Handelsbank AG, Proyezd Khudozhestvennovo Teatra 6/5, kv. 35, ph. 292-4839

Osterreichische Landerbank AG, Kalyayevskaya ul. 19, ph. 200-5221

Postipankki, Molochny per. 9/14, korpus 3, ph. 201-3714

Raiffeisen Zentralbank Austria, 1st Krasnogvardeyskiy proyezd, Exh. Complex, Pav. 2, ph. 256-7444

Skandinaviska Enskilda Banken, ul. Pushkinskaya 5/6, kv. 34, ph. 292-0338

Skopbank, Pereulok Sadovskikh 4, kv. 2, ph. 209-6836

Societe Generale, Krasnopresnenskaya nab. 12, Office 1009, ph. 253-5145

State Bank of India, Pokrovskiy bulvar 4/17, kv. 32, ph. 297-2190

Svenska Handelsbanken, Pokrovskiy bulvar 4/17, kv. 35, ph. 207-6018

Swedbank, Pereulok Sadovskikh 4, kv. 2, ph. 209-6836

Union Bank of Finland LTD, ul. Pushkinskaya 5/6, kv. 34, ph. 292-0338

Union Bank of Switzerland, Pokrovskiy bulvar 4/17, kv. 4, ph. 207-3429

Westdeutsche Landesbank Europa AG, Krasnopresnenskaya nab. 12, Office 1207-1208, ph. 255-6464

Yapi Ve Kredi Bankasi A.S., Krasnopresnenskaya nab. 12. Office 1206a, ph. 253-1947

BARS

Most major tourist hotels have hard currency bars. Some of the better choices are:

Brown Bear Pub, Mezhdunarodnaya hotel, ph. 255-2742

Cosmos Hotel: Heineken and Solaris bars

Die Bierstube, Olympic Penta hotel, ph. 971-6101

German Wine Bar, Ukraine hotel, third floor, ph. 253-2316

Heineken Bar: Zolotoe Koltso (Belgrade II) Hotel

Luks, Petrovskiy passage, open 10-19

Medusa Bar, aboard the Alexander Blok, ph. 255-9278

Moscow Commercial Club, ul. Bolshaya Kommunisticheskaya 2a, tel. 274-0081, open 9-24

Mozhayskiy disco, Mozhayskoe shosse 163, ph. 447-3294

Night Flight, ul. Tverskaya 17, happy hour 21-23 M-Th, ph. 229-4169

Novotel Lobby Bar, ph. 578-9407

Rossia Hotel, Jever-Bistro, East entrance, ph. 298-2923

Santa Lucia Bar, Intourist Hotel 3rd floor, ph. 203-1632

Savoy Hotel bar, ul. Rozhdestvenka 3, ph. 929-8555

Shamrock Pub, Novy Arbat 19

Spanish Bar, Moskva Hotel, ph. 292-2893

Taganka Bar, V. Radishevskaya 15, ph. 272-4351

Terrace Bar, Aerostar Hotel, ph. 155-5030

Liquor can be purchased at any hotel Beriozka as well as the shops listed under Food.

Embassy clubs are usually welcoming to Westerners (excluding the US bar as entrance requires US Embassy Association Membership):

Australian Down Under Club, Kropotkinskaya per. 13, Fridays 17:30-22:00

British Club, Kutuzovskiy prospekt 7/14, Saturdays 20-23:00, Sundays 12:30-14:30

Canadian Club, Starokonyushenny per. 23, Fridays 18:30-23:00

BOOKS

Western and Soviet books can be bought at (See also Newspapers/Magazines):

Books, in the Mezhdunarodnaya Hotel, ph. 253-2376; at ul. Vesnina 8/10, ph. 241-9587; and at ul. Tverskaya 18, ph. 200-0146

Dom Knigi (House of Books, for rubles) on Novy Arbat

Foreign Books (and prints), ul. Prechistenka 31, ph. 203-9263

Kniga Bookshops in the Cosmos, Pullman, Aerostar and Molodyozhnaya Hotels (open 8-20:00).

Mosgorspravka, ul. Tverskaya 7, next to Central Telegraph, for some good reference books and business newspapers.

Progress Bookshop (for rubles) offers that publisher's books for sale (they specialize in foreign language literature) at 17 Zubovskiy bulvar -- the Garden Ring, open 10:30 to 19:30

Sovaminco Shops in the National, Sovietskaya, and Peking hotels and in Dom Knigi

For used Soviet and Western books, try stopping into any Bukinist. For books in foreign languages, try:

Akademkniga, ul. Tverskaya 19, the Bukinist section on the second floor

Books and Prints, ul. Kropotkinskaya 31, ph. 203-9262, open 9-20

Innostrannaya Kniga Used Book Store, ul. Kachalova 16, ph. 290-4082, open 10-19

BOWLING

Kegelbahn in the basement of the Kosmos Hotel and the Bowling Bar at the Mezhdunarodnaya Hotel.

BRUNCH

With the opening of more and more joint venture hotels, the options for brunches are growing. The best bets are:

Aerostar Hotel, from 11:30 to 14:30 ($22);

Express Bar in the Mezhdunarodnaya Hotel, breakfast weekdays or weekends (about $5)

Jazz Brunch, Sundays at the Metropol from 11:30 to 16 ($35), ph. 927-6452 for reservations

Savoy Hotel, Sunday brunch ($26), from 11-3

Vienna Cafe in the Olympic Penta Hotel, from 10:30-2:30 (45DM)

C

CAR RENTAL

See also Limos

*A number of car rental opportunities are available. As in the West, your best bet is to call around and compare prices and models, and bargain. For fax and/or telex numbers of the compnaies below, see the Telephone Directory **(phone numbers in bold type are Sheremetevo desk phone numbers).***

Aerotour Car Rental, ph. 457-6678

Auto Sun, ph. 280-3600

AVIS Car Rental, ph. 205-7872; **578-5646**

Business Car, Ovchinnikovskaya nab. 18/1, ph. 231-8225

Europcar, Hotel Mezhdunarodnaya I, ph. 253-1369; Hotel Zolotoe Koltso, ph. 248-2657; **578-8278**

Fobit Car Rental, 1st Dorozhny proyezd 3a, ph. 315-0134

Hertz Car Rental, Leninskiy prospekt 152, ph. 434-5332; **578-7532**

InNis JV, 927-1187; 200-3207

InterAvto-M, 297-0003

Intourist Car Rental, Hotel Kosmos, ph. 215-6191; 235-6051

Intourservice Car Rental (with driver), ph. 203-0096

Iris Car Rental, ph. 488-8000

Moscow Commercial Club, ph. 274-0081

Mosrent Car Rental, Zemledelcheskiy per 14/17, str. 2, ph. 248-3607

Mosrentservice JV (FRG), ul. Krasnobogatyrskaya 79, ph. 963-8780; **578-8250**

Pullman-Iris Hotel (with driver), 488-8000

Rozec Car Rental, ul. Kulakova 20, ph. 145-1441

Rus-Otel, ph. 382-0586

Sovincenter Car Rental, Krasnopresnenskaya nab. 12, ph. 253-2477

Vesta Car Rental, Leningradskaya Hotel, room 61, ph. 248-2657

CAR PHONE

AMT Khoroshevskoye sh. 42a, ph. 941-3092

Moscow Cellular, Pokrovskiy bulvar 8, ph. 297-7783

CAR SALES

There are some possibilities for purchasing a car for delivery in Moscow, most of which are sourced out of Finland. There are also some new possibilities for on the spot purchase in Moscow (those which sell a particular make of auto are so indicated):

Accord Association, ph. 123-9362
Alankom, ul. Letchika Babushkina 26, ph. 186-5301 (Oldsmobile)
Auto-Bystrow, ph. 245-7257; 229-0775
Eurotax Moscow Bureau, Leningradskiy prospekt 64, room 203, ph. 155-0856
Fisherman's Harbor, Krasnobogatyrskaya 79, ph. 963-9077
Ford Motor Company, ul. Marx-Engelsa 8, ph. 203-9237; ul. Gorbunova 14, ph. 447-3804
Forto, ul. Mytnaya 11, ph. 236-4467
Gewika Industrieanlagen GmbH, Pushkinskaya ul. 9/10, ph. 200-1206; 292-1784; 292-6840 (BMW)
Interavtocom JV (Italy), Volgogradskiy prospekt 42, ph. 276-8824
Lada Export, Otkrytoye shosse 48a, ph. 168-2828
LogoVaz JV (Italy), ul. Prechistenka 17, str. 2, ph. 202-3468; 203-6664 (Fiat, Volvo)
Mercedes-Benz AG, Prospekt Vernadskovo 9/10, kv. 602, ph. 131-3448
Mosrentservice, Krasnobogatyrskaya 79, ph. 963-9173 (Mercedes)
MTDS Joint Venture, ul. Gorbunova 14, ph. 448-6728; 448-8035 (Volvo)
Nisso Boeki Co. Ltd, ul. Gilyarovskovo 8, kv. 13-16, ph. 284-4838; 284-5381; 284-5382 (Nissan)
Raduga Car Sales, ul. 1st Tverskaya-Yamskaya 46, 4-5 flr, ph. 251-0500 (Audi, VW)
Saab, Mr. Per Baeckman, Swedish Embassy, ph. 147-9009
Servoimport, Profsoyuznaya ul. 88/20, ph. 335-9866

CAR SERVICE

There are many foreign car service companies, mainly joint ventures. Most, as in the West, specialize in a particular make of car, and are so noted:

Emergency Towing Service
Novoryazanskiy per. 13, ph. 267-0113;
Varshavskoe shosse 87, ph. 119-8000, 119-8108, 240-2092

General Service
ABC Opel, ul. Sergeya Eyzenshteyna 2, ph. 181-0407
Autodesignservice JV (Japan), Trubnikovskiy prospekt 1, ph. 290-2327
Moscow X-Service, ul. Mytnaya 18, entrance 2, ph. 238-6634
Nefto Agip JV (Italy), Bolshoy Cherkasskiy per. 7, korpus D, ph. 930-7973
Sims & Klein, ul. Tverskaya 36, ph. 251-8950
Service Station #7, 2nd Selskokhozyaistvenny proyezd 6, ph. 181-1374, 181-2169
Sovinteravtoservice, 2/1 Institutskiy per, ph. 299-7773, 299-5900.
Spetzavtotsentr, Kiyevskaya ul. 8, ph. 240-2092, 240-4330

Audi, Volkswagen
Raduga, 1st Dorozhny proyezd 3a, ph. 315-3736

BMW
Spetzavtotsentr, Kiyevskaya ul. 8, ph. 240-2092, 240-4330

Mercedes
Service Station #7, 2nd Selskokhozyaistvenny proyezd 6, ph. 181-1374, 181-2169
Mosrentservice, Krasnobagatyrskaya 79, ph. 963-9168

Nissan and other Japanese makes
InNis Joint Venture, 7th Proyezd Maryinoi Roschi, ph. 971-0386, 971-6385, 200-3207

Opel
ABC Opel Service, ul. Sergeya Eyzenshteyna 2, ph. 181-0407

Saab
Volgogradskiy prospekt 177, ph. 379-6245, open M-F 8-17

Toyota, Volvo
MTDS, ul. Gorbunova 14, proyezd 5, ph. 448-8035

Each service provider has or can obtain spare parts for the make of cars it services. For easy purchase of basic spare parts (windshield wipers, oil, oil filters, jumper cables, etc.) the place to go is:

Stockmann Auto and Home Store, Lyusinovskaya ul. 70/1, ph. 954-8234

CASINOS/GAMBLING

Casino Aleksander Blok, Krasnopresnenskaya nab. 12, docking, ph. 255-9323, open 20-4

Casino Moscow, Leningradskaya Hotel, Kalanchevskaya ul. 21/40, ph. 975-1967

Casino Royale, Begovaya ul. 22, ph. 945-1410, open 20-4

Casino Valery, Ploshchad Indira Gandi 1, ph. 939-9611

Moscow Commercial Club, Bolshoy Kommunisticheskaya 2a, ph. 274-0081

Oriental Excelsior Club, Bombay Restaurant, Rublevskoye shosse 91, ph. 141-5504

Savoy Hotel, ul. Rozdestvenka 3, ph. 929-8555

CHAMBERS OF COMMERCE

British-Soviet Chamber of Commerce, Krasnopresnenskaya nab., Office 1904, ph. 253-2554; 253-7704.

Canada-USSR Business Council, Chapayevskiy per. 8, ph. 157-7619.

Finnish-Soviet Chamber of Commerce, Pokrovskiy bulvar 4/17, ph. 925-9001; 925-9092

Franco-Soviet Chamber of Commerce, Pokrovskiy bulvar 4/17, kv. 3, ph. 297-9092

Hungarian Chamber of Commerce, ph. 253-2921

Inter-Republican Universal Trade Exchange, ph. 208-6681

Italian-Soviet Chamber of Commerce, ul. Vesnina 7, ph. 241-5729; 241-6217; 241-6517

Japan-USSR Trade Association, ul. Mytnaya 1, ph. 237-2465

Moscow Chamber of Commerce, ul. Chekhova 13-17, ph. 299-7612

Russian Chamber of Commerce and Industry, ul. Ilyinka 6, ph. 924-5645; 923-4323; ul. Kuybysheva 6, ph. 921-0811

United States Commercial Office, Novinskiy bulvar 12-15, ph. 255-4848

US-USSR Trade and Economic Council, 3 Shevchenko nab., ph. 243-5470; 243-5621

CLOTHING

There are several places you can purchase clothing for hard currency:

AISI International JV (Italy), ul. Chekhova 8, ph. 209-7553

Alain Manoukian, ul. Druzhinnikovskaya 11, open 12-20, ph. 255-9140.

Atelier Modnie Golovnie Ubori, ul. Gertsena 16 (hats)

Alternative JV & IPLV, Orlyonok Hotel, ul. Kosygina 15, open 10-20 (clothing, toiletries, shoes)

Baginskiy Fashion, Hotel Mezhdunarodnaya mezzanine, open Mon-Sat 10-21, Sun 11-19, lunch 15-16 (clothing, shoes and accessories)

Benetton, west side of Moskva Hotel, Mon-Sat 10-20, ph. 924-2734 (credit cards only); GUM store open 11-20, ph. 921-5065

Dom Modi, Prospect Mira 55 (puts out racks of nice clothing designed and made on location every day for rubles)

Franca-Serra Italia, ul. Tverskaya 1, open Mon-Sat 11-14, 15-20

Interoko, Frunzenskiy nab. 30, ph. 242-8941, open Mon-Sat 10-18 (limited selection)

Intour, backside of Hotel National, ph. 203-8531, open 9-12, 12-20 (for jeans)

Jindo Rus, Hotel Intourist, first floor, open 8:30-20, ph. 203-9742; also in Hotel Kosmos, Mezzanine level, open 8:30-21, ph. 217-0025; 217-0990 (furs, leather)

Julius Meinl, Leninskiy prospekt 146, ph. 438-3444

La Pantera, Prospect 60-Letiya Oktabrya 10/1, ph. 126-1601; 126-4510, open Monday to Saturday 9-20.

Magazin del Mondo, Ukraine Hotel, 8th floor (shoes), ph. 243-4682

Malta, Prospekt 60-letiya Oktyabrya 12, ph. 126-8510, open 9-20 (furs, clothing, shoes)

Mia Shoe, Tikhvinskiy per. 1/50 (children's shoes)

Montana Centro, 17 Bolshoi Cherkassy per. (sportswear and electronics)

Moscow Duty Free, Sheremetevo Airport, ph. 578-9012

Peter Justesen Catalogue Orders, ph. 971-1178

Petrovskiy Passage, ul. Petrvoka 10 (indoor shopping mall)

Quelle Catalogue Orders, ul. B. Molchanovka 34, str. 2, ph. 291-4735(14 days for delivery)

Rifle Jeans Store, corner of ul. Neglinnaya and Kuznetskiy Most, open Mon-Fri 10-14, 15-19, ph. 923-2458

Rosfratex, ul. Vasilyevskaya 7, ph. 254-8772

Sadko, Kutuzovskiy prospect 9, open 10-14, 15-20, ph. 243-7502

Salentini JV, Dokuchayev per. 13, ph. 207-5607

Samos JV (Poland), Komsomolskiy prospekt 7, ph. 202-5955

Valentin Yudashkin Salon, Passage Department Store

Stockmann, Leninskiy prospekt 73/8, ph. 134-0386, open 7 days 10-20

Vera Moda, ul. Chekhova 8, ph. 209-7553, open 10-19, lunch 14-15

COFFEE SHOPS

Meeting for coffee in Moscow can be a real challenge if you don't know where to turn. Below are a few sure-fire places to get a cup of coffee or tea during the day:

Carpigiana, Hotel Mezhdunarodnaya lobby (excellent service)

Express bar, Hotel Mezhdunarodnaya, mezzanine level

Garden bar, Hotel Intourist lobby

Georgian Cultural Center, ul. Arbat 42

Metropol Hotel, Cafe/confectionary

Pekin hotel coffee bar, 3rd floor

Savoy bar, off the lobby of the Savoy hotel

Santa Lucia bar, Intourist hotel 3rd floor

Spanish bar, Hotel Moscow lobby

Tino Fontana, Hotel Mezhdunarodnaya

COMMERCIAL DEPARTMENT

See also Chambers of Commerce

Check with your embassy as to whether it has a commercial department to help you. The American, British, Canadian, Italian, German, and Finnish embassies (among others) all have Commercial counselors. (see "Embassy of..." in Telephone Directory for address, phone, fax and telex numbers).

COMPUTER SALES

Most of the following companies make only bulk sales, but a few, in particular MicroAge and Computerland, are also geared to individual purchases. Most can also help you with software purchases.

AF Computers JV (Italy), Sudostroitelnaya ul. 15, ph. 112-5090

Amstrad, ul. Tverskaya 22, Hotel Minsk, room 548/648, ph. 299-1548

Aquarius Systems Integral, Pushkinskaya ul. 32, ph. 200-0459

Avstrosoft JV, ul. Garibaldi 21b, ph. 128-8072

Computer Aided Technology JV (Switz.), Krutitskiy val 3, korpus 2, ph. 276-4714

Computer Automated Systems JV (UK), Studencheskaya ul. 39, k. 2, ph. 200-4671

Computer Systems and Technology JV (US), ul. Chernyshevskovo 10, ph. 924-5969

Computerland, ul. Kosygina 15 (Orlyonok hotel), open 10-20, ph. 939-8128

CSS Moscow, Kropotkinskaya ul. 35, dom 3, floor 2, ph. 202-0480

Demos, Ovchinnikovskaya nab. 6, ph. 231-2129

Dialogue JV, ul. Spartakovskaya 13, ph. 265-6212

Digital Equipment Corporation, ph. 253-2550

Hewlett Packard Company, Pokrovskiy bulvar 4/17, kv. 12, ph. 923-5001

IBM, ul. Bakhrushina 18, ph. 235-6602.

Informatika NPC JV, ul. Skhodnenskaya 6, ph. 497-6378

International Computers Limited, ul. Vavilova 83, kv. 5, ph. 134-9549

Interquadro JV, 2nd Novopodmoskovny per. 4, ph. 150-9201

Merisel/Computer Technologies JV, Krutitskiy val 3, korpus 2, ph. 276-4714

MicroAge Computers, Balaklavskiy prospekt 3, ph. 316-2111

Microinform JV (Hungary), Kozhevnicheskaya ul. 3, ph. 235-7700

Microprocessor JV (Bulgaria), 1st Rybinskaya ul. 3, ph. 264-2376

Ortex, Litovskiy bulvar 3a, ph. 427-1101

ParaGraph JV (US), Petrovskiy bulvar 23, ph. 924-1781

Silicon Technology Corporation, Prospekt Vernadskovo 82, ph. 433-2575

Steepler Ltd., Post Box 30, Moscow 103031, ph. 245-2194

Summit Systems Computers, ph. 265-5813

Valtex International Corporation, ph. 137-5197

Vektor SP Brokerage Firm, ul. Safonovskaya 17/43, ph. 415-7734

Wang Computer Systems, VDNKh Exhibition Complex, building 1, unit 17, ph. 188-4071; **(Service)**, Kolomenskiy proyezd 1/1, ph. 112-3324

West International, Lavochkina ul. 19, ph. 451-5364

ZPA C Akovice, ph. 250-1982

COMPUTER SERVICE

All of the companies in the previous listing can arrange computer repairs, as can:

Eksimer, Leninskiy prospekt 76a, ph. 930-7193; 127-3395

Salma Service Center, Zelyeny prospekt 2/19, ph. 306-0283

CONFERENCE ROOMS

Most of the finer hotels, including the Metropol, Slavyanskaya-Radisson, Aerostar and Olympic Penta can provide conference and meeting room facilities. In addition, try:

Comstar Business Center, ul. Petrovka 10 (Passage), Room 301, ph. 924-0892

Institute for Systems Studies, 60-Letiya Oktyabrya 9, 5th floor, ph. 135-4222

Moscow Business Centre, ul. Streletskaya 10, ph. 289-6464

Moscow Commercial Club, Bolshaya Kommunisticheskaya 2, ph. 274-0081

Sovincenter, (Hotel Mezhdunarodnaya), call the Service Bureau at 253-2760

CONSULTING FIRMS

See Legal Advice

See Accounting, Advertising

Listed below are only larger, better known firms:

Bain-Link, ul. Shcherbakovskaya 40-42, ph. 369-2643

ConsultAmerica, ul. Krasnokholmskaya 1/15, office 73, ph. 271-2580

McHugh & McCaffery International, Staropanskiy proyezd 4, ph. 924-9655

PBN Company, Berezhkovskaya nab. 2 (Radisson-Slavyanskaya), ph. 941-8489

Pencil Group, Pokrovskiy bulvar 4/17, kv. 25, ph. 230-2955

Vneshconsult, VDNKh, pavilion 4, ph. 181-4294

COPIERS

To buy a copier in Moscow, you can order from abroad or deal directly with:

C. Itoh & Co., LTD., Krasnopresnenskaya nab. 12, Office 602-605, ph. 253-8339

Konica Complex, ph. 277-3819; 279-0506; fax 200-5254

Rank Xerox Limited, 4th Dobryninskaya per. 6/9, ph. 237-6842

COPYING

AlphaGraphics Printshops of the Future, ul. 1st Tverskaya-Yamskaya 50, open Mon-Fri 9-18, ph. 251-1215, fax 230-2207; 230-2217, or the Kosmos Hotel, open 7 days 8-20, ph. 217-1085, fax 281-9551

Comstar Business Center, ul. Petrovka 10 (Passage), Room 301, ph. 924-0892

Copyrus, ul. Vavilova 11/19, open Mon-Fri 10-18, ph. 235-1475 (rubles)

Institute for Systems Studies, 60-Letiya Oktyabrya 9, 5th floor, ph. 135-4222

Moscow Business Centre, ul. Streletskaya 10, ph. 289-6464

Mezhdunarodnaya Hotel Service Bureau, open weekdays 9:30-17:30, ph. 253-2760

Reprocenter (Rank Xerox), All Russian Exhibition Center (VDNKh), ph. 181-2994; 181-3042; Ukraine Hotel, open 9-18, ph. 243-3007; Kutuzovskiy prospekt 22, ph. 243-1290

Savoy Hotel Business Center, ul. Rozhdestvenka 3, open 9-21, ph. 929-3780

COSMETICS

Christian Dior, ul. Tverskaya 4 (rubles); Hotel Mezhdunarodnaya (hard currency), ph. 253-9297

Estee Lauder, ul. Tverskaya 6 (rubles), ph. 292-8783

Nina Ricci, ul. Tverskaya 9, ph. 229-2967

Sadko, Kutuzovskiy prospekt 9, ph. 243-7502

Sana, Nizhnaya Pervomayskaya 65, ph. 464-1254

Siren, ul. Novy Arbat 44, ph. 291-1225

Zolotaya Roza, in the Hotel Moscow off Manezh Square (rubles), ph. 292-1194

CREDIT CARD LOSS

American Express: 254-4505

All other cards: call Intercreditcard, Grafskiy per. 10/12, str. 2, ph. 284-4151 or 284-4713 (can also report AMEX)

CUSTOMS

See also Shipping Agents

There are a large number of customs clearing agents. Some are listed below. For an up-to-date list, call InformVes at 220-1606. As well, most Western transport agencies with services to and from Moscow can provide such services.

Customs clearing agents:

Yeruslan coop (Sheremetevo): ph. 578-8879, fax 578-6539

Sofi JV: ph. 925-9587

Customs points:

Butovo: 548-7621; 548-7745; 548-7636; 548-7641

Sheremetevo: 578-2120

Moscow Central Customs, ul. Marinoy Roshchy 12, ph. 971-1178; 971-1196, fax 971-0105

Oktyabrskaya Tovarnaya Stantsiya, Komsomolskaya pl., ph. 975-4460

Other important numbers/addresses:

InformVES, Ovchinnikovskaya nab. 18/1, ph. 220-1606;

Ministry of Foreign Economic Relations, Smolskaya-Sennaya 32-34, 6th podyezd, ph. 244-1320.

D

DENTISTS

Dental-Beker JV (FRG), Kuznetskiy Most 9/10, ph. 923-5322

Intermed (Soviet-West German joint venture), ul. Durova 26, korpus 5, ph. 288-9679, 284-7403, hours 9-20.

Swiss Medical Interline, in the Hotel Intourist, ul. Tverskaya 5, room 2030-1, open Mon-Sat 9-20, ph. 203-9496; 203-8631

DRUG STORES

See also Medical Care

Diplomatic Polyclinic Drugstore, ph. 237-5335 (closed Sat & Sun)

Farmakon, ul. Tverskaya 4, ph. 292-0843

Fyodorov's Institute, 59a Beskudnikova bulvar, open Mon-Fri 10-17:30, ph. 905-4227.

Interoko, ul. Petrovka 10, ph. 292-3451

Kniga Bookshops, with locations in the Cosmos and Molodyezhnaya Hotels, ph. 217-0081 or 210-9311 (over the counter drugs only)

Medicine Man, The, ul. Chernyakhovskovo 4, ph. 155-7080; 155-8780

Sana JV, ul. Nizhnaya Pervomayskaya 65, open Mon-Sat 9-20, Sun 10-17, ph. 464-1254; 464-2563, fax 464-4563

Unifarm JV, Skaterny per. 13, ph. 202-5071.

VITA, ul. Poklonnaya 6, open Mon-Fri 10-19, Sat 11-16, lunch 14-14:30, ph. 249-9667; 249-7818; 249-9429

24 hour Soviet pharmacies

(closed at night, but ring the doorbell for access)

19/21 25th Octyabrskaya ul., ph. 924-6451

6 Tishinskaya Square, ph. 254-4610

14 Kutuzovskiy prospect, ph. 243-1601

10 Smolenskaya ploshchad, ph. 241-9882

ul. Tverskaya 4, ph. 292-0301

ul. Prechistenka 6, ph. 201-7568.

DRY CLEANING

Pick-up and delivery service

Infa Hotel Joint Venture (the Savoy Hotel), ph. 929-8693

Drop-off service

Mezhdunarodnaya Hotel, Service Bureau, ph. 253-2776

Based on recommendations, use also a local Khimchistka - one of the best is at ul. Vavilova 11.

Furniture or carpeting

Chimvak, ul. Ryabinovaya 8, #209, ph. 444-1071.

E

ELECTRONICS

Beriozka, Rossiya Hotel (just off Red Square), ph. 298-3620 (cameras, VCRs, TVs, tape players, kitchen appliances)

Beriozka, Krasnokholmskaya nab., 5/9, ph. 272-0474

Blue Belt, Kuntsevskaya ul. 4, korpus 1, ph. 417-9400

JVC Shop, Leninskiy prospect 86, ph. 137-2025 (VCRs, TVs, kitchen appliances (including refrigerators), tape decks, etc.)

Konica (Tokyo Boeki), ul. Leninskaya Sloboda 9, ph. 275-1674

Kvant, Olympiyskiy prospekt 30, ph. 288-8949

Mikrodin, Novozavodskaya ul. 18, ph. 145-9462

Montana Centro, Bolshoy Cherkasskiy per., 17 near GUM

Moskva Electronics Store, Kutuzovskiy prospekt 31

OLBI Store, ul. Dimitrova Ulyanova 3, ph. 135-6567

Optintorg, ul. Krzhizhanovskovo 16, korpus 1, ph. 124-8447

Panasonic Shop, ul. Polyanka 30, ph. 238-4424

Stockmann Home and Car Store, Lyusinovskaya ul. 70/1, ph. 954-8234 (audio, video, home applianceds, tools, kitchenware)

Supershop, Astrakhanskiy per. 5, ph. 280-2545

Sadko, Kutuzovskiy prospect 9, ph. 243-7502 (stereos, cameras, some video and appliances)

Shaeffer Shop/Interoko, Frunzenskiy nab. 30, pavilion 12, office electronics, microwaves, etc. ph. 242-8941, open Mon-Sat 10-18.

Tamada Duty Free, Hotel Moscow, ph. 292-2874, open 10-20.

ELECTRONIC MAIL

Prices and services are fast becoming very competitive in this, the easiest, cheapest and most reliable way to establish East-West (or East-East) communications. See Section VI on Communications for more details and for Western addresses of email service providers. Below are the Moscow addresses of major email services.

Glasnet, ul. Vesnina 9/5, ph. 241-8243

Infocom, Kuznetskiy most 4, ph. 925-1235; 925-4093

SovAm Teleport (MCI Mail, GEnie, Compuserve, SFMT, Sovset and other large email and bulletin board systems), Nezhdanova ul. 2a, ph. 229-3466 or 229-9663

Sprint (Telemail), ul. Tverskaya 7, entrance 7, at 201-6890

EMBASSIES

See the Telephone Directory under "Embassy of..." for addresses and complete listing of all embassies.

EXCHANGES

Thousands of exchanges have sprung up in the past year. These are just some of the major ones.

Alisa Commodity Exchange, Leninskiy prospekt 45, ph. 137-6514

All Russian Real Estate Exchange, ul. Yaroslavskaya 8, korpus 3, ph. 217-6009

AsA Interexchange Trading Company, ph. 210-9766

Association of Oil Brokers, Dealers and Traders, Nab. Morisa Toreza 26/1, ph. 233-8841

AVEX Commodities Exchange, ph. 921-1430

C.A. & Company Ltd., ul. N. Krasnoselskaya 35, ph. 267-4482

Chemical Goods Exchange, ph. 281-9258

Construction Exchange, ph. 128-9722

Fininvest, Suvorovskiy bulvar 8, ph. 203-2355

Hermes Tyumen-Moscow Exchange, ph. 245-6265

International Exch. of Information and Telecomm, Leningradskiy prospekt 80/2, ph. 158-7492

International Sports Exchange, ph. 201-1994

Kolyma Susuman Gold Exchange, ph. 262-4682

Moscow Biotech Exchange, ph. 159-3030

Moscow Central Real Estate Exchange, Trekhprudny per. 1, kv. 20, ph. 202-7287

Moscow Central Stock Exchange, ul. Granovskovo 5, kv. 37, ph. 229-7635

Moscow Commodity Exchange, VDNKh, Pavilion 4, ph. 187-8614; **(Energy Dept.)**, VDNKh, Pavilion 4, ph. 187-8505

Moscow International Agricultural Exchange, ph. 283-3693
Moscow Oil Exchange, ph. 233-8981
Moscow Regional Privatization Exchange, ph. 556-9862
Moscow Trade House, ul. Chekhova 2, ph. 299-1333
Moskovskiy Fondovy Dom, 1st Volokolamskiy proyezd 10, ph. 289-5355
Russian Auto Exchange, ph. 384-4101
Russian Commodity and Raw Material Exchange, Novaya ploshchad 3/4, ph. 262-8080; Business Channel, ph. 262-8080
Russian Fish Exchange, VDNKh, ph. 181-0918
Russian Forestry Exchange (Roslesbirzha), ph. 925-7295
Russian Fur and Leather Commodity Exchange, Kolpachny per. 14, ph. 227-1013
Russian Investment and Joint Stock Company, Novaya Ploshchad 3/4, entr. 6, ph. 936-0766
Stolitsa Trade House, ph. 924-0243
Transtrade, ul. Myasnitskaya 26, ph. 287-6741
Tyumen Commodity and Stock Exchange, ph. 261-1590
Umitec Exchange, ul. Profsoyuznaya 113, korpus 3, ph. 248-7643

EXPRESS MAIL

Several options are now available. The types and prices of services vary and not all will pick up and deliver. See Section VI in Russia Business Survival Guide on Communications (Express Mail) for more detailed information):

Barry Martin Travel offers courier services for letters and small packages to and from London. The courier leaves Moscow on Monday and arrives on Saturday (£15 for a letter or £40 for the first kilo and £15 for each additional), ph. 253-2940.
British Airways: ph. 253-2492.
DHL Express Mail, ul. Vesnina 1, ph. 201-2585; 202-8090 (20 kilo weight limit). Full services are also available through AlphaGraphics Printshops of the Future, ul. 1st Tverskaya-Yamskaya 50, ph. 251-1215 (delivery time to Europe or U.S. is 2-3 days; payment only in credit cards or by bank transfer)
Emery Worldwide, ul. Myaskovskaya 17/7, ph. 203-0119; 203-7049
Federal Express: counter near the bank in the International Trade Center: you must presently have a FedEx account in the West, ph. 253-1641; 255-6836.
Garantpost JV: Varshavskoe shosse 37 (International Post Office), ph. 117-0040 (2-3 days); a letter of one kilo or less costs $36; 1 kilo costs $56, each additional kilo costs $6.
Huolintakeskus (Moscow-Helsinki): ph. 299-7773; 299-5900.
Krasnaya Gorka (inside CIS only), ph. 381-2746; 947-4706
Prompt International, ul. Myaskovskaya 17/7, ph. 203-9945; 202-1868
TNT Express Worldwide, 3rd Baltiyskiy per. 3, ph. 156-5771; 156-5760. The Western addressee must pay shipping costs. delivery time is 2-4 days.
UPS Express Mail JV (Finland), Bolshaya Ochakovskaya ul. 15a, ph. 430-6373; 430-7069. Call before 11 am for same day pickup; 2 day delivery to the US, one day to Europe.

F

FAX

Most hotel service bureaus can send or receive faxes (see Telephone Directory for fax numbers), but the best places to go in the city are:

AlphaGraphics Printshops of the Future, ul. 1st Tverskaya-Yamskaya 50 (5 days/wk) or the Kosmos Hotel (7 days/wk): ph. 251-1215, **FAX:** 230-2207; (Cosmos) 288-9551
Central Telegraph, ul. Tverskaya 7 (for rubles -- long lines). Cost is 54 rubles per minute to the US, 36 rubles per minute to Europe.
Comstar Business Center, ul. Petrovka 10 (Passage), Room 301, ph. 924-0892; **FAX:** 975-2319
Moscow Business Centre, ul. Streletskaya 10, ph. 289-6464; **FAX:** 292-6511
Moscow Commercial Club, Bolshaya Kommunisticheskaya 2a, ph. 274-0081; **FAX:** 274-0080
Mezhdunarodnaya Hotel Service Bureau, open weekdays 9:30-17:30, ph. 253-2760
Savoy Hotel Business Center, ul. Rozhdestvenka 3, ph. 929-8500, open 9-21, **FAX:** 928-3780.

FILM

When buying film, always check the expiration date. Also, avoid purchasing ORWO NC-21 or DC-4 film, which can only be developed in Russia. For video film, see Video. For film developing, see Photo.

Kodak supplied kiosks in the Kosmos, Mezhdunarodnaya, Molodyozhnaya, Ukraine and National Hotels.

Kniga Bookshops in the Cosmos and Molodyozhnaya Hotels

Polaroid Shop, Leninskiy prospekt 70/11, ph. 930-9627, open 10-13

Sadko, Kutuzovskiy prospect 9, ph. 243-7502

Stockmann Stores, Leninskiy prospekt 73/8, ph. 134-0386; Lyusinovskaya ul. 70/1, ph. 954-8234; Zatsepkiy val 4/8, ph. 233-2602

Tamada Duty Free, Hotel Moscow, ph. 292-2874, open 10-20

FIRE DIAL 01

FLOWERS

Bouquets can be bought year-round for rubles at most major metro stations, usually in underpasses. Prices vary greatly from season to season. For the cheapest bouquets, look for vendors who seem to be selling from their own garden. The best flowers are consistently available at:

Belorusskiy flower market, next to Belorusskiy train station

Polskaya Gvozdika, Leninskiy prospekt 79, ph. 134-5416

Pushkin Square underpass.

Priroda, Kutuzovskiy prospekt 5/3, ph. 243-5528

Tsentralny Market, Tsvetnoy bulvar 15, open 7-18

FOOD

See also Shopping, Markets

Several hard currency grocery stores are now open:

A Markt, ul. A. Mitskevicha 27/29, ph. 291-7655

Alfa Shop, Nikolskaya ul. 2

Apollo Store, Arbat 32, ph. 241-6060

Arbat Irish House, Novy Arbat 21, ph. 291-7641 (cash or credit card w/pre-approval)

Food Orders Store, Biryulevskaya ul. 37, ph. 326-4477

Intercar Supermarket JV (FRG), ul. Bolshaya Sadovaya 5/1, ph. 209-6591; 251-6903 (cash or credit card)

Intermarket, ul. A. Mitskevicha 12, ph. 291-7655, open 10-20 (credit card)

Julius Meinl, Leninskiy prospekt 146, ph. 438-3444, open Mon-Sat 10-20; Sun 10-18 (credit card)

Kalinka Stockmann, Zatsepskiy val 4/8, ph. 233-2602, open 10-20 every day, (credit card only)

Moscow Cash and Carry, Leninskiy prospekt 95a, ph. 132-5510

Natalena, Petrovskiy passage, ul. Petrovka 10, ph. 924-9532

Sadko, Bolshaya Dorogomilovskaya 16, ph. 243-7501, open Mon-Sat. 10-20, Sun. 10-17, closed 15-16 for lunch (cash or credit card)

Tino Fontana Store, Hotel Mezhdunarodnaya II, ph. 253-1787, Open Mon-Sat 10-20; Sun 10-18, lunch 14-15 (cash, credit card or trav. check)

Other food stores of note

Australian-Soviet Bakery, 29/8 Pyatnitskaya ul. (great bread for rubles with long lines)

Baku-Livan Bakery: (cakes, baklava, and other baked goods) Tverskaya ul. 24, open 11-22.

Franca Serra: around the corner from the National Hotel, entrance from ul. Tverskaya, open 11-14, 15-20 (liquor)

French Bread bakeries: ul. Generala Glagoleva 30 or Lazarevskiy proyezd 4

Lavash (Georgian bread): set back from the ring road near the Pekin Hotel, Bolshaya Sadovaya 3, korpus 6

Morozko (frozen foods): ul. Lva Tolstovo 2, open Mon-Sat 10-20, lunch 13-14, ph. 246-0504, and ul. Kedrova 7a, open Mon-Sat 9-19, lunch 14-15.

Precarpazi, where Balaklavskiy prospekt meets Varshavskoye shosse (nuts, sausage, dried fruits and breads)

Slastyona Bakery (pastries): Krasnokazarmennaya 3, open 9-19, ph. 261-8626

Strastnoy 7: A Belgian-Soviet joint venture that offers catering. Strastnoy bulvar 7, open 12-23, ph. 299-0498

FOOD DELIVERY

The following options exist for delivery of fast food (some coop restaurants will also deliver). See also Pizza:

Intourservice, Okhotny ryad 16, ph. 287-3981
Konss, ph. 236-4845
McDonalds: ph. 200-1655 ($5 delivery fee if order less than $50)
Pettina (Finnish hamburgers, frozen processed food, pizza, cookies): ph. 286-5217
Russian Bread (bread, rolls, etc.), ph. 962-1665

FURS

If you are looking for a fur hat, you can try some of the farmers' markets, particularly Danilovskiy (ul. Mytnaya 74) or Rizhskiy (Prospekt Mira 94) markets (for rubles). For hard currency, try :

Beriozka, Hotel Rossia
Beriozka, Luzhnetskiy proyezd 25a
Jindo Rus, in the Hotel Intourist lobby and on the Mezzanine level of the Cosmos Hotel, open 8:30-20 and 8:30-21, respectively.
Kommisiony, 30 Pushkinskaya ul., open Mon-Sat 9-20, lunch 14-15 (rubles)

FURNITURE

See Office Supplies
See Hardware

For home furniture, try:

Dom Mebeli, Leninskiy prospekt 101, ph. 432-2986, 477-4185 (rubles)
Intermebel, ul Litvina-Sedova 26/9 ,ph. 259-6933 (hard currency)
Khudozhestvenny salon, ul. Dimitrova 54 (antique auctions every Saturday morning)
Kommissiony, Frunzenskaya nab. 54 (auctions every Wednesday afternoon)
Star-Progress, Frunzenskaya nab. 30, pavilion 15, ph. 248-4458, fax 230-2601
Swedish Furniture, Leninskiy prospekt 64, ph. 137-0291, open 10-19
Queen-Mosmebel, ul. Garibaldi 26, ph. 128-7835, open 10-18

G

GAS STATIONS

See also Car Service

Below is a list of Moscow city gas stations, by geographical location:

Center
ul. Trifonovskaya, 36/38 • Frunzenskaya nab. • Luzhnetskaya nab.

North
ul. Pryanishnikova, 10 • Sheremetevskaya ul. 85a • Signalny prospect • Dmitrovskoye shosse, 104 • ul. Rimskovo-Korskakova • ul. Abramtsevskaya 26.

Northwest
ul. Begovaya, 3a • Leningradskiy prospect, 43 • ul. Marshala Biryuzova, 2 • Staropetrovskiy per., 4 • 1st Krasnogorskiy prospect • ul. Festivalnaya • Belomorskaya ul. 2 • Svetlogorskiy prospect, 12 • Nemanskiy prospect, str. 14.

Northeast
ul. Dokukina, 4 • Izmailovskiy prospect, Gorodok Baumana • Ostashkovskoe shosse, at Outer Ring Road • Ostashkovskoe shosse • Rusakovskiy nab. • Yaroslavskoe shosse, 107 • 10th ul. Krasnoy Sosny

South
Varshavskoe shosse, 21 km • ul. Kakhovka, 28 • Varshavskoe shosse, 26 & 77 • 7th Kozhukhovskaya ul., 7 • Proletarskiy prospect, 60a • ul. Y. V. Andropova, 6 • Vostryakovskiy prospect, Outer Ring Road

Southwest
ul. Lobachevskovo, 92a • Leninskiy prospect, kvartal 42 • Leninskiy prospect, at Outer Ring Road

Southeast
ul. Lublinskaya • Volgogradskiy prospect, 166 & 135 • Shipilovskaya ul., 31a

East

ul. Semyonovskiy val, 4 • Poluyarovskaya nab. • ul. Stalevarov, 12a • Shchelkovskoe shosse, at Outer Ring Road • Sokolnicheskiy val

West

Khoroshovskoe shosse, 37/39 • Nizhnegorodskaya ul. 25 • Belobezhskaya ul. • Minskaya ul. • Kastanaevskaya ul. • 2nd Kuskovskaya ul., 16 • Vereyskaya ul. • ul. Gorbunova • ul. Konobalova, 9/2

If you have questions about the assortment of gasoline available at a certain station or about the location of a certain station, you can call 473-03-45 or 473-03-46 for such information. You can get oil and grease for Russian cars at stores located at: Dmitrovskoe shosse, 65b · Leningradskoe shosse, 21a • Volokolamskoe shosse, 83 • ul. Vilisa Latsisa, 16 • Taganskaya ploshchad • Krasnobogatyrskaya ul. • Rusakovskaya nab.

GOLF

Golf Club Tumba Moscow JV (Sweden), ul. Dovzhenko 1, ph. 147-6254

GOVERNMENT

Some government offices are listed here. For Russian ministries, see the Telephone Directory under "Ministry of..."

CIS

Committee for Cooperation of CIS States, ph. 925-9051

Russia

Presidium of the Supreme Soviet of the RSFSR, Krasnopresnenskaya nab. 2, ph. 205-6847

Russian Supreme Soviet - Reception, ph. 202-0185

RSFSR Council of Ministers, Krasnopresnenskaya nab. 2, ph. 205-5432

Ministry of Economics and Finance
- Okhotny Ryad 12, ph. 292-9139
- Foreign Economic Relations Committee, ph. 292-9656

Ministry of Foreign Affairs, ul. Smolenskaya-Sennaya 32/34, ph. 244-4314
- Visa Department, ph. 244-2459
- Foreign Companies Accreditation Department, ph. 244-4125
- Protocol Department;244-2987

Ministry of Foreign Economic Relations, ul. Smolenskaya-Sennaya 32/34, ph. 244-1046

Russian First Deputy Prime Minister, Staraya ploshchad 4, ph. 206-2629

Russian Deputy Prime Minister, Staraya ploshchad 4, ph. 206-2171

Russian Prime Minister
- Office: Kremlin, ph. 244-1886
- Administration: Staraya pl. 4, ph. 206-5064
  - Government Information Service;205-460
  - Information Department, ph. 206-4547
  - Press Center;206-3000

Moscow

Moscow City Council, ul. Tverskaya 13
- Executive Committee, ph. 229-5431
- Orgkomitet, ph. 203-2655
- Planning Committee, ul. Stanislavskovo 24, ph. 925-3123

Moscow Mayor's Office, ph. 290-8680
- Economic Department, ph. 299-4224
- Foreign Affairs Department, ph. 229-9325
- Protocol Department, ph. 229-9325

Prefectures

Central, Marksistskaya ul. 24, ph. 292-1635

Eastern, Preobrazhenskaya ploshchad 9, ph. 161-9887

North-Eastern, Prospekt Mira 18, ph. 281-4385

North-Western, ul. Svobody 13/2, ph. 490-4438

Northern, Timiryazevskaya 27, ph. 976-1008

South-Eastern, Aviamotornaya 10, ph. 362-4288

South-Western, Sevastopolskiy prospekt 28, korpus 4, ph. 128-2722

Southern, Avtozavodskaya 10, ph. 275-0636

Western, ul. Ivana Franko 12, ph. 443-4335

GYM

See also Swimming, Tennis

American Medical Center, Shmitovskiy proyezd 3,

Chaika Sports Complex, Turchaninov per. 1/3, ph. 246-1344

Ginseng (for women only): ul. Chernyshevskovo 32, 2nd Floor, ph. 227-1641, 227-1773

Olympic Penta Hotel, Olympiyskiy prospekt 18/1, ph. 971-6101

Mezhdunarodnaya Hotel, Krasnopresnenskaya nab. 12, ph. 255-6691

Slavyanskaya Health Club, Berezhkovskaya nab. 2, ph. 941-8027

H

HAIR CUTTING

Africana Beauty Center, ul. Zelenodolskaya 41, ph. 172-7671

Charodeika, Novy Arbat (Kalininsky) prospekt 25 in the same building at the Arbat Restaurant), ph. 290-5339

Ginseng, ul. Chernyshevskovo 32, 2nd floor, ph. 227-1641, 227-1773

Kudesnitsa, ul. Gertsena 37, ph. 291-2111; 290-2981

Metropol Hotel, ph. 927-6002

Mezhdunarodnaya Hotel, ph. 253-1789.

Nefertiti, Intourist hotel, 11th floor, ph. 203-1589, open 9-21, 14-14:30 lunch

Olympic Penta Hotel, Olympiyskiy pr. 18/1, ph. 971-6101

OSA, ul. Semashko 4, ph. 202-0282

Zhen Shen, Petrovskiy Passage, ph. 921-6460

HARDWARE

Intermarket Shop JV, ul. Mitskevicha 10, ph. 291-7656

Renlund Biurobin, ul. Ostrovskovo 39, ph. 237-7612, open Mon-Fri 9-15

Scanflot-Scanior Design, ul. Biryuzovaya 19, ph. 194-8811; 194-2542

Stockmann, Lyusinovskaya ul. 70/1, ph. 954-8234, 952-6513

HORSEBACK RIDING

See also Racing

Bitsa Horseback Riding Complex, Balaklavskiy prospect 33, ph. 318-1566, 318-2277

Moscow Tourist Club, ph. 203-1094

Rusispan JV, Maslovo Odintsovskiy district, ph. 143-8691

Yamskoy Dvor, Leninskiy prospect 35 ($10 per hour), ph. 135-8255

HOTELS

All major (and most minor) hotels are listed below. Following the address and phone of each is (in bold type) a map reference to the hotel's location (i.e. F15(10[17]) is map page 10, sector F15 or page 17, same sector). Numbers in brackets refer to the enlarged city center map. For fax and telex number, see the Telephone Directory.

Aeroflot Hotel, Leningradskiy prospekt 37, ph. 151-5624 **E10(5)**

Aerostar Hotel, Leningradskiy prospekt 37, korpus 9, ph. 155-5800 **E11(5)**

Akademicheskaya Hotel I, Leninskiy prospekt 1, ph. 238-0902 **I26(14)**

Altai Hotel, Botanicheskaya ul. 41, ph. 482-5703 **H4(4)**

Arbat Hotel, Plotnikov per. 12, ph. 244-7635 **H16(10[12])**

Arena Hotel, ul. 10-letiya Oktyabrya 11, ph. 245-2802 **[F18](10[21])**

Baikal Hotel, Selskokhozyaystvennaya ul. 15/1, ph. 189-7515 **K6(7)**

Belgrade (II) Hotel, Smolenskaya pl. 8, ph. 248-1643 **G16(10 [21])**

Budapest Hotel, Petrovskiye Liniye 2/18, ph. 921-1060 **J14(11 [19])**

Danilov Hotel, Danilov Monastery, Bolshoy Stary Danilov per., ph. 924-0294 **I20(14)**

Druzhba Hotel, Prospekt Vernadskovo 53, ph. 432-9629 **B24(13)**

Inflotel, Aboard the Aleksandr Blok, Krasnopresnenskaya nab., docking, ph. 255-9278 **F15 (10 [17])**

Intour-Penta JV (Holland), Olympiyskiy prospekt 18/1, ph. 288-9729 **J11(7)**

Intourist Hotel, ul. Tverskaya 3/5, ph. 203-4008 **I14(10 [19])**

Izmailovo Hotel, Izmaylovskoye shosse 71, ph. 166-0145 **R11(8)**

Kiyevskaya Hotel, Kiyevskaya ul. 2, ph. 230-1444 **F16(10 [21])**

Kosmos Hotel, Prospekt Mira 150, ph. 217-0786 **L7(7)**

Kuzminki Hotel, Volzhskiy bulvar 114a, korpus 9, ph. 179-0879 **R19(12)**

Leningradskaya Hotel, ul. Kalanchevskaya 21/40, ph. 975-3032 **L13(11) [20]**

Lokomotiv Hotel, ul. Bolshaya Cherkizovskaya 125, ph. 161-8133 **R9(8)**

Marco Polo Presnya, Spirodenevskiy per. 9, ph. 202-0381 **H14(10[18])**

Mayak Hotel, ul. Bolshaya Filevskaya 25, ph. 142-2384 **A16(9)**

Metropol Hotel, Teatralny proyezd 1, ph. 927-6000 **J14(11 [19])**

Mezhdunarodnaya Hotel I, Krasnopresnenskaya nab. 12, ph. 253-2760 **F15(10 [17])**

Mezhdunarodnaya Hotel II, Krasnopresnenskaya nab. 12, ph. 253-2761 **F15(10 [17])**

Minsk Hotel, ul. Tverskaya 22, ph. 299-1300 **I13(10 [19])**

Mir Hotel, Bolshoy Devyatinskiy per. 9, ph. 290-9519 **G15(10 [17])**

Molodyozhnaya Hotel, Dmitrovskoye shosse 27, ph. 210-4838 **G7(6)**

Moskva Hotel, Okhotny ryad 7 (Hotel Moskva), ph. 292-1100 **J14(11 [19])**

Mozhayskaya Hotel, Mozhayskoye shosse 165, ph. 447-3434

National Hotel, Okhotny ryad 14/1, ph. 203-6539 **J14(11 [19])**

Neptune Hotel, ul. Ibragimova 30, ph. 369-6383 **Q11(8)**

Novotel Hotel, Sheremetevo II Airport, ph. 578-9407

Olympic Penta Hotel, Olympiyskiy prospekt 18/1, ph. 971-6101 **J11(7)**

Orlyonok Hotel, ul. Kosygina 15, ph. 939-8845 **F20(14)**

Ostankino Hotel, ul. Botanicheskaya 29, ph. 219-2880 **H6(6)**

Pekin Hotel, ul. Bolshaya Sadovaya 1/5, ph. 209-3400 **H13(10 [18])**

President, ul. Dmitrova 24, ph. 238-7303 **I17([23])**

Pullman-Iris Hotel, Korovinskoye shosse 10, ph. 488-8000 **E2(3)**

Rossia Hotel, ul. Varvarka 6, ph. 298-5400 **J15(11 [19])**

Rossiyanka Hotel, ul. Donskaya 1, ph. 238-0508 **I18(10 [23])**

RusOtel JV (US), Varshavskoye shosse, 21st km, ph. 382-0586

Salyut Hotel, Leninskiy prospekt 158, ph. 438-6565 **A26(13)**

Savoy Hotel, ul. Rozhdestvenka 3, ph. 929-8555 **J14(11 [19])**

Sayani Hotel, Yaroslavskoye shosse 116, korpus 2, ph. 183-1456 **N4(2)**

Sevastopol Hotel, ul. Yushunskaya 1a, ph. 119-8182 **H26(14)**

Severnaya Hotel, ul. Sushchevskiy val 50, ph. 289-6413 **J11(7)**

Sheremetevo Hotel, Sheremetevo II, ph. 578-5753

Sovietskaya Hotel, Leningradskiy prospekt 32/2, ph. 250-2342 **G11(6)**

Soyuz Hotel, ul. Levoberezhnaya 12, ph. 457-9004 **A1(3)**

Soyuz II Hotel, 1st Krasnogvardeyskiy prospekt 25b, ph. 259-3004 **E15(9)**

Sport Hotel, Leninskiy prospekt 90/2, ph. 131-1191 **C24(13)**

Spros Hotel JV (Switz.), Leninskiy prospekt 95/15, ph. 133-4393 **D24(13)**

Sputnik Hotel, Leninskiy prospekt 38, ph. 938-7096 **G20(14)**

Tourist Hotel, ul. Selskokhozyaystvennaya 17/2, ph. 187-6018 **K6(7)**

Tsentralnaya Hotel, ul. Tverskaya 10, ph. 229-8589 **I14(10 [19])**

Tsentralny Dom Turista (Central House of Tourism), Leninskiy prospekt 146, ph. 434-2756 **B25(13)**

Ukraine Hotel, Kutuzovskiy prospekt 2/1, ph. 243-3020 **F15(10 [17])**

Universitetskaya Hotel, Michurinskiy prospekt 8/29, ph. 939-9731 **C20(13)**

Ural Hotel, ul. Chernyshevskovo 40, ph. 297-4258 **L14(11 [20])**

Varshava I Hotel, Leninskiy prospekt 2, ph. 238-1970 **I18(10 [23])**

Varshava II Hotel, Kotelnicheskaya nab. 1/15, ph. 227-4078 **K16(11 [24])**

Volga Hotel, Dokuchayev per. 10, ph. 280-7729 **K13(11 [20])**

Voskhod Hotel, Altufyevskoye shosse 2, ph. 401-9822 **H4(4)**

Yaroslavskaya Hotel, Yaroslavskaya ul. 8, ph. 283-1733 **L8(7)**

Yunost Hotel, ul. Khamovnicheskiy val 34, ph. 242-4861 **F18(10 [21])**

Yuzhnaya Hotel, Leninskiy prospekt 87, ph. 134-3065 **D23(13)**

Zagorye Hotel, ul. Yagodnaya 15, ph. 329-3011

Zolotoe Koltso (Belgrade I) Hotel, Smolenskaya ul. 15, ph. 248-6734 **G16(10 [21])**

Zolotoy Kolos Hotel, Yaroslavskaya 15, korpus 3, ph. 286-2703 **L7(7)**

Zvezdnaya Hotel, Zvezdny bulvar 42, ph. 215-4292 **J8(7)**

I

ICE CREAM

Baskin Robbins Ice Cream, West side of the Rossiya Hotel, just off Red Square, open 11-22; also for rubles on the Arbat **J15(11[19])**

Carpigiana, at the Hotel Mezhdunarodnaya has excellent service **F15(10[17])**

Pinquin Ice Cream (Soviet-Finnish JV) has several locations in Moscow (all for rubles): 1st Tverskaya-Yamskaya ul. 37 **H13(18)**; North Side of the Moscow Hotel **J14(11[19])**; Novokuznetskaya ul. 8, open 11-22; Gagarin ploshchad **G20(14)**

INFORMATION

Directory Assistance: 09

Information on companies, call InfoService Forepost: 555-5510

Intourist information: 203-6962

Several companies also provide a wide range of business information services. The range of services is very diverse and requires inquiry:

All Moscow JV (FRG), Chistoprudny bulvar 8, ph. 928-9429

ASU-Impuls, ul. Nelidovskaya 18, kv. 38, ph. 497-2047

Commersant -- Kiosk, ph. 202-9951

Fakt, ph. 299-0004

Forepost Information Service, ul. Skhodnenskaya 26, ph. 555-5510

Gosstatistika Information Center, ul. Kirova 39, ph. 207-4681

Information Moscow, Leninskiy prospect 45, kv. 426, ph. 135-1164

Moscow Central Address Information Bureau, Krasnoproletarskaya 10, ph. 258-2820

Russian Information Services, Bolshoy Kondryatevskiy pereulok 4, kor. 2, kv. 168, ph. 254-9275

INTERNATIONAL PHONE

See Telecom

See Car phone

International phones (in booths) payable by credit card or pre-pay card are available in the Cosmos, Mezhdunarodnaya, Pekin, Intourist, Savoy, Sovietskaya and Molodyezhnaya Hotels, and others. Always be sure of the costs before you dial; these booths are very expensive.

Long distance call booking: 8-194 or 8-196

Long distance call booking from a hotel: 333-4101

Also try calling from the Central Telegraph Office (for rubles – the crowd is commensurate, except early in the a.m.), at ul. Tverskaya. 7.

Certain business centers (i.e. Comstar, Moscow Commercial Club) and hotel service desks (i.e. Savoy, Slavyanskaya, Metropol, Aerostar, Mezhdunarodnaya) also have direct international lines which can be used for fax or phone calls (see the listing under Fax above).

INTOURIST

See Section I of Russia Business Survival Guide for Intourist offices abroad

General inquiries: 203-6962 (in Russian, English, German, and French, from 9-21:00)

UK department: 292-2973

US department: 292-2386

J

JAZZ

Call ahead to verify the program

Blue Bird Cafe (Sinyaya Ptitsa), ul. Chekhova 23, ph. 299-8702

Club na Taganke, ul. Chkalova 76, ph. 272-6331; 272-7320

Jazz Club, ph. 921-9744

La Francaise, Pullman Iris Hotel, features Jazz Quintet Sun-Thurs 7:30-12, ph. 488-8000

Metropol Hotel, Teatralny proyezd 1 (Sunday Jazz Brunch, 11:30-18, for $35), ph. 927-6452

Rock and Jazz Laboratory, ph. 923-1604

Sorok Chetyre, Leningradskoe sh. 44, ph. 159-9951

Victoria, Hard Rock Cafe, (more often Rock is featured) at the Zelyony theater in Gorkiy Park -- meals are also served, ph. 237-0709

L

LANGUAGE COURSES

See also Translation

The opportunities are virutally endless; call around, bargain for the best rate. Listed below are just a few of the potential options, those which have been most widely advertised and/or around the longest.

Many institutes and technical colleges also have courses which are very good.

Centre for Intensive Language Training, 291-3727; 248-0415
Idea International, 1st Krasnoselskiy per. 7/9, str. 5, kv 224, ph. 264-0664
Inform Invest, ul. Malaya Bronnaya 28/2, ph. 334-1921
Otema-Glaza, Proyezd Serova 4, ph. 207-8048; 924-8466
RaznoService, ph. 246-9587
RussLan, ul. Milukho-Maklaya 21, blok 9, ph. 434-7380
Service Globus, ul. Planetnaya 29, ph. 155-7295

LEGAL ADVICE

A number of Western legal firms now have offices in Moscow, should you need advice on such questions:

Baker & McKenzie, Bolshoy Gnezdnikovskiy per. 7, ph. 200-4906
Chadbourne & Parke, Maxim Gorkovo 38, ph. 231-1064
Clifford Chance, Yuzhinskiy per. 15a, ph. 973-2415
Coudert Brothers, ul. Petrovka 15, kv. 19-20, ph. 928-7838
Leboeuf, Lamb, Leiby & Macrae, Koroviy val 7, Suite 13a, ph. 230-1386
Steptoe and Johnson, c/o USCO, Novinskiy bulvar 15, ph. 255-4848
White & Case, ul. Tverskaya 7, entrance 7, ph. 201-9292

For Soviet legal advisers, your best bets are:
Inform-Pravo JV, ul. Druzhby 10/32, ph. 143-6771
Inyurcolleguia, ul. Tverskaya 5, ph. 203-6864
Moscow Legal Collegium, ul. Pushkinskaya 9, str. 6, ph. 229-9033
Stanbet JV (US), Sredne-Tishinskiy per. 14, str. 4, ph. 253-7011
Yuridicheskyie Uslugi, VDNKh, Metallurgy Pavilion, ph. 181-2517
Vnesheconomservis, ul. Ilyinka 6, ph. 259-3753

LIBRARIES

Russian State Library (formerly Lenin State Library), ul. Vozdvizhenka 3
This is the largest library in the world. You'll need a passport to get in. No roaming the stacks here, but you can request a book from the counter and they will bring it to you. Hours are 9 a.m. to 10 p.m. daily, except Sundays in summer and the last Monday of every month, when it is closed.
Foreign Literature Library, Ulyanovskaya ul. 1, open 10 to 10 every day except the first day of every month.

LIMOS

There are a number of options. You can go up to Lenin Hills or the tomb of the unknown soldier and recruit a Zil driver from among those driving wedding parties around to take you around on his day off (for rubles or hard currency). For a hard currency variant, try:
Intourservice (very expensive): ph. 203-0096

LIQUOR

See Food
See Shopping

All the joint venture food stores stock liquor, wine and beer, as do remaining Beriozkas (state run hard currency stores) in major hotels.

LOST PROPERTY

In the Metro, ph. 222-2085
In a taxi or public transport, ph. 923-8753

LUNCH

See Restaurants

Some restaurants are better than others for lunch. Among the better bets are: Savoy, U Pirosmani, Vltava, Livan, Spanish Bar, U Margarity, Strastnoy 7 and the Praga. Hotel restaurants in the Metropol, Olympic Penta and Aerostar are also very good. Addresses and phone numbers are in the Telephone Directory and Restaurant Listing. See the latter for a complete listing of the better cooperative, state and joint venture restaurants.

M

MAPS

See also Books

For the most detailed Moscow city map available (identical map to that in the back of this book, only full-sheet), contact Russian Information Services at 254-9275. For other maps of Russia try:

Atlas, Kuznetskiy most 9
Knigi, Kuznetskiy most 20
Dom Knigi, Novy Arbat
Mosgorspravka, ul. Tverskaya 5, around the corner from Central Telegraph.

MARKETS

The best farmers' markets (rubles) are:

Cheremushkinsky, Lomonosovskiy prosp. 1
Tsentralny, Tsvetnoy bulvar 15
Rizhsky, Prospekt Mira 94-6
Dorogomilovsky, ul. Mozhaiskiy val 10
Yaroslavsky, Prospekt Mira 122
Danilovsky, ul. Mytnaya 74

MASSAGE

Chaika Sports Complex, Turchaninov per. 1/3, ph. 246-8753 -- also has pool and gym
Ginseng (for women only): ul. Chernyshevskovo 32, 2nd flr., ph. 227-1641; 227-1773
JV Rozek: ul. Dovlatova 13, ph. 245-4661
Massage Russkaya America, Luzhnetskaya nab. 10, ph. 201-1680
Olympic Penta Hotel, Olympiyskiy prospekt 18/1, ph. 971-6101; 971-6301
OSA, ul. Semashko 4, ph. 202-0282

MEDICAL CARE

See also Drug Stores, Dentists

The health care alternatives have dramatically improved over the last year and several options now exist where none were present previously.

American Medical Center, Shmitovskiy proyezd 3, ph. 256-8212
Biocard Health Center JV (Belgium), 3rd Cherepkovskaya ul. 15a, ph. 149-0533
Botkin Clinic, 2nd Botkinskiy proyezd 5, korpus 5, ph. 945-0033
Diplomatic Polyclinic, 4th Dobryninskiy per. 4, ph. 237-8338
Euromedical Emergency Service, ph. 432-1616 (emergency evacuation services)
Medservice, Trifonovskaya ul. 61, kv. 65, ph. 288-5875;
Medservice International JV, ul. Lva Tolstovo 5/1, ph. 275-4390
Moscow Medical International Centre JV (FRG), ul. Obukha 14, ph. 297-1848
Sana JV (France), ul. Nizhnyaya Pervomayskaya 65, ph. 464-1254, open Tues-Sat 10-21, Sun 10-17
Tourist's (Foreigners') Clinic, Gruzinskiy proyezd 2, ph. 254-4396; 254-4326 for house calls

Embassy Doctors:

American Embassy Medical Clinic: 252-2451, ext 247 (Embassy personnel only: $50/visit)
British Embassy Doctor: 231-8511 ($75/visit)
French Embassy Doctor: 237-4655
Italian Embassy: 241-1533; 241-1534
Japanese Embassy: 202-3853

Other:

For an **Ambulance, dial 03**
To trace persons known to be in a hospital, call 928-9572; 208-9157
Information on hospitals: 208-7584

MONEY CHANGING

See Section IV on Money

With recent ruble devaluations, changing money can be more difficult. Some joint venture hotels offer exchange services to their clients only.

American Express has installed ATM machines that dispense travelers checks in US Dollars for holders of the American Express card. One is located at the American Express office at 21a Sadovo-Kudrinskaya, the other in the lobby of the Mezhdunarodnaya Hotel. They charge a 5% commission on exchange operations.

Many of the banks listed under Banks, Domestic above can also change money for individuals. There is also a change bureau in the Central Telegraph office (ul. Tverskaya 7).

Otherwise, your best bets are (call ahead to check availability of cash and hours of operation):

Dialog Bank, Slavyanskaya-Radisson Business Center, 941-8434

Kosmos Hotel, Prospekt Mira 150, ph. 217-1603

Olympic Penta Hotel, Olympiyskiy prospekt 18/1, ph. 971-6101

Rossiya Hotel, ul. Varvarka 6, ph. 298-0008

MOVIES

See Video Rental

There is no lack of movie theaters in Moscow, and often they are the showplaces for glasnost. The problem is, all the movies are in Russian. The exceptions are listed below.

There are also billboards with theater listings at strategic points throughout the city. You can also call theaters directly to find out their programs – you will find the address and phone of many Moscow theaters in the Telephone Directory.

Central Children's Film Theater (Tsentral'ny Detskiy Kinoteatr), (Foreign films in foreign languages once per month)

Illuzion, Kotelnicheskaya nab. 1/15, ph. 227-4339. (Occasional foreign films)

Kinotsentr, ul. Druzhinnikovskaya 15, ph. 205-7306

Mir-Espace, Tsvetnoy bulvar 11, ph. 200-1695

French embassy, (French films, Mondays and Wednesdays at 7 pm, call 236-0003 or 236-1223 to find out how you can attend.

MOVING

Heinrich Klingenberg International Moving, Prospekt Vernadskovo 103, korpus 1, kv. 58, ph. 434-2414

Interdean AG, Rublevskoye shosse 36, korpus 2, kv. 212, ph. 415-4296

John Nurminen Oy, ul. Bolshaya Ochakovskoye 15a, ph. 430-7861

MUSEUMS

See the Telephone Directory under the museum you wish to visit for address and telephone number. For guided tours of selected museums, call Intourist Moscow at 928-4515 or 927-1372.

MUSIC

See Books

You can purchase records and good quality CDs (made in Moscow on German and Dutch equipment) for rubles at the stores below. For dollars, you can buy them at most hard currency stores selling non-food items (See Electronics).

Melodiya, Novy Arbat (next to Dom Knigi) and at Leninskiy prospekt 11

Radio Technika, ul. Novokuznetskaya 17/19

N

NEWS

Live feed of ***CNN*** *is available at the Savoy Hotel, near Lubyanskaya ploshchad, the Bowling Bar in the Mezhdunarodnaya Hotel, and the Sovaminco Shop on the 7th floor of the Ukraina Hotel, and in most joint venture hotels.*

A nine-ruble antenna ("decimetrovy") bought at an electrical supply store will allow you to receive CNN in your apartment. Your television must get UHF reception. CNN is at 20-25 on the dial.

NEWSPAPERS/MAGAZINES

See Section I of Russia Business Survival Guide, under Periodicals

For business news, there are a number of good publications now available in English, which you can obtain in Moscow and/or subscribe to there. Most are available at the locations listed under books and some are available for rubles at Soyuzpechat kiosks:

Commersant (weekly) : $150 per year, ph. 253-8656. (Also available at Mosgorspravka, ul. Tverskaya 5)

Deloviye Lyudi (monthly): $85 per year, or for rubles at many Soyuzpechat kiosks, ph. 333-3340

Economist ($120/yr), ***International Herald Tribune*** ($600/yr), ***Le Monde*** ($675/yr), ***Die Welt, Neue Zuercher Zeitung and USA Today*** ($380/yr), contact Sovaminco at 923-5581

LA Times NewsFax, a same-day news digest of the Los Angeles Times, can be purchased at AlphaGraphics, ul. 1st Tverskaya-Yamskaya or Kniga Bookshops in the Cosmos Hotel

Moscow Magazine (monthly): ph. 203-3644, ($54 per year),

Moscow News (weekly): ph. 229-8186

Moscow Times (twice weekly) presently free, but subscriptions starting soon, 928-2515
Newsweek, ph.135-1164
Postfactum (daily, by fax): 941-0900
Russian Business Reports (weekly): contact East-West Information Consortium for Moscow delivery, at Leninskiy prospekt 39, kv. 42, ph. 135-8745, ($400 per year)

O

OFFICE SUPPLIES

See also Furniture, Copiers, Telecom

Beriozka, ul. Fersmana 5, ph. 124-5024 (open Monday-Saturday 9-20)
Planshop, Mezhdunarodnaya hotel, ph. 253-2773 (open Monday thru Friday, 9-19, closed 14-15)
Stockmann, Leninskiy prospekt73/8, ph. 134-0386, open 10-20
Shaeffer Shop/Interoko, Frunzenskaya nab., a Soviet-West German joint venture offers a complete line of office supplies and furniture by mail order, but which also has a limited number of supplies in stock, ph. 242-8941 (open Monday-Saturday 10-18).
Statfall, ul. 1905 goda 10a, 4th flr, ph. 252-0803

OPTICAL

For contact lens solutions or items related to eye care, try:

Mikrokhirugiya Glaza, Beskudnikovskiy bulvar 59a, ph. 484-8120
Optic Moscow, Arbat 30, ph. 241-1577
Sana, ul. Nizhnaya-Pervomayskaya 65, open Tues-Sat 10-21, Sun 10-17, ph. 464-1254

P

PAGING SYSTEMS

AMT, Khoroshevskoye shosse 42a, ph. 941-3092
Intermed, Bolshaya Kolkhoznaya ploshchad 5/1, ph. 928-5757

PARKS

If you're going to be staying in Moscow over a weekend, a park in Moscow is a nice place to spend a Sunday afternoon. Best among these are Izmailovskiy park, Sokolniki park, the Academy of Sciences Botanical Gardens, and, of course, Gorkiy Park. Kolomenskoe is a must. Also recommended is the view from Lenin Hills at the University. Most parks are open 10-22.

Three good places to rest outside the city are:

Sunny Forest JV (Spain), for camping, near Nikolina Gora, ph. 143-8691 ($6 per car per day.
Wilma Sanatorium, ph. 496-9810
Zavidovo Dacha, ph. 203-1033

PASSPORT PHOTOS

If you are not in a rush, most Photografia salons in the city offer one day service for passport photos (rubles), but black and white only.

For instant color photos, try:

AlphaGraphics, ul. 1st Tverskaya-Yamskaya 50, ph. 251-1215, 251-1208.
Kodak kiosk, Mezhdunarodnaya hotel

PHOTO

For 35 mm film developing, turn to Kodak for the best hard currency prices, with kiosks in the Mezhdunarodnaya Hotel, Ukraine, Kosmos, and others. A new kiosk is also open in Petrovskiy Passage. Try also:

Fuji, Novy Arbat 25, ph. 203-7307
Main Administration for the Diplomatic Services, Mezhdunarodnaya Hotel, ph. 253-1643;
PhotoSalon, ul. Arbat 43 (for rubles)

PIZZA

Astro Pizza, call-in and pick up service, ph. 245-1216
Pizza Hut
ul. Tverskaya 12, ph. 229-2013 (seating inside for hard currency only);
Kutuzovskiy prospekt 17(near Sadko, seating for rubles and hard currency), ph. 243-1727. You can call this location to order a pizza and then pick it up later

POLICE DIAL 02

See also Legal Advice
See Section IV, on Crime

Most hotels have a militia department attached or assigned to them. A need to call upon the police is rare among business travelers, but if you need to, you can call the militia by dialing 02.

POSTAL

Central Post Office, ul. Myasnitskaya 26, ph. 928-6311

Central Telegraph, ul. Tverskaya 7, ph. 924-9004

International Post Office, Varshavskoye shosse 37, ph. 114-4584

PRINTING

See also Copying

AlphaGraphics Printshops of the Future, ul. 1st Tverskaya-Yamskaya 50, ph. 251-1215 and 251-1208.

GlavUPDK Printing, ph. 203-2294

Moscow Magazine Design Bureau, Suvorovskiy bulvar 8a, House of Journalists, room 309, ph. 928-7083 (Desktop publishing and design services)

Offset Printshop, Nagornaya 12, ph. 127-2363

P&D, ul. Suvorovskaya 32/1, ph. 963-6097; fax 926-0671

Sovaminco, ul. Gertsena 11/4, str. 2, ph. 923-5581

R

RACING (HORSE RACING)

Hippodrome, ul. Begovaya 22. Races are held Sundays at 13:00 and Wednesdays and Saturdays at 18:00 (ruble entrance and betting).

RADIO

American Top 20: Radio Channel 3 on the second and fourth Saturdays of every month, from 19:30-21:10

BBC: The best short-wave frequencies are 12095 and 15070

Evropa plus Moskva: FM 69.8 mhz, 9-13 daily; MW 1116 khz daily after 7 pm

Radio Nostalgie (French): 11-15 daily at MW 300 meters, 963 kHz

RELIGIOUS SERVICES

To get times of services call the numbers listed below:

Baptist Services, Maly Vuzovskiy per. 3, ph. 297-5167

Bulgarian Orthodox Services, ul. Volodarskovo 29, ph. 271-0124

German Evangelical Church Services, German Embassy, ph. 238-1324

Greek Orthodox Services, Telegrafny per. 15a, ph. 923-4605

Jewish Synagogue, ul. Arkhipova 10, ph. 923-9697

Jewish Youth Cultural Center Tkhiya, ul. Bolshaya Tulskaya 44, ph. 234-5297

Morman Church Services, ul. Donskaya 37, ph. 240-6332

Moscow Patriarchate, Chistoprudny per. 5, ph. 201-3416

Protestant and Anglican Services, Leninskiy prospekt 78, ph. 143-3562

Roman Catholic Services, Kutuzovskiy prospekt 7/4, korpus 5, kv. 42, ph. 243-9621

Russian Orthodox Services, ph. 245-2013

Seventh Day Adventists Services, , ph. 297-5167

St. Andrew's Church, ul. Stankevicha 9, ph. 143-3562

St. George's Church, ul. Varvarka 12, ph. 298-3872

REPAIR SERVICES

Appliances and Office Equipment

GlavUPDK, ph. 202-2865; 201-2706; (office eqpt.) 143-1502

Dorin Electronics, ph. 571-8108

Eureka JV, ph. 943-0893

Olva, Leninskiy prospekt 132, ph. 434-9561

Raznoservice, ph. 246-9587

Phone repair

GlavUPDK, ph. 202-2706

General

Interstroy Service Division, ph. 450-9513

Dipservice, ph. 143-1502

RESTAURANTS

KEY:

c = coop
s = state restaurant
j = joint venture
h = hard currency only accepted
h/r = rubles for meals, hard currency for alcohol
* = recommended
Information in bold is map coordinates of the restaurant
(i.e. **F14(17)** = section F14, page 17)

AMERICAN

McDonald's, Bolshaya Bronnaya ul. 29, ph. 229-1811 {*,j}, **I14(10[19])**

Pettina Hamburgers, ul. Malaya Pereyaslavskaya 6, str. 12, ph. 286-5217 {j,h}, **L7(7)**

Pizza Hut, listed under Pizza

TrenMos Restaurant, Komsomolskiy prospekt 21, ph. 245-1216 {j,h}, **H18(10[22])**

ARMENIAN

Ayastan Restaurant, Flotskaya 3, ph. 456-7444 {c}, **C3(4)**

Moosh cafe, ul. Oktyabrskaya 2/4, ph. 284-3670 {*,c,h/r}, **J11(7)**

Sayat-Nova cafe, ul. Yasnogorskaya 17, korpus 1, ph. 426-8511 {c}

Tsakhkadzor cafe, ul. Lesnaya 15, ph. 251-0257 {c,h/r}, **H12(6)**

AZERI

Agdam cafe, Khlebnikov per. 4, str. 1, ph. 278-7146 {c}, **P14(12)**

Baku Restaurant, ul. Tverskaya 24, ph. 229-8506 {s}, **I13(10 [19])**

Farkhad cafe, Bolshaya Marfinskaya 4, ph. 218-4136 {c}, **H6(6)**

Karabakh, ul. Lipetskaya 52, 329-7100 {c,h/r}

Nargiz cafe, Lebedyanskaya 22, kor. 4, ph. 329-7187 {c}

CAUCASIAN

Abkhaskiy Dvor Restaurant, Nakhimovskiy prospekt 35, ph. 124-9833 {c}, **F23(14)**

Araks cafe, Sirenevy bulvar 11, korp. 2, ph. 164-3630 {c}

Bistro-Nedelya cafe, Oktyabrskaya ul. 18, ph. 288-9398 {c}, **J11(7)**

Dukhan Shavo Restaurant, Karamyshevskaya nab. 58, ph. 197-1975 {c,h/r}

Yakimanka cafe, Bolshaya Polyanka 2/10, Str. 1, ph. 238-8888 {*,c}, **J16(11 [23])**

CHINESE

Golden Dragon, Mezhdunarodnaya Exhibition Center, ph. 248-3602 {*,s}, **E15(9)**

Karina Restaurant, Solyanskiy proyezd 1-3, ph. 924-0369 {c}

Mei-hua Restaurant, ul. Rusakovskaya 2/1, str. 1, ph. 264-9574 {c,h/r}, **M12(7)**

Pekin Restaurant, ul. Bolshaya Sadovaya 1/7, ph. 209-1815 {*,j,h}, **H13(10 [18])**

DANISH

Glazur Restaurant, Smolenskiy bulvar 12/19, ph. 248-4438 {*,c}, **H16(10 [22])**

EUROPEAN/RUSSIAN

Aist cafe, Malaya Bronnaya 1/8, ph. 299-6692 {c}, **H14(10 [18])**

Anna Mons Restaurant, ul. Krasnokazarmennaya 3, ph. 261-3561 {c}, **N14(11)**

Antrakt cafe, Sirenevy bul. 2, ph. 166-7490 {c}

Arkadia Restaurant, Okhotny ryad 4a, ph. 926-9008 {c}, **J15(11 [19])**

Atrium Cafe, Leninskiy prospekt 44, ph. 137-3008 {c,CC}, **F20(14)**

Ayot cafe, ul. Obrucheva 45, ph. 331-5355 {c}, **E26(13)**

Bely Lebed cafe, Sivtsev Vrazhek 3, ph. 203-1283 {c}, **H15(10 [18])**

Beriozka cafe, Karamyshevskaya nab. 18, ph. 191-1089 {c}

Boyarskiy Restaurant, Hotel Metropol, 4th floor, ph. 927-6089 {*,j,h}, **J14(11 [19])**

Cafe Raduga, ul. Nizhegorodskaya 8, ph. 272-6680 {c}, **N17(11)**

Club na Taganka, Verkhne-Radishchevskaya 19, ph. 272-7320 {c}, **L16(11 [24])**

Continental Restaurant, Hotel Mezhdunarodnaya, ph. 253-9798 {s}, **F15(10 [17])**

DAB Beer Bar, Zolotoe Koltso Hotel, ph. 248-2696 {*,s,h}, **G16(10 [21])**

Dom na Tverskoy cafe, ul. Gotvalda 12, ph. 251-8419 {c}, **H12(6)**

Dubrava Restaurant, Hotel Kosmos, ph. 217-0495 {s}, **L7(7)**

Evropeiskiy Zal Restaurant, Hotel Metropol, ph. 927-6039 {*,j,h}, **J14(11 [19])**

Galaxy Restaurant and Pub, Selskokhozyaystvennaya pr. 2, ph. 181-2074 {s}, **L6(7)**

Glazur cafe, Smolenskiy bulvar 12, ph. 248-4438 {*,j,h}, **H16(10 [22])**

In Vino Restaurant, Ukraine Hotel, 2nd floor, ph. 243-2316 {j}, **F15(10 [17])**

Kareta cafe, Yermakova Roshcha 7a, ph. 256-2280 {c}

Kashtan Restaurant, Taganskaya ul. 40/42, ph. 272-6242 {c}, **M16(11)**

Kropotkinskaya 36 cafe, ul. Prechistenka 36, ph. 201-7500 {h,CC}, **H16(10 [22])**

Magarita cafe, Malaya Bronnaya 28, ph. 299-6534 {c}, **H14(10 [18])**

Moscow Commercial Club JV, ul. Bolshaya Kommunisticheskaya 2a, ph. 274-0081 {j,h}, **L16(11 [24])**

Moskovskiye Zori (Kozikhinsky) cafe, Malaya Kozikhinskiy per. 11, ph. 299-5725 {*,c,h/r}, **H14(10 [18])**

Moskva Restaurant, Okhotny ryad 7 (Hotel Moskva), ph. 292-6227 {s}, **J14(11 [19])**

Nevka cafe, Volokolamskoye shosse 15, ph. 158-1090 {c}, **A8(5)**

Olimp Restaurant, Luzhnetskaya nab., ph. 201-0148 {c}, **F19(10)**

Ordynka Restaurant, Bolshaya Ordynka 71, ph. 237-9905 {c}, **J17(11 [23])**

Orient cafe, Nikoloshchepovskiy per. 1/9, ph. 241-1076 {c,h/r}, **G15(10 [17])**

Peter's Place, Zemlyanoy val 72, ph. 298-3248 {c,h/r}, **L14(11 [20])**

Podvorye Restaurant, ul. Maroseika 9, ph. 923-8949 {c}, **K14(11 [20])**

Pokrovka cafe, ul. Chernyshevskovo 4, ph. 923-0282 {c,h/r}, **K14(11 [20])**

Prague Restaurant, Arbat 2, ph. 290-6171 {s}, **I15(10 [19])**

Razgulyai Restaurant, Spartakovskaya ul. 11, ph. 267-7613 {c,h/r}, **M13(11)**

Rossiya Restaurant, Hotel Rossiya, ph. 298-4133 {s}, **J15(11 [19])**

Rus Restaurant, Krasnozvozdnaya 13, Saltykova, ph. 524-4202 {c}

Ruslan cafe, Vorontsovskaya 32/36, ph. 272-0632 {c,h/r}, **L17(11 [24])**

Russkaya Izba cafe, Ilyinskoye village near Arkhangelskoye, ph. 561-4244 {c}

Russkiy Traktir Restaurant, Arbat 44, ph. 241-9853 {c}, **H15(10 [18])**

Ryleeva 9 cafe, Ryleeva 9/5, ph. 291-6063 {c,h/r}, **H16(10 [22])**

Savoy Restaurant, ul. Rozhdestvenka 3, ph. 928-0450 {*,j,h}, **J14(11 [19])**

Skazka Cafe, Tovarishcheskiy per. 1, ph. 271-0998 {c,h/r}, **L16(11 [24])**

Skazka II Restaurant, Yaroslavskoe shosse, 43rd km, ph. 184-3436 {*,s}

Slavyanskiy Bazaar Restaurant, ul. 25 Oktyabrya 13, ph. 921-1872 {*,s}, **J14(11 [19])**

Sorok Cheterie (44) cafe, Leningradskoye shosse 44, ph. 159-9951 {*,c,h}, **B7(5)**

Soyuz Pisateley (Writers' Union) Restaurant, ul. Vorovskovo 52, ph. 291-2169 {c,h}, **H14(10 [18])**

Soyuz Restaurant, Gospitalny val 22, ph. 360-7432 {c}

Stoleshniki Cafe, Stoleshniki per. 8, ph. 229-2050 {c}, **I14(10 [19])**

Supriz cafe, Medynskaya 5, korpus 1, ph. 384-4400 {c}

Taganka Bar, v. Radishchevskaya 15, ph. 272-4351 {c}, **L16(11 [24])**

Taiga Cafe, Aerostar Hotel, ph. 155-5030 {*,j,h}, **E11(5)**

Talisman cafe, ul. Shchepkina 1, 208-9055 {c}

Terrace Bar, Aerostar Hotel, ph. 155-5030 {*,j,h}, **E11(5)**

Theater cafe, ul. Tverskaya 5 {c}, **I13(10[19])**

Tsentralny Restaurant, ul. Tverskaya 10, ph. 229-0241 {s}, **I14(10 [19])**

U Kamina cafe, Chernyshevskovo 32, ph. 297-0840 {c}, **K14(11 [20])**

U Yosefa cafe, Dubininskaya 11/17, ph. 238-4646 {c,h/r}, **K18(11 [24])**

Vecherny Siluet Restaurant, Taganskaya pl. 88, ph. 272-1503 {*,c,h}, **L16(11 [24])**

Vienna Cafe, Olympic Penta Hotel, ph. 971-6101 {*,j,h}, **J11(7)**

Viktoria (Hard Rock Cafe) cafe, Zelyoni Theater, Kymskiy val 9, ph. 237-0709 {c}, **K17(11 [24])**

Viktoria Restaurant, Prospect Mira 78, ph. 971-0721 {c}, **K11(7)**

Vltava cafe, Vasilyevskaya 15/24, ph. 251-6898 {*,c}, **H13(10 [18])**

Zaidi Poprobui cafe, Prospect Mira 124, korpus 11, ph. 286-7503 {c}, **K8(7)**

Zamoskvorechie cafe, Bolshaya Polyanka 54, ph. 230-7333 {c}, **J17(11 [23])**

FRENCH

Champs Elysees Restaurant, Pullman Iris Hotel, ph. 488-8000 {*,j,h}, **E2(4)**

Le Cafe Francais, Pullman Iris Hotel, ph. 488-8000 {*,j,h}, **E2(4)**

Potel et Chabot, Hotel Mezhdunarodnaya, ph. 253-2760 {*,j,h}, **F15(10 [17])**

GEORGIAN

Aragvi Restaurant, ul. Tverskaya 6, ph. 229-3762 {s}, **I14(10 [19])**

Arena cafe, ul. 10-letiya Oktyabrya 11, ph. 245-2972 {c}, **F18(10 [21])**

Cafe Mziuri, Arbat 42 {c}, **H15(10 [18])**

Guria cafe, Komsomolskiy prospekt 7/3, ph. 246-0378 {*,c}, **H17(10 [22])**

Iveria Cafe, Minskoe shosse, 45th km, ph. 593-4159 {c}

Kolkhida cafe, ul. Sadovaya-Samotechnaya 6, ph. 299-6757 {c}, **J13(11 [19])**

U Pirosmani cafe, Novodevichy proyezd 4, ph. 247-1926 {*,c,h/r}, **F17(10 [21])**

GERMAN

Die Bierstube, Olympic Penta Hotel, ph. 971-6101 {*,j,h}, **J11(7)**

GREEK

Greek Restaurant, On board the Aleksander Blok, ph. 255-9278 {*,j,h}, **E15(9)**

Stanislavskovo 2 cafe, ul. Stanislavskovo 26a, ph. 291-8689 {c}, **I14(10 [19])**

INDIAN

Bombay Restaurant, Rublevskoye shosse 91, ph. 141-5504 {s}, **C18(9)**

Delhi Restaurant, ul. Krasnopresnenskaya 23b, ph. 255-0492 {*,j,h/r}, **G14(10 [17])**

ITALIAN

Arlecchino Restaurant JV (Italy), Druzhinnikovskaya ul. 15, ph. 205-7088 {*,j,h}, **G14(10 [17])**

Lasagne cafe, Pyatnitskaya ul. 40, ph. 231-1085 {c,h}, **J17(11 [23])**

Pescatore Restaurant, Prospekt Mira 36, ph. 280-0850 {*,h}, **L7(7)**

Tino Fontana Restaurant, Hotel Mezhdunarodnaya, 3rd floor, ph. 253-2241 {*,j,h}, **F15(10 [17])**

Villa Peredelkino JV (Italy), Solntsevskiy Rayon, 2nd Chobotovskaya alleya 2, ph. 435-1578 {j,h}

Vstrecha cafe, ul. Gilyarovskovo 3, ph. 208-4597 {j,h}, **K11(7)**

JAPANESE

Sakura Restaurant, Hotel Mezhdunarodnaya, ph. 253-2894 {j,h}, **F15(10 [17])**

Sappora Restaurant, Prospekt Mira 14, ph. 207-8253 {*,j,h}, **K12(7)**

KOREAN

Phen Huan Restaurant, 23/25 Sretenka, ph. 208-0654 {c}, **K13(11 [20])**

Zarya Vostoka cafe, ul. 26 Bakinskikh Komissarov 4, korpus 2, ph. 433-2201 {*,j}, **A25(13)**

LEBANESE

Baku-Livan-Nasr JV, ul. Tverskaya 24, ph. 299-8506 {*,j}, **I13(10 [19])**

PHILLIPINE

Manila Restaurant, The, ul. Vavilova 81, ph. 132-0055 {j}, **E23(13)**

PIZZA

Astro Pizza, ph. 245-1216 (take out)

Pizza Hut Restaurant

Kutuzovskiy prospekt 17, ph. 243-1727 {*,j,h/r}, **F15(10 [17])**

ul. Tverskaya 12, 229-2013 {*,j,h}, **I14([19])**

Take out: ph. 243-1727

SPANISH

Rincon Espanol Restaurant (El), Hotel Moskva, ph. 292-2893 {*,j,h}, **J14(11 [19])**

SWISS

Le Chalet Restaurant, Korobeynikov per. 1/2 (Chaika Tennis Club), ph. 202-0106 {*,j,h}, **I17(10 [23])**

TATAR

Serebryany Slonyonok cafe, Bolotnikovskaya 52, ph. 121-2011 {c}

VIETNAMESE

Kuilong cafe, Litovskiy bulvar 7, ph. 425-1111 {j}

S

SAUNAS

See also Massage, Swimming

Most of the newer joint venture hotels have saunas and swimming pools. For public baths, try:

Sandunovskaya Sauna (*banya*) is located at 1st Neglinnaya pereulok, 1a, around the corner from the Bolshoy Theater and across from TSUM, ph. 925-4631 (Moscow's oldest sauna)

SECURITY

Delta Force, ph. 231-4782 (bodyguards and security guards)

Dorin Electronics, Khimkiy, ph. 571-8108 (installation of electric locks)

Intermarket, ul. A. Mitskevicha 10, ph. 291-7656 (full assortment of locks and home security devices)

Medservice JV, ph. 288-5875 (steel apartment doors)

Moscow Security Van Department, 5th Roshinskiy per. 7/8, ph. 234-1838 (armoured vans)

SHIPPING AGENTS

See also Moving, Customs

Anglo-Soviet Shipping Co. Ltd., Pokrovskiy bulvar 4/17, kv. 25, ph. 207-5954

Baltes Moebelspedition, Vekovaya ul. 5, kv. 14, ph. 274-0746

BMT Transport, Mezhdunarodnaya II, room 940, ph. 253-9406

Finnair Cargo, Sheremetevo II, ph. 578-2718

Huolintakeskus, ph. 299-7773

Interdean, Rublyovskoe shosse 36, korpus 2, kv. 212, ph. 415-4296;

International Shipping Lines, Novy Arbat 21, ph. 291-9331

Intertransservice, Rabochaya ul. 93, ph. 278-0102;

John Nurminen, ul. B. Ochakovskaya 15a, ph. 430-7861, 548-7809

Lufthansa Airlines Cargo, Sheremetevo II Cargo Terminal, ph. 578-6758

Moscow Diplomatic Transport Service JV (Sweden), ul. Gorbunova 14, ph. 448-8035

MosTransEurope, Butyrskiy val 22, kom. 46-7, ph. 973-0076

Oy Huolintakeskus AB, Institutskiy per. 2/1 (Sovinteravtoservice), ph. 230-1386; 230-1387;

Scan-Cargo, Head Office, Institutskiy per. 2/1, ph. 200-1522; Butovo, 548-7144

SeaLand, ph. 926-1733

Sofi Courier Services JV (Finland), ul. Myasnitskaya 22, room 404, ph. 925-9587

Sovfrakht, ul. Rozhdestvenka 1/4, ph. 926-1032

Sovmortrans JV, ul. Rozhdestvenka 1/4, ph. 926-1142

Sovtransavto, Institutskiy per. 2/1 (Butovo), ph. 971-3663; Oktyabrskaya ul. 2/4, ph. 292-8965

Sovtransservis, ul. B. Ochakovskaya 15a, ph. 430-7867; Butovo 548-7675

Soyuzvneshtrans, Gogolevskiy bulvar 17, ph. 203-1179

SHOPPING

See also Food, Souvenirs, Electronics, Books

Shopping hours throughout Moscow can vary greatly. Beware the afternoon break, which usually falls between 13-14:00 or 14-15:00. Most all shops, however, are open six days a week and some stores, particularly food stores and bread stores, are open on Sundays.

Typical hours for food stores are 9-20:00, while for central department stores it is 8-21:00. Beware also the infamous "sanitary day", "closed for technical reasons" or "closed for inventory". These days occur at random and mean the store is closed for the entire day. They are more likely to happen at the start of the month.

SOUVENIRS

In addition to the Beriozka stores and other kiosks in your hotel (and of course in addition to checking out the Vernisage at Izmailovskiy Park and the Arbat open air mall), you may want to venture out and buy souvenirs for rubles in state stores. Some of the better ones are:

Art and Print Salon, ul. 1st Tverskaya-Yamskaya 56b

Art and Icon Salon, 6 ul. Arbat, Mon-Sat 11-14, 15-19

Detskiy Mir (Children's World), Teatralny proyezd 2, Mon-Sat 8-21
Dom Farfora, Leninskiy prospekt south of Ploshchad Gagarina
GUM, On Red Square, Mon-Sat 8-21
Khrystal i Farfor, Tverskaya ul. 15, Mon-Sat 8-14,15-20
Podarki, Tverskaya ul. 4, Mon-Sat 9-21
Pushkinskaya Lavra, Kuznetskiy most 5, Mon-Sat 10-14, 15-19
Russkiy Souvenir, Kutuzovskiy prospect 9, Mon-Sat 11-14, 15-20
Tadzhikistan, ul. 1st Tverskaya-Yamskaya 52

STORAGE

Transcargo, Putevoy proyezd 3, ph. 253-1182

SWIMMING

Outdoor

The Moscow outdoor pool, located on the river embankment about a quarter mile from the Kremlin (on the former site of the Cathedral of Christ the Savior), is open year round 7 a.m.-11 p.m. 202-4725
Serebyrany bor (a lake near Moscow outskirts -- Polezhayevskaya metro, then any bus West about a mile or two)

Indoor pools

(reservations required; *In all instances, bathing caps are recommended)*

Chaika Sports Complex, Turchaninov per. 1/3, ph. 246-1344, open 7-24.
Kosmos Hotel Pool, Prospekt Mira 150, ph. 217-1183
Lenin Stadium Swimming Pool, Luzhniki, ph. 201-0764
Mezhdunarodnaya Hotel Pool, Mezhdunarodnaya Hotel, ph. 255-6691
Olympic Penta Hotel Pool, Olympiyskiy prospekt 18/1, ph. 288-1333
Olympic Complex Swimming Pool, Olympiyskiy prospekt 16, ph. 288-1333
Slavyanskaya-Radisson Pool, Berezhkovskaya nab. 2, ph. 941-8027
Swimming Pool of TsSKA, Leningradskiy prospekt 39, ph. 213-2583

T

T-SHIRTS

Sovaminco Joint Venture, ul. Gertsena 11/4, str. 2, ph. 923-5581
Spantek JV (US), Tatarskaya ul. 7, kv. 37, ph. 233-5019

TAILORS

GlavUPDK Tailor, ph. 280-5451
Mayers International, ph. 255-1089

TAXIS

Taxi Reservations, 9am - 6pm, ph. 457-9005; 975-5101; 975-3101
Taxi Reservations, 24 hours a day, ph. 927-2108; 927-0000

When reserving a taxi, you will be asked the time and place where you wish to be met and where you will have the taxi take you. You will also give your name and phone number. About 15-20 minutes before the cab is to arrive, you will receive a call, often from the driver himself, telling you the cab's plate number. The additional charge for booking a cab is 20 rubles in the day and 25 rubles at night.

Private taxi hire services are available at widely varying rates from (at the time of printing):

Avtotechnik, ph. 256-5698
Consulting Co., ph. 322-8198
Demos, ph. 516-8587
Galaktika, ph. 304-1968
Gostinichni, ph. 256-5212
Izvoschik, ph. 399-0440
Mosavtolegtrans (state), ph. 923-8052
Mozayka, ph. 297-0003; 297-6075
Service Globus, ph. 155-7295
Technikom, ph. 245-4169
Victoria, ph. 235-6863

TELECOM

See Electronic Mail
See International Phone

The companies listed below offer services related to obtaining telecommunications equipment and services for firms setting up offices and/or communications capabilities.

Alcatel, Pokrovskiy bulvar 4/17, kv. 21, , ph. 207-9998 (equipment)
AT&T, Nastasinskiy per. 7, ph. 299-6482
Belcom, ul. Usacheva 35, ph. 245-5766 (remote communications)
Bell Atlantic, Degtyarny per. 2, ph. 209-6256
Capricone International S.P.R.L., ph. 113-2933
Combellga, Kutuzovskiy prospekt 7/4, office 252, ph. 243-3578 (PBX)
Comstar, 3rd Tverskaya-Yamskaya ul. 39/5, ph. 250-1730 (direct dial international lines and city lines)
Elektroprovod, Malaya Kommunisticheskaya ul. 21, ph. 297-4897
Infatel JV (Japan), ul. Tverskaya 7, ph. 201-9174
Infocom JV (Finland), Kuznetskiy Most 4, ph. 925-1235 (email)
Morsvyazsputnik, Novoslobodskaya 14/19, ph. 258-7045
Moscow Cellular Communications, Pokrovskiy bulvar 8, ph. 297-7783 (cellular)
Moscow City Telephone Network, Degtyarny per. 6, ph. 299-4745 (local city lines)
Siemens, 1st Donskoy proyezd 2, ph. 237-6476 (equipment)
SovAm Teleport, ul. Nezhdanovoy 2a, ph. 229-9663 (email and leased lines)
Sovamer Trading Company, ph. 337-3441
Sovintel, Dubovoy Roshchi 25, ph. 215-6097 (international direct dial lines)
Sprint Networks, ul. Tverskaya 7, entrance 7, ph. 201-6890 (email)
Teleset Service, ph. 166-9763

TELEGRAM/TELEX

Central Telegraph Office at ul. Tverskaya 7
Communications House, Novy Arbat 22

Both are open 24 hours (your hotel will also have telex services through the Service Bureau). For costs and more information, see Section VI of Russia Business Survival Guide, Communication.

Dictate a telegram by phone (in Russian) by calling 927-2002.

TENNIS

Chaika Tennis Courts, Turchaninov per. 1/3, ph. 246-1344
Indian Embassy, ul. Obukha 6-8, ph. 297-0820 (to play squash) . ($30 registration fee.)
Luzhniki Courts, 201-1655
Petrovskiy Park Tennis Club, 36 Leningradskiy prospekt, ph. 212-8351; 383-3174 (also have tennis supplies).
Sokolniki Palace of Sports, Sokolniki val 1b, ph. 268-0079; 268-0285

THEATER/BALLET

The service desk in your hotel (often a separate theater desk exists) is the best place to turn to for tickets. For places like the Bolshoy, you can often hang around outside the theater the day of the performance and buy tickets from scalpers, but this means is not recommended. For Russian speakers, try the Teatralniye kassi (the kiosks on the street). Also try:

IPS Theater Box Office, Hotel Metropol Lobby, Teatralny proyezd 1/4, ph. 927-6729

TIME DIAL 100

Seasonal time changes are as follows: clocks are set one hour ahead the last weekend of March and back one hour the last weekend in September. Check time differences across Russia on the map on pages 2 and 3 of Russia Business Survival Guide.

TRAIN INFORMATION

General: 266-9000; 266-9999
Order train tickets over the phone and have them delivered to your home or office (C.O.D.) by calling 266-8333; 262-8684

TRAIN STATIONS

Byelorusskiy Train Station, Tverskaya zastava 7, ph. 266-9213
Kazan Train Station, Komsomolskaya ploshchad 2, ph. 266-2843
Kiev Train Station, Ploshchad Kiyevskovo Vokzala, ph. 240-7345
Leningrad Train Station, Komsomolskaya ploshchad 3, ph. 266-9111
Paveletskiy Train Station, Leninskaya ploshchad 1, ph. 233-0040
Rizhskiy Train Station, Rizhskiy ploshchad, ph. 266-9535
Savyolovskiy Train Station, Ploshchad Savyolovskovo Vokzala, ph. 266-9007
Yaroslavskiy Train Station, Komsomolskiy ploshchad 5, ph. 266-0218

TRANSLATION

Services of this nature are widely available and have a very wide quality range. For best results, make sure the service can draw on native speakers of the language you are having something translated into. The better written and oral translation services available are listed below.

AT&T offers a unique over-the-phone translation service. You call them up, any time day or night, in the US at (800) 628-8486, and for $3.50 per minute plus long distance charges, you can have a translated telephone conversation. From outside the US, call (800) 843-8420.

Berlitz (Sovincenter), Krasnopresnenskaya nab. 12, ph. 253-8223

Book Boutique/Knizhny Znak, 1st Kadashevskiy per. 12, ph. 231-1020

Central Bureau of Interpreters, Leningradskiy prospekt 23, ph. 250-1723

Dialekt, ul. Novozavodskiy 27, kom 27, ph. 145-8956; 145-8915

Inlingua, Semenovskaya nab. 2/1, ph. 360-0874

Intourist-Moscow Translation Services, Stoleshnikov per. 11, ph. 928-4515

Intrakon, 3rd Neglinny per. 5, ph. 200-6921

Katyusha, Semenovskaya nab. 2/1, ph. 360-0874

Polyglot, ul. Rybalko 13, ph. 194-7781

RussLan JV (US), ul. Miklukho-Maklaya 21, blok 9, ph. 299-1549

Service Globus (US), ul. Planetnaya 29, ph. 155-7295

World Bible Translation Center, Krylatskiye Kholmy 34, ph. 413-8294

TRAVEL AGENCIES

Most Western travel agencies in Moscow exist to serve their clients when they are in Moscow. But they can often help you solve travel-related problems while in the Commonwealth or help you arrange travel to other parts of the Commonwealth. The major agencies with offices in Moscow are listed below.

Aerotour Joint Venture: Hotel Soyuz-1, suite 211, ph. 458-5786

American Express, ul. Sadovaya Kudrinskaya 21a, ph. 254-4305

Area Travel Agency Ltd., Rozhdestvenka ul. 3, ph. 929-8665

BalkanTourist, Kuznetskiy Most 1/8, ph. 292-7042

Barry Martin Travel, Mezhdunarodnaya II, room 940, ph. 253-2940

Business Tour, Mezhdunarodnaya II, office 701, ph. 255-0584

Cedok, 4th Tverskaya-Yamskaya ul. 35/9, ph. 258-8932

Europaeishes Reiseburo GmbH, ul. Bolshaya Spasskaya 12, ph. 280-6438

Express-Boyd, ph. 203-2675

GlavUPDK Travel and Tickets, ph. 202-2725

Griphon Travel, Hotel Ukraine Service Bureau, ph. 243-2595

Ibusz, ul. Medvedeva 5, ph. 299-7402

Inatours, ph. 253-1529

Intourservice, Hotel Ukraine, ph. 243-2690

Intourtrans, ul. Petrovka 15/13, room 429, ph. 927-1197, fax 200-3207

Intravel, Hotel Kosmos, Mezzanine level, ph. 215-6780

Kaleva Travel Agency Ltd., Hotel Intourist, room 801, ph. 203-6108

Lufthansa Airlines, Olympic Penta Hotel, Olympiyskiy prospekt 18/1, ph. 975-2501

Nur-Touristik, ph. 203-5397

Olympia Reisen, ph. 263-0057

Orbis Travel, ul. 1st Tverskaya-Yamskaya 56, kv. 88, ph. 250-1780

Soviet Travels, ph. 248-3607

Spate-Moscow, Ukraine Hotel, office 221, ph. 243-6550

Sputnik Tourist Agency, Maly Ivanovskiy per. 6, str. 2, ph. 925-9278

Thomson Holidays, Intourist Hotel, room 1120, ph. 203-4025

Travelco, TBA JV (US), Izmailovo Hotel, Bldg. B, room 1733, ph. 166-2882

TrekKingtour JV (FRG), ul. Malaya Yakimanka 2/1, ph. 230-7426

U

UPDK

Main Administration for Servicing the Diplomatic Corps, ul. Prechistenka 20, ph. 201-2326; 201-2964 (protocol).

V

VETERINARIAN

Large pets, ph. 212-8076.
Vet pharmacy, ul. Kirova 34, ph. 923-6659

VIDEO

Blank video tapes can be purchased at Kodak supplied kiosks in the Kosmos, Molodyozhnaya, Mezhdunarodnaya, and National hotels. Western video rental is possible if you have friends in the US Embassy.

For rental of video films, try:

Elektronika, Leninskiy prospekt 87
Forum Videotheque, Sadovo-Sukharevskaya 14
Video Force, lobby of the Mezhdunarodnaya office building, entrance 7, open Mon-Sat 11-20, lunch 13:30-14:30, ph. 253-7708
Videotheques at Arbat 51 or ul. Staraya Basmannaya 15

VISA OFFICE

See also Section II of Russia Business Survival Guide, on Visas & Visa Support

For registration problems/questions, turn to :

UVIR, ul. Chernyshevskovo 42, ph.207-0113 (private visa); 207-0239 (business visa), open Mon, Tues, Th 10-18, lunch 13-15; open Fri 10-13, 15-17.

W

WATCH BATTERIES

To get the batteries changed on watches, try the kiosks (which usually have in stock Western batteries, of the right size too) at Danilovskiy Market or at the Souvenir store on ul. 1st Tverskaya-Yamskaya, a half-block from the Peking Hotel, away from the Kremlin.

Z

ZOO

By most accounts a very disappointing zoo. You can miss this one. If you cannot, it is located near the US Embassy:

Moscow Zoo, ul. Bolshaya Gruzinskaya 1, open 9-17 in winter, 9-20 in summer.

Moscow Business Telephone Directory

City Codes Within the CIS

To direct-dial long distance within the Commonwealth of Independent States, dial 8, wait for a dial tone, then dial the city code as listed below and then the local number. You will often need to add zeroes to the local portion of a phone number to make a total of 7 digits, but not always.

Alma-Ata	327
Arkhangelsk	818
Ashkabad	363
Astrakhan	85100
Baku	8922
Barnaul	3952
Bishkek	331
Blagoveshensk	41622
Borodino	39168
Bratsk	39531
Brest	01622
Bryansk	08322
Bukhara	365
Cheboksari	8350
Cherkassy	0472
Chelyabinsk	351
Chita	30222
Dagomys	8620
Dnepropetrovsk	0562
Donetsk	0622
Dushanbe	3772
Ekaterinenburg	3432
Fergana	373
Gomel	02322
Grozny	8712
Ivanovo	09322
Irkutsk	3952
Izhevsk	3412
Kazan	8432
Kaliningrad	01122
Kaluga	08422
Karaganda	3210
Kaunas	0127
Kemerovo	38422
Khabarovsk	4210
Kharkov	0572
Kiev	044
Kirov	833
Kishinev	0422
Kostroma	09422
Krasnodar	861
Krasnoyarsk	3912
Kuibishev	8462
Kurgan	35222
Kursk	07100
Lipetsk	0740
Lvov	0322
Magadan	41300
Magnitogorsk	35137
Minsk	0172
Moscow	095
Mozhaisk	238
Murmansk	815
Narva	01435
Nikolaev	0510
Nizhny Novgorod	8312
Noginsk	251
Novgorod	8160
Novosibirsk	3832
Odessa	048
Omsk	38122
Orel	0860
Orenburg	35300
Pavlodar	3182
Penza	8412
Perm	3422
Petropavlovsk	3150
Petrozavodsk	81400
Pinsk	01653
Poltava	05322
Pskov	81122
Riga	0132
Rostov	08536
Rostov-on-Don	8632
Rovno	0360
Ryazan	0912
St. Petersburg	812
Samarkand	366
Saratov	8452
Saransk	8342
Simferopol	06522
Semipalatinsk	3222
Sergeyev Posad	254
Sevastopol	0690
Simferopol	0652
Smolensk	08100
Sochi	8620
Stavropol	86522
Sukhumi	88122
Sumgait	89264
Suzdal	09231
Syktyvkar	82122
Taganrog	86344
Tallin	0142
Tambov	07522
Tartu	01434
Tashkent	3712
Tbilisi	8832
Termez	37622
Tiraspol	04233
Tomsk	38222
Tula	0872
Tver	08222
Tyumen	3452
Ulan-Ude	30122
Ulyanovsk	84222
Ufa	3472
Uralsk	31122
Vilnius	0122
Vitebsk	02122
Vladimir	09222
Volgograd	8442
Vologda	81722
Volokolamsk	236
Voronezh	0732
Vyborg	278
Vyru	01441
Yakutsk	41122
Yalta	0600
Yaroslavl	0852
Yerevan	8852
Zaporozhe	0612
Zhitomir	041

• For other cities, or if you have difficulties with dialing, call:

271-9118

A

	Phone	Fax	Telex
A Markt, ul. Mitskevicha 27/29	291-7655		
A.C.P., see Litwin			
A.C.P. Amca Chimie et Plastiques, see Groupe Litwin			
A.S.K. JV (Austria), Partiny per. 1	231-5201		
ABB Asea Brown Boveri AG, Pokrovskiy bulvar 4/17, kv. 7	207-1393	230-2833	413229
ABB Stromberg Oy, Pokrovskiy bulvar 4/17, kv. 7	227-1496	230-2833	413229
Abbott Laboratories, Gruzinskiy per. 3, kv. 162	254-1774	230-2462	413340
ABC Opel, ul. Sergeya Eyzenshteyna 2	181-0407		
Abkhaskiy Dvor Restaurant, Nakhimovskiy prospekt 35	124-9833		
Abramtsevo Museum, from Yaroslavskiy Railway Stn.	2-543-2470		
Academinvest JV (Austria), Leninskiy prospekt 1 (filial)	238-4993		
Academinvest JV (Austria), ul. Gubkina 14, kv. 11	129-0443	938-2278	
Academy of Agricultural Sciences, All-Union, Bolshoy Kharitonyevskiy per. 21	208-6015	207-3762	
Academy of Medical Sciences of the USSR, see Russian Academy of Medical Sciences			
Academy of Pedagogical Sciences, Pogodinskaya 8	245-1641		
Academy of Sciences of the USSR, see Russian Academy of Sciences			
Academy of the Arts, ul. Prechistenka 21	201-4031		
Accord Association	123-9362	200-2216	
Acotech JV, Bolshaya Kommunisticheskaya ul. 36, str. 4	272-3282		
Ad-Opus JV, Bolshaya Molchanovka 23, kv.38	291-3929		
Adan JV (US), Leninskiy prospekt 1, k. 1	238-2163		
ADC JV (FRG), ul. Bolshaya Ordynka 14	231-9342		
Adventure Tours	292-2791		
AEC	250-9974	251-1538	
AEG Aktiengesellschaft, Pokrovskiy bulvar 4/17, korpus 3, 1st flr.	208-5413	230-2313	413265
Aero Traders Pvt. Ltd., Krasnopresnenskaya nab. 12, Office 1105a	255-5751	253-2675	413069
Aeroart, ul. Smolenskaya 6	241-7707		
AeroConcept, Novoryazanskaya ul. 26	267-6545	292-6511	
Aerofirst JV, Sheremetevo II	578-5749	230-2351	411954
Aeroflot, Leningradskiy prospekt 37	245-0002		411969
Sheremetevo II	578-9101		
Arrivals	578-7518		
Departures	578-7816		
Aeroflot Airport Information	155-0922		

All numbers and addresses in the Telephone Directory were individually verified prior to printing and are therefore judged to be the best available at the time of printing. Given the swift nature of change in Moscow, it is expected that some numbers will not be correct even soon after printing. If you have corrections or additions to suggest to the Telephone Directory, please call Russian Information Services at (Moscow) 254-9275 or (US) 802-223-4955.

	Phone	Fax	Telex
Aeroflot Bank, Leningradskiy prospekt 37-A	292-5822	155-5991	
Aeroflot Bank, ul. Pushkinskaya 4/2	292-0759		
Aeroflot Hotel, Leningradskiy prospekt 37	151-5624		
Aeroflot-Lufthansa and Partners JV, Sheremetevo I Airport, K-340	578-0540	578-2743	
Aeroimp JV (Canada), Leningradskiy prospekt 37, korpus 9	152-8810	155-6614	
Aeromar JV (UK), Sheremetevo I Airport	578-2094	578-2714	
Aeronica	143-0631		
Aeroprima JV, A-167, Leningradskiy prospekt 37	155-6685	155-6647	
Aeroservice JV (Japan), Sheremetevo II Airport	578-9187	578-2753	911718
Aerosovital JV (Italy), Leningradskiy prospekt 37			
Aerostar Hotel, Leningradskiy prospekt 37, korpus 9	155-5800	151-8630	411108
Aerotour Car Rental	457-6678		
Aerotour JV (Greece), ul. Levoberezhnaya 12, office 211	458-5786	200-2205	411162
Aerovokzal, Leningradskiy prospekt 37a	155-0922		
AF Computers JV (Italy), Sudostroitelnaya ul. 15	112-5090		411700
AFceica S.A., ul. Bolshaya Ordynka 46	233-5941	237-0777	411640
African National Congress/Mission to the USSR, ul. Konyushkovskaya 28, kv. 9	252-3295		413583
Africana Beauty Center, ul. Zelenodolskaya 41	172-7671		
Africargo JV (France), Leningradskiy prospekt 37	155-6631		411969
Aftenposten, Kutuzovskiy prospekt 9/2, kv. 119	243-6632	243-6747	413193
Aftonbladet, ul. Marksistskaya 1, korpus 1, kv. 53	274-0016		
AG fuer Industrielle Elektronik (AGIE), see Galica AG			
AG Marketing, Kutuzovskiy prospekt 7/4, kv. 300	243-7111		
Agat-Credit JV (USA), Krymskiy val 10/14	238-8558	230-2576	
Agdam cafe, Khlebnikov per. 4, str. 1	278-7146		
Agence France Presse, ul. Sadovaya-Samotechnaya 12/24, kv. 67-68	292-3175	200-1946	413321
Agency Commercial Information, Granovskaya ul. 2, str. 4, kv. 13	202-7151		
Agenzia Nazionale Stampa Associata (ANSA), Kutuzovskiy prospekt 9, kv. 14	243-7393	243-0673	413451
Agotour JV (FRG), Leningradskiy prospekt 37, office 303	155-6626		411475
Agreal JV (France), ul. Arkhitektora Vlasova 3	281-8855	975-2016	411624
Agrica Commercial Bank, Ulyanovskaya ul. 34	277-1041		
Agrika JV (Poland), ul. Profsoyuznaya 128	338-7266		412152
Agro-Tes JV (France), ul. Bakhrushina 10, str.1	258-9066	230-2115	
Agroavtomatika-Oof JV Filial, ul. Verkhnaya 34	257-7852	257-0884	411027
AgroEngineering JV, ul. Bolshaya Sadovaya 2/46	254-8842	253-9203	411756
Agroimpex JV (France), ul. Lesnaya 43	258-1742	288-9559	411274
Agrokhim Association, ul. Gritsevetskaya 2/16	203-2352		
Agrokhimbank, ul. Gritsevitskaya 2/16	202-3847		
Agromark JV (Austria), Novogireyevskaya 24, korpus 1, kv. 6	176-9572		
Agroprombank, ul. Neglinnaya 12	928-0084	921-7646	421301
Agropromservice, Pereulok Chernyshevskovo 4	281-2201	975-2016	411624
Agrosputnik JV (FRG), ul. Lesnaya 45a	258-7502	258-7504	412116
Agrotechnics Steel JV (Syria), Dmitrovskoye shosse 107	483-4510	332-8555	412186

	Phone	Fax	Telex
Ahlstrom ABB Stromberg, Per. Sadovskikh 4, kv. 3	209-6417	200-0254	413483
Aideks JV (Italy),			
1st Krasnoselskiy per. 7/9, str.5, kv. 224	264-0664		411700
Aikon JV (UK), Uglovoy per. 27	972-3135	200-9216	413523
AIOC Corporation, Kutuzovskiy prosp. 9/2, kv. 113-114	243-6718		
Air Algerie, Koroviy val 7, section 11	237-5257		
Sheremetevo II	578-3386		
Air China, ul. Druzhby 6	292-3387		413080
Sheremetevo II	578-2725		
Air France, Koroviy val 7	237-2325		
Sheremetevo II	578-2757		
Air India, Koroviy val 7, section 4	237-7494		
Sheremetevo II	578-2747		
Air-BI JV, Sheremetevo II Airport	578-8268	578-2784	
Airline Ticket Booking	155-5003		
AISI International JV (Italy), ul. Chekhova 8	209-7553	200-4287	
Aisi JV (Bulgaria), Kuznetskiy most 4	925-7158		
Aist cafe, Malaya Bronnaya 1/8	299-6692		
Aitiem-Dok JV (FRG), ul. Novaya Perevedenovskaya 8	388-8018	388-8018	
Akademicheskaya Hotel I, Leninskiy prospekt 1	238-0902		
Akademicheskaya II Hotel, see Rossiyanka Hotel			
Akademkniga, ul. Tverskaya 19			
Akahata, ul. 2nd Brestskaya 43, kv. 70	251-8736		413093
Akatekh JV, Tsvetnoy bulvar 32, kv.6	209-2998		
Akonis JV (FRG), ul. Radio 17	267-2022		
AKOR JV (India), Volkhonka 5/6	202-1129	203-4390	
AKPS Marcom VT JV (Austria), ul. Grodnenskaya 13	443-7333	200-0260	
Aktsia Art Gallery, ul. Gertsena 19	291-7509		
Akvales JV Filial, Bolshoy Kiselny per. 13/15	200-4282		411647
AKZO JV, Rublevskoye shosse 26, korpus 1, kv. 1	415-4251	415-2945	413612
Al-Hayat, Rublevskoye shosse 26, korpus 1, kv. 18	415-4253	415-4254	
Alain Caumon S.A., Gruzinskiy per. 3, kv. 75-76	254-6927	230-2432	413945
Alain Manoukian, ul. Druzhinnikovskaya 11	255-9140		
Alankom, ul. Letchika Babushkina 26	186-5301		
Albatros JV (FRG), Zolotorozhskiy val 34	362-6852		
Alcatel Trade International,			
Pokrovskiy bulvar 4/17, kv. 21	207-9998	230-2688	413115
Alexander Blok Hotel, see Inflotel			
Alfa Shop, Nikolskaya ul. 2			
Alfa-Echo JV (Switz.), ul. Novatorov 7, korpus 2	936-3001	936-2526	411792
Alfa-Laval, Pokrovskiy bulvar 4/17, kv. 29	207-6478	230-2146	413355
Alfa-Systems JV (FRG), ul. Vorontsovskaya 35A	271-9005		
Alfacommerz Handelgesellschaft Gmbh	253-2407		
Algemeen Dagblad, ul. Akad. Koroleva 4, kor. 2, kv. 79-80	215-1966	215-1966	413644
Algerian Press Service, Leninskiy prospekt 148, kv. 27	434-4679		413900
Alisa Commodity Exchange, Leninskiy prospekt 45	137-6514		
Alisa Stock Exchange, Leninskiy prospekt 45	137-0006	137-6525	
Alisa System of Exchanges, Leninskiy prospekt 45	137-6819		
Alitalia, ul. Pushechnaya 7	923-9840		
Sheremetevo II	578-2767		
All Moscow JV (FRG), Chistoprudny bulvar 8	928-9429	925-4274	
All Nippon Airways, Mezhdunarodnaya II, room 825	253-1546	253-1549	
Sheremetevo II	578-5744	578-2720	

	Phone	Fax	Telex
All Russian Exchange Bank, B. Matrosskiy per. 1/1	268-8203	268-8205	
All Russian Exhibition Center (VDNKh) Prospekt Mira	181-9162		
All Russian Real Estate Exchange, ul. Yaroslavskaya 8, korpus 3	217-6009	217-6051	
All Union Copyright Agency, ul. Bolshaya Bronnaya 6a	203-4115		
Alla JV (Switz.), Sokolnicheskiy val 1	268-5430	268-9117	
Allimpex JV (FRG), 1st Varshavskiy proyezd 2	111-8497	111-7178	207301
Almaz Cinema, ul. Shabolovka 56	234-1002		
Almazyuvelirexport, Zubovskiy bulvar 25	245-3420	200-5267	411115
Almega Service JV (Finland), ul. Ordzhonikidze 3	335-8821		
Almeko JV, Leningradskiy Prospekt 80	158-7466	158-5671	
Alogar JV (Switzerland), ul. Maly Ulyanovoy 8, kv.36			
Alpa JV, ul. Kosmonavta Volkova 16	450-3322	943-0072	411080
Alpha Systems JV (FRG), ul. Solyanka 1/2	924-4161		
Alpha Technologiya, Trifonovskaya ul. 61, str. 1	281-1857		
Alphabet Russian Language Center	235-5717		
AlphaGraphics Printshops of the Future, Kosmos Hotel, Prospekt Mira 150	217-1085	281-9551	
ul. 1st Tverskaya-Yamskaya 50	251-1215	230-2207	
Altai Cinema, Kubanskaya ul. 29	350-4033		
Altai Hotel, Botanicheskaya ul. 41	482-5703		
Altair JV (France), Profsoyuznaya ul. 84/32	333-3145		411498
Alternativa JV (Sweden), Seliverstov per. 2	207-5758	207-0187	
Alternative JV & IPLV, Orlyonok Hotel			
Alto JV, Baltiyskaya ul. 7			
Altromash JV (Austria), 2nd Vladimirskaya ul. 6, korpus 2	176-1472	176-2130	414712
Alybiross JV, ul. Gertsena 47, str. 2	291-5639	230-2571	
Ambulance	03		
AMCA International, see Litwin			
American Broadcasting Company, Kutuzovskiy prospekt 13, kv. 52	243-0572	243-0497	413427
American Express, ul. Sadovaya-Kudrinskaya 21a	254-4305	253-9372	413075
American Medical Center, Shmitovskiy proyezd 3	256-8212	973-2142	911626
American Store, ul. Profsoyuznaya 84/32	333-2313	333-6466	
American Trade Consortium, Nab. Shevchenko 3	243-6628	243-1661	412100
American-Soviet Trade & Economic Council, see US-USSR Trade & Economic Council			
Amerkand JV, 3rd Cherepkovskaya ul. 15a			
Amfora JV (Austria), Gogolevskiy bulvar 14	291-1688	291-2911	
Amigo JV (Spain), Komsomolskiy prospekt 19	248-2225		412164
Amiko International Ltd JV (US), Kremlevskaya. nab. 1/9	451-3090	451-3090	
Amixt, Novinskiy bulvar 18a	281-7514		
AMK Anlagen und Maschinenvertrieb Korff GmbH, Hotel Intourist 2013	203-1323	200-1211	413661
AMMO JV (Holland), ul. Kosygina 4	137-8241	938-2156	112790
Amro Bank, Krasnopresnenskaya nab. 12, Office 1707	253-1476	230-2284	413301
Amru-Star JV (US), ul. Aviamotornaya 53	273-9388	273-1937	412176
Amskort International JV (US), Prospekt Mira, VDNKh, Pavilion 4	187-8842	200-2278	411089
Amsovinvest JV (US), ul. Mytnaya 18	238-5485	230-2360	

	Phone	Fax	Telex
AmSovMed JV (USA), ul. Dostoyevskovo 4	288-9837		
Amstrad, ul. Tverskaya 22, Hotel Minsk, room 548/648	299-1548	299-1206	411640
AMT JV (Finland), Khoroshevskoye shosse 42a	941-3092	253-9911	412225
Amtel Exports Private Ltd., Krasnopresnenskaya nab. 12, Office 503L	253-1944	253-1949	411636
Amtex GmbH, Hotel Soyuz II	256-2975	256-2975	
Amtorg, Trubnikovskiy per. 19	202-5794		
ANA, see All Nippon Airways			
Anatolian News Agency, Rublevskoye shosse 26, kv. 279	415-2934		413641
Andre & Cie S.A., Pokrovskiy bulv. 4/17, korpus 3, kv. 2	207-2959	274-0028	413203
Andrei Rublyov Museum (Museum of Early Russian Art), Ploshchad Pryamikova 10	278-1429		
Angara Cinema, Chongarskiy bulvar 7	110-5602		
Anglican Church Services, see St. Andrew's Church			
Anglo-American School, Devyatinskiy per. 9	255-0326		
Anglo-American School, Leninskiy prospekt 78	131-8700		
Anglo-Soviet Shipping Co. Ltd., Pokrovskiy bulvar 4/17, kv. 25	207-5954	230-2955	413158
Anglo-Soviet Trade-Industrial Service JV, Verkhny Taganskiy tupik 2	272-1176		411700
Angolan Airlines, see Linhas Aereas de Angola			
Angolan Radio, see Embassy of Angola			
ANGOP News Agency, see Embassy of Angola			
Angstrome JV, Prospekt Mira, VDNKh			
Animal Theater, ul. Durova 4	281-2914		
Aniral Utek, 2nd Novopodmoskovny per. 4	150-4201	943-0059	413560
Anna Mons Restaurant, ul. Krasnokazarmennaya 3	261-3561	267-9726	
Annik JV, Leningradskiy prospekt 47			
Antareks Stroy JV, ul. Petrovka 19	923-3378	928-6674	412160
Antarex SU JV (Italy), ul. Obrucheva 36	120-3575	420-2250	412160
Antenne 2, Leninskiy prospekt 45, kv. 427	135-1172	230-2010	413304
Antey JV (FRG), ul. Lva Tolstovo 2/22, str.6	247-3229	202-5318	
Antique Store, ul. Verkhne-Radishchevskaya 9a	227-0550		
Anton Ohlert, ul. Mytnaya 1, 5th flr	230-0576	230-2157	413416
Antrakt cafe, Sirenevy bulvar 2	166-7490		
APCO, see Most JV (USA)			
APN (Novosti News Agency), see IAN			
Apollo Store, Arbat 32	241-6060	241-3434	411043
Apsheron JV (Syria), 1st Neopalimovskiy per. 6	248-4725		
APV Pasilac, Pereulok Sadovskikh 4, Office 6	209-2823	200-0241	413308
Aquarius Systems Integral, Pushkinskaya ul. 32	200-0459	229-8459	
Arab League, ul. Konyushkovskaya 28	253-9270		
Arab School, Mosfilmovskaya 60	147-4083		
Aragvi Restaurant, ul. Tverskaya 6	229-3762		
Araks cafe, Sirenevy bulvar 11, korp. 2	164-3630		
Arbat Hotel, Plotnikov per. 12	244-7635		
Arbat Inc. 90 JV, ul. Durova 36	921-2820	200-2265	
Arbat International JV (Jordan), Arbatskiy per. 6/2	291-5904	291-6078	411700
Arbat Irish House, Novy Arbat 21	291-7641		
Arbeiderbladet, Leninskiy prospekt 148, kv. 43	434-4697		
Arbitration Board, Moscow City Council, Zemlyanoi val 48a	297-7583		

	Phone	Fax	Telex
Moscow Regional Council, Prospekt Sapunova 9	228-8388		
Arch Technology Corporation, Vernadskovo prosp. 41	431-0554		
Architecture Museum (Shchusev Museum)			
Don Monastery, Donskaya ploshchad 1	232-0221		
ul. Vozdvizhenka 5	291-2109		
Area Travel Agency Ltd., Rozhdestvenka ul. 3	929-8665		
Arena cafe, ul. Desyatovo Oktyabrya 11	245-2972		
Arena Hotel, ul. 10-letiya Oktyabrya 11	245-2802		
Arendmash JV (Finland),			
ul. Zoi i Aleksandra Kosmodemyanskikh 26/21	150-9700	943-0050	411085
Argeville, Gruzinskiy per. 3, kv. 75-76	254-6927	230-2432	413945
Argoteknics Stil JV (Syria), Dmitrovskoye shosse 107	485-5536		
Argumenti i Fakti, Myasnitskaya 42	923-3541	200-2252	
Argus JV Filial, 1st Shchipkovskiy per. 26	235-1158		
Argus JV Filial (Chelek JV), Petrovskiy bulvar 3	200-6630		
Argus Trading Ltd., ul. Skakovaya 9, kv. 4	945-2777	945-2765	413376
Ariana Afghan Airlines, Koroviy val 7, flr 2, kv. 8a	238-9779		414459
Sheremetevo II	578-2719		
Arif JV (US), Krasnovorotskiy pr. 36	252-2281	252-1605	
Ariplan, International Association JV, ul. Vavilova 15			
Arkadia Restaurant, Okhotny ryad 4a	926-9008		
Arkom JV (Holland), ul. Simonova 3b	152-0717		411263
Arksim JV Filial (China), ul. Lunacharskovo 3/14	241-9124	241-6858	
Arktika Cinema, ul. Menzhinskovo 6	472-5979		
Arlecchino Restaurant JV, Druzhinnikovskaya ul. 15	205-7088	973-2029	411070
Arlekin, Inc., Bolshaya Kharitonyevskiy per. 14, kv. 8	928-6841	476-3841	
Armadillo Ltd., Leninskiy prospekt 2	237-2237	253-1340	411663
Armed Forces Museum, ul. Sovetskoy Armii 2	281-1880		
Armoury Palace, Kremlin	221-4720		
ART, Leninskiy prospekt 93, kv. 42	138-3477		
Art and Electronics JV, Sadovaya-Triumfalnaya 14-12	209-6247	200-2232	
Art Gallery of the USSR, see State Tretyakov Art Gallery			
Art Moderne Gallery, ul. Bolshaya Ordynka 39	242-0175	230-2800	
Art Salon, Ukrainskiy bulvar 6-185	264-4109		
Art-Business-Centre JV, Skatertny per. 23a	291-2668	200-4240	411030
Arthur Andersen JV (FRG), ul. Novoryazanskaya 40	298-6456	265-3341	911580
Artibank	248-3188		
Artpramo JV (Czech.), Starokonyushenny per. 6	946-4549		411418
Artromed International JV (Australia),			
2nd Tverskaya-Yamskaya ul. 52, kab. 6	450-3811	200-2217	411700
AS JV (France), Proyezd Serova 4	445-0787		411630
As-Partner JV (Austria), 3rd Cherepkovskaya ul. 15A	307-7605		
AsA Interexchange Trading Company	210-9766		
Asahi Shimbun, Kutuzovskiy prosp. 7/4, korpus 6, kv. 63	243-0989	230-2772	413383
Asco Insurance Company	459-7570		
Ascom JV, Prospekt Mira, VDNKh	181-9240		
Asea Brown Bauer, see ABB Asea			
Ases Moscow (Austria), Zubovskiy bulvar 4	201-3548	201-4545	411323
ASET Consultants, Inc., ul. Vernadskovo, 33/153	201-5021	201-7247	412230
Ashkhabad Cinema, Chertanovskaya ul. 17a	315-1268		
Ashwini Kumar Consultants	269-0636		
Asikulo JV (Finland), ul. Kachalova 16, kv.4	258-8957		411700

	Phone	Fax	Telex
Ask American-Soviet Cinema Initiative JV (US), Smolenskiy bulvar 17	244-0042	230-2200	411939
ASK JV (Austria), Tverskoy bulvar 13	433-0981	433-0981	
Askad JV (Switz.), ul. Lesnaya 45a	258-7502		
Asko Consulting, Petrovskaya ploshchad 12	209-1208		
Asko Moden JV (FRG), Dmitrovskoye shosse 7	216-4729	216-2809	
ASKO-Service, Post Box 346, Moscow 103009	120-1183	457-2123	411867
Askom JV (FRG), Prospekt Mira	181-9240		
Askot JV (Switz.), Suvorovskiy bulvar 11	291-3218	200-2284	
Asmaral JV (UK), Kotelnicheskaya nab. 1/15, kv. 28, korpus V	928-9760	227-4286	411823
Aspect JV, ul. Ryleyeva 25	241-2206	230-2658	412156
Aspek JV (Spain), ul. Fedotovoy 11/2, kv. 14	241-9500	291-6880	
Assess-Moskva JV (Austria), Zubovskiy Bulvar 4	201-3548	201-4545	
Associated Press, Kutuzovskiy prospekt 7/4, korpus 5, kv. 33	243-5153	230-2845	413422
Association Amikst JV (France), ul. Chaykovskovo 18a	924-11175	230-2884	
Association of Oil Brokers, Dealers and Traders, Nab. Morisa Toreza 26/1	233-8841		
Asta JV (US), ul. Belomorskaya 26	200-4555	310-7024	
Asteis JV (UK), Verkhny Taganskiy tupik 2	272-1176		411355
Astek JV (Australia), ul. 3rd Cherepkovskaya 15a	414-6932	415-2962	112454
Astiko JV (US), ul. Tverskaya 5	291-9924	200-3210	
Asto (Avtoexport-Satra) JV, ul. Marksa-Engelsa 8	203-5430	202-6075	411135
Astra International JV, ul. Kotlyakovskaya 3	111-8184		
ASU-Impuls, ul. Nelidovskaya 18, kv. 38	497-2047		
AT & T, Nastasinskiy per. 7	299-6482		
Atel JV (Switzerland)	939-3784		
Atelier Modnie Golovnie Ubori, ul. Gertsena 16			
Atemi JV, ul. Trubnaya 4	207-3113		
Athens News Agency/ET-2 TV/NEA, Rublevskoye shosse 36, korpus 2, kv. 255-6	415-4306	415-4306	
Atlant Commercial Bank, Prospekt Mira 50	280-1302		
Atlant JV (Yugoslavia), ul. Krasikova 32	129-0933	310-7026	411163
Atlantik International JV, ul. Vavilova 44, k. 2	236-0555		
Atlantikstrom JV, Pushkinskaya ul. 9	292-4917		
ATM-DOK JV (FRG), Kirovogradskaya 21	388-8018		
Atochem, see Elf Aquitaine			
Atoll Firm, Kashirskoye shosse 66, korpus 1, entrance 2	324-0728	324-3020	
Atoll MM JV, ul.Pogodinskaya 4, k. 235	248-0022		
Atomenergoexport, Ovchinnikovskaya nab. 18/1	220-1436	230-2181	411397
Atrium Cafe, Leninskiy prospekt 44	137-3008		
Audi Sales and Service, see Fisherman's Harbor			
Auditing Council of the USSR	206-7187		
Aurora 80, Lavrushinskiy per. 17, kv. 83	231-3507		413616
Australian Broadcasting Corporation, Rublevskoye shosse 26, kv. 19	415-4015	415-2904	413639
Australian Down Under Club, Kropotkinskaya per. 13			
Australian-Soviet Bakery, 29/8 Pyatnitskaya ul.			
Austrian Airlines, Krasnopresnenskaya nab. 12, # 1805	253-1670	253-1669	413127
Sheremetevo II	578-2734	578-2770	413901
Auto Sun JV (Japan), Grokholskiy per. 29	280-3600	280-4428	414753
Auto-Bystrow	245-7257		

	Phone	Fax	Telex
Auto-Lux International JV (FRG), ul. Oktyabrskaya 6	288-8785	970-2015	412126
Autodesignservice JV (Japan), Trubnikovskiy prosp. 1	290-2327	290-4519	
Avangard Cinema, ul. Generala Belova 18	394-7900		
Avangard JV (France), ul. Tverskaya 9, pod. 6, 6th flr	229-0315	200-4244	
AVEX Commodities Exchange	921-1430		
Aviabank, Ulanskiy per. 16	207-5856	207-5897	411761
Aviaexport, Trubnikovskiy per. 19	290-0176		
Avicenna JV, 2nd Romyatnicheskiy per. 11/16	229-5593	288-9563	411685
AVIS Car Rental	578-5646		
Avitsenna JV (Syria), 2nd Syromyatnicheskiy per. 11/16	227-1607	288-9563	
Avkom JV, Sheremetevo II, K-340	578-5212		
Avrora Cinema, ul. Profsoyuznaya 154	337-2600		
Avrora Publishers, Sushchevskiy val 64	971-0245		
Avstrokop-Lisow AG, Mezhdunarodnaya II, room 1548	253-1317	253-9090	
Avstrosoft JV, ul. Garibaldi 21b	128-8072	310-7060	
Avto JV (UK), ul. Marksa-Engelsa 8	203-5430		411436
Avtobank, ul. Lesnaya 41	258-9090		
Avtoexport, ul. Marksa-Engelsa 8	203-0662	202-6075	411135
Avtokhozyaistvo, Dmitrovskoye shosse 98	488-3112		
Avtokomp JV (UK), Bulvar Matrosa Zheleznyaka 3-1-70	162-3385		
Avtopromimport, Pyatnitskaya 50/2	231-8126		411961
AvtoVAZ Bank			411961
Axel Johnson AB, Kutuzovskiy prospekt 13, kv. 131-132	243-5025	243-9563	413154
Axelsen Industries Ltd., Mezhdunarodnaya II, room 621	253-2621	253-9481	411432
Ayastan Restaurant, Flotskaya 3	456-7444		
Ayot cafe, ul. Obrucheva 45	331-5355		
Azerbaidjan Trading House, ul. Malaya Gruzinskaya 52/a-54	253-4269	255-9729	
Azia-Tsentr JV (Pakistan), ul. Kropotkinskaya 10	202-4314	202-4258	

B

	Phone	Fax	Telex
Babcock, see Deutsche Babcock			
Baginsky Fashion, Mezhdunarodnaya Hotel, Mezzanine			
Bai JV (US), Altufyevskoye shosse 2	401-1422		
Baikal Cinema, Mikhalkovskaya ul. 4	154-1324		
Baikal Hotel, Selskokhozyaystvennaya ul. 15/1	189-7515		
Baikonur Cinema, ul. Dekabristov 21	404-5119		
Bain-Link, ul. Shcherbakovskaya 40-42	369-2643	369-5947	
Bakas AB JV, ul. Nagornaya 7, korpus 3	127-6829		
Baker & McKenzie, Bolshoy Gnezdnikovskiy per. 7	200-4906	200-0203	413671
Bakhrushkin Theater Museum, ul. Bakhrushina 31/12	235-3787		
Baku Cinema, ul. Usiyevicha 12/14	155-0006		
Baku Restaurant, ul. Tverskaya 24	229-8506		
Baku-Livan Bakery, ul. Tverskaya 24			
Baku-Livan-Nasr JV, ul. Tverskaya 24	299-8506		
Balkan Air, Kuznetskiy Most 3	921-0267		
Sheremetevo II	578-2712		
BalkanTourist, Kuznetskiy Most 1/8	292-7042	200-0202	414560
Baltes Moebelspedition, Vekovaya ul. 5, kv. 14	274-0746	200-2217	411700
Baltika Cinema, Khimkinskiy bulvar 54	493-4331		

	Phone	Fax	Telex
Baltimore Sun, ul. Sadovaya-Samotechnaya 12/24, kv. 18	200-2153	200-0265	413426
Banca Commerciale Italiana, Per. Sadovskikh 6, kv. 9	209-6518	209-6569	413482
Banca CRT Sovitcom JV (Italy), Kuznetskiy Most 16	921-3525	928-7262	
Banca Nazionale Del Lavoro, Krasnopresnenskaya nab. 12, Office 1602	253-1802	253-9472	413500
Banco Central - Madrid, ul. Mytnaya 1, Office 4	230-0388		413042
Banco di Napoli, Krasnopresnenskaya nab. 12, Office 1008	253-2590	230-2952	413105
Banco di Roma, Pereulok Sadovskikh 4, kv. 8	209-6625	200-0233	413294
Banco do Estado de Sao Paulo, Koroviy Val 7, kv. 220	238-9724	230-2034	413964
Banco Exterior de Espana, Krasnopresnenskaya nab. 12, Office 1408	253-2263		413345
Banco Hispano Americano, Krasnopresnenskaya nab. 12, Office 1301	253-8176		413302
Bank fur Gemeinwirtschaft AG, Proyezd Khudozhestvennovo Teatra 6/5, kv. 35	292-4839	200-0215	413955
Bank of America NT & SA, Krasnopresnenskaya nab. 12, Office 1605	253-7054		413189
Bank of Scotland, Pokrovskiy bulvar 4/17, kv. 34	207-5998	230-2386	413121
Bank-Melli-Iran, Smolenskiy bulvar 22/14, kv. 3	248-2153		
Banque Nationale de Paris, Pokrovskiy bulvar 4/17, kv. 19	207-5888	274-0054	413243
Banque Paribas, Pokrovskiy bulvar 4/17, kv, 31	297-5511	230-2188	413209
BANSO Real Estate Agency, ul. Novozavodskaya 21	148-0806		
Baptist Services, Maly Vuzovskiy per. 3	297-5167		
Barass JV, Perovskoye shosse 9	173-8352	975-2008	
Barbers International Ltd., ul. Chernyshevskovo 2/1	928-7084		
Barclays Bank PLC, Pereulok Sadovskikh 4, kv. 14	209-6452		413224
Barrikadi Cinema, Barrikadnaya ul. 21	252-0680		
Barry Martin Travel, Mezhdunarodnaya II, room 940	253-2940	253-9374	413197
Bars JV, Rublevskoye shosse 16, korpus 4	415-9818		
Barus Video JV (Holland), Skatertny per. 20	290-4258	200-1286	411114
BASF AG, Bolshoy Gnezdnikovskiy per. 7	200-2749	200-0206	413167
Baskin Robbins Moscow JV (US), ul. Metallurgov 29	305-3610	305-7990	
Bat Cabaret Theater, Bolshoy Gnezdnikovskiy per. 3	229-8661		
Bayer, ul. Mytnaya 1, 9th flr, Office 22-3	230-0042		413947
Bayerische Hypotheker u. Wechselbank AG, see Hypo Bank			
Baytur Construction and Contracting Co., Krasnopresnenskaya nab. 12, Office 422	253-1095	253-9506	413593
BBC TV News, Gruzinskiy per. 3, kv. 1-2	253-9360	253-1144	413613
BBDO Marketing, VDNKh, Gidrometerologia pavilion	181-9997	187-8296	411238
Beirut JV	248-4725		
Belcom, ul. Usacheva 35	245-5766	205-0653	
Belgian Air, see Sabena Belgian World Airlines			
Belgrade Hotel, Smolenskaya pl. 8	248-1643		
Belgrade I Hotel, see Zolotoe Koltso Hotel			
Belka Trading International, see Quinta			
Bell Atlantic, Degtyarny per. 2	209-6256		
Bely Lebed cafe, Sivtsev Vrazhek 3	203-1283		
Bennetton, GUM Department Store	921-5065		
Bennetton, Moskva Hotel, West entrance	924-2734		
Bering Air	373-9664		
Beriozka, Krasnokholmskaya nab. 5/9	272-0474		
Beriozka, Luzhnetskiy prospekt 25a	246-2742		

	Phone	Fax	Telex
Beriozka, Rossia Hotel	298-3620		
Beriozka, ul. Fersmana 5	124-5024		
Beriozka, ul. Prechistenka 31	203-9262		
Beriozka cafe, Karamyshevskaya nab. 18	191-1089		
Beriozka Cinema, Martenovskaya ul. 25	302-0362		
Berosil JV (Australia), ul. Bolshaya Maslovka 21	212-8482	212-8202	
Bet JV (UK), ul. Profsoyuznaya 86	334-2365		
BET Trading Associates Limited	203-5303		
Bezopasnost Joint Stock Company, see Security Joint Stock Company			
BfG:Moskau, see Bank fur Gemeinwirtschaft AG			
Bicar JV, ul. Vavilova 15	135-7189	134-7429	
Biocard Health Center JV (Belgium), 3rd Cherepkovskaya ul. 15a	149-0533		411355
BioChimMak JV (Austria), GSP-3 Leninskiye Gory	939-2421	939-0997	411483
Biology Museum (Timiryazev Museum of Biology), Malaya Gruzinskaya ul. 15	252-0749		
Biplan JV (Spain), Maly Vuzovskiy per. 4-6	297-7069		
Birusinka Cinema, Bulatnikovskaya ul. 9	383-8292		
Birzhevaya Gazeta	256-9575		
Birzhevie Novosti	262-8988		
Bison Bahre & Greten, ul. Mytnaya 1, Office 29	230-0665	230-2375	413295
Bistro-Nedelya cafe, Oktyabrskaya ul. 18	288-9398		
Bitsa Horseback Riding Complex, Balaklavskiy prospekt 33	318-6820		
Blue Belt, Kuntsevskaya ul. 4, korpus 1	417-9400		
BMT Transport, Mezhdunarodnaya II, room 940	253-9406	253-9374	413197
BNL, see Banca Nazionale Del Lavoro			
BNP, see Banque Nationale de Paris			
Bochako GmbH, Krasnopresnenskaya nab. 12, #1407	253-2260	230-2685	413271
Bodigard JV (US), ul. Kedrova 15	129-0927	253-9382	
Boge Larsen Oy AB, ul. Konyushkovskaya 28, kv. 6	253-9671		413575
Boliden Allis, Krasnopresnenskaya nab. 12, Office 901	253-2970	253-2971	413491
Bollus JV, Skakovaya ul. 32	945-2824	945-6369	
Bolshaya Rossiyskaya Entsiklopedia Publishers, Pokrovskiy bulvar 8	297-7483		
Bolshoy Theater, Teatralnaya ploshchad 1	292-9986		
Bombay Restaurant, Rublevskoye shosse 91	141-5504		
Bominflot, Pereulok Sadovskikh 4, Office 5	200-0284		413123
Book Boutique, 1st Kadashevskiy per. 12	231-1020		
Book Chamber International,, ul. Ostozhenka 2	202-6911		
Books and Prints, Kropotkinskaya ul. 31	203-9262		
Books, Moskniga, Mezhdunarodnaya Hotel	253-2376		
Tverskaya, ul. 18	200-0146		
Vesnina, ul. 8	241-9587		
Bordiga Art-Image JV (Italy), ul. Tverskaya 29A	249-6007	200-2211	411030
Bordiga Soyuz JV (Italy), Podkolokolny per. 8, str. 2	925-1922	924-4193	
Borodino Cinema, Mozhayskoye shosse 5	443-7459		
Borodino JV (UK), Kutuzovskiy proyezd 2	249-6774	249-6774	
Borodino Panorama, Kutuzovskiy prospekt 38	148-1967		
Bosch, see Robert Bosch AG			
Bosmosco, Chistoprudny bulvar 8	921-0735		
Boston Globe, Smolenskaya nab. 2A, kv. 106	244-0406	415-2937	

	Phone	Fax	Telex
Botkin Clinic, 2nd Botkinskiy proyezd 5, korpus 5	945-0033		
Boyarskiy Restaurant, Hotel Metropol, 4th floor	927-6089		
BR-Soviet International JV, Ogorodny proyezd 16	218-2345		
Bremco Exporters, Rublevskoye shosse 26, korpus 1, kv. 56-7	415-2902	415-2914	413622
Brest Cinema, Yartsevskaya ul. 21	141-6448		
Bricom, Mezhdunarodnaya II, room 940	253-2115	253-9374	413197
Brigitte, Kutuzovskiy prospekt 9, kv. 5	243-7895		
British Airways,			
Krasnopresnenskaya nab. 12, Office 1905	253-2492		
Sheremetevo II	578-2936		
British Broadcasting Corporation, ul. Sadovaya-Samotechnaya 12/24, kv. 9	200-0245	200-0296	413498
British Club, Kutuzovskiy prospekt 7/4			
British Petroleum, ul. Kalyayevskaya 19	200-5228	200-3258	413701
British Playgroup, Kutuzovskiy prospekt 7/4, kv. 11	243-4811		
British-Soviet Chamber of Commerce, Krasnopresnenskaya nab. 12, Office 1904	253-2554	230-2358	413523
Broadway and Company	243-2575		
Brown Bear Bar, Mezhdunarodnaya Hotel	255-2742		
Brown, John, PLC, see Jonh Brown			
Bruel and Kjaer Export A/S, Leninskiy prospekt 63/2, room 2321	135-8616	135-9003	411637
BT-Master JV (Switz.), ul. Moskvina 6	200-6896		
Budapest Cinema, ul. Leskova 14	407-2783		
Budapest Hotel, Petrovskiye Liniye 2/18	921-1060		
Buhler AG and GmbH, ul. Timiryazevskaya 1, kv. 411	211-0947	973-2047	413749
Bulgarian Civil Airlines, see Balkan Air			
Bulgarian Orthodox Services, ul. Volodarskovo 29	271-0124		
Bulgarian Tourist Information, Kuznetskiy Most 1/8	292-3125	200-0202	414560
Bull S.A., ul. Konyushkovskaya 28, kv. 4	253-9713	253-9281	413574
Bulletin of Foreign Commercial Information, ul. Pudovkina 4	143-0478		
Bulletin of Legis. Acts of Ministries and Govt Dept, Zemlyanoi val 38/40	297-8583		
Bulvar Yana Rainisa Exhibition Center, Bulvar Yana Rainisa 19	493-1467		
Burda Moden JV (FRG), ul. Pushechnaya 3	230-2815	230-2292	411941
Burevestnik Cinema, Dobryninskaya ploshchad 3a	236-3136		
Business and Banks Newspaper,			
ul. Dekabristov 10, korpus 1	907-8210		
ul. Timura Frunze 8/5	245-3509	245-0226	
Business Car, Ovchinnikovskaya nab. 18/1	231-8225	231-4924	
Business Contact, ul. Kakhovka 31, korpus 2	331-9555		
Business in the USSR JV, Profsoyuznaya ul. 73	333-3340	330-1568	414741
Business MN	200-0851		
Business Tour, Mezhdunarodnaya II, office 701	255-0584	253-9072	413697
Business Week, Kutuzovskiy prosp. 9, korpus 2, kv. 122	243-6600	230-2512	413155
Butek Narodny Concern, Yartsevskaya ul. 30	149-3200	149-0903	
Butovo Customs Point	548-7621		
Byelorusskiy Train Station, Tverskaya zastava 7	266-9213		

C

	Phone	Fax	Telex
C. Itoh & Co., LTD., Krasnopresnenskaya nab. 12, Office 602-605	253-8339	230-2224	413381
C.A. & Company Ltd., ul. N. Krasnoselskaya 35	267-4482	264-5545	
Cable News Network (CNN), Kutuzovskiy prospekt 7/4, kv. 256-8	243-0909	243-7095	413953
Cafe Mziuri, Arbat 42			
Cafe Raduga, ul. Nizhegorodskaya 8	272-6680		
Camco, Ltd., Mezhdunarodnaya II, room 1340	253-1575	253-1340	413523
Canada-USSR Business Council, Chapaevskiy per. 8	157-7619	157-5161	
Canadian Broadcasting Corporation, Gruzinskiy per. 3, kv. 163	250-5264		413149
Canadian Club, Starokonyushenniy per. 23			
Canadian Press, Rublevskoye shosse 26, korpus 1, kv. 130	415-4211	415-2946	413631
Canadian Television, Rublevskoye shosse 36, korpus 2, kv. 287-288	415-4280	415-2957	
Canadian Tribune, Smolenskaya nab. 5, kv. 9	244-7332		413066
Capricone International S.P.R.L.	113-2933	310-7095	
Caravella JV (France), Leninskiy prospekt 90/2	131-8185		
Cargill Enterprises, Inc., Berezhkovskaya nab. 2, room 3006	941-8278	941-8260	6504552
Cariplo, Bolshoy Gnezdnikovskiy per. 7, 4th flr	200-4191	200-4295	413675
Carl Schenk AG, Krasnopresnenskaya nab. 12, Office 1502	253-2458	253-9908	413646
Carlisle Syntec Systems, ul. Neglinnaya 17	200-3736		
Carpigiana, Mezhdunarodnaya Hotel			
Casino Aleksander Blok, Krasnopresnenskaya nab. 12, docking	255-9323		
Casino Moscow, Leningradskaya Hotel	975-1967		
Casino Royale, Begovaya ul. 22	945-1410		
Casino Valery, Ploshchad Indira Gandi 1	939-9611		
Caterpillar Overseas S.A., Pokrovskiy bulvar 4/17, kv. 13	207-1007	230-2777	413202
Catharsis	238-8018		
Catholic Services, see Roman Catholic Services			
CBS Radio, ul. Sadovaya-Samotechnaya 12/24, kv. 38	100-2992		
CECA S.A., see Elf Aquitaine			
Cedok, 4th Tverskaya Yamskaya 35/39	258-8932		414442
Center for Intensive Language Training	291-3727		
Center for Scientific-Technical Exchange JV (US), ul. Krasikova 3	129-0744	310-7015	411076
Center for Soviet American Dialog, Prospekt Mira 36	280-4166		
Center for Study of Russian JV (FRG), 2nd Minaevskiy per. 2	258-9101		411798
Central Bank of Russia, ul. Zhitnaya 12	237-5145	237-5055	412312
Central Chess Club, Gogolevskiy bulvar 14	291-0641		
Central Children's Theater, Ploshchad Sverdlova 2/7	292-0069		
Central Exhibition Hall (Manezh), Manezhnaya ploshchad 1	202-9304		

	Phone	Fax	Telex
Central House of Art Workers Kuznetskiy Most metro	921-9744		
Central House of Artists, Krymskiy val 10	238-9843		
Central House of Tourism, see Tsentralny Dom Turista			
Central News Service and New Age, ul. Pravdy 7/9, kv. 35	213-7209		413248
Central Post Office, ul. Myasnitskaya 26	928-6311		
Central Puppet Theater, ul. Sadovaya-Samotechnaya 3	299-3310		
Central Telegraph, ul. Tverskaya 7	924-9004		
Telegrams	927-2002		
CentreCanadSovstroy JV, Leninskiy prospekt 42			
Centrobank Commercial Bank, ul. Narodnaya 7	272-0612		
Centrocredit Commercial Bank, 2nd Kolobovskiy per. 9/2	299-6090		
Cerasi and Company, Mezhdunarodnaya II, kv. 1601	253-1601		
CFF, see Compagnie Francaise des Ferralles			
CGM/Unitramp, see Compagnie Generale Maritime			
Chadbourne & Parke, Maxim Gorkovo 38	231-1064	233-5298	
Chaika JV, Kropotkinskaya nab. 3-5	202-3461		
Chaika Sports Complex, Turchaninov per. 1/3	246-1344		
Cham-MEI JV, ul. Energeticheskaya 8	362-6821	361-1620	411610
Chamber Music Theater, Leningradskiy prospekt 71	198-7204		
Champs Elysees Restaurant, Pullman Iris Hotel	488-8000		
Chance JV (FRG), ul. Butlerova 24B	334-2470	334-2560	
Channel 4, ul. Marksistskaya 1, korpus 1, kv. 45-46	270-6688	274-0004	413543
Charodeika, Novy Arbat 25	290-5339		
Chase Manhattan Bank N.A., Krasnopresnenskaya nab. 12, Office 1709	253-2865	230-2174	413912
Chastnaya Zhizn, see Private Life			
Chekhov House, Sadovaya-Kudrinskaya ul. 6	291-6154		
Chekhov's Theater, see Moscow Theater of the Arts (Old)			
Chelek Agroplast JV filial (Chelek JV), 4th Parkovaya ul. 12, korpus 1	165-9243		
Chelek Agroplast JV filial (Intercross JV), Bolshoy Sukharevskiy per. 21	207-0101	200-0294	
Chelek JV (Denmark), ul. Raskovoy 4	257-0810		411172
Chelovek i Zakon, Olympiyskiy prospekt 22	281-6995		
Chelovek Studio Theater, Skatertny per. 23a	291-2668		
Chemical Goods Exchange	281-9258		
Chemie Holding AG, Krasnopresnenskaya nab. 12, office 1106	253-1480	230-2862	413437
Chemimetal	227-4039		413499
Chemimpex Pvt. Ltd, ul. Mytnaya 1, 7th flr	230-0832	230-0521	413001
Chemos JV (Finland), ul.Petrovka 17, str. 10	119-5968		
Cheppel JV (Finland), ul. Tverskaya 55, str. 1, kv. 2	250-1319	292-6511	
Cheremushki Cinema, ul. Garibaldi 21	120-9003		
Chetek	206-5735		
Chevron Overseas Company, Krasnopresnenskaya nab. 12, office 1603a	255-1557	253-9516	411646
Chicago Tribune, Kutuzovskiy prospekt 7/4, kv. 138	243-9593	253-9012	413436
Children's Fund, Armyanskiy per. 11/2	925-1376		
Children's Music Theater, Prospekt Vernadskovo 5	130-5243		
Chilewich International Corp., Kursovoy per. 9, kv. 2	203-8157	200-1215	413211
Chillinger Vika JV (Austria), Uglovoy per. 2/120	972-4231	274-8420	

	Phone	Fax	Telex
Chimmashexport, Bezbozhny per. 25	288-3690		411032
Chimvak, ul. Ryabinovaya 8, #209	444-1071		
Chinar Exports Ltd.,			
Krasnopresnenskaya nab. 12, Room 1404B	253-2196		413998
Chori Co. Ltd., ul. Pushkinskaya 9, kv. 9	292-4841	200-0249	413407
Chosonminhang (N.Korean Airways),			
ul. Mosfilmovskaya 72	143-6307		413636
Sheremetevo II	578-7580		
Christian Dior, Mezhdunarodnaya Hotel	253-9297		
ul. Tverskaya 4			
Christian Science Monitor,			
ul. Sadovaya-Samotechnaya 12/24, kv. 53	200-0281		413423
Christmas JV (US), ul. Kalyayevskaya 23a	251-8844	251-8844	
Chunichi Shimnun & Tokyo Shimbun,			
Kutuzovskiy prospekt 9, kv. 25	243-1671	230-2888	413388
Church of Saint George, ul. Varvarka 12	298-3872		
Church of the Trinity in Nikitniki			
(Museum of 17th Century Art), Nikitnikov per. 3	298-3451		
CIBA Corning Diagnostics Ltd., Yuzhinskiy per.15	973-2121		413377
CIBA-Geigy AG, Pokrovskiy bulvar 4/17, kv. 37	973-2110	230-2666	413133
Yuzhinskiy per. 15	973-2121		
CIC-Union Europeenne, I'ntl ET CIE.,			
Krasnopresnenskaya nab. 12, Office 609	253-1182	230-2104	413375
Cifal, Trekhprudny per. 11/13, kv. 4	299-2272	200-1232	413037
Cinebridge JV (USA), ul. S. Eisensteina 8	181-6200		411841
Circus (New) on Lenin Hills, Prospekt Vernadskovo 7	930-2815		
Circus (Old), Tsvetnoy bulvar 13	200-0668		
Circus-Europe JV (France),			
3rd Frunzenskaya ul. 10, kv. 88	424-8004		411230
Cleopatra JV (Egypt), ul. 1st Tverskaya-Yamskaya 46b	250-8813	938-8038	411030
Clifford Chance, Yuzhinskiy per. 15a	973-2415	973-2236	413777
Club Kachalova-27 JV, ul. Kachalova 27	202-5611	202-1213	411153
Club na Taganka, Verkhne-Radishchevskaya 19	272-7320		
Cluster JV (Finland), Bolshoy Vuzovskiy per. 3/12	925-1085	925-1085	
CNN, see Cable News Network			
Co-op Trade Japan Ltd., Bolshoy Gnezdnikovskiy per. 7	200-2535	200-4293	
Co-Star JV (US), Valdayskiy proyezd 16	457-8186		411474
Cobra Bank, Maly Gnezdnikovskiy per. 9	229-0028		
Coca-Cola	253-2037		
Coe & Clerici S.p.A., 4th Dobryninskiy per. 6/9	237-6892	230-2683	413281
Cogolo S.r.L., ul. Timiryazevskaya 1	257-8814	200-3223	413603
Cole Corette and Abrutyn	245-5718		
Columb JV (Panama),			
ul. 4th Tverskaya-Yamskaya 13, kv. 9	251-9817	973-2049	125267
Columbia Broadcasting System,			
ul. Sadovaya-Samotechnaya 12/24, kv. 38	200-2992	299-2631	413435
Colve GmbH, ul. Delegatskaya 16/1	281-8447	281-8447	
Combellga, Kutuzovskiy prospekt 7/4, office 252	243-3578	244-9558	
Combustion Engineering, Leningradskiy prospekt 47	158-6401		
Comecon, see Int'l Org. of Economic Cooperation			
Comef S.A., ul. Mytnaya 1, Office 24	230-0022	230-2712	413046
Comfortobuv JV (Austria), Elektrozavodskaya ul. 46	963-4100		

	Phone	Fax	Telex
Commercial Bank of International Integration, Olympiyskiy prospekt 32	284-4987		
Commersant, Khoroshevskoye shosse 41	941-0900		411712
Kiosk	202-9951		
Commerzbank Aktiengesellschaft, Pereulok Sadovskikh 4, kv. 9	209-6440	200-0246	413274
Committee for Antimonopoly Policy, Prospekt Vernadskovo 41	434-8466		
Committee for Cooperation of CIS States	925-9051		
Committee for Security and Cooperation in Europe, ul. Prechistenka 3	203-6271		
Committee of Youth Organizations, ul. Maroseika 7/8	206-8542		
Commodity-Credit Partnership	271-0730	271-1372	
Communication-Adjusting, Novoslobodskaya ul. 55	258-3689		
Compagnie Francaise des Ferralles, ul. Gubkina 14, kv. 79	938-2824		414771
Compagnie Generale de Geophysique, ul. Mytnaya 1, Office 28	230-2071	230-2663	413568
Compagnie Generale Maritime, Serpukhovskiy val 8, kv. 201	232-4835	230-2296	413100
Computer Aided Technology JV (Switz.), Krutitskiy val 3, korpus 2	276-4714	274-0097	
Computer Automated Systems JV (UK), Studencheskaya ul. 39, k. 2	200-4671		
Computer Partner JV (Austria), ul. Kiyevskaya 21	144-2274		
Computer Systems and Technology JV (US), ul. Chernyshevskovo 10	924-5969	923-0748	412166
Computerland, ul. Kosygina 15	939-8128	930-7820	
Comstar Business Center, ul. Petrovka 10 (Passage), Room 301	924-0892	975-2319	
Comstar JV (UK), 3rd Tverskaya-Yamskaya ul. 39/5	250-1730	200-3283	414708
Concern Mairan, Hotel Belgrad, room 1827	248-7270		
Concert Hall in the Church of Pokrova v Filyakh, Novozavodskaya 6	148-4552		
Concert JV, ul. Neglinnaya 15	423-4275	288-9588	411124
Concord JV (US), ul. Smolenskaya 10			
Coneco, Mezhdunarodnaya II, room 439	253-1353		
Congress of Business Circles of Russia, Novy Arbat 29	291-3409		
Congress of Exchanges	262-3619		
Congress of the Russian Business Community	291-7601		
Connect International JV, ul. Bolshaya Filevskaya, 37/17	248-7273	144-0558	
Conoco Overseas Oil Company, Kudrinskiy per. 13/2	973-3101		
Conservatory, ul. Gertsena 13	229-8183		
Consortium JV, ul. Kachalova 27	202-5611	200-1213	411153
Constanta JV (FRG), Rublevskoe sh. 26, korp. 1, kv. 305	254-4087	415-4080	
Construction Exchange	128-9722		
Construction Exhibition, Frunzenskaya nab. 30	242-8968		
Construction Marketing and Trading Inc.	972-4662		
ConsultAmerica, ul. Krasnokholmskaya 1/15, office 73	271-2580	230-2101	413205
Consulting Construction Company JV, Golovinskoye shosse 12	331-3055		

	Phone	Fax	Telex
Contact JV (Lichtenstein), ul. Pyatnitskaya 73	230-8908	230-2345	
Contemporary Art Center, ul. Dimitrova 6	238-9666		
Continental Airlines, Kolokolnikov per. 11	924-9050		
Continental Restaurant, Hotel Mezhdunarodnaya	253-9798		
Continentalinvest JV (France), VDNKh Expo Center	181-1377	181-4133	411418
Control Data Corporation, Krasnopresnenskaya nab. 12, Office 2006	253-8379	253-9004	413311
Convent, Sukharevskaya ploshchad	234-5678	234-5678	411700
Conversbank Commercial Bank, Bolshaya Ordynka ul. 24/26	239-2620		
Conversion Concern	268-6643		
Converta, Pokrovskiy bulvar 4/17, kv. 17	207-3470	298-4490	413065
Cooper and Lybrand, Pokrovskiy bulvar 4/17, kv. 33	318-5754	230-2244	
Cooper Industries Inc., Pereulok Sadovskikh 4, kv. 12	209-6520		413376
Copechim Trading A.G., Pokrovskiy bulvar 4/17, str. 3, kv. 1	208-7642	200-2243	413157
Copyrus, ul. Vavilova 11/19	235-1475		
Corinth JV, ul. T. Makorovoy 12	231-1204	230-2729	
Corona JV, Bolshaya Gruzinskaya 4/6, str.2	254-0401	253-9484	411117
Correo Espanole (El)/El Pueblo Vasco, Rublevskoye shosse 26, korpus 1, kv. 229	415-2919		
Corriere Della Sere, Kutuzovskiy prospekt 9, kv. 15	243-1309	243-5276	413456
Corstjens, ul. Gertsena 54, kv. 7	290-6872	256-7396	414521
Cosmos Hotel Indoor Pool	217-1183		
Coudert Brothers, ul. Petrovka 15, kv. 19-20	928-7838	200-0268	413310
Cox Newspapers, Kutuzovskiy prospekt 7/4, kv. 138	243-0930		413436
Credit Lyonnais, Pokrovskiy bulvar 4/17, kv. 18	207-6489	230-2288	413228
Creditanstalt, Krasnopresnenskaya nab. 12, Office 1108	253-2752	253-2852	413556
Credito Italiano, Pokrovskiy bulvar 4/17, kv. 40	207-0389	230-2724	413266
Credo Card Department	131-9292		
Credobank, ul. Osipenko 15/2	220-3435	975-2154	412308
Crokus International JV (US), ul. Grimau 10a	126-2635	310-2140	
CSS Moscow, Kropotkinskaya ul. 35, dom 3, floor 2	202-0480		
Cubana de Avacion, Koroviy val 7, sect. 5	238-0223		
Sheremetevo II	578-2704		
Cultural Initiative International Fund, Bolshaya Kozlovskiy per. 13/17	928-6422		
Culture and Heritage JV, see Kultura i Naslediye JV			
Cummins Engine Co. Inc., Krasnopresnenskaya nab. 12, Office 2006	253-8379	253-9004	413311
Customs License and Quota Dept	246-1350		
Czechoslovak Airlines, 2nd Brestskaya 21/27	250-4571		
Sheremetevo II	578-2704		

D

	Phone	Fax	Telex
D'Arcy Masius Benton and Bowler, Tverskoy bulvar 13	200-7286	200-6937	411943
D'Meismus Benton & Bowls JV, Tverskoy bulvar 13			
DAB Beer Bar, Zolotoe Koltso Hotel	248-2696		
Daewoo, ul. Kachalova 27	202-8142	202-7797	411153

	Phone	Fax	Telex
Dagens Industri, Kutuzovskiy prospekt 14, kv. 14	243-0036	243-0036	413382
Dagens Nyheter, Kutuzovskiy prospekt 13, kv. 95	243-1759	230-2589	413280
Daily Telegraph, ul. Sadovaya-Samotechnaya 12/24, kv. 25	229-0628	229-7437	413429
Daiwer-Sifaid Business Moscow JV, ul. Gertsena 47	132-3492	230-2571	411700
Dalkon Trading JV, ul. Sadovaya-Kudrinskaya 19, kv. 17	254-6179		
Dallas Morning News, Rublevskoye shosse 26, kv. 109	415-4244		
Dan News Agency, ul. Bolshaya Polyanka 3/9, kv. 25	238-6022		413361
Danieli & C S.p.A. Buttrio, ul. 2nd Baumanskaya 9/23	267-9936	975-2049	413665
Danilov Hotel, Danilov Monastery, Bolshoy Stary Danilov per.	924-0294		
Danish Radio, ul. Sadovaya-Samotechnaya 12/24, kv. 64	200-0770	200-2200	413351
Danish TV, Kutuzovskiy prospekt 7/4, kv. 130-131	243-5165	253-9179	413365
Dansk Industri Syndikat A/S, see DISA Technologies			
Daru Handelsgesellschaft mbH, Hotel Soyuz II, kv. 3	253-9594	253-9571	413625
Darwin Museum, Malaya Pirogovskaya ul. 1	246-6470		
DAS JV (Italy), ul. Nametkina 106			
Daval, ul. Lunacharskovo 7, kv. 3	203-6161		413165
Davy Corporation, Krasnopresnenskaya nab. 12, Office 703b	253-1263	253-9861	413070
DBM JV (Belgium), ul. Gertsena 47, str.2	132-3492	230-2571	411700
Def JV (US), Yakimanskaya nab. 10/2	238-9021		
Degussa AG, ul. Gilyarovskovo 65	971-6728	971-6726	412319
Dek JV, ul. Ferganskaya 25	376-1435		
Delhi Restaurant, ul. Krasnopresnenskaya 23b	255-0492		413561
Delovaya Rossiya, Klenovy bulvar 3	112-1310		
Delovaya Volna Radio Company	217-9162		
Delphin JV (FRG), Leninskaya sloboda 26	275-1130	243-6714	413420
Delphin-Service JV Filial, ul. Trofimova 1/17	279-0829		
Delta Airlines, Krasnopresnenskaya nab. 12, #1102a	253-2660		413089
US Embassy Ticket Office	253-9871		
Sheremetevo II	578-2738		
Delta Consulting Medical, Berezhkovskaya nab. 12, pod. 15	245-9999		212257
Delta Express Service JV (France), Sheremetevo II	208-7419		
Delta Force	231-4782	133-0674	
Delta Industrieberatung GmbH, Kursovoy per. 9, 4th flr	201-2018	200-1242	413021
DEM JV (France), ul. Bolshaya Ordynka 34	243-2886		4139995
Demag AG, see Mannesmann AG			
Demos, Ovchinnikovskaya nab. 6	231-2129	233-5016	
Demos JV (Switz.), Mosfilmovskaya ul. 25	143-4892		
Den norske Bank, ul. Pushkinskaya 5/6, kv. 34	292-0338	200-0237	413286
Dengi i Kredit, Neglinnaya 12	921-5286		
Dental-Beker JV (FRG), Kuznetskiy Most 9/10	923-5322	924-9601	8874639
Depark JV (Brazil), ul. Sovkhoznaya 10	357-0180	207-5859	411672
Depars JV (Argentina), Ilovayskaya ul. 10	357-0241	207-5859	411672
Dernieres Nouvelles D'Alsace (Les), see Le Figaro			
Desta JV (Austria), Bolshaya Ochakovskaya 15a	430-6880	430-7862	411927
Detective Theater, see Moscow Detective Theater			
Deutsche Babcock, Pereulok Sadovskikh 6, kv. 7	209-2837	200-0222	413226
Deutsche Bank AG, ul. Ostozhenka 23	201-2988	200-1227	413073

	Phone	Fax	Telex
Deutsche Genossenschaftsbank, Hotel Intourist, room 2009	203-1621	200-2224	411823
Deutsche Presse Agentur (DPA), Kutuzovskiy prospekt 7/4, kv. 210	243-9790		413122
DG Bank, see Deutsche Genossenschaftsbank			
DHL Express Mail, ul. Vesnina 1	201-2585	201-2490	
Olympic Penta Hotel	971-6101		
Diag International JV (Switz.), Volzhskiy bulvar 114a, korpus 9	179-3597		
Diagraf JV Filial (UK), Bolshaya Tulskaya ul. 52	234-0021	230-2029	
Dialekt, ul. Novozavodskaya 27, kom. 27	145-8956		
Dialog Bank, Slavyanskaya-Radisson Business Center	941-8434		
Staropanskiy per. 4	921-9104	923-6556	
Dialog JV (US), ul. Spartakovskaya 13	265-6212	329-4711	411498
Dialog Magazine, ul. Pravdy 24	257-2691		
Diamex Studio JV Filial (FRG), Volzhskiy bulvar 114a, korpus 9	179-3045		
Diana, ul. Mytnaya 74	230-3614		
Diana JV Filial (Japan), ul. Dubninskaya 27	235-4916		
Diaplus JV (Switz.), Nauchny proyezd 8	332-6440	302-6557	
Diario-16/Cambio-16/El Observodor, ul. Sr. Pereyaslavskaya 14, kv. 86-87	280-0298		
Dibrok Brokerage Firm, ul. Osipenko 19/1	233-5441		
Die Bierstube, Olympic Penta Hotel	971-6101		
Digital Equipment Company, Hotel Mezhdunarodnaya II, room 803	253-2880		
Dina International, ul. Akad. Pilyugina 14, kor. 3, kv. 953	936-2011	936-2700	413550
Dinaelektronik JV (FRG), ul. Sadovniki 4	111-4255	200-5822	412272
Dinamika JV, Tsvetnoy bulvar 26	200-6651	230-3090	411389
Dinamo Sports Palace, ul. Lavochkina 32	453-6501		
Dinamo Stadium, Leningradskiy prospekt 36	212-7092		
Dinamo Swimming Pool, Leningradskiy prospekt 36	212-8483		
Diomides Inc., ul. Bryanskaya 12, kv. 128	240-6430		
Dipace Arredamenti s.r.l., Krasnopresnenskaya nab. 12, Office 321	253-2321		411432
Diplomatic Polyclinic, 4th Dobryninskiy per. 4	237-8338		
Diplomatic Polyclinic Drugstore, 4th Dobryninskiy per. 4	237-5335		
Directory Assistance	09		
DISA Technologies, Prosp. Vernadskovo 9/10, kv. 635-8	131-3393	938-2117	413079
Discovery JV (FRG), ul. Sadovaya-Samotechnaya 3	230-2392	230-2392	411730
Diversified Business Moscow JV, ul. Gertsena 47	132-3492	230-2571	
Djamdani in Moscow JV, Mantulinskaja ul. 5	299-0161		
Djamirco JV, ul. Pyatnitskaya 22, str.2			
DMB&B, see D'Arcy Masius Benton and Bowler			
DMM JV (Italy), Novocheremushkinskaya 58	120-8590	120-4244	411688
Dom Biruni JV (Jordan), ul. Rozhdestvenka 12	924-7220		412157
Dom Khudozhnikov (House of Artists), Krymskiy val 10	238-9634		
Dom Mebeli, Leninskiy prospekt 101	432-2986		
Dom Modi, Prospekt Mira 55			
Dom na Tverskoy cafe, ul. Gotvalda 12	251-8419		
Dom Uchonikh (House of Scientists), ul. Prechistenka 16	201-4555		
Dominus, Petrovskiy bulvar 7	200-6694		

	Phone	Fax	Telex
Domodedovo Airport	234-8656		
Donau-Bank AG, Wien, 1st Krasnogvardeyskiy proyezd, Exh. Complex, Pav. 2	256-7444	253-9483	413599
Dorin Electronics, Khimkiy	571-8108		
Dostoyevskiy House Museum, ul. Dostoyevskovo 2	281-1085		
Dow Chemical Company, Pokrovskiy bulvar 4/17, kv. 9	297-0074	230-2933	413217
DowElanco, ul. Gertsena 26, kv. 54	202-4597	200-4257	414776
Drager, Mezhdunarodnaya II, room 749	253-1555	253-1661	413312
Dragun GmbH, Rublevskoye shosse 36, korpus 2, kv. 212	415-4296	415-2959	413587
Drama Theater on Malaya Bronnaya, Mal. Bronnaya 4	290-4093		
Dresdner Bank AG, Krasnopresnenskaya nab. 12, Office 1708	253-2681		413183
Dresser Industries Inc., ul. Lunacharskovo 7, kv. 16-17	203-0055	200-1284	413166
Dresser Marketing, ul. Lunacharskovo 7, kv. 16	203-7924	200-1225	413337
Dresser Soviet Engineering JV (US), Okhotny Ryad 18, korpus 8	202-5866		
Drevko JV, Bolshoy Sergiyevskiy per. 18	925-2736		
DRT Inaudit, 2nd Samotechnaya per. 1/23	281-6646	971-6419	
Druzhba, Luzhnetskaya nab. 10	201-1655		
Druzhba Cinema, ul. Waltera Ulbrikhta 16/1	943-4182		
Druzhba Hotel, Prospekt Vernadskovo 53	432-9629		
Druzhba Narodov, ul. Vorovskovo 52	202-5203		
Druzhba-Filia JV (Cyprus), Prospekt Vernadskovo 53	431-7812	924-5021	412170
Dubrava Restaurant, Hotel Kosmos	217-0495		
Dukhan Shavo Restaurant, Karamyshevskaya nab. 58	197-1975		
DUMEZ (Societe), ul. Bolshaya Dorogomilovskaya 14, korpus 1, kv. 39	243-3948	243-5264	413315
Dupont, see E.I. Dupont De Nemours and Co.			
Durov Corner, ul. Durova 4	281-2914		
Dusseldorfer Messegesellschaft M.B. H. Nowea, Hotel Soyuz II	256-7395	230-2505	413509
Dzhuna JV (FRG), ul. Lyusinovskaya 12	238-4101		

E

	Phone	Fax	Telex
E.I. Du Pont De Nemours & Co., Inc., Krasnopresnenskaya nab. 12, flr 15, Office 1503a	253-2498	253-9047	413555
E.M. Industrie Consulting and Handels GmbH, Krasnopresnenskaya nab. 12, Office 504	253-1365	253-9383	411636
E.T.P.M., ul. Bolshaya Dorogomilovskaya 14/1, kv. 39	243-3948		413315
East-European Investment Bank, Nagornaya ul. 22, korpus 5	166-1383	166-1289	
East-West Auto-Corp JV (Austria), ul. Yuzhnoportovaya 22	354-8954	354-9854	
East-West Creative Association, ul. Stankevicha 9	229-6901	200-4249	411417
East-West Information Consortium, Leninsky prospekt 39, kv. 42	135-8745		
East-West Project JV (Belgium), ul. Shcherbakovskaya 40/42	369-5987		
Eastern Express Publishing and Commercial Assn., ul. Sadovaya-Kudrinskaya 9	244-8820	292-3690	
EastLight Art JV (Austria), B. Ovchinnikovskiy per. 20, K-104	299-5957		

	Phone	Fax	Telex
Echo Planety, Tverskoy bulvar 10-12	202-6748		
Echo-Trends JV (US), Sivtsev-Vrazhek per. 4, korpus 2	241-9547		
Echoconsta JV, 1st Krasnogvardeyskiy proyezd 1	255-2536		
Echomed JV, Perevedenovskiy per. 4, str.3	261-4149	267-8143	
Echomin JV, Zvenigorodskoye shosse 9			
Echor JV, ul. Kedrova 8, korpus 1	125-5282		
Echosintez JV, ul. Krupskoy 4, korp.1	200-2289	200-2289	
Eclipse JV (UK), Prospekt Vernadskovo 95, kor. 3, kv. 122	433-1507	433-1507	
Ecoenergetika JV (US), GSP Leninskiy prospekt 19	234-0005	234-4250	
EconEx	243-6948		
Economic Daily, Kutuzovskiy prospekt 14, kv. 99	243-3739		
Economika Publishers, Berezhkovskaya nab. 6	240-4877		
Economist, The, ul. Akad. Koroleva 4, korpus 2, kv. 78	215-2574		
Econotech	125-5434		
Ecorambus Corporation, Petrovsko-Razumovskiy prospekt 27	212-5679	213-2629	
Edland JV (Austria), Balaklavskiy prospekt 1	316-0181	316-0511	411418
EFE Agency, ul. Sadovaya-Samotechnaya 12/24, kv. 23	200-1532	200-0219	413114
Egli AG, see Joseph Agli AG			
Ehlsid JV, Leningradskoye shosse 18	150-9775		
EHXA JV (Yugoslavia)	277-4283		
EKA Corporation, Kursovoy per. 9, Office 6	202-1441	200-1259	413176
Ekhsso JV, 2nd Brestskaya ul. 31	254-3974		
Ekonomicheskaya Gazeta, Bumazhny proyezd 14	212-2389	200-2297	
Ekonomika i Zhizn, Bumazhny proyezd 14	212-2389	200-2290	
Ekoplast JV, Dmitrovskoye shosse 102a	483-7500		
Ekopsi JV (US), Shosse Entuziastov 6	246-6151	246-2211	
Eksimer, Leninskiy prospekt 76a	930-7193		
Ekster International JV (US), Stremyanny per. 28	231-1357	270-6360	
Ekstra Newspaper, Kutuzovskiy prospekt 9, korpus 2	243-6718	243-6718	413420
El-Trol JV, Leninskiy Prospekt 99	434-5253	434-5253	
Elative	272-6257		
Elba JV (US), ul. Rokotova 1/12, pom. 120	425-2724		41532
Elbrus Cinema, Kavkazskiy bulvar 17	321-1796		
Elders Australia and New Zealand, see Sovenz New Zealand			
Electricite de France Internationale, ul. Mytnaya 1, office 24	230-0022	230-2712	413046
Electronics and Engineering JV (Lichtenstein), Podkopayevskiy per. 7, str. 2, kv. 16	227-1449	237-2635	414357
Eleftherotypia, ul. Bolshaya Pereyaslavskaya 7, kv. 41	280-5441		413931
Elegant JV (Canada), Moskva Hotel	928-6212		
Eleks-Vest JV (Norway), Leninskiy prospekt 6	288-9552		411622
Elektrobank, ul. Trubnaya 19/12, str. 2	208-1211	208-6703	
Elektrofarfor, Shosse Entuziastov 17	273-7896	291-4281	411003
Elektroimport, Trekhprudny per. 11/13, 2nd flr	299-6682	200-0234	
Elektrointorg, ul. Usiyevicha 24/2	155-4026		
Elektromatik JV (Austria), ul. Bolshaya Semenovskaya 49	369-2893		
Elektronika Research Institute, Prospekt Vernadskovo 39	432-9223		411668
Elektroninvest JV, ul. M. Kaluzhskaya 8	315-3574		
Elektronmatik JV (Austria), ul. B. Semenovskaya 49	369-7911	369-7911	
Elektronorgteknika, ul. Gertsena 24	205-0033	205-3901	411385
Elektrontex JV (Bulgaria), Shukhova 14	236-4695		
Elektropribor, ul. Ogareva 5	229-6110		

	Phone	Fax	Telex
Elektroprovod, Malaya Kommunisticheskaya ul. 21	297-4897	297-6555	
Elend JV (Italy), Leningradskoye shosse 18			
Elf Aquitaine, ul. Gertsena 47	291-8412	200-0258	413519
Elf Lub, see Elf Aquitaine			
Eli Lilly & Elanco GmbH, Hotel Pekin, Suite 1001	209-4141	200-2202	413685
Eliada JV (Cyprus), Krymskij val 9	237-0709		
Elkat JV (Finland), 2nd Kabelnaya ul. 2	361-4393	247-0058	
Elkom JV, ul. Dorozhnaya 38	921-0888	921-0442	411700
ELM, VDNKh, Pavilion 3, Moskva Center	162-5511	181-0448	
Elmako JV, Starokonyushenny per. 6	201-7602	201-7357	411418
Elnor JV, ul. 16 Parkovaya 26	468-5404	468-5404	
Elogar JV, ul. Novaya Basmannaya 23a	261-5764	202-9056	
Eloks JV (France), ul. 25 Oktyabrya 17	928-7614	921-2040	111122
Eloylgeo JV (India), ul. Narodnovo Opolcheniya 39, kor. 3	192-8071		
Elpav JV, ul. Petrovka 26	200-4151		
Eltech JV (Austria), Nab. Morisa Toreza 30	214-7811	214-7803	414727
Eltemek, ul. Bolshaya Spasskaya 1/2	208-2837	208-2745	411003
Elza, ul. Elektrozavodskaya 21	369-3078	963-9765	411589
Embassy of			
Afghanistan, Sverchkov per. 3/2	923-5515	924-0478	413270
Albania, ul. Mytnaya 3, kv. 23	230-1722		
Algeria, Krapivenskiy per. 1a	200-6642		413273
Angola, ul. Olaf Palme 6	143-6324		143402
Commercial Office	143-6335		
Argentina, ul. Sadovaya-Triumfalnaya 4/10	299-0367		413259
Armenia, Armanksiy per. 2	924-1269		
Australia, Kropotkinskiy per. 13	246-5012	230-2606	413474
Austria, Starokonyushenny per. 1	201-7317	230-2365	413398
Commercial Office	201-7308		413399
Azerbaidjan, ul. Stanislavskovo 16	229-1649		
Bangladesh, Zemledelcheskiy per. 6	246-7900	248-3185	413196
Belarus, ul. Maroseika 17/6	924-7031		
Belgium, ul. Malaya Molchanovka 7	203-0531	291-6005	413471
Benin, Uspenskiy per. 4a	299-2360	200-0226	413645
Bolivia, Lopukhinskiy per. 5	201-2508		413356
Brazil, ul. Gertsena 54	290-4022		413476
Bulgaria, ul. Mosfilmovskaya 66	147-9000		
Commercial Office	147-9007		
Burkina Faso, ul. Meshchanskaya 17	971-0620		413284
Burma, see Embassy of Union of Myanmar			
Burundi, Uspenskiy per. 7	299-7200		413316
Cambodia, Starokonyushenny per. 16	201-4736	201-7668	413261
Commercial Office	132-7074		413987
Cameroon, ul. Vorovskovo 40	290-6549		413445
Canada, Starokonyushenny per. 23	241-5882	241-4400	413401
Cape Verde, Bolshaya Spasskaya 9	208-0856		413929
Central African Republic, ul. 26-Bakinskikh-Komissarov 9, kv. 124-125			
Chad, Rublevskoye shosse 26/1, kv. 21	415-4139		413623
Chile, ul. Yunosti 11, korpus 1	373-9176		413751
China, ul. Druzhby 6	143-1540		413981
Commercial Office	938-2005		
Columbia, ul. Burdenko 20	248-3042	248-3025	413206

	Phone	Fax	Telex
Congo, Kropotkinskiy per. 12	246-0234		413487
Costa Rica, Rublevskoye shosse 26, kv. 58-59	415-4042		413963
Cuba, ul. Mosfilmovskaya 40	147-4312		
Commercial Office	290-6230		
Cyprus, ul. Gertsena 51	290-2154	200-1254	413477
Czech and Slovak Republic, ul. Yuliusa Fuchika 12/14	251-0540		
Commercial Office	250-8403		
Denmark, Pereulok Ostrovskovo 9	201-7860	201-7860	413378
Commercial Office	238-6930	230-2072	413928
Ecuador, Gorokhovskiy per. 12	261-5544		413174
Egypt, Skatertny per. 25	291-6283	291-4609	413276
Commercial Office	243-0363	230-2114	413200
Equatorial Guinea, Kuznetskiy prospekt 7/4, korpus 5, kv. 37	243-9611		
Estonia, Kalashnyi per. 8	290-3178		
Ethiopia, Orlovo-Davydovskiy per. 6	230-2036		413980
Finland, Kropotkinskiy per. 15/17	246-4027	230-2721	413405
France, ul. Dimitrova 45	236-0003		413290
Commercial Office	237-8740		413325
Gabon, ul. Vesnina 16	241-0080		413245
Georgia, yl. Paliashvilv 6	290-6902		
Germany, ul. Bolshaya Gruzinskaya 17	252-5521	253-9276	413412
Ghana, Skatertny per. 14	202-1870		413475
Greece, ul. Stanislavskovo 4	290-2274	200-1252	413472
Commercial Office	290-4753		
Guinea, Pomerantsev per. 6	201-3601		413404
Guinea-Bissau, ul. Bolshaya Ordynka 35	231-7928		413055
Guyana, 2nd Kazachiy per. 7	230-0013		413071
Hungary, ul. Mosfilmovskaya 62	148-8611	143-4625	414428
Commercial Office	252-0001		
Iceland, Khlebny per. 28	290-4742	200-1264	413181
India, ul. Obukha 6-8	297-0820		413409
Indonesia, ul. Novokuznetskaya 12	231-9549	230-2213	413444
Iran, Pokrovskiy bulvar 7	227-5788		413493
Iraq, ul. Pogodinskaya 12	246-5506	230-2922	413184
Economic Bureau	246-4061		
Ireland, Grokholskiy per. 5	288-4101		413204
Commercial Office	280-6500		413512
Israel, ul. Bolshaya Ordynka 56	238-1346	238-1346	
Italy, ul. Vesnina 5	241-1533	253-9289	413453
Commercial Office	248-3152		
Ivory Coast, Molochny per. 9/14	201-2400		413091
Jamaica, Koroviy val 7, kv. 70-71	237-2320		413358
Japan, Kalashny per. 12	291-8500		413141
Jordan, Pereulok Sadovskikh 3	299-9564	299-4354	413447
Kazakhstan, Chistoprudny bulvar 3a	208-9852		
Kenya, ul. Bolshaya Ordynka 70	237-3462	230-2340	413495
Kirgizstan, ul. Bolshaya Ordynka 64	237-4882		
Korea (North), ul. Mosfilmovskaya 72	143-6249		413272
Commercial Office	143-6241		413279
Korea (South), ul. Gubinka 14	938-2802		
Kuwait, 3rd Neopalimovskiy per. 13/5	248-5001	230-2423	413353

	Phone	Fax	Telex
Laos, ul. Bolshaya Ordynka 18/1	233-2035		413101
Commercial Office	231-2862		
Latvia, ul. Chaplygina	925-2707		
Lebanon, ul. Sadovaya-Samotechnaya 14	200-0022	200-3222	413120
Libya, ul. Mosfilmovskaya 38	143-0354	143-7644	143443
Lithuania, ul. Pisemskovo 10	291-2643		
Luxembourg, Khruschevskiy per.3	202-2171	200-5243	413131
Madagascar, Kursovoy per. 5	290-0214		413370
Malaysia, ul. Mosfilmovskaya 50	147-1514	147-1526	413478
Mali, ul. Novokuznetskaya 11	231-0655		413396
Malta, Koroviy val 7, kv. 219	237-1939	237-2158	413919
Mauritania, ul. Bolshaya Ordynka 66	237-3792		413439
Mexico, ul. Shchukina 4	201-4848	230-2042	413125
Moldova, Kuznetsky Most 18	928-5405		
Mongolia, ul. Pisemskovo 11	290-6792		
Commercial Office	229-5407		
Morocco, Pereulok Ostrovskovo 8	201-7395	230-2067	413446
Mozambique, ul. Gilyarovskovo 20	284-4007		413369
Myanmar (Burma), ul. Gertsena 41	291-0534	291-0163	413403
Namibia, ul. Konyushkovskaya 28, kv. 10	252-2471	253-9610	413567
Nepal, 2nd Neopalimovskiy per. 14/7	244-0215		413292
Netherlands, Kalashny per. 6	291-2999	200-5264	413442
New Zealand, ul. Vorovskovo 44	290-1277	290-4666	413187
Nicaragua, ul. Mosfilmovskaya 50, korpus 1	938-2701		413264
Niger, Kursovoy per. 7/31	290-0101	200-4251	413180
Nigeria, ul. Kachalova 13	290-3783		413489
Norway, ul. Vorovskovo 7	290-3872	200-1221	413488
Commercial Office	202-3484		413563
Oman, Pereulok Obukha 6	928-6418	975-2174	411432
Pakistan, ul. Sadovaya-Kudrinskaya 17	250-3991		413194
Palestine, Kropotkinskiy per. 26	201-4340		413126
Peru, Smolenskiy bulvar 22/14, kv. 15	248-7738		413400
Commercial Office	246-6836		
Philippines, Karmanitskiy per. 6	241-0563	230-2534	413156
Poland, ul. Klimashkina	255-0017	254-2286	414362
Commercial Office	254-3421		
Portugal, Botanicheskiy per. 1	230-2435	280-3134	413254
Qatar, Koroviy val 7, kv. 197-8	230-1577	230-2240	413728
Romania, ul. Mosfilmovskaya 64	143-0424		
Rwanda, ul. Bolshaya Ordynka 72	237-4626		413213
Senegal, ul. Donskaya 12	236-2040		413438
Sierra Leone, ul. Paliashvili 4	203-6200		413461
Singapore, Pereulok Voyevodina 5	241-3702	230-2937	413128
Somalia, Spasopeskovskaya ploshchad 8	241-8624		413164
Spain, ul. Gertsena 50/8	202-2160	200-1230	413220
Commercial Office	202-7772	200-1226	413900
Sri Lanka, ul. Shchepkina 24	288-1651		413140
Sudan, ul. Vorovskovo 9	290-3993		413448
Sweden, ul. Mosfilmovskaya 60	147-9009	147-8788	413410
Switzerland, Pereulok Stopani 2/5	925-5322	200-1728	413418
Syria, Mansurovskiy per. 4	203-1521		413145
Tadzhikistan, Skaterny per. 19	290-6102		
Tanzania, ul. Pyatnitskaya 33	231-8146	230-2968	413352

	Phone	Fax	Telex
Thailand, Eropkinskiy per. 3	201-4893		413309
Togo, ul. Shchuseva 1	290-6599		413967
Tunisia, ul. Kachalova 28/1	291-2858		413449
Turkey, Vadkovskiy per. 7/37	972-6500	200-2223	413731
Commercial Office	972-6500		413148
Turkmenia, Pereulok Aksakova 22	291-6636		
Uganda, Pereulok Sadovskikh 5	251-0060		413473
Ukraine, ul. Stanislavskovo 18	229-2804		
United Arab Emirates, ul. Olaf Palme 4	147-6286		413547
United Kingdom, Nab. Morisa Toreza 14	231-8511		413341
Commercial Office	248-2001		413314
United States of America, Novinskiy bulvar 19/23	252-2451		413160
Commercial Office	255-4848	230-2101	413205
Uruguay, Lomonosovskiy prospekt 38	143-0401	938-2045	413238
Uzbekistan, Pogorelskiy per. 12	230-0076		
Venezuela, ul. Yermolova 13/15	299-9621	200-0248	413119
Vietnam, ul. B. Pirogovskaya 13	245-0925		
Commercial Office	250-4852		
Yemen, 2nd Neopalimovskiy per. 6	246-1814		413214
Yugoslavia, ul. Mosfilmovskaya 46	147-4106		
Commercial office, INA Commerce, Krasnopresnenskaya nab. 12, office 107	253-1253	253-1270	414451
Zaire, Pereulok N. Ostrovskovo 10	201-7673	201-7948	413479
Zambia, Prospekt Mira 52a	288-5001		413462
Zimbabwe, Serpov per. 6	248-4367	230-2497	413029
Emergency Towing Service, Novoryazanskiy per. 13	267-0113		
Emergency Towing Service, Varshavskoe shosse 87	119-8000		
Emery Worldwide, see Inservice			
Emita JV (Italy), ul. Mytnaya 1, kv.31	238-9714	230-2093	413507
EMS Garantpost JV, Varshavskoye shosse 37	114-4584	230-2719	
Ener JV (US), ul. Nezhdanovoy 8/10, korpus 2			
Energobigmach JV, ul. Oktyabrskaya 5, str. 8			
Energomashexport, Bezbozhny pereulok 25A	288-8456	288-7990	411965
Enervek JV (Greece), Potapovskiy per. 5, str. 3	927-5506	230-2898	411776
Engineering VO- Investment Center JV, ul. Nametkina 10a	172-9710	172-9708	
ENI - Ente Nazionale Idrocarburi, ul. Sadovaya-Samotechnaya 12/24	203-8166	200-1204	413136
Enichem, Krasnopresnenskaya nab. 12, Office 1302	253-2146	230-2723	413940
ENICO, Krasnopresnenskaya nab. 12, Office 2009	253-2066	253-9070	414440
Enims, 5th Donskoy proyezd 21b	234-2300		411928
Enix JV (India), Kirovogradskaya 11	315-3904		
ENKA, ul. Yelanskovo 2	248-5042	288-9521	4133379
Enka Pazarlam, ul. Petrovka 12	928-8547	288-9521	413379
Enthusiast JV (Bulgaria), Vspolny per. 4	203-3706	200-2216	
Entuziast Cinema, ul. Vishnyakovskaya 18	373-5000		
EP Companies, Presnenskiy val 19	252-0671		
Epek JV (FRG), ul. Kirova 20	928-5655		
Epsilon JV (India), Leninskiy prospekt 53	132-5917		411479
Epson, see Seiko Epson Corporation			
Erma International JV, Rublevskoye sh. 28, korpus 3	415-5207	415-2973	
Ermitage Theater, Karetny Ryad 3	209-6742		
Ernst & Young, Koroviy val 7, office 10, 2nd flr.	237-1250	230-2202	413950

	Phone	Fax	Telex
Erten JV (France), 5th Donskoy proyezd 21b	230-2991	230-2991	
ESAB AB Sweden, ul. Usacheva 35	245-5735	245-5070	413743
Esme JV, ul. Skakovaya 17	945-5161	945-5071	
Esso-Gutzeit Oy, see Valmet Oy			
Estafeta Cinema, ul. Timiryazevskaya 17	211-3553		
Estee Lauder, ul. Tverskaya 6	921-5873		
Esteti JV (Italy), ul. Verkhnyaya Radishchevskaya 9A	297-7297		
Estrada Theater, Bersenevskaya nab. 20/2	230-0444		
Etex Ligne Reguliere, Pokrovskiy bulvar 4/17, kv. 1	297-4835		413326
Ethical Pharmaceuticals Limited, ul. Dovatora 13	245-7906	200-2216	
Sheremetevo 2, Office 641	578-2717		
Eureka JV	943-0893		
Eurintrade S.A., ul. Lunacharskovo 7, kv. 10-11	202-8511	253-9502	413163
Eurobank, 1st Krasnogvardeyskiy proyezd, pav. 2, tower 3	256-7444	253-9483	413599
Eurodeal JV (Luxemburg), Gorokhovskiy per. 19	265-3908	975-2234	412817
Euroimpex SrL, Kursovoy per. 9, Office 1	202-1858	200-1245	413535
Euroline JV, Volgogradskiy prospekt 139	175-2450	172-1927	
Euromedical Club	431-8755		
Euromedical Emergency Service	432-1616		
Euronetics JV (Italy), ul. Dubninskaya 65, str.447	235-2251	253-1665	
Euronews Moscow, Bolshoy Tishinskiy per. 2-19	254-9049	230-2298	
Europ Assistance, Berezhkovskaya nab. 12, pod. 15	240-9999	230-2432	212257
Europaeishes Reiseburo GmbH, ul. B. Spasskaya 12	280-6438	280-6066	
Europalette JV (FRG), ul.Vavilova 9a	135-1726		
Europcar, Hotel Mezhdunarodnaya 1	253-1369		
Hotel Zolotoe Koltso	248-2657		
Sheremetevo II	578-8278		
Europe JV (Switzerland), ul. Karla Marksa 15a	131-1579	200-2278	
Europe Plus JV, ul. Akademika Koroleva 19	215-9938	217-8986	
Eurosov Petroleum, ul. Grimau 7/1, kv. 18	126-6527		
Eurostron JV (France), ul. Luganskaya 4, korpus 1	322-4757	292-5611	
Eurotax Moscow Bureau, Leningradskiy prosp. 64, rm 203	155-0856		
Evangelischer Pressedienste (EPD),			
Kutuzovskiy prospekt 7/4, kv. 301	243-4046		
Evik JV, ul. Mikhalkovskaya 34	456-5156	453-6004	
Evko JV (FRG), ul. Vyborgskaya 16	150-2684	150-9935	
Evricom JV, ul. Lva Tolstovo 5/1	157-1857		
Evrodil JV (Luxemburg), ul. Chernyshevskovo 17	923-6285		
Evropalet, ul. Vavilova 9a	135-1726		
Evropeiskiy Zal Restaurant, Hotel Metropol	927-6039		
Evrostron JV (France), Luganskaya ul. 49	322-4757		
Ewald Budde, Krasnopresnenskaya nab. 12, Office 1247	253-1763		
Excelsior, Gruzinskiy per. 3, kv. 266	250-4165		413013
Exhibition Hall of			
Moscow Artists' Trade Union, ul. M. Gruzinskaya 28	253-7355		
Academy of Arts, ul. Prechistenka 21	201-3052		
Union of Artists of the RSFSR, ul. Tverskaya 25/9	299-2289		
Begovaya ul. 7-9	213-8314		
ul. 1st Tverskaya-Yamskaya 46b	250-1412		
ul. Kuznetskiy Most 20	928-1844		
EXI International Ltd., Shchukinskaya ul. 12/1	190-7772		
Exotic-Tour JV (France), ul. Chkalova 57	227-0412		
Expertek JV (US), ul. Krasikova 32	129-1633		

	Phone	Fax	Telex
Expo-Consta JV (Finland), 1st Krasnogvardeyskiy pr.1	255-2536	253-9513	411865
Expocenter, Sokolnicheskiy val. 1	268-1340		
Export License Department of Russia, Staraya pl. 4	206-3387		
Exporters' Association of Russia, ul. Gertsena 22/7	202-7089		
Exportkhleb, Smolenskaya-Sennaya 34/32	244-4701	253-9069	
Exportles, Trubnikovskiy per. 19	291-6116	200-1219	411299
Exportsamotsveti, ul. Narodnovo Opolcheniya 29/1	197-5401		
Expovestrans JV (FRG), 1st Krasnogvardeyskiy pr. 12	256-7323	256-5571	411591
Express Bar, Mezhdunarodnaya Hotel			
Express Credit Commercial Bank, 3rd Pryadilnaya ul. 3	367-2979		
Express-Boyd	203-2675		
Expressen, ul. Bolshaya Dorogomilovskaya 14, kv. 66	243-7232		

F

	Phone	Fax	Telex
F & C Trade Corporation	281-2964		
F. Hoffmann-La Roche LTD, Per. Sadovskikh 4, kv. 13	209-6808	200-4275	413090
Fabeg JV (FRG), ul. Dobroslobodskaya 7/1, str. 4, kv. 33	267-6962	200-2216	411700
FABSA International Trading and Consulting, Kutuzovskiy prosp. 7/4, korpus 6, kv. 19	243-9293	230-2027	413026
Face to Face JV, Proyezd Serova 4	288-8354		411630
Fairn & Swanson Ltd., Krasnopresnenskaya nab. 12	253-9408		
Leninskiy prospekt 78	131-9129		
Fakel Cinema, Shosse Entuziastov 15/16	362-1168		
Fakt, Khrovoshevskoye shosse 41	299-0004	941-0900	411712
Falkon JV (US), Kutuzovskiy prospekt 2/1, Hotel Ukraina	243-3256	200-2171	411172
Fambris JV (UK), ul. Zoy i Alexandra Kosmedemyyanskikh 31	159-6356	159-6356	
Famiglia Cristiana, Kutuzovskiy prospekt 14, kv. 50	243-1932		413064
Fantest, ul. Plekhanova 17/1	368-4769	369-1065	
Far Eastern Economic Review, Rublevskoye sh. 36, kv. 257-258	415-4318	415-2937	
Farkhad cafe, Bolshaya Marfinskaya 4	218-4136		
Farmakon, ul. Tverskaya 4	292-0843		
Farmitalia Carlo Erba, Koroviy val 7, office 1	237-2622	230-2032	413460
FATA European Group SrL, Koroviy val 7, Office 6	236-2141	230-2477	413916
Faxon International, ul. Kuusinena 21b	987-7431	943-0089	
Fazis-Moscow JV Filial (FRG), ul. Sadovaya-Triumfalnaya 12	200-2792	253-9316	411169
Federal Express, Krasnopresnenskaya nab. 12, flr. 1, Ent. 3	253-1641	253-1066	413904
Fel Funk - Electronic Labor, Koroviy val 7, kv. 100	238-9995	230-2824	413017
Femker JV, ul. Dubninskaya 83/4	928-2492		
Fer-Chip JV (Singapore), Maly Karetny per. 4			
Ferrostaal, see MAN AG, Munchen			
Festo-Didactic JV (Austria), 2nd Baumanskaya ul. 5	263-6098	267-4984	
Fexima, ul. Sadovaya-Samotechnaya 4a	923-8001	200-2280	413186
Fiat, Trekhprudny per. 11/13, 2nd flr	299-0229	200-0289	413458
Fidimage JV (US), ul. Gertsena 19	291-4536		
Fifth Floor Studio (Na Pyatom Etazhe), Kostomarovskiy per. 3	297-6564		
Filer Joint Stock Company	562-0166		

	Phone	Fax	Telex
Financial and Business News, ul. Bozhenko 14/4	417-0479	417-1229	
Financial Times, Kutuzovskiy prospekt 14, kv. 1	230-2267		413300
Finansovaya Gazeta, ul. Krzhizhanovskovo 14	124-3802		
Finansy i Statistika Publishers, ul. Chernyshevskovo 7	925-4709		
Finatec S.A., Krasnopresnenskaya nab. 12, #2001-2002a	253-7183	253-9904	413920
Fininvest, Suvorovskiy bulvar 8	203-2355	291-5550	
Finistbank, Khamovnicheskiy val	242-0282		
Finmeccanica Group, ul. Mytnaya 1, kv. 33	230-1110	230-2769	413233
Finn-Stroi Oy, Koroviy val 7, Office 10	237-1250	230-2202	413950
Finnair, Proyezd Khudozhestvennovo Teatra 6	292-8788	200-1288	413902
Sheremetevo II	578-2718		413902
Finnart JV (Finland), Petrovsko-Razumovskiy proyezd 17	214-5277		
Finnboard, see Finnpap-Finnbumaga			
Finncell, see Finnpap-Finnbumaga			
Finnish Radio & TV, Koroviy val 7, kv. 122	237-1047	230-2876	413054
Finnish School, Kropotkinskaya per. 15/17	246-4027	230-2721	413405
Finnish-Soviet Chamber of Commerce, Pokrovskiy bulvar 4/17, kv. 2	925-9001	230-2711	413406
Finnpap-Finnbunaga, Pokrovskiy bulvar 4/17, korpus 4a	227-0022	200-3293	413976
Finprogetti, see Programma 2000			
Finpromerchant, see Programma 2000			
Finsider, see ILVA/Finsider			
Fire (Emergency Assistance)	01		
First Gallery, The, Strastnoy bulvar 7	299-0498		
Fish Development Service Company JV (FRG), Rozhdestvenskiy bulvar 9	926-5828	230-2487	
Fisherman's Harbor, ul. 1st Tverskaya-Yamskaya 46A	251-3379	250-1302	
Service, Krasnobogatyrskaya 79	963-9077		
Fitil Cinema, Frunzenskaya nab. 12	245-0438		
Flakt Suomen Puhallintehdas Oy, Per. Sadovskikh 4, kv. 3	209-3726	200-0253	413483
Flamingo Hotel, see Inflotel			
Flamingo JV Filial, ul. Sushchevskiy val 50	289-2566		
Flash Telecomm, see Sovamer Trading Company			
Flax Union JV, Rublevskoye shosse 36, korpus 2			
Fleet Street International Ltd., Novy Arbat 56, Kv. 1108-1109	290-8527		
Flora JV (Austria), ul. Vavilova 15	209-8855		411045
Flying Mouse Cabaret, see Lyetuchaya Mysh Cabaret			
FMC Corporation, Gruzinskiy per. 3, kv. 201-202	254-4119	200-2221	413979
Fobit Car Rental, 1st Dorozhny proyezd 3a	315-0134		
Fonon International JV, ul. Buzheninova 16	963-0180	288-9598	412243
Food & Toy Processing JV (Australia), Aviatsionny per. 5	152-1800		
Food Orders Store, Biryulevskaya ul. 37	326-4477		
ForbesProgress JV (USA), ul. Malogvardeyskaya 41	140-1970	140-0562	
Ford Motor Company, ul. Gorbunova 14	447-3804		
ul. Marx-Engelsa 8	203-9237		
Foreign Books, ul. Prechistenka 31	203-9263		
Foreign Correspondents Association, Suvorovskiy bulvar 6, room 308	203-3616		
Foreign Literature Library, Ulyanovskaya ul. 1	227-8810		
Foremost Progress JV (Canada), Staraya Basmannaya ul. 20, str. 8	261-3530		411255

	Phone	Fax	Telex
Forepost Information Service, ul. Skhodnenskaya 26	555-5510	420-2459	
Formula Information Technologies Center, 3rd Neglinny per. 5	925-6897	432-9294	
Forto, ul. Mytnaya 11	236-4467		
Fortuna JV (Spain), ul. Markhlevskovo 13/1	925-3679	230-2387	411211
Fortune, Kutuzovskiy prospekt 14, kv. 3-4	243-1511	243-3752	413433
Forum Cinema, Sadovaya Sukharevskaya 14	208-2220		
Fotopro JV (FRG), 2nd Smolenskiy per. 2/3	241-0861		
Foundation for Economic Development of Russia, Maly Gnezdnikovskiy per. 4	229-9558		
Framatome, Pereulok Sadovskikh 4, kv. 4	209-2838	243-7262	413285
Francaise, Le, Pullman Iris Hotel	488-8000		
Franco-Serra Italia, ul. Tverskaya 1			
Franco-Soviet Chamber of Commerce, Pokrovskiy bulvar 4/17, kv. 3	297-9092	230-2277	413326
Frankfurter Algemeine Zeitung, Kutuzovskiy prospekt 7/4, korpus 5, kv. 28	243-5388		413313
Franki Gritop JV (Italy), ul. B. Cheremushkinskaya 19b	126-3506	200-4212	
French Bread Bakery, Lazarevskiy proyezd 4 ul. Generala Glagoleva 30			
French School, Spasonalivkovskiy per. 12/16	237-4636		
Frezenius JV (FRG), Kolomenskiy proyezd 4	118-8347	288-9567	
Froesch, see Hemaks			
FTI JV, Chapayevskiy per. 14	157-0672	231-3094	
Fuji Photo Store, Novy Arbat 25	203-7307		
Fuji TV, ul. Bolshaya Dorogomilovskaya 14, kv. 86	230-2514	230-2349	413198
Furniture Store, Leninskiy prospekt 64	137-0291		
Fyodorov's Institute, see Mikrokhirugiya Glaza			

G

G.K. Etno JV (Hong Kong), ul. Ulyanova 4, korpus 1	335-0267		
G.V.F. Company Ltd.	275-4081	275-4081	
Gala-Disk JV (FRG), Mozhayskoye shosse 5	443-7805	443-8644	413017
Gala-Kameron JV (UK), Zemlyanoi val 54	297-2381		
Galaxy Restaurant & Pub, Selskokhozyaystvennaya per. 2	181-2074		
Galika AG, Krasnopresnenskaya nab., Office 717	253-2717	253-9160	
Galla International, Bolshaya Filevskaya 14-2, kv. 11	145-4821	145-0634	
GAM-Impianti SA, Krasnopresnenskaya nab., Office 1447	253-1777	253-9703	
Gamma-Agence Photo, ul. Obrucheva 4, kor. 2, kv. 155-156	936-4173		
Gamos JV (US), ul. Dimitrova 7/8	230-1208	253-9703	411691
Garanti Bank, Mezhdunarodnaya II, room 1425	253-1589	253-1425	
Garantpost JV, Varshavskoye shosse 37	117-0040		
Garden Bar, Intourist Hotel Lobby			
Garmonia JV (India), ul. Petrovka 25	200-6375	230-2057	411653
Gasagroprom of Russia, Orlikov per. 3	208-5833		
Gazkro JV, ul. Verkhnyaya Radishchevskaya 17	272-1600	271-1029	
Gazprom Concern, Maly Stroiteley ul. 8/1	133-1300		
Gazprombank, ul. Stroiteley 8	131-0971	133-8490	
GE-CGR Medical Systems, Krasnopresnenskaya nab. 12, office 1542	253-1542	253-9402	413904

	Phone	Fax	Telex
Gebr. v.d. Berg Moving and Storage	140-6571		
GEC Alsthom, Pokrovskiy bulvar 4/17, kv. 21	207-7002	230-2688	413115
Gemeenschappelijke Pers Dienst (GPD), Rublevskoye shosse 36, kv. 239	415-4312	415-4309	
General Business JV (Italy), ul. Ostuzheva 7, str. 2	202-8501	200-2217	
General Electric Co., Pokrovskiy bulvar 4/17, kv 20	297-2995	230-2882	413236
Generale Bank, Krasnopresnenskaya nab. 12, #1705-1706	253-7572	253-9778	413904
Gennaya Inzheneriya, ul. Miklukho-Maklaya 16/10	335-1800		
Geo, Kutuzovskiy prospekt 7/4, kv. 314	230-2748		
Geokor JV (Thailand), Teterinskiy per. 12/2	297-5514		
Geonora JV (FRG), ul. Sovetskoy Armii 6	288-9190		411700
Georam JV, Leninskiye gory, MGU, Geography Faculty	939-3772	939-0126	
Georgian Cultural Center, ul. Arbat 42			
Geosoft JV (Austria), Podsosenskiy per. 26, korpus 1,2	256-2610	230-2390	414455
Geotim JV, ul. Miklukho-Maklaya 23	433-6265		
Gerate und Reglerwerk, Leipzig GmbH, Leninskiy prospekt 95a	132-5347	132-5347	414500
German Evangelical Church Services, German Embassy	238-1324		
German School, Novinskiy bulvar 20	291-8079		
German Wine Bar, Hotel Ukraine, 3rd floor	253-2316		
Gewika Industrieanlagen GmbH, ul. Pushkinskaya 9, #10	292-1784	292-6840	413162
Ghtumya, ul. Mytnaya 1, Office 21	230-0465		413049
Gildemeister AG, Krasnopresnenskaya nab. 12, Office 1501	253-5968	253-9908	413995
Ginseng, ul. Chernyshevskovo 32	227-1641		
Giza S.p.A., ul. Sadovaya-Sukharevskaya 2/34	925-3255		413208
Glasnet, ul. Vesnina 9/5	241-8243		
Glavk Ltd.	120-9568		
Glavmoskod JV, Sovetskaya pl. 2/6	921-0056	200-3212	
GlavUPDK, ul. Prechistenka 20	201-2326		
Accommodation Department	201-2398		
Appliance Repair	202-2865		
Gas Coupons	240-9680		
Home Service	201-2706		
Legal Department	563-8850		
Office Equipt. Repair	143-1502		
Phone Repair	202-2706		
Printing	203-2294		
Spetzavtotsenter, Kiyevskaya ul. 8	240-2092		
Supply Depot, ul. Durova 32	288-1263		
Tailor	280-5451		
Travel and Tickets	202-2725		
Glazur cafe, Smolenskiy bulvar 12	248-4438		
Glinka Concert Hall, ul. Fadeyeva 4	251-1066		
Glinka Museum Hall, ul. Fadeyeva 4	972-3237		
Global Edge, Gorokhovskiy per. 18	267-1850		
Global-System JV, ul. Bolshaya Serpukhovskaya 5			
Globaltest JV (US), Nagornaya ul. 24/9, kv. 2	127-6677	253-9771	413996
Globe and Mail of Canada, Kutuzovskiy prosp. 7/4, kv. 60	243-1362		413044
Gnesin Institute Opera Studio, ul. Vorovskovo 30/36	290-6737		
Goethe Institute Moscow, Leninskiy prospekt 95a	936-2457	243-1744	
Gogol Theater, ul. Kazakova 8a	261-5528		
Golden Dragon, Mezhdunarodnaya Exhibition Center	248-3602		

	Phone	Fax	Telex
Golden Dragon JV, 1st Krasnogvardeyskiy proyezd 12	255-2510		
Golden Lion JV, ul. Letchika Babushkina 26			
Golden Lotus JV (China), Krasnopresnenskaya nab., Expocenter	248-3602		
Golden Star Trading Company, Krasnopresnenskaya nab. 12, Office 703a	253-1265	253-9180	413541
Golf Club Tumba Moscow JV, ul. Dovzhenko 1	147-6254	200-2264	611700
Golodetz, see M. Golodetz (Overseas) Ltd.			
Good Luck JV (Holland), Izmaylovskoye shosse 69a	166-0363		
Gorizont Cinema, Komsomolskiy prospekt 21/10	245-3143		
Gorkiy House Museum, ul. Kachalova 6/2	290-0535		
Gorkiy Museum of Literature, ul. Vorovskovo 25a	290-5130		
Gorkiy Park Enterprises JV (UK), Krymskiy val 9	232-5385	237-3435	
Gorkom Grafikov, see Moscow Graphic Arts Society			
Gosstatistika Information Center, ul. Kirova 39	207-4681		
Gosstrakh, Nastasinskiy per.3, korpus 2	299-2942		
Gosstrakh RSFSR, Neglinnaya 23	200-2995		
Gotabanken, Pokrovskiy bulvar 4/17, kv. 4	207-3429	230-2456	413188
Grat JV (FRG), ul. Kastanayevskaya 8	145-2123		
Greek Orthodox Services, Telegrafny per. 15a	923-4605		
Greek Restaurant, On board the Aleksandr Blok	255-9278		
Greenfield JV (Malta), Raushskaya nab. 4	318-2218	975-2165	
Griphon Travel, Hotel Ukraine Service Bureau	243-2595		
GRW Leipzig, see Gerate und Reglerwerk, Leipzig GmbH			
Guangming Daily, Kutuzovskiy prospekt 7/4, kv. 146	243-1779		413086
Guardian, The, Gruzinskiy per. 3, kv. 75-76	254-4354		413945
Guelman Gallery, ul. Dimitrova 2/6	238-8492		
Gummerus Publications, ul. Alabyana 10, kv. 347	198-6138		413094
Guria cafe, Komsomolskiy prospekt 7/3	246-0378		
Gutehoffnungshutte, see Man AG			
GVM International, ul. Marshala Vasilevskovo 1, korpus 2	196-6150	943-0023	
Gypsy Theater 'Romen', Leningradskiy prospekt 32/2	250-7353		

H

H.G.S. JV (Austria), ul. Petrovka 26	925-6112	200-6308	411238
Haagsche Courant, ZOP, ul. Marksistskaya 1, kv. 1	270-1539		413544
Habaford (FRG), ul. Osipenko 77	231-8122	231-3094	
HAKA Corporation, see EKA Corporation			
Halliburton Company, 3rd Tverskaya-Yamskaya 29/6, kv. 8	251-3461		
Hankkija, see Novera			
Hanoi Cinema, Litovskiy bulvar 7	425-6101		
Hanoi JV (Vietnam), Prospekt 60-letiya Oktyabrya 20/21	125-6001		
Hantarex S.U., ul. Obrucheva 36	334-2974	420-2250	412160
Hantarex Vek, Maly Gnezdnikovskiy per. 2/4	229-3861	420-2250	412160
Hanver JV, ul. Simonovskiy val 12	274-5466		
Hard Rock Cafe, see Viktoria (Hard Rock Cafe) cafe			
Hatha Osthandels GmbH	124-9120		
Havana Cinema, ul. Sheremetevskaya 6	281-9464		
Heinrich Klingenberg International Moving, Prospekt Vernadskovo 103, korpus 1, kv. 58	434-2414		
Helsingin Sanomat, ul. 26th Bakinskikh-Komissarov 9, kv. 6	434-3685	230-2421	413053

	Phone	Fax	Telex
Hemaks, Krutitskiy val 3, korpus 2, kv. 105	276-9792		413440
Herman Berstorff Machinenbau GmbH, Sh. Frezer 17	170-3101	170-4550	413600
Hermes Tyumen-Moscow Exchange	245-6265		
Hertz Car Rental, Leninskiy prospekt 152	434-5332		
Sheremetevo II	578-7532		
Hewlett Packard, VDNKh Technopark, Building 2	181-8002		
Pokrovskiy bulvar 4/17, kv. 12	923-5001	230-2611	413225
High-Tech Stroi JV, 2nd Zachatyevskiy per. 2, str. 18	201-4839		
Hines Interests, Leninskiy prospekt 146	434-2666		
Hiruta Co., Ltd. Japan, ul. Mytnaya 1	238-4955	230-2648	413907
Historical Museum, Krasnaya ploshchad 1/2	928-8452		
History of Moscow Museum, Novaya ploshchad 12	924-8490		
Hitachi, Krasnopresnenskaya nab. 12, Office 2004	253-5960	253-1854	
HiTechStroi JV (Finland), 2nd Zachatyevskiy per. 2, str. 13	941-6057		
Hoechst, ul. Kalyayevskaya 17	973-2451	973-2375	
Hoechst Pharma, Trekhprudny per. 11/13	299-8285	200-2206	413138
Hokkaido Shimbun, Kutuzovskiy prospekt 9, kv. 24	243-6998	230-2390	
Hollming, Kursovoy per. 9, Office 6	202-1441	200-1259	413176
Holographic Systems, Inc., ul. Novokuznetskaya 17/19	231-0426		
Homatek JV (FRG), ul. Ordzhonikidze 11	234-9869	230-2227	411025
Honda, Petrovskiy Passage, 1st line, ul. Petrovka 10	921-6503		
Honeywell, Inc., Trekhprudny per. 11/13, 3rd flr	299-6543		413255
Hopf Service	255-2709		
Horse-breeding Museum, Timiryazevskaya ul. 44	216-1003		
Hotel-Sovetskiy JV (France), Leningradskiy prosp. 32/2	250-7255		411671
House of Trade Unions (Kolonny Zal),			
Pushkinskaya ul. 1	292-0178		
Huhtamaki Oy, ul. Mytnaya 1, kv. 15	230-0443	230-2245	413993
Humbolt-Zab Zementanlagenbau GmbH,			
ul. Kalanchevskaya 6/2, korpus 1	262-8299	975-1915	413704
Hungarian Chamber of Commerce	253-2921	252-0930	
Hungarian School, ul. Olaf Palme 5, korpus 2	143-6057		
Hungexpo, ul. Vorovskovo 21	291-1845	202-8241	414340.
Hunstman-Aeromar JV, Sheremetevo II, K-340	578-3132	578-2714	
Hunter Douglas Europe B.V.,			
Stary Petrovsko-Razumovskiy proyezd 2	212-5112	213-5354	413677
Huolintakeskus	299-7773		
Hurriyet, Kutuzovskiy prospekt 7/4, kv. 151	243-1489		
Hypo Bank, Bolshoy Gnezdnikovskiy per. 7, 4th flr	200-4627	200-4295	413675
Hyundai, Krasnopresnenskaya nab. 12, Office 1809	253-1683	253-1682	413698
HZZ-Moskau, see Humbolt-Zab Zementanlagenbau GmbH			

I

I-Kub-K JV (US), ul. Nezhdanovoy 2a	229-9862		411809
I.M.S. Corp. JV (USA), ul. Svobody 8/4	491-8412		
I.V.K. International, Main Office: Hotel Intourist	203-9439	203-9355	
2nd Pugachevskaya ul. 10, korpus 1	161-2954		
IAEG	253-1765		
IAN, see ITAR (Novosti Information Agency)			
Iarus JV, ul. Shchuseva 3	290-3294		

	Phone	Fax	Telex
Iberia, Kuznetskiy Most 3	921-9293	230-2242	
Sheremetevo II	578-2791	578-2789	
Ibis JV (UK), ul. Rozhdestvenka 11	923-4632		411488
IBM Corporation, ul. Bakhrushina 18	235-6602	230-2733	413232
Ibris JV (Brazil)	921-2683		
Ibusz, ul. Medvedeva 5	299-7402	299-8876	414400
ICL, see International Computers Limited			
Idea International JV (Canada),			
1st Krasnoselskiy per. 7/9, str. 5, kv. 224	264-0664	200-2217	
IHI, see Ishikawajima-Harima Heavy Industries			
III (Information, Research & Publishing International),			
Prospekt Vernadskovo 84	436-0758		
Ikarus-Cooperation JV (Hungary), Kropotkinskiy per. 7	245-2300	230-2469	414336
IKEA International A/S, ul. Obrucheva 4, korpus 2	936-2677	936-2198	
Ikon JV (UK), ul. Moskovrechye 31, korpus 2	362-8774	230-2574	
IKON, KRO (Radio & TV), TROUW,			
Leninskiy prospekt 45, kv. 427	135-1172	230-2010	413304
Ikpa JV (Finland), ul. Tverskaya 23	291-9491	253-9794	411238
Il Giornale, ul. Mytnaya 3, kv. 50-1	938-2176		413949
Il Giorno, Kutuzovskiy prospekt 13, kv. 43	243-1550	243-4744	413664
Il Sole/24 Ore, Rublevskoye shosse 26, korpus 1, kv. 7	415-4034		413634
Illuzion Cinema, Kotelnicheskaya nab. 1/15	227-4339		
ILM Handleskontor GmbH & CO KG,			
Podkopayevskiy per. 9, str. 2	297-6839	230-2302	414357
ILVA/Finsider, ul. Mytnaya 1, kv. 32-33	230-1110	230-2769	413233
Imatran Voima OY, Pereulok Sadovskikh 4, kv.1	209-6856	200-1277	413247
Imax Show International JV (US), Trekhgorny val 6	205-7233	205-7438	
IMC JV (US), ul.Svobody 8/4	491-8412		
IMM-Bivest JV (UK), ul. Seleznevskaya 13	258-8602	258-6802	
IMO JV (FRG), Yakimanskaya nab. 10/2	238-9021		
Imperial Chemical Industries PLC,			
Krasnopresnenskaya nab. 12, Office 1209	253-2056	230-2044	413241
Imporleste Representacoes, S.A.,			
ul. Bolshaya Ordynka 50, kv. 3-4	233-8597	230-2814	416222
Impulse-Apparat JV (Korea), Vspolny per. 13	290-4269	290-4269	412201
In Vino Restaurant, Ukraine Hotel, 2nd floor	243-2316		
Inatours	253-1529		
Inbio JV (FRG), ul. Bolshaya Kommunisticheskaya 27	271-1269	253-9310	411432
Inbiser, ul. Belomorskaya 26	455-9210		
Inbor-Induro JV (FRG),			
Rublevskoye shosse 44, korpus 2, kv. 294	413-0359		414756
Incomtrade JV, Podsosenskiy per. 28	113-2157	310-7016	
Independent Radio News,			
ul. Akad. Koroleva 4, korpus 2, kv. 19-20	215-1147		
Independent Television News,			
ul. Marksistskaya 1, kv. 47-48	270-6688	274-0004	413543
Independent, The, ul. Marksistskaya 1, kv. 27	270-7232	270-7232	413525
Independiente (El), Rublevskoye shosse 26, kor. 1, kv. 294	415-4138	415-2936	413630
Indian School, Dorogomilovskaya 32	240-6437		
Indonesian School, Novokuznetskaya 12	231-9549		
Induro, Krasnopresnenskaya nab. 12, Office 807	253-2807	253-1577	
Industrie Pirelli SpA, Krasnopresnenskaya nab. 12, #1003	253-2568		413023

	Phone	Fax	Telex
Industrieberatung Wilkening,			
ul. Bolshaya Molchanovka 34, bdg. 2	291-4735	200-2263	411775
Ineko JV (US), ul. Kalibrovskaya 22a	281-4622		
Inex JV (Japan), Hotel Orlenok, room 514-515	939-8016	253-9506	413593
INEX Russian Language Center	126-0016		
Infa-Otel JV (Finland), ul. Rozhdestvenka 3	928-9169	230-2186	411620
Infatel JV (Japan), ul. Tverskaya 7	201-9174	292-0616	414793
Infiks JV, ul. Yablochkova 5	210-2832		
Infinit JV (Austria), ul. Pyatnitskaya 29/8	231-3805	230-2062	
Inflotel, Krasnopresnenskaya nab. 12, docking	255-9278		
Info-Global JV (FRG), Tikhvinskaya per. 10/12	241-3228		
Infocom JV (Finland), Kuznetskiy Most 4	925-1235	200-3219	
Inforcom Consulting, Merzlyakovskaya per. 8	925-6644		
Inform-Pravo JV, ul. Druzhby 10/32	143-6771	938-2120	411734
Informarket JV (Holland),			
ul. Krzhizhanovskovo 14, korpus 3	124-4504		
Informatika NPC JV, ul. Skhodnenskaya 6	497-6378	497-7200	
Information Computer Enterprise JV (US),			
VDNKh, Pavilion 4	187-9331	187-8830	411665
Information Moscow, Leninskiy prospect 45, kv. 426	135-1164	230-2010	413199
Informbank, ul. Timura Frunze 8/5	245-0213	245-0226	
Forminvest JV (Switz.), ul. Malaya Bronnaya 28/2	299-0587	334-1921	412196
Informlitsenzreklama JV (FRG),			
Leninskiy prospekt 146, office 1901	438-8100	230-2818	411670
Informprogress JV (US), ul. Kosygina 15	939-8412		
InformVES, Ovchinnikovskaya nab. 18/1	220-1606		
Ingersoll-Rand Company,			
Krasnopresnenskaya nab. 12, Office 1101	253-7151	253-9075	413969
Ingosstrakh Insurance Company, ul. Pyatnitskaya 12	231-1677	230-2518	411144
INIOR Institute	262-8988		
Inko Ltd. JV (Finland), Novy Arbat 16	290-6922	200-1209	411286
Inkom Bank -- Central Division,			
Nametkina, ul. 14, korpus 1	332-0699	331-8833	
Sibirskiy proyezd 2, korpus 2	270-9290		
Inkom JV, Zubovskaya ploshchad 3	299-4937		
Inkomeks JV, ul. Myasnitskaya 45	921-1085	200-2258	
Inkompex JV, ul. Krivorozhskaya 33	113-2025	310-7016	
Inkoros	928-4739	928-4739	
Inlingua, Semenovskaya nab. 2/1	360-0874	360-0874	
Inmet JV (Switz.), Tsvetnoy bulvar 16	200-2779	253-9904	413920
InNis JV (Japan), 7th Proyezd Maryioni Roschi	971-0386		
ul. Bolshaya Ordynka 32	927-1187	200-3207	411449
Innostrannaya Kniga, ul. Prechistenka 31	203-9263		
Used Book Store, ul. Kachalova 16	290-4082		
Innovation Land Bank, ul. Krasikova 32, room 605	129-1211		
Innovation, Information, Intellect & Communication,			
ul. Nezhdanovoy 2a	229-4668	229-3237	411809
Inpred, Krasnopresnenskaya nab. 12	253-7075	253-9913	411486
Inpribor JV (Austria), ul. Koshtoyantsa 1A	432-0975		
Inprogress JV, Pereulok Voyevodina 2/1, kv. 3	241-1690	241-5927	
Inrosspreus JV (FRG), ul. Skakovaya 17	945-5030	253-9001	
Inrosvet JV (Spain), ul. Udaltsova 67a	133-8528	288-9522	411466
Inservice, ul. Myaskovskaya 17/7	203-9945	200-1295	411044

	Phone	Fax	Telex
Institute for Systems Studies, 60-Letiya Oktyabrya 9, 5th floor	135-4222		
Institute of Public Health Managers	289-4055		
Instituto Bancario San Paolo di Torino, 1st Krasnogvardeyskiy Proyezd, Exh. Complex, Pav. 2	256-7444	253-9483	413599
Inta JV (Spain), ul. Novoalekseyevskaya 16	283-5718	288-9522	
Intark JV (FRG), Sechenovskiy per. 6, str. 1	273-2361		
Intarkor International JV (FRG), Nizhniy Taganskiy tupik 11, str. 2	271-2934		
Intekkom JV (Finland), ul. Usiyevicha 22	155-4535		
Intekkom JV (Switz.), Shosse Entuziastov 5	277-4060		411024
Inteko JV (Austria), ul. Lesnaya 41	258-6787	258-4411	411072
Intel Technologies, ul. Pyatnitskaya 18/5	231-9083		
Intelmas JV (FRG), ul. Prechistenka 37, str. 2	231-7596		
Inter Aks JV, Volzhskiy bulvar 114a, korpus 9	179-3045		
Inter MTD JV, Seliverstov per. 8	208-2880	233-1711	
Inter Oceanic Factors Agency Inc., Bezbozhny per. 16, kv. 38	280-8731		413277
Inter Techno Corporation, Stary Petrovsko-Razumovskiy proyezd 6/8-3, kv. 76	214-9801	361-7555	
Inter-Republican Universal Trade Exchange	208-6681		
Inter-Verso JV (UK), ul. Sadovo-Spasskaya 20	207-6793	200-2204	
Interagra, ul. Pushkinskaya 9, kv. 8	292-3036	230-2233	413182
Interagrokompleks JV (Austria), Mozhayskoye shosse 24	449-5840		
Interagrosystems JV (FRG), ul. Yartsevskaya 30, kom. 1107	141-3396		
Interagrotex JV (Sweden), ul. Pryanishnikova 31	482-4613	973-2417	411624
Interalpha	151-1168	245-6473	
Interastro JV (Hungary), ul. Profsoyuznaya 32/34			
Interatlantic JV, ul. Izhorskaya 7	486-4746	288-9529	207301
InterAvto M	297-0003		
Interavtocom JV (Italy), Volgogradskiy prospekt 42	276-8824		411333
Interbite JV, Leninskiy prospekt 52	137-4769		
Interbook JV (Yugoslavia), 2nd Smolenskiy per. 1/4	241-6399	230-2403	411871
Intercar JV (FRG) -- offices, ul. Akademika Pilyugina 14	936-2469		
Supermarket JV, ul. Bolshaya Sadovaya 5/1	209-6591		413597
Interclub Moscow JV (FRG), ul. Begovaya 22, kv. 1	481-7772		
Intercom JV (Austria), ul. Bolshaya Ordynka 41	231-1502	239-1240	
Interconcepts, Inc., ul. Dovzhenko 12, korpus 1	143-7511	938-2123	413610
Intercontact Agroservice JV (Holland), ul. Bolshaya Filevskaya 37, korpus 1	144-6818	144-0558	411311
Intercoop, Krasnopresnenskaya nab. 12, Office 1517	253-1517	253-9173	
Intercreditcard, Grafskiy per. 10/12, str. 2	284-4151		
Intercross JV, see Chelek Agroplast JV filial			
Intercross Trading Corporation, Zubovskiy bulvar 4	201-8837	230-2170	411323
Interdean AG, Rublevskoye shosse 36, korpus 2, kv. 212	415-4296	415-2959	413587
Interdepartmental Council for Foreign Advertising, ul. Kuybysheva 6	231-8428		
Interdesign JV, Dokuchayev per. 2	200-4254	200-4254	411672
Interdum Corporation JV, ul. Im. Kurchatova 182	190-5171		411594
Intereco JV (UK), Kursovoy per. 9	172-7674	200-2018	

	Phone	Fax	Telex
Interexpert JV, Berezhkovskaya nab. 6	240-5883	240-4869	
Interexpo, Krasnopresnenskaya nab. 12, Office 1335	253-1335	253-9067	413649
Interexpressia JV (Switz.), ul. Neglinnaya 27/2/26	299-5894		
Interface JV, ul. Klimashkina 9	253-3453		411429
Interfax	250-9257		
Interferma JV, ul. Timura Frunze 34, Ship Vermont	243-7855	200-3220	
Interflug, ul. Bolshaya Spasskaya 12	280-7233		
Intergeomodel JV, see PPS-Intergeomodel JV			
Interglekors	190-8858		
Intergrafservice JV (FRG), Sushchevskiy val 49	289-7253	219-8431	
Intergraph Corp., Frunzenskaya nab. 8, kv. 47	246-6328		
Interimpex-Engineering JV, ul. Novocheremushkinskaya 60, korpus 2	332-6931	420-2002	
Interimpulse JV, Prospekt Mira 114b	287-2022		
Interinform JV (Austria), ul. Petrovka 26	921-1971	290-6002	412211
Interinformset JV (Australia), ul. Tverskaya 5/6	203-7571	200-4256	411666
Interinvest JV, Mozhayskoye shosse 41	443-1835		
Interjuris JV, ul. Kirova 24, str. 3-4	923-5604	923-5485	
Interkeramika JV (Finland), ul. Ozernaya 48	430-7770		
Interkholod JV, ul. Kostyakova 12	210-3601		411581
Interkinofototekhnika JV (Switzerland), Leningradskiy prospekt 47, Nikfi	157-2923		
Interkinotcentr JV (FRG), ul. Druzhinnikovskaya 15	255-9420		
Interkom JV (Bulgaria), Prospekt Vernadskovo 4	490-3721		411088
Interkontakt JV, ul. Chaykovskovo 11	255-4613	243-5126	41172
Interkoop JV (Italy), Pereulok Gorkovo 3/1	127-5695	310-7057	
Interkor JV (Austria), Internatsionalnaya ul. 10	297-0809		
Interkous JV, Malaya Kolkhoznaya pl. 6, str. 2	250-8993		
Interkovent JV (Sweden), Ulyanovskaya ul. 38/23	227-0700		411700
InterLazerLeasing JV (UK), ul. Gertsena 22/26, rooms 26-8	291-4870	230-2309	
Interling JV (US), Shosse Entuziastov 62	305-0239		
Interlink JV (FRG), ul. Narodnovo Opolcheniya 34	946-8711	943-0087	411683
Interlink JV (Sweden), ul. Izhorskaya 7	486-2696	486-4748	
Intermarket Shop JV, ul. Mitskevicha 10	291-7656		
Intermebel JV, ul. Litvina-Sedova 26/9	259-6933		
Intermechanika JV (Hong Kong), Lomonosovskiy prospekt 24	939-3262	939-0186	411483
Intermed, ul. Dimitrova 31	238-2312		414380
Intermed Dental Clinic, ul. Durova 26, korpus 6	284-7403		
Intermed JV (FRG) Head Office, Kolkhoznaya pl. 5/1	928-5757	208-1738	
Intermedbio-IMB JV (US), Leninskiy prospekt 156	434-1020	434-1020	411649
Intermedia International S.r.L., Begovaya alleya 11, k. 629	945-2764	946-1100	
Intermedservice JV, Hotel Intourist, rooms 2030-2031	203-8631	200-8282	411271
Intermedtest JV (Switz.), Abrikosovskiy per. 1	248-5317	292-6511	
Intermet Engineering JV, Leninskiy prospekt 2a	238-3536	230-2223	208266
Intermetod JV, Frunzenskaya nab. 30	242-8881		413832
Intermicro JV (Austria), Nizhnyaya Krasnoselskaya 39	264-2927	200-2238	411035
Internal Affairs with Moscow City Council, Main Dep., Petrovka 38	200-8342		
International Association of Business Cooperation, Shelepikhinskoye shosse 11, kv. 64	259-6788		

	Phone	Fax	Telex
International Bank of Economic Cooperation, Kuznetskiy Most 15	928-9906		
ul. Mashi Poryvayevoy	975-3861	975-2202	
International Center for Small Enterprise Development, MGU, Humanities Faculty, korpus 2, k. 473	939-3555	939-0877	
International Computers Limited, ul. Vavilova 83, kv. 5	134-9549	938-2016	413074
International Exch. of Information and Telecomm., Leningradskiy prospekt 80/2	158-7492	230-2819	411127
International Exhibition Complex, Krasnopresnenskaya nab.	268-1340		
International Federation of Peace and Consensus, Prospect Mira 36	280-0850		
International Food Exchange	455-4782	186-1338	
International Foundation for the Survival and Dev. of Humanity, ul. Vesnina 9/5	241-8243		
International Fund of Goodwill and Health, Chernyshevskovo ul. 22-1	297-4999		
International Health Care, Gruzinskiy per. 3, korpus 2	253-0703		
International Information Service JV (Italy), ul. Sivashskaya 4/2	110-5702		411195
International Interest Group, Inc., ul. Sadovaya-Samotechnaya 9, kv. 34	979-7065		
International Investment Bank, ul. Mashi Poryvayevoy	975-4008	975-2070	411358
International Medical Center JV, ul. Obukha 14	297-1453		
International Moscow Bank JV, ul. Plyushchikha 37	246-2567		411174
International Organization of Economic Cooperation, ul. Novy Arbat 56	290-9111		411141
International Post Office, Varshavskoye shosse 37	114-4584		
International Processing Systems	209-6095		
International Sports Exchange	201-1994	142-5915	
International Women's Club, c/o US Embassy	252-2508		
Interoko, ul. Petrovka 10	292-3451		
Interoko JV (FRG), Frunzenskaya nab. 30	242-8941		
Interolimp JV (FRG), Staropanskiy per. 1/5	928-3381	923-3545	411791
Interperiodika JV (US)	129-2900		
Interplastica, Hotel Leningradskaya, room 439	975-5328	230-2234	
Interpravo JV (Austria), Kholodilny per. 3	232-5922		
Interprint JV (Bulgaria), Butikovskiy per. 12	291-9597		
Interproekt JV (Italy), Novoslobodskaya ul. 58	258-9700	253-9702	
Interprogress JV, Miklukho-Maklaya 55a	241-7911		
Interprokom JV (FRG), Savvinskaya nab. 25	246-1105	247-1052	111541
Interquadro JV, 2nd Novopodmoskovny per. 4	150-9201	943-0059	413560
Interrocks JV, 2nd Shlyuzovoy per. 5/1	313-0769	290-3452	
Interrols JV (US), Krivokolenny per. 12	925-6951	924-1240	
Interros FTO	207-1275	207-2229	
Interrunis JV (Austria), ul. Myasnitskaya 24, str. 3-4	923-5604		911557
Interscrap JV (US), ul. Ostozhenka 26	299-8648	943-0052	413094
Interservice JV (FRG), Shlyuzovaya nab. 6	235-1347	230-2157	
Intershelf JV (UK), Kozhevnicheskaya ul. 11	235-5925	230-2301	411782
Intershtrikhkod JV (UK), Strastnoy bulvar 8	229-1933	229-3511	411871
Intersignal JV (US), Profsoyuznaya ul. 82	330-6528	333-1088	
Intersoft JV (US), Lomonosovskiy prospekt 18	930-5570	310-7050	411853
Intersoyuz JV (FRG), Pushkinskaya ploshchad 5	209-3755	230-2330	111121

	Phone	Fax	Telex
Intersputnik, 2nd Smolenskiy pereulok 1/4	244-0333		411288
Interstroy Service Division	450-9513		
Interstroy Standard JV, ul. Krzhizhanovskovo 13	124-3768		
Interstroyindustria JV, ul. Pyatnitskaya 2	233-4643	200-4256	
Interstroykompleks JV, ul. Sadovo-Sukharevskaya 2/34	925-2184		
Intersurdo JV (Sweden), Seliverstov per. 8	208-2821		
Intertap JV (Poland), Krasnoprudnaya ul. 24/2	264-2585	264-4116	412557
Intertechnologia JV Filial, Michurinskiy proyezd 1	939-3262		
Intertes JV (US), ul. Narodnovo Opolcheniya 34	947-8560		411683
Intertest JV (US), Telegrafny per. 9	923-1959		
Intertex JV, Nab. Novikova-Priboya 9, korpus 2	197-9195	273-1937	412176
Intertop JV (New Zealand), Tsvetnoy bulvar 21, str. 8	200-3009	200-3341	
Intertorg, Inc., Gruzinskiy per. 3, kv. 63-64	254-3162	253-9771	413996
Intertrade JV (Belgium), ul. Natashi Kovshovoi 16	925-6404		
Intertrest JV (US), Sadovnicheskaya nab. 1/15	233-0626		
Interunity JV (Panama), Novinskiy bulvar 40a	202-2082	230-2035	413932
Interural JV (Switzerland), ul. Tverskaya 9a, str.7	229-6688	973-2083	
Intervils JV (Australia), ul. Gorbunova 3	488-1361		
Intervodavtomatika JV (Bulgaria), ul. Khmeleva 7	208-5339		
Intour-Penta JV (Holland), Olympiyskiy prospekt 18/1	288-9729	288-2634	
Intourconsult JV (Austria), Kronshtadtskiy bulvar 43a	454-0039	454-3071	
Intourist, ul. Mokhovaya 16	292-5230		411331
Car Rental, Hotel Kosmos	215-6191		
Information	203-6962		
Intourist Hotel, ul. Tverskaya 3/5	203-4008		411823
Intourist Moscow, Stoleshnikov per. 11	923-5763	928-4813	
Museum Tours, Stoleshnikov per. 11	928-4515		
Translation Services, Stoleshnikov per. 11	928-4515		
Intourservice, Hotel Kosmos	215-7880		
Belinskovo, ul. 4a	203-5637	200-1243	411211
Car Rental	203-0096		
Central Excursion Bureau, ul. Tverskaya 1	203-0096		
Goods Delivery	287-3981		
Hotel Mezhdunarodnaya	253-2362		
Hotel Rossiya	298-1753		
Hotel Ukraine	243-2690		
Okhotny ryad 16	292-2365	200-1243	411211
Intourtrans, ul. Petrovka 15/13	927-1181	973-2045	411449
Intourtransavto	928-8614		
Intraco, ul. Timiryazevskaya 1/3	979-6895	210-0012	413686
Intrade A/S, Serebryany Bor, 19, line 4	947-7777		
Intrakon, 3rd Neglinny per. 5	200-6921		
Intravel, Hotel Kosmos, Mezzanine level	215-6780		411488
Intur-Kone JV, ul. 26 Bakinskikh Komissarov 9	434-5219		
Invemo JV, ul. Bakhrushina 28			
Investronic Holland b.v., Hotel Pekin, room 1103	200-5219	200-4222	413297
Invino JV (FRG), Kutuzovskiy prospekt 2/1	243-3000		411654
Invipo JV (FRG), ul. Bolshaya Molchanovka 34, str. 2	291-4713	200-2263	411775
Inyurcolleguia, ul. Tverskaya 5	203-6864	203-0826	411811
Inzhmebel JV (FRG), 2nd ul. Marinoy Roshchi 22	971-4288	961-6372	
Inzhplast GmBH JV, Perovskiy proyezd 35	273-7388		
Ipatco BRT S.A., ul. Petrovka 15, kv. 19-20	923-9330	200-1228	413267
IPS Theater Box Office, Hotel Metropol Lobby	927-6729		

	Phone	Fax	Telex
Iraqi Airways, ul. Pyatnitskaya 37	231-2974		
Sheremetevo II	578-2707		
Irik JV (Cyprus), ul. Gasheka 12, korpus 7, kv. 51	250-9563	230-2502	413072
Iris Car Rental	488-8000		
Iris JV (France), Beskudnikovskiy bulvar 59b	905-4381	485-5954	411856
Irish Times, ul. Marksistskaya 1, korpus 1, kv. 57-58	274-0051	274-0397	413537
IRSOTR, Serpukhovskiy val 8, kv. 69-70	232-4975		413566
Ishikawajima-Harima Heavy Industries Co., Inc., ul. Mytnaya 1. Office 7	230-1032	230-2756	413087
Iskra Cinema, ul. Kostyakova 10	216-2724		
Iskra Industry Co., Ltd., Pokrovskiy bulvar 4/17, kv. 30	298-5014		413239
Iskusstvo i Elektronika (Arts & Electronics) JV (US), ul. Gotvalda 10	251-0131	200-2232	
Issko JV (FRG)	152-5916		411432
Istok JV (India), ul. Granovskovo 2, bulvar 4-5	924-7434		411778
Istok-K Computer Network	245-5165		
Istros JV (Syria), Pereulok Sadovskikh 10	207-4406	291-0608	
IT Comercio Internacional, SA, see Imporleste Representacoes			
Italian School, ul. Lobachevskovo 38	431-4966		
Italian-Soviet Chamber of Commerce, ul. Vesnina 7	241-6517	230-2414	413171
Italimpex, ul. Mytnaya 1, kv. 16	230-0787	230-2696	413237
Italimpianti, ul. Mytnaya 1, kv. 31	238-9714	230-2093	413507
Italsovmont JV (Italy), see Italimpianti			
ITAR (Novosti Information Agency), Zubovskiy bulvar 4	201-2424	201-2119	411321
ITC, see Inter Techno Corportion			
Iteko JV (Switz.), 2nd Frunzenskaya ul. 10	242-0323	253-2736	411432
ITM JV (India), ul. Dovatora 12, korpus 2	247-0938		
Itoman & Co., LTD., ul. Mytnaya 1, 2nd flr	230-2605		413085
ITTM JV (Canada), Krasnopresnenskaya nab. 12, #736	253-1666	253-2736	411432
IVB Industrievertretungen GmbH, Leninskiy prospekt 95a, office 533	936-2446	936-2446	414500
Iveria Cafe, Minskoe shosse, 45th km	593-4159		
Izdatbank			
Izmailovo Concert Hall, Izmaylovskoye shosse 71	166-7844		
Izmailovo Hotel, Izmaylovskoye shosse 71	166-0145		
Izmailovo JV (Canada), Izmaylovskoye shosse 71	166-0165	166-2563	
Izmailovo Universal Exch.of Tourist & Resort Services and Goods, Ozerkovskaya nab. 50	235-6567	235-6063	
Izopleks JV (UK), ul. Shchinskaya 12, korpus 1	196-9315		
Izvestia-Burda JV (FRG), Pushkinskaya ploshchad 5	200-3462	230-2303	
Izvestiya, Pushkinskaya ploshchad 5	209-9100		

J

	Phone	Fax	Telex
J K Enterprises LTD., ul. Bolshaya Spasskaya 15	207-2931	208-8302	413621
Janayugom, ul. Akademika Anokhina 30, korpus 4, kv. 854	430-4517		
Japan Air Lines, Kuznetskiy Most 3	921-6448		413111
Sheremetevo II	578-2942		413922
Japan Sea Corporation, ul. Mytnaya 1, 2nd flr	237-2349	230-2790	413907
Japan-USSR Trade Association, ul. Mytnaya 1	237-2465		
Japanese School, Leninskiy prospekt 78	131-8733		
JAT (Yugoslav Airlines), Kuznetskiy Most 3	921-2846		

	Phone	Fax	Telex
Jazz Brunch, Metropol Hotel	927-6452		
Jazz Club, Kuznetskiy Most Metro	921-9744		
Jerusalem Company, ul. Bolshaya Ordynka 46	233-5941	233-0777	411640
Jever-Bistro, Rossiya Hotel, East entrance	298-2923		
Jewish Drama Studio Theater, Varshavskoye shosse 71	110-3758		
Jewish Music Theater, Taganskaya ploshchad 12	272-4924		
Jewish Synagogue, ul. Arkhipova 10	923-9697		
Jewish Youth Cultural Center Tkhiya, ul. Bolshaya Tulskaya 44	234-5297		
Jiji Press, ul. Sadovaya-Samotechnaya 12/24, kv. 21	200-1017	200-0231	413137
Jindo Rus, Hotel Intourist, 1st flr	203-9742		
Kolpachny per. 14	203-9742	227-1013	412130
Kosmos Hotel, Mezzanine	217-0025		
John Brown PLC, Pokrovskiy bulvar 4/17, kv. 27	207-3269	230-2315	413419
John Nurminen Oy, ul. Bolshaya Ochakovskoye 15a	430-7861	430-7862	411927
Joint Way JV (US), ul. Timiryazevskaya 4/12	216-8223	216-8627	
Josef Schmitter, Mezhdunarodnaya II, room 1207	253-1207	253-9361	411432
Joseph Egli AG, Leningradskaya Hotel, room 913	975-1752	975-4987	
Journal de Geneve (Le), ul. Bolshaya Spasskaya 12, kv. 30-2	230-2464		
Journal of Commerce/Knight-Ridder, ul. Karetny Ryad 10/5, kv. 43	299-1174	200-2216	
Journalists' Union Photocenter, see Photocenter of the Journalists' Union			
Julius Meinl Store, Leninskiy prospekt 146	438-3444		
Jupiter, Butyrskiy val 7	250-2300		
Jurakon International Agency JV, 1st Khoroshevskiy proyezd 14, korpus 3, kv. 86	946-0838	200-2217	411700
JV Medialink, Olympic Village, ul. Pelshe 3	462-1281		411424
JVC Shop, Leninskiy prospekt 60	137-2025		
Jyllands Posten, Rublevskoye shosse 26, korpus 1, kv. 117	415-2925		413553

K

	Phone	Fax	Telex
Kabelbel JV (Austria), ul. Belomorskaya 26	458-3486		
Kaleva Travel Agency Ltd., Hotel Intourist, room 801	203-6108		
Kalinka Stockmann, see Oy Stockmann AB			
Kamernaya Tsena Theater, Zemlyanoi val 64	297-3718		
Kamir Advertising Agency, ul. Goncharova 17a	219-0101		
Kamneft JV (FRG), ul. Narodnovo Opolcheniya 40, kor. 3	192-8057		114444
Kamos JV (Poland), Okhotny Ryad 18	203-2505	292-6511	411429
Kampo Mos JV (Spain), ul. Zorge 5	943-3913		
Kanematsu Corporation, Krasnopresnenskaya nab. 12, Office 1508	253-2485	253-9907	413480
Kansallis-Osake-Pankki, Pokrovskiy bulvar 4/17, kv. 4	207-3429	230-2456	413188
Kansan Uutiset, ul. Bolshaya Cherkizovskaya 5a, kv. 12	168-2524		413095
Karabakh, ul. Lipetskaya 52	329-7100		
Kareta cafe, Yermakova Roshcha 7a	256-2280		
Karina Restaurant, Solyanskiy proyezd 1-3	924-0369		
Kashtan Restaurant, Taganskaya ul. 40/42	272-6242		
Kastilia JV (Spain), Ozerkovskaya nab. 26			
Kato Aromatic, Krasnopresnenskaya nab. 12, office 1005	253-2581	253-2583	413714
Katyusha, 2/1 Semenovskaya nab.	360-0874	360-6317	911508
Kaufmann's Handel-Maatschappij N.V., Stary Petrovsko-Razumovskiy proyezd 2	212-2341	213-5354	413677

	Phone	Fax	Telex
Kaukomarkkinat Oy, Pokrovskiy bulvar 4/17, kv. 10	207-4144	298-4490	413278
Kawakami Trading Company, Ltd., ul. Pushkinskaya 9, kv. 9	292-9435	200-0249	413407
Kazakhstan Cinema, Leninskiy prospekt 105	433-4165		
Kazan Train Station, Komsomolskaya ploshchad 2	266-2843		
KBA-Planeta AG, Leninskiy prospekt 95a, room 531	132-5955	434-2072	414500
Kemira Oy, Koroviy val 7, kv. 12	236-0519	230-2354	413918
Keram-Optic Systems JV, ul. Vavilova 38	135-0387		
Kerch Cinema, ul. Biryulevskaya 17	326-1666		
Khelar Aasar, Leninskiy prospekt 148, kv. 138	434-4051		413946
Khemos JV (Finland), ul. Petrovka 17, str. 10	119-5968		
Khimbank, ul. Myasnitskaya 20	927-7701	928-4978	
Khoros JV (Sweden), Koptevskaya ul. 26, korpus 2	238-5946		
Khudozhestvenny Cinema, Arbatskaya ploshchad 14	291-9624		
Kiev Train Station, Ploshchad Kiyevskovo Vokzala	240-7345		
Kinokom JV, ul. Lesnaya 27	251-7189		411700
Kira JV, ul. Alexandra Tolstovo 22/2	202-6019	200-1269	
Kirgizia Cinema, Zelyony prospekt 81	301-4246		
Kishinev Cinema, ul. Yunykh Lenintsev 12	179-3747		
Kiteksim JV (Poland), ul. Fadeyeva 1	299-3157	253-9794	411238
Kiyev Cinema, Kutuzovskiy prospekt 30/32	249-3864		
Kiyevskaya Hotel, Kiyevskaya ul. 2	230-1444		
Klein, Schanzlin & Becker AG, Krasnopresnenskaya nab. 12, Office 1502	253-2456	253-9908	413646
Klinchayan Brokerage Company	378-0768		
Klingenberg, see Heinrich Klingenberg International Moving			
KLM Royal Dutch Airlines,			
Krasnopresnenskaya nab. 12, Office 1307	253-2150		
Sheremetevo II	578-2762		
Klockner & Co., AG, Pokrovskiy bulv. 4/17, korpus 3	208-9942	230-2516	413296
Klockner-Humbolt-Deutz AG, ul. Kalanchevskaya 6/2, korpus 1, 4th flr	975-1902	975-1915	413704
Klodiks JV (China), Profsoyuznaya ul. 65	334-9211	334-9110	411899
Klont JV, Leninskiy prospekt 55	135-9581		
Kloos-Niitavtoprom-Avtosvarka JV, Prospekt Andropova 22/30	118-7092	118-3555	412158
Kniga Bookshops			
Kosmos Hotel	217-0081	288-9550	
Molodyozhnaya Hotel	210-9311		
Pullman Iris Hotel	488-8100		
Kniga Printshop JV (Canada), ul. 1st Tverskaya-Yamskaya 50	251-1210	230-2207	411871
Kniga Publishers, ul. 1st Tverskaya-Yamskaya 50	251-6003		
Knizhnaya Palata, Oktyabrskaya 4, str. 2	288-9238		
Knizhnoye Obozreniye, Sushchevskiy val 64	281-6266		
Knizhny Znak, see Book Boutique			
Kobe Steel LTD, Krasnopresnenskaya nab. 12, Office 1807	253-2645	253-2648	413632
Kobelco, see Kobe Steel LTD			
Kobus JV, MGU, 2nd Uchebny, korpus au406-407	939-1028	939-2914	
Kodak Film Developing, Mezhdunarodnaya Hotel	253-1643		
Kokusai Koeki Co., LTD, Krasnopresnenskaya 12, #1102	253-7612	253-9694	413022
Kolkhida cafe, ul. Sadovaya-Samotechnaya 6	299-6757		

	Phone	Fax	Telex
Kolnish/Bonner Rundschau, Kutuzovskiy prosp. 14, kv. 102	243-1189	243-9941	413319
Kolomenskoye, Proletarskiy prospekt	115-2309		
Kolyma Susuman Gold Exchange	262-4682		
Komatsu LTD, Krasnopresnenskaya nab. 12, #1503-1504	253-7550	253-9773	413975
Komed JV (US), ul. Pravdy 7/9	214-3260	200-0209	411267
Komel JV (FRG), 1st Cheremushkinskiy proyezd 5	230-1568		
Kometika CLK JV (UK), Leningradskoye shosse 46	251-9249		
Komfactory JV (FRG), ul. Eyzenshteyna 8	233-8998		
Komintertek JV, ul. Verkhnyaya Krasnoselskaya 3	264-4298		
Komipex JV (Switzerland), ul. Rustaveli 15			
Kommercheskiy Vestnik, Kolpachny per. 7, str. 3	227-2232		
Kompania Jever Stube Rossia JV, Studencheskaya ul. 30 kv. 2	200-4671		
Kompar JV (Austria), ul. 1905 goda 10	259-4171		
Kompat JV (FRG), Proyezd Serova 5	923-6173	200-2203	411693
Kompleks Inc. JV, ul. Durova 36	921-2829	200-2265	
Kompleksniye Systemy Trade House, Kerchenskaya ul. 1a, korpus 3	122-0092		
Komplektimport V/O Rosvneshtorg, Barrikadnaya ul. 8/5	254-8050	253-9576	411060
Komplex JV (Switz.), ul. Krzhizhanovskovo 6	129-8166	938-2153	
Kompro JV (UK), ul. Ordzhonikidze 3	234-6370		
Komserv GmbH JV (FRG), Rozhdestvenskiy bulvar 9	925-2639		
Komsomolskaya Pravda, ul. Pravdy 24	257-2139		
Komsomolyets Cinema, Dmitrovskoye shosse 49	488-6946		
Komtek JV (Singapore), ul. Kosmonavta Volkova 16	202-7171	943-0072	411080
Komtorgbank, ul. Myasnitskaya 47	207-7096		
Komvek JV, Volokolamskoye Shosse 1	158-9743		
Kone, see NOKO			
Konfort JV (India), Leninskiy prospekt 36	246-4868		411432
Konica (Tokyo Boeki), ul. Leninskaya Sloboda 9	275-1674	275-2775	
Konica Complex	277-3819		
Konss	236-4845		
Kontakt JV, Pyatnitskaya 73	230-8908	230-2345	
Kontinent Bank, ul. Gostinichnaya 9, korpus 4	485-1654	482-2627	
Kontinent JV (China), Kadashevskaya Nab. 12	441-7041		
Kontrakt JV Filial, Sirenevy bulvar 2	166-1381	166-4945	
Kontur JV (Finland), Prospekt Mira 188	187-1976		
Konversbank, ul. Bolshaya Ordynka 24/26	239-2093		
Koopbank Tsentrpotrebsoyuza, B. Cherkasskiy per. 15	923-2790		
Kopris and M JV (Lichtenstein), ul. Tamanskaya 2a	199-3600	934-0096	
Kor-United JV, Starokonyushenny per. 5/14	242-1454		
Korall JV (FRG), Kutuzovskiy prospekt 9, korpus 9, kv. 113	243-6728	243-6718	413420
Korean Air (South Korea), Hotel Kosmos, room 1629	217-1627	578-2729	
Sheremetevo II	578-2728	578-2729	
Korean Airways (North Korea), see Chosinminhang			
Korolyov House Museum, 6th Ostankinskiy per. 2/28			
Korona JV, Tikhvinskaya per. 10/12, korpus 9	251-0673		
Korus JV, 2nd Silikatny proyezd 8	256-8648	253-9310	
Kosmos Cinema, Prospekt Mira 109	283-5636		
Kosmos Export-Import GmbH	253-1721		
Kosmos Hotel, Prospekt Mira 150	217-0786		411488
Kotra, Mezhdunarodnaya II, room 747	253-1569	253-1698	413657

	Phone	Fax	Telex
Kozikhinskiy cafe, see Moskovskiye Zori cafe			
KP-Emag JV (FRG), ul. Butlerova 17	330-2574		411017
Krafts Technologies JV (US/FRG), ul. Vavilova 13	923-1150	924-5114	411630
Kramis JV (Spain), ul. Tikhvinskaya 1/13	972-6846		411069
Krasnaya Gorka	381-2746		
Krasnaya Presnya Cinema, ul. Mantulinskaya 5	256-6566		
Krasnaya Presnya Museum, Bolshevitskaya ul. 4	252-3035		
Krasnaya Zvezda, Khoroshevskoye shosse 38	941-2158		
Krasny Proletary, Malaya Kaluzhskaya 15	330-9882		
Kremlin Palace of Congresses, Kremlin	926-7901		
Krestyanka, Bumazhny proyezd 14	212-1239		
Krokodil, Bumazhny proyezd 14	250-1086		
Krone-Iskra JV (FRG), Ploshchad Kurchatova	196-7213		
Kropex JV, ul. Prechistenka 36/21	203-1738	200-3217	
Kropotkinskaya 36 cafe, ul. Prechistenka 36	201-7500		
Krouni JV, ul. Narodnovo Opolcheniya 10, korpus 2, kv. 46	238-3409	230-2406	411610
Krovtex JV, ul. Neglinnaya 17	200-4555	200-4495	411191
Krugovaya Panorama Cinema, VDNKh	181-9525		
Krugozor, Pyatnitskaya ul. 25	241-6767		
Krupp GmbH, Krasnopresnenskaya nab. 12, Office 1304	253-2074	230-2835	413941
Krylatskoe Olympic Sports Center, Krylatskaya ul. 10	140-7369		
KSB Pumpen, see Klein, Schanzlin & Becker AG			
Kudesnitsa, ul. Gertsena 37	291-2111		
Kuilong cafe, Litovskiy bulvar 7	425-1111	421-0222	
Kultura, Novoslobodskaya 73	285-7802		
Kultura i Naslediye JV, Vspolny per. 14	290-3338		
Kuntsevo Cinema, ul. Ivana Franko 14	444-0115		
Kuskovo (Ceramics Museum), ul. Yunosti 2	370-0160		
Kutuzov Hut, Kutuzovskiy prospekt 38	148-1967		
Kuzminki Hotel, Volzhskiy bulvar 114a, korpus 9	179-0879		
Kuznetskiy Most JV (Italy), Kuznetskiy Most 10	928-5525	923-2458	
Kvant, Olympiyskiy prospekt 30	288-8949		
Kvorri Master-Lamas JV, ul.Platovskaya 4	240-4347		
Kyodo News Service, Kutuzovskiy prospekt 14, kv. 13	230-2367	253-9774	413382
Kyoho Tsusho Kaisha, LTD, Krasnopresnenskaya nab. 12, Office 1007	253-2587	230-2312	413147

L

L'Evenement Du Jeudi, Kutuzovskiy prospekt 7/4, kv. 304	243-7050		
L'Humanite', ul. Alabyana 10, kv. 192	943-0055		413307
L'Unita, ul. Pravdy 7/9, kv. 11	214-4259	253-9278	413490
La Pantera, Prospekt 60-Letiya Oktyabrya 10/1	126-1601		
Labomed GmbH	253-2142		
Labtam Limited, Mezhdunarodnaya II, room 1547	253-1778	253-9285	
Lada Export, Otkrytoye shosse 48a	168-2828	168-2715	414902
Ladoga Cinema, ul. Shirokaya 12	479-5856		
Lady of Hope Chapel (Roman Catholic), Kutuzovskiy prospekt 7/4, korpus 5, kv. 42	243-9621		
Lal JV (Sweden), ul. B. Kommunisticheskaya 23	272-0069	272-4682	411738
Lando JV (Syria), Leninskiy prospekt 146, (CTH) room 1001	438-5866		411823
Lanit JV, ul. Sivashskaya 4, korpus 2	110-5752	119-8804	411195

	Phone	Fax	Telex
Larsen Oy, see Borge Larsen Oy AB			
Lasagne cafe, Pyatnitskaya ul. 40	231-1085		
Lavalin International Inc., Krasnopresnenskaya nab. 12, office 608	253-1187	253-1181	413752
Lavash Bakery, Bolshaya Sadovaya 3, korpus 6	251-7888		
LB International Trade Services	200-5224		
Le Cafe Francais, Pullman Iris Hotel	488-8000		
Le Chalet Restaurant, Korobeynikov per. 1/2	202-0106		
Le Figaro, ul. Bolshaya Spasskaya 12, kv. 32	230-2464		413323
Le Soir, ul. Bolshaya Spasskaya 12, kv. 10	280-0380		
League of Commercial Banks	921-4415		
Leboeuf, Lamb, Leiby & Macrae, Koroviy val 7, Suite 13a	230-1386	230-2101	413205
Lebrus S.V.G. JV (FRG), Leningradskiy prospekt 63	157-3317		
Legstroininvest, ul. Novaya Basmannaya 24/1	267-7987		417316
LEKO	143-3282		
Lemos JV, Prospekt Mira, Vdnkh	181-9931	188-6356	
Lenin Funeral Train, Leninskaya ploshchad 1	235-2898		
Lenin Library, see Russian State Library			
Lenin Museum, Ploshchad Revolyutsii 2	295-4808		
Lenin Museum in Gorkiy (Gorkiy Leninskiye)	136-2334		
Lenin Stadium, Luzhniki	246-5515		
Swimming Pool, Luzhniki	201-0764		
Leningrad Cinema, ul. Novopeschanaya 12	157-6014		
Leningrad Train Station, Komsomolskaya ploshchad 3	266-9111		
Leningradskaya Hotel, ul. Kalanchevskaya 21/40	975-3032		411659
Lenkom Theater, ul. Chekhova 6	299-0708		
Lesinvest, Lt JV, ul. Kuybysheva 15	206-0318	208-4193	
Lexica JV (Syria), Pushkinskaya ul. 23/8	229-0534	972-4426	411796
LG Associates, Bolshaya Spasskaya ul. 12, kv. 49-50	280-0426	230-2992	612205
Liberation, ul. Gilyarovskovo 8, kv. 69	288-9533	288-9533	413652
Libre Belgique, Krutitskiy val 3, korpus 2, kv. 107	276-9974		413332
Libyan Arab Airlines, Koroviy val 7, ent. 2	237-2976		413606
Sheremetevo II	578-2730		
Liebherr-Holding GmbH, Pereulok Sadovskikh 6, kv. 10	209-6679	200-0235	413372
Lignacon, Mezhdunarodnaya II, room 1050	253-1711		
Likes-Moscow JV Filial (USA), ul. Usacheva 11	246-9350		
Liko-Raduga JV (Japan), see Auto Sun			
Line JV (Canada), ul. Rimskovo-Korsakova 3	281-9892	975-2027	411815
Lingua	390-1250		
Lingvotekhnika JV (Bulgaria), Kargopolskaya 17	402-8984		
Linhas Aereas de Angola (Angolan Airlines), Koroviy val 7, Office 8	237-0010		
Sheremetevo II	578-2773		
Linia Grafic	245-6074		
Liniya-Poligraf Advertising Firm, ul. Sovkhoznaya 2	351-6173		
Link JV (Switz.), ul. Shcherbakovskaya 40/42	369-2643	369-5947	
Liron JV (Sweden), ul. Sretenka 20	207-0003	207-0008	
Liskun Museum, see Animal Husbandry Museum			
Literary Gazette International JV (US), Kostyanskiy per. 13	208-8594	200-0238	411294
Literary Museum, ul. Petrovka 28	221-3857		
Literaturnaya Gazeta, Tsvetnoy bulvar 30	924-1168		

	Phone	Fax	Telex
Litmond Trade House and INCO, Ltd., ul. Solyanka 1/2, str. 1	928-8186	975-2372	412370
Litpharm JV (Switzerland), ul. 1st Aeroportovskaya 5	155-7722	943-0012	
Litsenzintorg, Minskaya 11	145-2700		
Litsom k Litsu, see Face to Face			
Little Mermaid Restaurant, Smolenskiy bulvar 12/19	248-4438	230-2319	
Litva Cinema, Lomonosovskiy prospekt 29/8	147-2282		
Litwin, Koroviy val 7, Office 16	238-4922	230-2930	413210
Lloyds Bank PLC, Krasnopresnenskaya nab. 12, #1808	253-8174		413057
LogoVaz JV (Italy), ul. Prechistenka 17, str. 2	202-3468	200-4224	412182
Lokomotiv Hotel, ul. Bolshaya Cherkizovskaya 125	161-8133		
Lomos Finance & Credit Consortium JV (Finland), ul. Tverskaya 23, str.2	299-6519	253-9794	411238
Los Angeles Times, ul. Sadovaya-Samotechnaya 12/24, kv. 37	200-0204	299-2304	413421
LOT Polish Airlines, Koroviy val 7, Office 5	238-0003		
Sheremetevo II	578-2706		
Lotintorg JV (Lichtenstein), Savvinskaya nab. 3	247-4859	943-0096	412148
Lubimex Holland B.V., ul. Lunacharskovo 7, kv. 1	241-0414	230-2115	413948
Luch Concert Hall, Varshavskoye shosse 71	110-3758		
Lucky-Goldstar	299-8777		
Lufthansa Airlines, Olympic Penta Hotel	975-2501	971-6784	413608
Sheremetevo II Cargo Terminal	578-6758	578-9276	
Sheremetevo II	578-3151	578-2771	413078
Luks, Petrovsky passage			
Luna Trading Inc., Krutitskiy val 3, korpus 2, kv. 97	276-4906	276-4890	413179
Lunacharskiy House Museum, ul. Vesnina 9/5	241-0877		
Lurgi GmbH Frankfurt/Main, Koroviy val 7, Office 9	230-2324		413097
Luzhniki Tennis Courts	201-1655		
Lyetuchaya Mysh Cabaret, B. Gnezdnikovskiy per. 10	229-7087		

M

	Phone	Fax	Telex
M & M Ferrous America, Ltd., Koroviy val, kv. 174	238-7363	238-7363	413660
M J Exports LTD, Mezhdunarodnaya II, room 441	253-2441	253-9475	413584
M&T Chimie, see Elf Aquitaine			
M. & D. Gertner K.G., ul. Mytnaya 1, 3rd floor	230-1010	230-2372	413173
M. Golodetz (Overseas) Ltd., Per. Sadovskikh 4, Office 11	299-2883	200-0227	413344
MacLean's Magazine, Kutuzovskiy prospekt 13, kv. 128	243-9604		413585
Madjess JV (Lebanon), ul. Markhlevskovo 3-31	205-6150		
Magarita cafe, Malaya Bronnaya 28	299-6534		
Magazin del Mondo, Ukraine Hotel, 8th floor	243-4682		
Magra, ul. Pushkinskaya 9, kv. 19	292-5142	230-2388	413152
Mainichi, Kutuzovskiy prospekt 7/4, kv. 1	253-9005	230-2484	413390
Malev Hungarian Airlines, Pr. Khudozhestvennovo Teatra 6	292-0434		414489
Malta, Prospekt 60-letiya Oktyabrya 12	126-8510		
Maly Theater, Teatralnaya ploshchad 1/6	924-4083		
Maly Theater (filial), ul. Bolshaya Ordynka 69	237-6420		
Malysh Grupo Libro International JV, ul. Davydkovskaya, 5	443-0654		
Malysh Publishers, Davydskovskaya 5	443-0655		
MAN AG, Munchen, Pereulok Sadovskikh 4, kv. 7	209-6674	200-0205	413185

	Phone	Fax	Telex
Manager, ul. Yablochkova 5	210-4030		
Manager Service JV (Denmark), Frunzenskaya nab. 30	242-8927	242-8973	414737
Manezh, see Central Exhibition Hall			
Manila Restaurant, The, ul. Vavilova 81	132-0055		
Mannesmann AG, ul. B. Dorogomilovskaya 14, kv. 28-31	243-0791	230-2306	413172
Mantigo JV, ul. Novocheremushkinskaya 60, korpus 2	274-0048	240-2002	
Manusonik JV Filial, ul. Perekopskaya 9A	122-3336		
Manvik JV, ul. Krzhizhanovskovo 14, korpus 2	124-3531	125-1753	411237
MAPA, Koroviy val 7, Office 220	230-2034		413965
Marathon Oil Company, ul. Petrovka 15, Office 19-20	924-5893		
Marc Rich & Co. AG, Kuznetskiy Most 3	921-4365	230-2026	413988
Marchi-Intensiv	928-1269	921-1240	
Marco Polo Presnaya Hotel, Spiridonevsky 9	202-0381	230-2704	414748
Marex, Severnoye Chertanovo 7, korpus 5, kv. 50	318-2739	200-2216	411700
Mari JV (Austria), ul. Kapitsy 34	429-1500		
Maria-Trazer JV (Italy), ul. Baumanskaya 57	265-0180		
Marine Resources Company International, Hotel Budapest, room 201	921-7971	200-1214	413052
Marketing Information Center JV (Finland), Kolpachny per. 7	924-7941	923-2856	
Marketing Research and Consulting JV, ul. Tverskaya 16/2	941-0900	200-0267	411712
Marmer GT JV, 2nd Vladimirskaya ul. 62a	309-4748	306-3415	
Marposs S.p.A., Trekhprudny per. 11/13	299-0932	200-0234	413938
Mars Cinema, Beskudnikovo ul. Inzhenernaya 1	901-0588		
Mars Gallery, Malaya Filevskaya ul. 32	146-2029	253-9794	411283
Marubeni Corporation, Krasnopresnenskaya nab. 12, #1908	253-1817	230-2731	413391
Marx and Engels Museum, ul. Marksa i Engelsa 5	203-3182		
Mashinoexport, ul. Mosfilmovskaya 35	147-1542	938-2116	411207
Mashinoimport, ul. Mosfilmovskaya 35	143-8927	938-2116	411242
Mashintorg-Lida, ul. Stavropolskaya 70, kv. 99	351-5459		
Mashpriborintorg, ul. Smolenskaya-Sennaya 32/34	244-2775		
Massage Russkaya America, Luzhnetskaya nab. 10	201-1680		
Master JV (France)	299-1184		
Mateko JV, ul. Novo-Basmannaya 10	299-1909	253-9098	
Matimport S.A., Bezbozhny per. 25	288-8610		
Matsushita Electric Industrial Co., LTD, Mezhdunarodnaya II, room 1047	255-6983	253-9013	
Mayak, ul. Pogodinskaya 4	248-0022		
Mayak Hotel, ul. Bolshaya Filevskaya 25	142-2384		
Mayakovskiy House Museum, Proyezd Serova 3/6	921-9387		
Mayakovskiy Theater, ul. Gertsena 19	290-6241		
ul. Khmeleva 21	208-3196		
Mayekawa Kawasho Corporation, ul. Mytnaya 1, kv. 8	230-0132	230-2112	413118
Mayers International	255-1089		
MBM JV, Tikhoretskiy bulvar 1	358-7228	358-1167	414789
McCall Tours	138-0738		
McDermott International, Inc., ul. Petrovka 15, kv. 19-20	928-9394	200-2237	413267
McDonald's, Bolshaya Bronnaya ul. 29	229-1811	200-3205	
Delivery Service	200-1655		
McHugh & McCaffery International, Staropanskiy pr. 4	924-9655	265-5714	
MCM International Services	288-7788		

	Phone	Fax	Telex
MD-Seis JV, ul. Narodnovo Opolcheniya 38/3	192-8087	943-1105	
Mebelintorg, Bolshaya Filevskaya 35	146-3672		
Mebinvest JV (USA), ul. Taneyevykh 7a, kv. 4	554-8972	244-0749	
Mechta Cinema, Kashirskoye shosse 42/2	324-8577		
MECOF S.p.A., Varshava Hotel, room 501	238-9582		411663
Medchoice Moscow JV, ul. Shchukinskaya 1	193-8654	292-6511	
Medecho JV, Shelkovskoye shosse 29	462-1281	462-0104	411424
Medexport, Kakhovka 31	331-8200	311-8988	411247
Media ISI, Oleny val 24, korpus 2, kv. 146	962-1444	288-9572	413577
Medialink JV (Finland), Novinskiy bulvar 7	205-2000		411424
Medical International JV (US), ul. Zhuravleva 2/8-1	213-6678		
Medicine Information Technology JV, ul. Sadovaya-Kudrinskaya 5	135-3027	310-7050	
Medicine Man, The, ul. Chernyakhovskovo 4	155-7080	151-4506	
Medigrant JV (India), Abrikosovskiy per. 2	248-0926	230-2480	
Medikor JV (Vietnam), ul. Yaroslavskaya 5	489-5990		
Medipart, ul. Gasheka 12, korpus 7	251-2626	973-2053	
Meditsinskaya Tekhnika	290-1143		
Medrex Instruments JV (US), Leninskiy prospekt 113	434-4438		
Medservice, Trifonovskaya ul. 61, kv. 65	288-5875		
Medservice International JV, ul. Lva Tolstovo 5/1	275-4390	284-5149	
Medtech JV, Simferopolyskiy bulvar 8	113-2351	113-2633	
Medtrade JV, 2nd Troitskiy per. 6a			
Medusa Bar, Inflotel	255-9278		
Mei-hua Restaurant, ul. Rusakovskaya 2/1, str. 1	264-9574		
Mekhatron JV, ul. Pyatnitskaya 48	231-0730		412824,
Mekong cafe, see Kuilong cafe			
Melar, Post Box 013, Moscow 103159	175-0647	975-2208	
Melar JV (Sweden), ul. Pyatnitskaya 48	231-0730		411576
Menatep Commercial Investment Bank, ul. Dubininskaya 17a	235-5925		
Menatep Financial Corporation, ul. Dubininskaya 17a	235-8815		
Menon, ul. Usacheva 35	245-5846	246-4434	
Menonsovpolygraph JV (India), ul. Nikitinskaya 5a	165-0265	165-5865	412213
Mercantile Oy, ul. Mytnaya 1, Office 21	230-0465		413049
Mercedes-Benz AG, Prospekt Vernadskovo 9/10, kv. 602	131-3448	230-2522	413346
Merck, Sharp & Dohme, Slavyanskaya-Radisson Hotel, room 3013-14	941-8275		
Mercury Garments Industries, Kursovoy per. 9, Office 3	203-1851	230-2540	413522
Merian Publishers, Kutuzovskiy prospekt 14, kv. 122	243-2218		
Merisel/Computer Technologies JV, Krutitskiy val 3, korpus 2	276-4714	274-0097	
Merloni Finanziaria S.p.A., Pereulok Sadovskikh 6, kv. 1	209-6840	200-0236	413215
Messaggero, Kutuzovskiy prospekt 7/4, korpus 5, kv. 34	243-0658		413457
Messemagazin International, Leningradskiy prospekt 28, kv. 122	212-9033		413986
Metal Hammer, Obydenskiy per. 14	202-5747		
Metallgesellschaft AG, Leninskiy prospekt 95a, kv. 601-603	132-5855	310-7066	413328
Metapress Agency, 4th Tverskaya-Yamskaya ul. 4	972-6453	972-6250	
Meteor Cinema, ul. Svobody 10	491-1397		
Meteor Ltd.	231-6174		
Metmashikoss JV, Ryazanskiy prospekt 8a	171-0247	274-0023	
Meton-Etep, Staropetrovskiy proyezd 11, korpus 2	153-9461	943-0025	

	Phone	Fax	Telex
Metorg GmbH and Co. KG, Mezhdunarodnaya II, room 1233	253-1233	253-9384	
Metra, ul. Lunacharskovo 7, kv. 2	203-1602		413502
Metropol Hotel, Teatralny proyezd 1	927-6000		
Metroreklama JV (FRG), Prospekt Mira 41	288-0309		
Metros JV (FRG), Prospekt Mira 41	288-0588	288-0791	
Mexican Television, ul. Akad. Koroleva 4, korpus 2, kv. 212	286-4411	283-4333	
Mezhbirzhevaya Torgovaya Kompaniya, see AsA Interexchange Trading Company			
Mezhdunarodnaya Hotel I, Krasnopresnenskaya nab. 12	253-2760		411432
Mezhdunarodnaya Hotel II, Krasnopresnenskaya nab. 12	253-2761		411446
Dry Cleaning	253-2776		
Indoor Pool	255-6691		
Service Bureau	253-2762		
Mezhdunarodnaya Kniga, ul. Dimitrova 39	238-4600		
Mezhdunarodnaya Prodovolstvennaya Birzha, see International Food Exchange			
Mezhdunarodnaya Zhizn, Gorokhovskiy per. 14	265-3781		
Mezhdunarodnye Otnosheniya, ul. Sadovaya-Spasskaya 20	207-6793		
Mezhnumismatika JV (FRG), ul. Pushkinskaya 9	292-0177	200-0270	411717
MGL International JV (Spain), ul. Davydkovskaya 5	443-0654	200-226	411700
MGU (Moscow State University), Leninskiye Gory	203-6565		
Mia Shoe, Tikhvinskiy per. 1/50			
MIAT Mongolian Airlines, Spasopeskovskiy per. 7/1	241-0754		
Sheremetevo II	578-2759		
MicroAge Computers, Balaklavskiy prospekt 3	316-2111	316-2118	
Microcomputersystem JV (FRG), ul. Pushkinskaya 32	229-4491		
Micrograf-Moscow JV Filial, Tokmakov per. 14	261-1911		
Microinform JV (Hungary), Kozhevnicheskaya ul. 3	235-7700	253-1053	411660
Microprocessor JV (Bulgaria), 1st Rybinskaya ul. 3	264-2376	292-6511	
Middle East News Agency (MENA), Sokolnicheskiy val 24, korpus 2, kv. 176	264-8276	288-9527	
Midland Montagu, Krasnopresnenskaya nab. 12, #1305	253-2144	230-2003	413108
Mig JV (US), Pakgauznoye shosse 1	153-1021	943-0007	
Mikora, ul. Taganskaya 5/9	332-9857	278-2009	
Mikrodin, Novozavodskaya ul. 18	145-9462		
Mikrokhirugiya Glaza, Beskudnikovskiy bulvar 59a	484-8120	485-5954	411856
Mikromed-Moscow JV Filial, ul. Timiryazevskaya 1	211-1722		411267
Miks JV (US), Ruzheyny per.4	247-5338		
Milbari JV, ul. Yuzhnoportovaya 7A	279-2813		
Milena Inform JV Filial, Hotel Intourist, room 1320	253-6052		
Military-Industrial Investment Company, Novaya ploshchad 3/4, entrance 6	262-7767	262-4406	411952
Milliyet, ul. Donskaya 18/7, kv. 136	236-2483	236-1344	
Milo JV (Italy), ul. Krasnobogatyrskaya 2	168-1728		
Miloserdie, ul. Admirala Makarova 15	452-4190		
Mineralogy Museum (Fersman Museum of Mineralogy), Leninskiy prospekt 18, korpus 2	232-0067		
Minerma JV (Luxemburg), ul. B. Ordynka 49, korpus 1	233-5992	230-2465	
Ministry of			
Agriculture, Gorlikov per. 3	204-4828	288-3580	411021
Automobile and Farm Machinery Manufacturing, Kuznetskiy Most 21/5	925-1132		

	Phone	Fax	Telex
Automobile Roads, ul. Bochkova 4	287-3600		
Automobile Transport, ul. Sadovaya-Samotechnaya 10	200-0803		
Aviation Industry, Ulanskiy per. 16	207-0025		
Bread Production, ul. Krzhizhanovskovo 6	129-6600		
Chemical and Oil Processing Industry, ul. Gilyarovskovo 31	281-9479		
Civil Aviation, Cargo Transport Division			411969
Leningradskiy prospekt 37	155-5009		412297
Civil Construction, see Rosgrazhdanrekonstruktsiya Concern			
Coal Industry, Novy Arbat 23, korpus 2	202-6943		
Communications, Delegatskaya 5	292-7070		
ul. Tverskaya 7	229-6966	230-2097	
Construction for Oil and Gas Ind., ul. Zhitnaya 14	238-5000		
Construction in the North and Western Region, ul. Stroiteley 8, korpus 2	930-4229		
Construction in the Southern Region, ul. Petrovka 14	200-4535		
Construction Materials Indust, ul. Krzhizhanovskovo 13	124-3177		
Culture, Arbat 35	241-0709		
Kitayskiy proyezd 7	925-1195		
Defense, ul. Myasnitskaya 37	296-8900		
Ecology & Natural Resources, ul. B. Gruzinskaya 4/6	254-7683	943-0013	
Economics and Finance, Okhotny Ryad 12	292-9139	975-2052	
Foreign Economic Relations Committee	292-9656		
Education, Leninskiy prospekt 6	927-0568		
Electronic Industry, Kitayskiy proyezd 7	220-6744		
Electrotechnical Ind. and Equipment, ul. Ogareva 5	229-7154		
Energy and Electricity, Kitayskiy proyezd 7	220-5500		
Fisheries, Rozhdestvenskiy bulvar 12	923-7634		
Foreign Affairs, Foreign Companies Accreditation Department	244-4125		
Foreign Affairs, ul. Smolenskaya-Sennaya 32/34	244-4314	244-1969	
Prospekt Mira 49a	281-1011		
Protocol Department	244-2987		
Visa Department	244-2459	244-3068	
Foreign Economic Relations, ul. Smolenskaya-Sennaya 32/34	244-1046	244-3068	
Forestry, Pyatnitskaya ul. 59/19	231-6844		
Telegrafny per. 1	208-0056		
Fuel and Energy, Kitasky proyezd 7	220-5200	206-8107	
Fuel Industry, see Russian State Fuel Association			
General Automobile Industry, Myusskaya ploshchad 3	251-9483		
Geology, ul. Bolshaya Gruzinskiy 4/6	254-6824		
Health Care, Rakhmanovskiy per. 3	928-4478		
Vadkovskiy per. 18-20	289-3065		
Heavy Automobile Industry, Nizhniy Kislovskiy per. 5	203-0437		
Industry, ul. Petrovka 14	209-8282	200-4534	
Internal Affairs	222-6093		
ul. Zhitnaya 16	237-7585		
Law, ul. Obukha 4	206-0554		
ul. Yermolovoy 10a	209-6173		
Light Industry, see Roslegprom Association			
Local Industries, see Rossoyuzmestprom			
Machinery and Equipment, see State Joint Stock Assoc. for Mach. and Equip.			

	Phone	Fax	Telex
Metallurgy, Ploshchad Nogina 2/5	220-8180		
Maritime Shipping, Rozhdestvenka 1/4	926-1000		
Medical Industry, Proyezd Khudozhestvennovo Teatra 2	292-9623		
Nuclear Power Industry, ul. Bolshaya Ordynka 24/26	239-4753		
Press and Mass Media, Strastnoy bulvar 5	209-6026	200-2281	
Public Education, Chistoprudny bulvar 6	924-7112		
Public Services, Shabolovka 4	236-4482		
ul. Stanislavskovo 7	290-1638		
Radio Industry, ul. Myasnitskaya 35	207-9842		
Residential Buildings, ul. Myasnitskaya 13	924-6734		
River Transport, see Rosrechflot Concern			
Ship Building, ul. Sadovaya-Kudrinskaya 11	255-0941		
Special Construction, ul. Bolshaya Sadovaya 8	209-1009		
Textile Industry, ul. Profsoyuznaya 3	129-9117		
Trade, ul. Myasnitskaya 47	207-7000		
ul. Varvarka 14	298-4864		
Trade and Resources, Orlikov per. 5	204-0178	975-3273	
Transport, ul. Sadovaya-Samotechnaya 10	200-0803	200-2678	
Transport Construction, ul. Sadovaya-Spasskaya 21	262-9901		
Water Projects Construction, Novaya Basmannaya 10	265-9109		
Water Resources, ul. Semashko 1/12	202-3286		
Minneftegasprom, Nab. Maurice Toreza 26/1	239-8800		
Minsk Cinema, Mozhayskoye shosse 54	447-0200		
Minsk Hotel, ul. Tverskaya 22	299-1300		
Mir Association, Borynsky Post 7	253-4863		
Mir Cinema, Tsvetnoy bulvar 11	200-1695		
Mir Hotel, Bolshoy Devyatinskiy per. 9	290-9519		
Mirbis JV (Italy), ul. Zatsepa 41	236-5103	237-3430	
Mission of the Israeli Federation of Chambers of Commerce, Krasnopresnenskaya nab.12, Office 809	253-2809		
Mitranss JV, Tsvetnoy Bulvar 21	200-2870	200-3341	412202
Mitsubishi Corporation, Krasnopresnenskaya nab. 12, Office 702-710	253-1278	230-2554	413387
Mitsubishi Heavy Industries, LTD, Bolshoy Gnezdnikovskiy per. 7, 2nd flr	200-2551	200-3232	
Mitsui & Co., LTD, Krasnopresnenskaya nab. 12, Office 1804	253-1592	253-9273	413395
Mivaro JV (Italy), Proyezd Serova 25	928-1869		
MkhAT Moscow Theater of the Arts see Moscow Theater of the Arts			
MkhAT Museum, see Moscow Theater of the Arts Museum			
MKS Plus JV, ul. Pionerskaya 12	190-5427	944-7471	
MKT-Inter JV, ul. Akademika Koroleva, korpus 2	215-2156	225-2056	
MKTS-Hertel JV (FRG), ul. Polkovaya 13	289-7385		
MM International JV (Spain), Bulvar Matrosa Zheleznyaka 23, k. 2, pom. 3	450-9160		
MMM, Gazgoldernaya ul. 10	171-0397		
Moag JV (Sweden), ul. Lesnaya 59	251-2535		
Mobil Oil Company Limited, Krasnopresnenskaya nab. 12, Office 504	253-1000	253-1040	411633
Moda JV, ul. Tikhvinskaya 1/13, str. 2	258-9738	972-4426	411796
Moda-Plast JV, Bolshoy Cherkasskiy per. 15	924-1620		411127
Moden JV (Italy), ul. Vodnikov 2	190-4788		141719

	Phone	Fax	Telex
Modern Ross JV, ul. Nikitinskaya 1a	165-1356	292-6511	
Modus Vivendi Press Agency, ul. Granovskovo 5	299-0502	230-2297	411795
MOES, see International Organ. of Economic Cooperation			
Molkom JV (FRG), ul. Verkhnaya Radishchevskaya 12	227-8535	200-3279	414731
Molodaya Gvardiya Publishers, Sushchevskiy 21	972-2200	972-0582	411261
Molodyozhnaya Hotel, Dmitrovskoye shosse 27	210-4838		
Molodyozhny Cinema, ul. Lyublinskaya 11	177-9010		
Molodyozhny Commercial Bank, Khamovnicheskiy val 34	242-0282		
Monde (Le), Kutuzovskiy prospekt 13, kv. 3	243-7242	230-2942	413367
Monde Diplomatique (Le), Rublevskoye shosse 26, korpus 1, kv. 221-222	415-2912		
Mongolian Airlines, see MIAT Mongolian Airlines			
Monolit JV (Denmark), ul. Yunosti 5/1	374-6933		
Monsanto, Volkov per. 19	255-0001	255-5001	413314
Montana Centro, Bolshoy Cherkasskiy per. 17			
Monte Dei Paschi di Siena, Krasnopresnenskaya nab. 12, Office 1105-1106a	253-2677	253-9087	413092
Montedison, Koroviy val 7, Office 1	237-2622	230-2032	413460
Montero JV (Belgium), ul. Novocheremushkinskaya 60, korpus 2	331-2170	420-2002	
Moosh cafe, ul. Oktyabrskaya 2/4	284-3670		
Morbank, Bolshoy Koptevskiy prospekt 6	151-5674	151-5674	411197
Morgan Grenfell & Co. Ltd, Pokrovskiy bulvar 4/17, kv. 34	207-5998	230-2386	413121
Morikawa Shoji Kaisha LTD, ul. Lunacharskovo 7, kv. 18	203-0041	200-1273	413283
Morman Church Services, ul. Donskaya 37	240-6332		
Morozko, ul. Kedrova 7a, ul. Lva Tolstovo 2	246-0504		
Morsea, ul. Bolshaya Pereyaslavskaya 15, kv. 1-2	280-9654	230-2841	413102
Morsvyazsputnik, Novoslobodskaya 14/19	258-7045		
Mosbiznessbank, Kuznetskiy Most 15	921-8582	230-2124	411864
Mosbudproekt JV (Poland), ul. Smolnaya 34a	251-8221	459-8338	911532
Moscomissintorg, Bolshoy Cherkasskiy per. 2/10	923-1444		
MosComputerTrade JV (US), ul. Novokuznetskaya 17/19	231-0426		411386
Moscow Adventure Tours	132-7313		
Moscow Artists' House Hall, Kuznetskiy Most 11	925-4264		
Moscow Ballet Theater, ul. Skakovaya 3	251-3221		
Moscow Biotech Exchange	159-3030		
Moscow Bird JV (US), Kutuzovskiy prospekt 17	243-9796		
Moscow Boston International Ltd., Novobasmannaya ul. 13/2-3	267-1302		
Moscow Business (Moskovskiy Bizness) Magazine JV, Zubovskiy bulvar 4	201-7475	230-2667	411323
Moscow Business Centre, ul. Streletskaya 10	289-6464	292-6511	
Moscow Cash and Carry, Leninskiy prospekt 95a	132-5510	936-2237	414500
Moscow Cellular Communications, Pokrovskiy bulvar 8	297-7783	227-0250	
Moscow Center for Scientific-Technical Information, Proyezd Serova 5	928-6605		
Moscow Center JV, Frunzenskaya Naberezhnaya 54	242-3069		
Moscow Central Address Information Bureau, Krasnoproletarskaya 10	258-2820		
Moscow Central Customs, ul. Marinoy Roshchy 12	971-1178	971-0105	
Moscow Central Real Estate Exchange, Trekhprudny per. 1, kv. 20	202-7287	299-3240	

	Phone	Fax	Telex
Moscow Central Stock Exch., ul. Granovskovo 5, kv. 37	229-7635		
Moscow Chamber of Commerce, ul Chekhova 13-17	299-7612		
Moscow Charity Movement, ul. Volkhonka 5/6, str.7	203-0219		
Moscow City Council			
Executive Committee, ul. Tverskaya 13	229-5431		
Interagency Commission	202-2782		
Internal Affairs, ul. Petrovka 38	200-8342		
Planning Committee, ul. Stanislavskovo 24	925-3123		
Orgokomitet	203-2655		
Moscow City Telephone Network, Degtyarny per. 6	299-4745	200-3208	
Moscow Commercial Club JV,			
ul. Bolshaya Kommunisticheskaya 2a	274-0081	274-0080	411211
Moscow Commodity Exchange, VDNKh, Pavilion 4	187-8614	188-9601	
Energy Dept., VDNKh, Pavilion 4	187-8505		
Moscow Conservatory, ul. Gertsena 13	229-7412		
Moscow Consulting Center JV, Kolokolnikov per. 22/19	207-1441	253-1601	
Moscow Contact JV (France), ul. Chekhova 2	299-5213	229-0962	411655
Moscow Detective Theater, ul. Dzerzhinskovo 13	222-5213		
Moscow Diplomatic Transport Service JV (Sweden),			
ul. Gorbunova 14	448-8035		
Moscow Duty Free, Sheremetevo II	578-9089	230-2351	411954
Moscow Engineering-Construction Institute JV,			
Yaroslavskoye Shosse 26	183-4692		
Moscow Fair JV, Sokolnicheskiy val 1, pavilion 4	269-3076	268-0891	412802
Moscow Graphic Arts Center, Malaya Gruzinskaya ul. 28	253-7605		
Moscow Guardian, Khoroshevskoe shosse 17	940-0227	941-0900	
Moscow Illustrated Press JV, Suvorovskiy bulv. 8a	203-3644	291-1787	411421
Moscow Industrial Bank, ul. Zhitnaya 12	230-7962		
Moscow Institute for the Economy (MINKh),			
Stremyanny per. 28	237-8508		
Moscow International Agricultural Exchange	283-3693		
Moscow International Bank,			
Pokrovskiy bulvar 4/17, kv. 32	207-5998		
Proyezd Khudozhestvennovo Teatra 6	292-0709	975-2214	
Pushkinskaya, ul. 5/6	292-8341		
Moscow International Peace Marathon JV (US),			
ul. Markhlevskovo 18	924-0824	200-2264	
Moscow Interregional Bank, Leningradskiy prospekt 9	251-5777		
Pereulok Markhlevskovo 3, kv. 5	251-5777	250-5633	
Moscow Legal Collegium, ul. Pushkinskaya 9, str. 6	229-9033		
Moscow Legis International JV, see Computer Systems and Technology			
Moscow Magazine, Suvorovskiy bulvar 8a	928-7083	291-1787	411421
Moscow Management Int'l JV, Petrovskiy bulv. 25	924-7416	200-5241	
Moscow Mayor's Office	290-8680	200-2265	
Economic Department	299-4224		
Foreign Affairs Department	229-9325		
Protocol Department	229-9325		
Moscow Medical Center	432-1616		
Moscow Medical Int'l Centre JV (FRG), ul. Obukha 14	297-1848		
Moscow Metro Museum, Sportivnaya metro	222-7309		
Moscow Museum (Museum of the History &			
Reconstruction of Moscow), Novaya ploshchad 12	924-8490		
Moscow Narodny Bank, Pokrovskiy bulv. 4/17, kv. 34	207-5998	230-2386	413121
Moscow News, ul. Tverskaya 16/2	292-2072	200-0267	

	Phone	Fax	Telex
Moscow Oil Exchange	233-8981		
Moscow Outdoor Swimming Pool, Kropotkinskaya nab. 38	202-4725		
Moscow Patriarchate, Chistoprudny per. 5	201-3416		
External Dept, Danilovskiy val 22	235-0708		
Publishing House, Pogodinskaya 20	246-9848		
Moscow Pizza JV, Kutuzovskiy prospekt 43	243-9964	243-1994	
Moscow Project Management JV (USA), Bolshaya Pereyaslavskaya 50	280-3435	280-9005	411660
Moscow Puppet Theater, Spartakovskaya ul. 26	261-2197		
Moscow Regional Privatization Exchange	556-9862	556-9817	
Moscow School for Banking, ul. Kibalchina 1	283-7961		
Moscow Security Van Dept., 5th Roshinsky per. 7/8	234-1838		
Moscow State University, see MGU			
Moscow Theater of the Arts - New, Tverskoy bulvar 22	203-8773		
Old, Proyezd Khudozhestvennovo Teatra 3	229-8760		
Filial, ul. Moskvina 3	229-9631		
Museum, Proyezd Khudozhestvennovo Teatra 3a	229-0080		
Moscow Times, Suvorovskiy bulvar 8a	928-2515		
Advertising, ul. Bogdana Khmelnitskovo 10/1-2	928-2515		
Moscow Tourist Club	203-1094		
Moscow Trade House, ul. Chekhova 2	299-1333		
Moscow Trade Union Sport Consulting JV (FRG), Bobrov per. 6	925-5290		
Moscow University Students Theater, ul. Gertsena 1	203-6876		
Moscow Volvo Rentals, see MTDS JV			
Moscow Wood JV, ul. Udaltsova, 22a	131-0560		
Moscow X-Service, ul. Mytnaya 18, entrance 2	238-6634	230-2459	
Moscow-Ashok Company JV, ul. Krasnaya Presnya 23b	200-4153		
Moscow-Bilifeld Machine Building JV (FRG), 2nd Irtyshskiy proyezd 4/6	462-0150		411681
Moscow-Buud JV (Australia), ul. Udaltsova 22a	131-0560		
Moscow-Carroll JV (UK), Presnenskiy val 1/5	238-0635		
Moscow-City Business Center	299-6360		
Moscow-Color JV (Belgium), Prospekt Marksa 7	262-9215		
Moscow-McDonalds JV (Canada), ul. Bolshaya Bronnaya 29	299-1811	934-2183	411770
Moscow-Milan System JV (Italy), Leninskiy prospekt 6	236-9556		
Moscow-Tours JV, Kalanchevskaya ul. 21/40	975-1850		
Mosdam JV, Vorontsovskiy Park 5	936-0014		
Moseniko-Invest JV (Switz.), Krasnopresnenskaya nab. 12, Office 2009	253-2066	253-9070	414440
Mosgorspravka, ul. Tverskaya 7			
Mosimedia JV (France), Kalashny per. 14	925-3476	975-2322	413182
MosJohnStroy JV, Sovetskaya ploshchad 2/6	921-0056	200-3212	
Moskniga Books, see Books, Moskniga			
Moskompeksim JV (Switz.), 1st Tverskaya-Yamskaya 37a	251-3376		
Moskovskaya Pravda Newspaper, ul. 1905 Goda 7	259-8233		
Moskovskaya Pravda Publisher, ul. 1905 Goda 7	256-9294		
Moskovskaya Regionalnaya Birzha Privatizatsii, see Moscow Regional Privatization Exchange			
Moskovskaya Tsentralnaya Birzha Nedvizhimosti, see Moscow Central Real Estate Exchange			

	Phone	Fax	Telex
Moskovskiy Fondovy Dom, 1st Volokolamskiy proyezd 10	289-5355	289-5355	
Moskovskiy Kommercheskiye Vesti	299-7225		
Moskovskiy Mezhdunarodny Bank, see Moscow International Bank			
Moskovskiye Zori cafe, Malaya Kozikhinskiy per. 11	299-5725		
Moskovsksaya Yarmarka JV (FRG), Sokolnicheskiy val 1	268-0183		
Moskva Cinema, Ploshchad Mayakovskovo 2	251-7222		
Moskva Electronics Store, Kutuzovskiy prospekt 31			
Moskva Hotel, Okhotny Ryad 7	292-1100		
Moskva Restaurant, Okhotny ryad 7 (Hotel Moskva)	292-6227		
Moskvich, Volgogradskiy prospekt 42	276-8200		
Moskviya, Leninskiy prospekt 64/2	925-1665		
Mospari JV (France), 2nd Brestskaya ul. 46	251-4049	251-6409	
Mosrent Car Rental, Zemledelcheskiy per 14/17, str. 2	248-3607	248-0251	411762
Mosrentservice JV (FRG), ul. Krasnobogatyrskaya 79	963-8780	162-1675	414766
Sheremetevo II	578-8250		
Mossoviet Cinema, Preobrazhenskaya pl. 4/2	963-0332		
Mossoviet Theater, Bolshaya Sadovaya 16	229-2035		
Sivtsev Vrazhek 44	241-0225		
Khamovnicheskiy val 2	242-1707		
Mosstroybank, ul. Chekhova 21/18	299-5860		
Mosstroyeconombank, ul. Vavilova 81	132-2897	132-2893	
Most JV (Japan), Sretenskiy tupik 1/34	208-1206	434-1020	
Most JV (USA), ul. Obrucheva 34/63	333-9070	420-2262	411135
MosTransEurope, Butyrskiy val 22, kom. 46-7	973-0076	975-2027	411815
Mosvart JV (Austria), Leningradskoye shosse 16	156-7525	930-1033	417343
Mosven JV, ul. Tverskaya 10	241-7580	244-7234	
Mosvneshinform, Krasnopresnenskaya nab. 1/2	205-1423	205-7873	412151
Moven Joint Stock Company, ul. Plekhanova 17	309-3373		
Mozhayskaya Hotel, Mozhayskoye shosse 165	447-3434		
Mozhaysky Disco, Mozhayskoe shosse 163	447-3294		
MPS, see Monte Dei Paschi di Siena			
MS-Group JV (US), Pyatnitskaya ul. 43	231-0759	231-6262	
MSZ-Wendt JV, Sushchevskiy val 3/5	289-2223	288-9541	
MTDS Moscow Volvo Rentals, ul. Leninskiy prospekt 152	434-5332		
Service Center, ul. Gorbunova 14	448-8035	448-6728	412255
MTIS GmbH, Kolominskiy prospekt 1a	112-5540	943-0068	411700
MTS JV (France), Bolshaya Serpukhovskaya 14/13, str. 8	236-4631	230-2900	911615
Multidesign JV (FRG), ul. Gilyarovskovo 17	284-3718		
Multiservice JV, ul. Bolshaya Polyanka 50	238-1032		
Mundo (El), ul. Osipenko 21, kv. 48	231-5330		
Museum of Applied Folk Art, Delegatskaya ul. 5	221-0139		
Museum of Folk Art, ul. Stanislavskovo 7	291-8718		
Museum of Oriental Art, Suvorovskiy bulvar 12a	291-9614		
Museum of Russian Revolutions, ul. Tverskaya 21	299-5217		
Museum of the October Revolution, see Museum of Russian Revolutions			
Music Museum (Glinka Museum of Music Culture), ul. Fadeyeva 4	972-3237		
Musical Comedy Theater (Operetta Theater), Pushkinskaya ul. 6	292-0405		
Musika Publishers, Neglinnaya 14	923-0497	925-6949	
Muslim Mosque, Vypolzov per. 7	281-3866		
Mysl JV Filial, Proyezd Serova 4	298-3723		

N

	Phone	Fax	Telex
N.H.K. TV & Radio, ul. Sadovaya-Samotechnaya 12/24, kv. 20	200-1568	299-7358	413393
N.V. Philips' Gloeilampenfabrieken, ul. Mytnaya 1, Office 18	230-0410	230-0410	413961
Na Doskakh Studio Theater, Vspolny per. 21, str. 2	290-1917		
Nachrichten Fur Aussenhandel, ul. Vavilova 85, kv. 57	134-9312		413268
Naidunia, Zemlyanoi val 52, kv. 158	227-8897		413320
Nalco Chemical Company, Mezhdunarodnaya II, room 732	255-6807	253-2732	411432
Nargiz cafe, Lebedyanskaya 22, korpus 4	329-7187		
Nashe Naslediye (Our Heritage), 1st Neopalimovskiy per. 4	244-0106		
Natalena, ul. Petrovka 10	924-9532		
Natali-Flora-Service JV, ul. Bolshiye Kamenshchiki 8	271-3003	200-2216	
National Broadcasting Company (Russia), Pyatnitskaya ul. 25	250-9257		411130
National Broadcasting Company (US), Gruzinskiy per. 3, kv. 217-220	230-2675		413428
National Committee of the Int Council of Museums, Pereulok Sivtsev Vrazhek 30	241-7210		
National Hotel, Okhotny Ryad 14/1	203-6539		
National Iranian Steel Corporation, ul. Bolshaya Spasskaya	280-3360		
National Public Radio, ul. Dmitriya Ulyanova 16, kv. 212	124-1457		
National Publishers' Association	921-6088		
National Westminster Bank PLC, Pokrovskiy bulvar 4/17, kv. 33	207-5739	230-2244	413258
Nauka i Zhizn, ul. Myasnitskaya 24	924-1835		
Nauka Publishers, ul. Profsoyuznaya 90	334-7610	420-2220	411612
Nauka v SSSR, Maronovskiy per. 26	238-2166		
Nauktekhinform JV (UK), ul. Usiyevicha 20a	152-5711	943-0060	411249
Nedelya, Pushkinskaya ploshchad 5	200-3479		
Nefertiti, Intourist Hotel, 11th flr	203-1589		
Nefte-Interoko JV, ul. Pivchenkova 1/3	144-7577		
Neftegazstroy Concern, Zhitnaya ul. 14	238-6877		
Neftegazstroybank, ul. Zhitnaya 14	238-6474		
Neftekhimbank, ul. Myasnitskaya 20	928-9580	927-7747	
Neftexhimexport, Gilyarovskiy ul. 31	284-8614	288-9584	411615
Nefto Agip JV (Italy), B. Cherkasskiy per. 7, korpus D	930-7973		
Nefto Agip JV (Italy), Leningradskoye shosse 63	457-2013		
Neglinka JV, Hotel Budapest, room 439	203-4551	200-3246	413581
Nemirovich-Danchenko House Museum, ul. Nemirovicha-Danchenko 5/7	209-5391		
Neo-Shag Gallery, Petrovskiye liniye 1/20	200-0562		
Neolab	253-2139		
Neptune Hotel, ul. Ibragimova 30	369-6383		
Neptune JV (Sweden), Budapest Hotel, room 439	921-4269	288-9557	413581
Nest International Ltd.	921-5100		
Neste Oy, Pokrovskiy bulvar 4/17, kv. 38	207-7473	207-7693	413067
Netherlands Press Association, see Gemeenschapperijke Pers Dienst			

	Phone	Fax	Telex
Neue Zuercher Zeitung, Kutuzovskiy prospekt 7/4, kv. 221-222	230-2273		413144
Neva Cinema, Belomorskaya ul. 16a	457-4221		
Nevka cafe, Volokolamskoye shosse 15	158-1090		
New Information Technology JV (Bulgaria), Bolshoy Savvinskiy per. 14	248-4148	943-0072	411080
New York Journal of Commerce, Kutuzovskiy prospekt 14, kv. 5	243-0032		
New York Times, ul. Sadovaya-Samotechnaya 12/24, kv. 56	973-2052	200-0240	413431
Newbridge Soviet Telecom JV, ul. Stankevicha 12	299-2935	200-4233	
Newbridge Systems JV (Canada), ul. Novokuznetskaya 17/19	231-0426		
News Agency of Sweden, Norway, Denmark & Finland, Kutuzovskiy prospekt 7/4, kv. 196	243-0674		413469
News-Burda Advertising-Information Service JV, Pushkinskaya ploshchad 5	209-3674	230-2303	411121
Newsday, ul. Marksistskaya 1, korpus 1, kv. 55	274-0014	270-9115	413548
Newstar, ul. Tverskaya 6	292-5057		
Newsweek, Kutuzovskiy prospekt 14, kv. 2	243-1773		413434
Niarmedik JV (UK), ul. Gamaley 18	190-6691		
Nichimen Corporation, Krasnopresnenskaya nab. 12, Office 1609	253-1915	230-2283	413985
Nidera Argentina S.A., Koroviy val 7, kv. 64	238-9146		413932
Night Flight, ul. Tverskaya 17	229-4169		
Nihon Keizai Shimbun, Koroviy val 7, kv. 137	230-2782	230-2330	413389
Nikkonor	383-7553		
Nina Ricci, ul. Tverskaya 9	229-2967		
Nipek	205-6137		
Nissho Iwai Corporation, Krasnopresnenskaya nab. 12, Office 908	253-1440	230-2325	413110
Nisso Boeki Co., LTD, ul. Gilyarovskovo 8, kv. 13-16	284-5381	230-2607	413169
Nit JV (FRG), ul. Sadovo-Kudrinskaya, 5			
Nitro-Sibir JV (Sweden), pr.Kalinina, 23	202-1147		
Noka JV (FRG), Suvorovskiy bulvar 12	290-1498	253-9460	413183
Nokia, see NOKO			
NOKO, Chisty per. 11/7	201-3079	230-2422	413002
Nord JV, ul. Bolshaya Ordynka 39	231-6907		
Nord-Piligrim	459-0960		
Nordbanken, Molochny per. 9/14, korpus 3	201-3714	200-1289	413018
Nordick-Monolit JV, ul. Leytenanta Boyko 104	578-3701		
NordOst	201-2851		
Normos-JV (Norway), ul. Babayevskaya 4	280-5311	200-0259	413432
Norrskensflamman, ul. Sadovaya-Spasskaya 21, kv. 261	923-4525		413020
Norsk Data AS, Astrakhansky per. 5, kv. 69	280-0604	280-0604	411001
Norsk Hydro A.S., ul. Usacheva 35	246-4948	245-5039	
NORT, see Noviye Razrabotki i Technologiy			
Nortex JV (Canada), ul. Pyatnitskaya 17	118-3447		
North Korean Airways, see Chosonminhang			
North-Eastern Joint Stock Commercial Bank, Prospekt Mira 9/18	207-7783	207-3168	
Northern River Port, Leningradskoye shosse 51	457-4050		
Norvit JV (Canada), Dmitrovskoye shosse 62-2	211-5933	200-2216	

	Phone	Fax	Telex
Norwegian Broadcasting Corporation, ul. Obrucheva 4, korpus 2, kv. 79	936-2121		413909
Norwegian TV, Kutuzovskiy prospekt 7/4, kv. 130	243-5165		
Nosbi JV, Nagatinskaya ul. 3a	111-5155		
Notary			
3rd Novomikhalkovskiy proyezd 5	154-0562		
Altufyevskoye shosse 24	401-3600		
Beringov prospekt 1	186-1756		
Berzarina, ul. 17, korpus 2	946-8331		
Bobrov per. 6, str. 3	928-4749		
Bogdanova, ul. 42	435-8736		
Bolshoy Komsomolskiy per. 8	921-6941		
Bulvar Yana Rainisa 1, korpus 1	497-7807		
Dmitrovskoye shosse 149	483-0645		
Dnepropetrovskaya, ul. 1	312-3864		
Frunzenskaya nab. 44/2	242-5471		
Krasnodonskaya 2, ul., korpus 1	350-2636		
Leningradskiy prospekt 14	214-1332		
Leningradskiy prospekt 75	158-5265		
Luganskaya, ul. 8	321-2938		
Lyusinovskaya 41	237-1154		
Malaya Yakimanka 22	238-8701		
Marksistskiy per. 1/32	272-1218		
Miklukho-Maklaya, ul. 20	335-0066		
Miklukho-Maklaya, ul. 32, korpus 2	330-5851		
Mozhayskoye shosse 41	443-0694		
Mytishchi, ul. Mira 4	581-0100		
Nagorny bulvar 14	123-6269		
Novy Arbat 31	205-2017		
Okskaya 20, korpus 2	177-5551		
Oseny bulvar 2	413-1105		
Pervomayskaya 44/20	367-5042		
Petrovka 23/10	200-6524		
Plekhanova, ul. 28, korpus 5	368-7186		
Prospekt Olminskovo 3	282-0531		
Prospekt Vernadskovo 127	438-7492		
Schelkovskoye shosse 21	164-4804		
Sergeya Makeyeva, ul. 8	259-1751		
Soldatskaya, ul. 10	363-4390		
Vorontsovskaya 30b	272-0164		
Zelenograd, 338b, kv. 74	535-1676		
Nova JV (FRG), Kuznetskiy most 19	926-0765		
Novamet JV, ul. 2nd Baumanskaya 9/23	261-7386	261-7386	411580
Novasider, Trekhprudny per 11/13, 2nd flr	299-0932	200-0234	413452
Novator Cinema, Spartakovskaya ploshchad 1/2	261-7530		
Novaya Zarya, ul. Pavla Andreyeva 23	236-7180		
Novera Group, Koroviy val 7, Office 14	230-1388	230-2810	413040
Novick Link Corp., Leninskiy prospekt 122, kv. 117	431-6809		
Novintech JV, ul. Nezhinskaya 13	442-5792	943-0072	411080
Novintex JV (Bulgaria), Malaya Kommunisticheskaya 4	272-0980	272-0801	
Noviye Razrabotki i Technologiy, Post Box 27, 117311	151-3497	371-0292	
Novoclub JV (US), ul. Karamzina 9	298-5800		
Novodevichy Convent, Novodevichy prospekt 1	245-3268		

	Phone	Fax	Telex
Novoexport, ul. Chekhova 2	128-6859		
Novoimpex JV Filial, ul. Sadovaya-Kudrinskaya 19	254-4049		
Novorossiysk Cinema, ul. Chernyshevskovo 47/24	297-6657		
Novosti Information Agency, see ITAR			
Novotel Hotel, Sheremetevo II Airport	578-9407	578-2792	911620
Lobby Bar	578-9407		
Novoye Vremya (New Times), M. Putinkovskiy per. 1/2	229-8872		
Novoye Vremya Hotel, ul. Avtozavodskaya 17, korpus 1	274-4694		
Novy Drama Theater, ul. Prokhodchikov 2	182-1977		
Novy Mir, Malaya Putinkovskiy per. 1/2	200-0829		
Nowea, see Dusseldorfer Messegesellschaft			
Nowitex GmbH	253-2804		
NRC-Handelsblad, Krutitskiy val 3, korpus 2, kv. 173	274-0008		413958
NTV, Kutuzovskiy prospekt 9, kv. 26	230-2389	253-9708	413109
Nuovo Pignone, Krasnopresnenskaya nab. 12. Office 1302	253-2084	230-2723	413940
Nur-Touristik	203-5397		
Nurminen, see John Nurminen Oy			
Nutech Trading Ltd., Prospekt Vernadskovo 41, kv. 502	437-6280	434-8455	413005
NY Dag, Bezbozhny per. 6, kv. 30	975-2011		413615

O

	Phone	Fax	Telex
O Salonen Oy, Pokrovskiy bulvar 4/17, kv. 2	925-9001	297-8356	
O. Tabakov's Studio Theater, ul. Chaplygina 1a	928-9685		
O.M.T. SpA, Hotel Volga, korpus 4, room 147-148	280-3779	975-2023	
Oblastnoi Teatr Yunovo Zritelya, Prokhladnaya ul. 28	321-6277		
Obraztsov Puppet Theater, see Central Puppet Theater			
Observador, El, ul. Sr. Pereyaslavskaya 14, kv. 87	280-0298		413570
Observer, The, ul. Bolshaya Spasskaya 12, kv. 127	280-5511		413962
Occidental Petroleum Corporation, Krasnopresnenskaya nab. 12, Office 1409	253-2270		413168
Octopus Technical Trade Center, Frezer shosse 17	170-3101	274-0057	413600
Odessa Cinema, ul. Kakhovka 21	122-3375		
Offis	120-5017		
Offset Printshop, Nagornaya 12	127-2363		
Ogonyok, Bumazhny proyezd 14	212-2269		
Oilfield Technology International, Hotel Pekin, Suite 401-402	209-4601	200-1261	413977
Okobank, Koroviy val 7, Office 13a	230-1387	230-1386	413056
Oktrabrskaya Tovarnaya Stantsiya, Komsomolskaya ploshchad	975-4460		
Oktyabr Cinema, Novy Arbat 42	202-1111		
Oktyabr Concert Hall, Kalininskiy prospekt 42	291-1261		
Oktyabrskaya Hotel I, see President Hotel			
Oktyabrskaya Hotel II, see Arbat Hotel			
OLBI Store, ul. Dimitrova Ulyanova 3	135-6567		
Oliks JV, ul. Profsoyuznaya 65	334-8751		411899
Olimp Restaurant, Luzhnetskaya nab.	201-0148		
Olimpia AMROS JV, ul. Dm. Ulyanova 37, str. 1	129-3853	129-3853	
Olimpo SRL, Hotel Pekin, room 901	209-3535		411661
Olivetti, Krasnopresnenskaya nab. 12, Office 904-905	253-8347	253-2993	413076
Olivier S.A., Pereulok Sadovskikh 6, kv. 5	209-6705	200-2256	413253

	Phone	Fax	Telex
Olmed JV, ul. 3rd Kabelnaya 1	273-1915	273-1708	411700
Olympia JV, Olympiyskiy Prospekt, 26	284-3031		
Olympia JV (Japan), Prospekt Mira 12	208-8667		
Olympia Reisen	263-0057		
Olympic Penta Hotel, Olympiyskiy prospekt 18/1	971-6101	230-2597	411061
Health Club	971-6101		
Olympic Sports Complex, Olympiyskiy prospekt 16	288-3777		
Olympic Complex Pool	288-1333		
Olympic Village Concert Hall, ul. Pelshe 1	437-5650		
Omarus Company, Ltd., ul. Markhlevskovo 4	928-6850	928-9174	
OMC, see Overseas Marketing Corporation Limited			
Omnisoft JV (Cyprus), ul. Sadovaya-Kudrinskaya ul. 18	290-0709		
OMV AG, Krasnopresnenskaya nab. 12, Office 1104-6	253-1480	230-2862	413437
OMV Gruppe, Krasnopresnenskaya nab. 12, Office 1106	253-1480	230-2862	413437
Onegin Hall, Konstantine Stanislavskiy Museum, ul. Stanislavskovo 6	299-2855		
Optic Moscow, Arbat 30	241-1577		
Optika Moscow Center JV, Frunzenskaya nab. 54	243-3069		
Optim-Mavet JV (FRG), Maly Tishinskiy per. 19, kv. 22	253-5023		411055
Optimum Commercial Bank, Krymskiy val 9	238-0000		
Optintorg, ul. Krzhizhanovskovo 16, korpus 1	124-8447	310-7074	411098
Orbikon JV (FRG), Podsosenskiy per. 20a	297-6559	297-6559	
Orbis Travel, ul. 1st Tverskaya-Yamskaya 56, kv. 88	250-1780		414330
Orbita Bank, 2nd Spasonalivkovskiy per. 6	238-8720	230-0128	
Orbita Cinema, ul. Novinki 2	115-6580		
Orbita JV (Poland), ul. Tverskaya 50		250-0489	411069
Orbita-Limosine Service JV, ul. Ryabinovaya 43a	447-0042		
Orbita-Service, Krivorozhskaya ul. 33	113-4490		
Orbotek JV (FRG), 4th Tverskaya-Yamskaya 21, str. 3	251-9151	200-3253	412178
Ordynka JV (FRG), Bolshaya Ordynka 40	238-1312		
Ordynka Restaurant, Bolshaya Ordynka 71	237-9905		
ORF (Radio & TV), Koroviy val 7, kv. 68	230-2603		413159
Orfey JV	973-0005		
Orgkomitet Joint Stock Company, ul. Ogareva 1/12, str. 2	203-2655	291-6773	
Orgmediko JV Filial, Polyanka 52	238-4742	200-2264	
Orient cafe, Nikoloshchepovskiy per. 1/9	241-1076		
Orient Co., Ltd., Mezhdunarodnaya II, room 1001	253-1001	255-5775	413702
Oriental Art Museum, Suvorovskiy bulvar 12a	202-4555		
Oriental Excelsior Club, Bombay Restaurant, Rublevskoye shosse 91	141-5504		
Orion Cinema, ul. Letchika Babushkina 28	470-6738		
Orion JV (Austria), ul. Skakovaya 36	257-6526	257-6526	
Orion-Yhtyma Oy, ul. Mytnaya 1, kv. 21	230-0465	230-2167	413049
Orlyonok Cinema, ul. Rusakovskaya 23	264-0729		
Orlyonok Hotel, ul. Kosygina 15	939-8845		
Ortex, Litovskiy bulvar 3a	427-1101	427-6410	131310
OSA, ul. Semashko 4	202-0282		
Ost-West Corporation JV (Switz.), Krasnopresnenskaya nab. 12-704	253-2702		414794
Ost-West Handelsbank AG, Proyezd Khudozhestvennovo Teatra 6/5, kv. 35	292-4839	200-0215	413955
Ostafievo Estate Museum, Sherbink	119-7300		

	Phone	Fax	Telex
Ostankino Hotel, ul. Botanicheskaya 29	219-2880		
Ostankino Museum (Museum of Serf Art), 1st Ostankinskaya ul. 5	283-4575		
Ostermann, Kuznetskiy Most 3	292-5110	230-2142	413468
Osterreichische Landerbank AG, Kalyayevskaya ul. 19	200-5221	200-4271	
Ostrovskiy Museum (N.A. Ostrovskiy), ul. Tverskaya 14	229-8552		
Ostwirtschaft Intern News Service, Rublevskoye shosse 26, korpus 1, kv. 186	415-4145		
Otchizna, Bolshoy Kharitonyevskiy per. 10	928-8283		
Otema Glaza JV (Luxembourg), Proyezd Serova 4	924-8466	207-8048	411630
Otis Elevator	208-9714		
Otto Wolff Aktiengesellschaft, Koroviy val 7, Office 3	237-1236		413227
Outokumpu Oy, see Kemira Oy			
Overseas Marketing Corporation Limited, Mezhdunarodnaya II, Room 1250	253-1701	253-9487	413672
Oversize JV (Australia), Gruzinskiy val 16	205-0709		
Ovimex JV (FRG), Rublevskoye shosse 28, korpus 3	413-9145	413-9144	
OVK JV, Krasnopresnenskaya nab. 12, Office 704	253-2702		
OWEG GmbH, ul. Tverskaya 36, kv. 2-3	251-8950	230-2078	413252
Oy Partek AB, ul. Mytnaya 1, kv. 15	230-0443	230-2245	413993
Oy Stockmann AB,			
Fashion and Business Store, Leninskiy prospekt 73/8	134-0386		
Grocery Supermarket, Zatsepskiy val 4/8	233-2602		
Home and Car Store, Lyusinovskaya ul. 70/1	954-8234		
Ozdorovlenie JV (FRG), Bolshoy Tishinskiy per.	252-3950	200-6166	

P

	Phone	Fax	Telex
P & D Research and Development, ul. Suvorovskaya 32/1	963-6097	962-0671	
P.L. JV (Sweden), Peschany per. 1a	412-9551		
P.R. Lotus Trading GmbH	973-0602	973-2057	
Pacific Union Investment Corp. JV (Panama), ul. 1st Dubrovskaya 1	276-4204	276-5039	411766
Pais (El), Kutuzovskiy prospekt 14, kv. 107	243-7073		413944
Pakistani School, ul. Sadovaya-Kudrinskaya 17	254-7201		
Palace JV (Bulgaria), ul. Solyanka, 9	427-2333	291-4281	173238
Palace of the 16-17th Centuries in Zaryadye, ul. Varvarka 10	298-3235		
Paleontology Museum, Leninskiy prospekt 16	234-2985		
Palet JV (Bulgaria), Grokholskiy per. 12a	265-5911		
Panalpina Inc., Gogolevskiy bulvar 17, Suite 209	203-1814	203-1814	411411
Panasonic Shop, ul. Polyanka 30	238-4424		
Panav-Moscow JV, ul. Marksa-Engelsa 8	203-2208	202-6075	411135
Paninter JV, ul. Lyusinovskaya 40, str. 7/8	237-2755		
Pantomime Theater (Mimiki i Zhesta), Izmaylovskiy bulvar 39/41	163-8130		
ParaGraph JV (US), Petrovskiy bulvar 23	924-1781	928-2768	
Parallel JV (UK), Pestovskiy per. 16	268-5512		
Paris Match, Leninskiy prospekt 13, kv. 73	237-3887		
Partek, see Oy Partek AB			
Pasilac, see APV-Pasilac			
Patriot Cinema, ul. Salyama Adilya 4	199-3888		

	Phone	Fax	Telex
Paurat, Mezhdunarodnaya II, room 1739	253-1739	253-9381	
Paveletskiy Train Station, Leninskaya ploshchad 1	233-0040		
PB-Technic, Nab. T. Shevchenko	243-4005	243-3933	
PBN Company, Slavyanskaya-Radisson Hotel	941-8489	240-2535	
PCB Tools JV (Switzerland), ul. B.Pionerskaya, 4			
Peja Chemie/Aussenhandel, Krasnopresnenskaya nab. 12, Office 1704	253-2163	253-2161	413036
Peja Holding N.V., Pokrovskiy bulvar 4/17, kv. 39	297-5813	200-1279	413207
Pekin Hotel, ul. Bolshaya Sadovaya 1/5	209-3400		
Pekin in Moscow JV, ul. Bolshaya Sadovaya 1/7	209-1387	209-1863	
Pekin Restaurant, ul. Bolshaya Sadovaya 1/7	209-1815		
Pencil Group, Pokrovskiy bulvar 4/17, kv. 25	230-2955		
People's Daily World, ul. Pravdy 11/13, kv. 47	212-7343		413514
Pepsi-Cola International, Kutuzovskiy prospekt 17	243-9428		
Perekop Cinema, ul. Kalanchevskaya 33	280-4077		
Perestroika JV (Finland), ul. Kosmonavtov 2/4			
Perestroika JV (US), Malaya Bronnaya 15b	299-3177	288-9574	411742
Peresvetov 4 Gallery, Peresvetov per. 4	275-2228		
Pergamos JV, Simonovskiy Pr, 3/1	203-7815		
Perspektiva Kronomarsk Global Marketing Services JV, 1st Dubrovskaya ul. 1	276-5039		411766
Pervomayskiy Cinema, ul. Pervomayskaya 93/20	465-7575		
Pescatore Restaurant, Prospekt Mira 36	280-0850		
Pet Holding, Mezhdunarodnaya II, room 925	253-2925	253-9232	
Peter Justesen	971-1178		
Peter's Place, Zemlyanoy val	298-3248		
Petrofoyt JV, Bezbozhny per. 25	288-2129		
Petrovskiy Park Tennis Club, Leningradsky prospekt 36	212-8351		
Petrovsky Passage, ul. Petrovka 10			
Pettina Hamburgers, ul. Malaya Pereyaslavskaya 6, str. 12	286-5217	286-5531	
PGD JV (US), ul. Amurskaya 44	165-4892	975-2098	411787
Pharma-Eks JV (FRG), ul. Bolshaya Pirogovskaya, 2/6	248-5727		
Phen Huan Restaurant, 23/25 Sretenka	208-0654		
Philadelphia Inquirer, ul. B. Dorogomilovskaya 14, kv. 6	243-4697	230-2842	413954
Philbro Energy, see Philipp Brothers Inc.			
Philipp Brothers Inc., Pokrovskiy bulvar 4/17, kv. 22	207-8734	230-2532	413219
Philips', see N.V. Philips' Gloeilampenfabriken			
Phillip Morris, Yuzhinskiy per. 13/2	973-4001		
Phoenix Company Lt JV, ul. Buzheninova, 16	963-0180	963-5137	412243
Phoenix International, Tamanskaya ul. 55	199-0690		
Phoenix JV (FRG), Promyshlenny proyezd 3	145-4667	975-3273	411656
Phoenix Overseas Limited, Mezhdunarodnaya II, #1450	253-1319	253-9998	413710
Phoenix Publishing JV (France), Proyezd Khudozhestvennovo Teatra 3	229-1161		4111030
Photocenter of the Journalists' Union, Suvorovskiy bulvar 8a	290-4188		
Photopro JV (FRG), Kutuzovskiy prospekt 4	148-6609		411700
Pilenga Godo JV Filial, Pr. Cherepanovykh 72, korpus 1	482-5803	928-2620	
Pilot, Leninskiy prospekt 45, kv. 427	135-1164		
Pioneer Cinema, Kutuzovskiy prospekt 21	249-2816		
Pirelli, see Industrie Pirelli SpA			
Pizza Hut Restaurant, Kutuzovskiy prospekt 17	243-1727		
ul. Tverskaya 12	229-2013		

	Phone	Fax	Telex
Pizza Hut Take-out, Kutuzovskiy prospekt 17	243-1727		
Pizza JV (Canada), ul. Myasnitskaya 43	248-2448		
PL/USSR-Sweden JV (Sweden), Peschany per. 1a	412-9551		
Plamya Cinema, Ploshchad Vosstaniya 1	255-4673		
Planeta Cinema, ul. Nezhinskaya 11	441-8201		
Planeta Publishers, ul. Petrovka 8/11	923-0470		
Planeta-Centre, ul. Tverskaya 6	292-6927	292-6732	
Planetarium, Sadovaya-Kudrinskaya ul. 5	254-1838		
Planshop, Hotel Mezhdunarodnaya	253-2773		
Plast-Service JV, ul. Pyatnitskaya 46, str. 2	231-2441		
PLE Pipeline Engineering GmbH, Mezhdunarodnaya II, room 1739	253-1739	253-9381	
Pleiades Publishing Inc., ul. Krasikova 32	129-2900		
Plus International JV (USA), ul. Varvarka 8b	298-3398	361-4497	
Pobeda Cinema, ul. Abelmanovskaya 17a	270-0321		
Podium International JV, Samokatnaya ul. 3/8, korpus A	362-1819	292-6511	
Podium JV (Hungary), ul. Neglinnaya 14	433-7955		
Podvorye Restaurant, ul. Maroseika 9	923-8949		
Poisk, Sukharevskaya ploshchad 3, korpus 1	207-8204		
Pokrovka cafe, ul. Chernyshevskovo 4	923-0282		
Polar Construction Corporation, Komsomolskiy prospekt 42	242-2279	230-2574	411619
Polar Star JV, see Polyarnaya Zvezda JV			
Polarny Cinema, ul. Polyarnaya 9	477-0033		
Polaroid Shop, Leninskiy prospekt 70/11	930-9627		
Polish Airlines, see LOT Polish Airlines			
Polish School, ul. Mosfilmovskaya 60	147-1354		
Politiken, Rublevskoye shosse 26, korpus 1, kv. 118-119	415-2961		
Politizdat Publishers, Myusskaya ploshchad 7	251-4594		
Polsib JV Filial, ul. Mosfilmovskaya 54	147-6488		
Polskaya Gvozdika, Leninskiy prospekt 79	134-5416		
Polyarnaya Zvezda JV (Canada), Olympiyskiy prospekt 26	457-0462		
Polyglot, ul. Rybalko 13	194-7781		
Polygraph Handelsgesellschaft mbH, Leninskiy prospekt 95a	936-2612	434-2063	414500
Polyot, Vorontsovskaya 35a	274-0013		
Polyot Cinema, ul. Nelidovskaya 10	492-8125		
Polytechnical Museum, Novaya ploshchad 3/4	923-0756		
Polyus International JV, ul. Razina, 8b	298-3398	361-4497	
Posad JV, Lyalin per. 21, str. 2	297-8825	929-8652	414519
Postfactum News Agency, Khoroshevskoye shosse 41	253-8656	941-0900	411712
Postipankki, Molochny per. 9/14, korpus 3	201-3714	230-2048	413018
Potel & Chabot, Hotel Mezhdunarodnaya			
Povtornovo Filma Cinema, ul. Gertsena 23	202-4942		
PPS-Agro JV, ul. Chkalova 27/2, entrance 9	266-4543	427-5822	411614
PPS-Intergeomodel JV (Bulgaria), Shosse Entuziastov 36	924-1450		207348
Prague Cinema, ul. Zdeneka Neeldy 1	945-4211		
Prague Restaurant, Arbat 2	290-6171		
Pralin JV, Altufyevskoye shosse 27	401-0084		
Pravda, ul. Pravdy 24	251-7386		
Pravda Cinema, ul. Lyusinovskaya 67	237-3665		
Pravda Publishers, ul. Pravdy 24	257-5111	200-2295	417529

	Phone	Fax	Telex
Prefecture of the			
Central District, Marksistskaya ul. 24	292-1635		
Eastern District, Preobrazhenskaya pl. 9	161-9887		
North-Eastern District, Prospekt Mira 18	281-4385		
North-Western District, ul. Svobody 13/2	490-4438		
Northern District, Timiryazevskaya 27	976-1008		
South-Eastern District, Aviamotornaya 10	362-4288		
South-West District, Sevastopolskiy prosp. 28, korpus 4	128-2722		
Southern District, Avtozavodskaya 10	275-0636		
Western District, ul. Ivana Franko 12	443-4335		
Prensa y Diplomacia, Rublevskoye shosse 26, korpus 1, kv. 294	415-4138	415-2936	413630
Present JV (Italy), ul. Koroleva 5	930-4118		
President Hotel, ul. Dimitrova 24	238-7303		
Presidium of the Russian Supreme Soviet, Krasnopresnenskaya nab. 2	205-6847		
Press Trust of India, ul. B. Pereyaslavskaya 7, kv. 133-134	280-2749		413319
Press-Kontakt JV, ul. Marshala Novikova 10/1, k. 9	193-4281	943-0005	
Pressa Publishers, ul. Pravdy 24	257-2884		
Preussag AG, 4th Dobryninskaya per. 6/9	237-7035	230-2527	413363
Price Waterhouse, Bolshoy Strochenovskiy per. 22/25	276-5902	230-2936	414724
Prima JV (Italy), Pleteshkovskiy per. 22	267-3124	975-2050	911570
Prioritet JV (US), see PRIS			
Priroda, Kutuzovskiy prospekt 5/3	243-5528		
PRIS JV (US), 1st Troitskiy per. 12/2, str. 4	284-8920		413590
Private Life, Proyezd Serova 11	928-1097		
Privatization Committee	928-6213		
Priziv Cinema, Kutuzovskiy prospekt 25	249-2907		
Procordia, Krasnopresnenskaya nab. 12, Office 903	253-2980	253-9086	413921
Procter and Gamble, Pullman Iris Hotel	906-0063		
Prodintorg, ul. Smolenskaya-Sennaya 32/34	244-2629		
Proekt JV, ul. Lesnaya 13, kv. 12	251-3280		
Proektsofin JV (Finland), Komsomolskiy prospekt 42	245-6015	230-2574	411619
Profil, ul. Donskaya 18/7, kv. 112	236-1296		
Prognoinfo JV (Hungary), ul. Sretenka 20	207-0003	207-0008	251246
Programma 2000, Pereulok Sivtsev-Vrazhek 15/25, kv. 123	241-3290	253-9711	
Programming Systems for Agriculture JV (Bulgaria), Bolshoy Tishinskiy per. 8	254-4497		411614
Progress Bookstore, Zubovskiy bulvar 17			
Progress Cinema, Lomonosovskiy prospekt 17	133-1664		
Progress Publishers, Zubovskiy bulvar 17	246-9032	230-2403	411800
Progress Trading Co., LTD, ul. Mytnaya 1, Office 30	230-1075	230-2226	413394
Project Kampo JV, Leninskiy prospekt 146	133-1041	200-1227	413073
Prokop JV (France), ul. Stanislavskovo 24	265-9001	200-2265	
Promen JV, ul. Vavilova, 38			
Promita JV (Sweden), Chermyansky proyezd 5a	200-2285	200-4417	413614
Prompoligraphmash, Ovchinnikovskaya nab. 18/1	231-4224	230-2111	111874
Prompt International, ul. Mayakovskaya 17/7	203-9945		
Promstroybank of the USSR, Tverskoy bulvar 13	200-7910	200-3273	411843
Promstroyimport, Novinskiy bulvar 13	203-0577		
Promtex JV (Canada), Perovskoye shosse 43	171-7628	288-9554	411623
Prosovart JV (Switz.), Izvestkovy per.3	928-2431		
Prospect JV, Lesnaya ul. 13, kv. 12			

	Phone	Fax	Telex
Prosvetitel JV (FRG), Petropavlovskiy per. 4/6	246-4517		
Protestant Services, Leninskiy prospekt 78	143-3562		
Provincias (Las), Krutitskiy val 3, korpus 2, kv. 95	276-7146	274-0010	
Publitalia '80 SpA			413482
Pullman-Iris Hotel, Korovinskoye shosse 10	488-8000	906-0105	413656
Puolimatka International, Koroviy val 7, Office 14	230-1388	230-2810	413040
Pushkin Drama Theater, Tverskoy bulvar 23	203-4221		
Pushkin Museum, ul. Prechistenka 12/2	202-3293		
Pushkin Museum of Fine Art, Volkhonka ul. 12	203-7998		
Pushnik JV (Venezuela), B. Strochenovskiy per. 22/25, str. 1	236-4493		
Put, ul. Sretenka 27/29	262-9215		
Puteshestviye v SSSR, Neglinnaya 8	928-3901		
Putnik JV (Venezuela), B. Strochenovskiy per. 22/25, str. 1	237-5902		
PVK JV (Bolivia), ul. Tverskaya 23, str.2			

Q

Qorri Master-Lamas JV (Finland), ul. Platovskaya 4		240-4347	
Quality Products, Bolshaya Bronnaya ul. 19, kv. 49	229-8290		
Que Pasa, see Dan News Agency			
Queen-Mosmebel JV (Egypt), ul. Garibaldi 26	128-7835	299-5676	412275
Quelle Catalogue Sales, ul. B. Molchanovka 34, str 2	291-4735	200-2263	411775
Quest Automation PLC, Koroviy val 7, Office 4	236-2135	230-2488	413905
Quinta, Bolshoy Cherkovskiy prospekt	923-1403	288-9501	
Quorum JV (US), ul. Yelanskovo 2	248-6822		

R

R.C.B. Product International JV (US), Prospekt Mira 5, kv. 29a	291-3848		
Rabotnitsa, Bumazhny proyezd 14, 10th flr	212-2039		
Radio Monte Carla, Rublevskoye shosse 26, kor. 1, kv. 10	415-4266	415-2916	
Radio Nacional de Espana, Krutitskiy val 3, kor. 2, kv. 93	276-6865	274-0006	413096
Radio Peking, ul. Bolshaya Pereyaslavskaya 7, kv. 105	280-8687		
Radio Suisse Romande/Schweitaer Radio, Gruzinskiy per. 3, kv. 212	230-2443		413336
Radio-France & Television Francaise 1, Gruzinskiy per. 3, kv. 223	250-2505	253-9294	413322
Radio-Maximum	200-1088		
Radioexport, ul. Kirova 35	923-7949	923-7941	411386
Radiotelevisione Italiana (RAI), Prospekt Mira 74, kv. 160	280-7689		413218
Radisson-Slavyanskaya Hotel, see Slavyanskaya-Radisson Hotel			
Raduga	253-1777		
Raduga Car Sales, ul. 1st Tverskaya-Yamskaya 46, 4-5 flr	251-0500		
Raduga Car Service, 1st Dorozhny proyezd 3a	315-3736		
Raduga Publishers, Zubovskiy bulvar 17	245-0151	230-2403	411826
Raiffeisen Zentralbank Austria, 1st Krasnogvardeyskiy proyezd, Exh. Complex, Pav. 2	256-7444	253-9483	413599
Raketto-SU JV (Italy), Sredne-Ovchinnikovskiy per. 8	216-0885	216-3617	
Ramax JV (Holland), ul. Kedrova 20, kv. 1	301-1610		
Rank Xerox Limited, 4th Dobryninskaya per. 6/9	237-6842	230-2728	413139

	Phone	Fax	Telex
Rantarin JV Filial, Orlikov per. 3	204-4814		
Rasma JV (Belgium), ul. Lesnaya 43	250-8763	288-9577	411273
Rasoni JV (Finland), Staraya Basmannaya ul. 18, str. 1	263-2655	267-9147	
Rassvet Cinema, ul. Zoi i Alexandra Kosmodemyanskikh 23	450-0213		
RAU, see Russian American University			
Rauma-Repola Oy, Pereulok Sadovskikh 6, kv. 8	209-2817	200-0214	413223
Rautaruukki Oy, see Valmet Oy			
Razgulyai Restaurant, Spartakovskaya ul. 11	267-7613		
Raznoexport, Verkhnaya Krasnoselskaya 15	264-5656		411408
Raznoimport, Ovchinnikovskaya nab. 18/1	220-1849		411118
Raznoservice Coop	246-9587		41118 R
Nursery School, Olsufyevskiy per. 8, korpus 5	243-6232		
Razvitie JV Filial (Australia), ul. Profsoyuznaya 61	334-8249	230-2606	413474
Razvitrie Management School	210-4030		
RCM International, Shevchenko nab. 3	195-2853	195-2853	
Real Estate, Suvorovskiy bulvar 5/1	290-1457		
Realta Sovietica, ul. Chernyakhovskovo 8a, kv. 19	158-8317		
Record Cinema, Lenin Stadium	246-6309		
Redaktor, ul. Fadeyeva 2, kv. 262	251-9647		
Redo Joint Stock Company, Post Box 33, 107005	274-1005	292-6511	411700
Referat, Basmanny tupik 10/12	263-1855		
Reformiz JV (FRG), ul. Bolshaya Semenovskaya 42	369-0260	369-0505	421298
Regie Nationale Des Usines Renault,			
ul. Lunacharskovo 7, kv. 12	202-0360		413327
REI Adventures	365-4563		
Reichhold Chemie GmbH, Mezhdunarodnaya II, #1736	253-1736	253-9302	
Rekon JV (Finland), Koroviy val 7, pom. 10	237-1250	230-2202	413950
Rektime JV (Japan), ul. Gavrikova 3/1m, str. 1, kv. 98	264-2799	972-6250	
Rena, 142771 Mosk. Obl. P/O Mosrentgen	339-6021		
Renault, see Regie Nationale Des Usines Renault			
Rendezvous-Khungun JV (Hungary),			
Frunzenskaya nab. 36/2	242-4178		
Renlund Biurobin, ul. Ostrovkovo 39	237-7612		
Renova JV, Kashirskiy Proyezd, 21	113-9407		
Reprocenter JV (UK), ul. Fadeyeva 1	181-2994	288-9561	411860
Reprocenter (Rank Xerox), Kutuzovskiy prospekt 22	243-1290		
Ukraine Hotel	243-3007		
VDHKh	181-3042		
Republica (La), Kutuzovskiy prospekt 14, kv. 12	243-6778		413485
Research & Commercial Medical Center JV,			
Bolshaya Kolkhoznaya ploshchad 3	207-1425	207-0533	
Resource Development Ltd.	290-3293		
Rest-Ital, Vorotnikovskiy per. 11	299-2116		413466
Retatorg, Krasnopresnenskaya nab., Office 503A	253-9191	253-9200	411813
Reuters PLC, ul. Sadovaya-Samotechnaya 12/24, kv. 55	200-0264		413342
Reynolds International Inc.,			
Leninskiy prospekt 2, kv. 218-219	231-0346		
Rheinische Post, Leninskiy prospekt 45, kv. 490	135-1358		413195
Rhone-Poulenc SA, ul. Mytnaya 1, Office 9	230-0232		413117
RIA, see Russian Information Agency			
Rida JV Filial, Rogozhskiy val 7	278-5502		
Rifle Jeans Store, Ul. Neglinnaya & Kuznetskiy Most	923-2458		
Riga Cinema, ul. Botanicheskaya 39	482-2360		

	Phone	Fax	Telex
Rikon JV, ul. Bolshaya Molchanovka 23	291-8000	291-8000	
RINAKO, see Russian Investment Joint Stock Company			
Rincon Espanol Restaurant (El), Hotel Moskva	292-2893		
Ring JV Filial, ul. Bolshaya Serpukhovskaya 30	237-1492		
Rio Excel Technologies Group JV (Canada), 1st Khoroshevskiy proyezd 10, korpus 2, podyezd 5	945-6128	200-2217	411700
Rio-Tinto	459-8105		
RITM Trading House	262-1311	975-1297	
River Boat Tickets, Leningradskiy prospekt 1	257-7109		
Rizhskiy Train Station, Rizhskiy ploshchad	266-9535		
Rizospastis, ul. Krasnaya Presnya 23, kv. 178	252-2963		413153
Road Technologie Sam JV, ul. Bolshaya Pionerskaya 4	264-5534		
Robert Bosch AG, ul. Mytnaya 3, Office 4	253-2166	253-2173	413556
Roche, see F. Hoffmann-La Roche LTD			
Rock and Jazz Laboratory	923-1604		
Rodel U.K. Limited, ul. Gasheka 12, korpus 7	251-2626	973-2053	
Rodina Cinema, Semenovskaya ploshchad 5	369-1781		
Rolba Co., LTD, Krasnopresnenskaya nab. 12, Office 504	253-1880	253-9383	411636
Rolls-Royce PLC, Pereulok Sadovskikh 4, kv. 12	209-6520		413376
Roman Catholic Services, Kutuzovskiy prospekt 7/4, korpus 5, kv. 42	243-9621		
Romanian Air Transport, ul. Mosfilmovskaya 64	143-2640		
Sheremetevo II	578-2716		
Romen Gypsy Theater, see Gypsy Theater Romen			
Romos JV, Staropanskiy per. 1/5	921-9392		411697
RON JV, ul. Razina 6	298-0552		
Ros-Marketing JV (FRG), Lubyanskaya ploshchad 22	923-2045	921-6367	
Rosart Amorim JV (Portugal), Vorontsovskiy per. 5/7	272-3990		
Rosavtobirzha, see Russian Auto Exchange			
Rosbiznessbank, Tomakov per. 14	261-1911		
Rosbri International Ltd. JV (UK), Garazhnaya ul. 6	366-8110	144-0562	411311
Roscom JV (US), Presnenskiy val 19, kv. 306	252-0671		
Rosenlew, see Imatran Voima Oy			
Rosfratex, ul. Vasilyevskaya 7	254-8772	230-2303	
Rosgrazhdanrekonstruktsiya Concern, Skakovaya 17	945-3669		
Rosinform	214-3235		
Rosinkas, Sretenskiy bulvar 1/4	928-3030		
Rosinterbank, Orlikov per. 3	204-4350		
RosInterTeatr JV (USA), Strastnoy bulvar 10	924-5496		411738
Roslegprom Association, Zubovskiy bulvar 2/39	246-3343		411621
Roslesbirzha, see Russian Forestry Exchange			
Rosneftegaz, Nab. Morisa Toreza 26/1	239-8800		
Rosplemkonzavod, 2nd Smolenskiy per. 3/4	248-1956	241-6774	
Rospromstroybank, Prospekt Mira 84	281-8936		
Rosrechflot Concern, ul. Petrovka 3/6	927-8135		
Rosselkhozbank	923-1032		
Rossia Cinema, Pushkinskaya ploshchad 2	229-2111		
Rossia Concert Hall, Moskvoretskaya nab. 1	298-1124		
Rossia Hotel, ul. Varvarka 6	298-5400		
Restaurant	298-4133		
Rossia JV (USA), 4th Tverskaya-Yamskaya ul. 4	972-6453	972-6250	
Rossiyanka Hotel, ul. Donskaya 1	238-0508		

	Phone	Fax	Telex
Rossiyskoye Investitsionnoye Aktsionernoye Obshchestvo, see Russian Investment Joint Stock Company			
Rosskommunbank, ul. Mysanitskaya 13	921-3950		
Rosso JV (Poland), ul. Akademika Koroleva 8, korpus 1	181-7329	181-7329	
Rossoyuzmestprom, ul. Krzhizhanovskovo 21/33	124-7642		
Rossteklo JV (FRG), ul. Kedrova 15	129-0909		
Rosstroyimpex, Shmitovskiy proyezd 3	256-8068		
Rosvneshtorg, Barrikadnaya 8/5	255-1342	253-9576	411060
Rosvneshtorgbank, Kuznetskiy Most 16	925-5231	973-2096	414726
Rosvostokstroi, Prospekt Vernadskovo 41	430-8809		
Rotary Club, Dmitrovskoye shosse 27	333-9070		
Rotel-Mikma JV (Switz.), Malaya Cherkizovskaya ul. 66	168-3796	975-2047	
Rovina Andorra, S.L., Balaklavsky prospekt 5a	316-0590	316-8834	
Rovstar JV, ul. Kuybysheva 3/8 ,Stroenie 1	925-0265		
Royal Jordanian Air	299-4344		
Rozec Car Rental, ul. Kulakova 20	145-1441	286-5204	
Rozek Advertising Agency JV Filial, Sushchevskiy val 50	289-0346	216-4714	
Rozek JV, ul. Dovatora 13	245-4661		
RT International Corp., ul. Kirova 13	927-2319		
Rubens Gallery of Modern Art, Verkhnaya Krasnoselskaya ul. 34	264-8292		
Rubin Cinema, ul. Nizhegorodskaya 76	278-2584		
Rundfunk Nachrichten Agentur (RUFA), Leninskiy prospekt 148, kv. 117	938-2109	938-2185	413666
Rurik Lt JV, ul. Gertsena, 22 kv.60	229-0268		
Rus Restaurant, Krasnozvozdnaya 13, Saltykova	524-4202	524-2311	
Rus-Ellada JV (Greece), Strastnoy bulvar 9	299-2387		
Rusalochka Restaurant, see Little Mermaid			
Ruscan JV (Canada), Smolenskaya-Sennaya ul. 27/29	244-0568		
Rusganza JV (UK), see Intercontact Agroservice JV			
Rushmin Trust & Trade JV, ul. Dubininskaya, 17a			
Rusispan JV (Spain), Maslovo, Odintsovsky District	143-8691	263-2162	
Ruslan cafe, Vorontsovskaya 32/36	272-0632		
Ruslit Publishers, Kutuzovskiy prospekt 1	243-4043		
RusOtel JV (US), Varshavskoye shosse, 21st km	382-0586	382-2162	
Russia, Government of			
Council of Ministers, Krasnopresnenskaya nab. 2	205-5432		
Deputy Prime Minister, Staraya ploshchad 4	206-2171	206-3528	
First Deputy Prime Minister, Staraya ploshchad 4	206-2629	206-2183	
Prime Minister, Kremlin	244-1886	206-3961	
Administration, Staraya ploshchad 4	206-5064	206-2431	
Government Information Service	205-4601		
Information Department	206-4547		
Press Center	206-3000	206-2988	
Russian Academy of Medical Sciences, Solyanka 14	297-0504	297-0523	
Russian Academy of Sciences, Leninskiy prospekt 14	234-2153		
Russian American University	496-4114		
Russian Army Theater, Ploshchad Kommuni 2	281-5120		
Russian Auto Exchange	384-4101	382-1162	
Russian Bread, ul. Elektrozavodskaya	926-1665		
Russian Business Reports, Leninsky prospekt 39, kv. 42	135-8745		
Russian Chamber of Commerce and Industry, ul. Kuybysheva 6	921-0811		411126

	Phone	Fax	Telex
Russian Club of Young Millionaires, Leninskiy prosp. 45	137-0006	137-6525	
Russian Commerce Agency	246-4763		
Russian Commercial Bank, Leningradskoye shosse 84	452-1143		
Russian Committee for Foreign Economic Relations, Ovchinnikovskaya nab. 18/1	220-1214		
Russian Commodity and Raw Material Exchange, Novaya ploshchad 3/4	262-8080	262-5757	
Business Channel	262-8080		
Russian Federation Chamber of Commerce, ul. Ilyinka 6	924-5645		
Russian Fish Exchange, VDNKh	181-0918		
Russian Forestry Exchange (Roslesbirzha)	925-7295		
Russian Fur and Leather Commodity Exchange, Kolpachny per. 14	227-1013		
Russian Information Agency, Zubovskiy bulvar 22/39	245-1772	230-2475	412324
Russian Information Services, Bolshoy Kondryatevskiy pereulok 4, kor. 2, kv. 168	254-9275	254-9275	
Russian Insurance Bank, Studeny proyezd 1	476-9471	292-6511	
Russian International Cultural Fund, Gogolevskiy bulvar 6	202-6984		
Russian Investment and Joint Stock Company, Novaya Ploshchad 3/4, entr. 6	936-0766	936-7545	
Russian Kompozitor Publishing Association, ul. Sadovaya-Triumfalnaya 14-12	209-2384		
Russian Language Studies Center JV, 2nd Minaevskiy per. 2	972-6200		411798
Russian Library Concert Hall, ul. Vozdvizhenka 3	222-8373		
Russian Orthodox Services	245-2013		
Russian Real Estate Exchange, see All Russian Real Estate Exchange JV			
Russian State Fuel Association, ul. Sadovaya-Chernogryazskaya 8	207-3370		
Russian State Library, ul. Vozdvizhenka 3	202-5790		
Russian Supreme Soviet - Reception	202-0185		
Russian Television and Radio, ul. Myasnitskaya 13, kor. 4	924-2005		
Russkaya Izba cafe, Ilyinskoye village near Arkhangelskoye	561-4244		
Russkaya Kniga, Prospekt Sapunova 13/15	921-3913		
Russkiy Traktir Restaurant, Arbat 44	241-9853		
Russkiy Yazyk Publishers, Staropanskiy per. 1/5	928-3755		
Russkoe Voisko, see Fifth Floor Studio			
Russky Strakhovoi Bank, see Russian Trading Bank			
RussLan JV (US), ul. Miklukho-Maklaya 21, blok 9	299-1549	299-1206	411640
Rybcomflot JV, Rozhdestvenskiy bulvar 9	925-8750		411208
Ryleeva 9 cafe, Ryleeva 9/5	291-6063		
Rynok Newspaper, Staropansky per. 5	290-7988		
Ryugen, ul. Malygina 9a	474-4433		
RZB: Raiffeisen Zentralbank Austria	256-7444		

S

S3 Technologies JV (US), ul. Ferganskaya 25	377-0206		
Saab, Mr. Per Baeckman, Swedish Embassy	147-9009		
Saab Service, Volgogradskiy prospekt 177	379-6245		
Saaek JV (Finland), Tverskaya ul. 23	299-6519	253-9794	411238

	Phone	Fax	Telex
SAAEK JV (US), ul. Malaya Bronnaya 26	202-3876		
Sab-Scray, Inc. JV (US), ul. Granovskovo 2, korpus 1	203-7631	203-6023	
Sabena Belgian World Airlines, Belgrade Hotel, rm 721	248-1214		
Sheremetevo II	578-2713		
Sabin Metal Corporation, ul. 1812 Goda 2, kv. 57	148-9116		
Sacramento Bee, ul. Vorovskovo 23a, kv. 3	291-6064		
Sadko, Bolshaya Dorogomilovskaya 16	243-7501		
Kutuzovskiy prospekt 9	243-7502		
Sadovniki Gallery, ul. Akademika Millionshchikova 35	112-1161		
SAGMAR, ul. Sr. Pereyaslavskaya 14, kv. 111, 144	971-1726		413305
Saico S.R.L., ul. Bolshaya Pirogovskaya 2-6	246-3499	248-2788	413726
Sais JV (US), ul. Menogina 4	259-8261	292-6511	
Sako-200 JV, ul. Vavilova, 53, korp. 1			
Sakura Restaurant, Hotel Mezhdunarodnaya	253-2894		
Salentini JV, Dokuchayev per. 13	207-5607	292-6511	
Salma Service Center, Zelyeny prospekt 2/19	306-0283		
Salomon Inc., see Philipp Brothers Inc.			
Salonen Oy, see O Salonen Oy			
Salyut Cinema, ul. Kedrova 14, korpus 3	125-0135		
Salyut Hotel, Leninskiy prospekt 158	438-6565		
Salzgitter AG, 4th Dobryninskaya per. 6/9, 4th flr	237-7035	230-2527	413363
Saman JV (US), Ryazanskiy prospekt 99, korpus 3	174-5754	273-8560	
Samer JV (Cyprus), Stremyanny per. 28	237-8351		
Sametko JV (UK), Rublevskoye shosse 26, kor. 1, kv. 305	415-4241	415-4080	412181
Samos JV (Poland), Komsomolskiy prospekt 7	202-5955		
Samsung Co., LTD, Krasnopresnenskaya nab. 12, #1104	253-2671	253-2670	413607
Samsung-Glavortsnab JV, Leninskiy Prospekt 90/2	131-2288	248-0814	
Samtes JV, 2nd Kozhevnicheskiy per. 4/6	235-3674	235-5267	411602
Samuel M. Spiro and Associates, Ltd.,			
Novokonyushenny per. 14	248-0683	248-3277	
San Paolo, see Instituto Bancario San Paolo di Torino			
Sana JV (France), ul. Nizhnyaya Pervomayskaya 65	464-1254	464-4563	412240
Sandoz A.G., ul. Lunacharskovo 7, kv. 4	203-1043	253-9511	413380
Sandunovskaya Sauna, 1st Neglinnaya per. 1a	925-4631		
Sandvik AB, ul. Usacheva 35	245-5770	245-1383	416913
Sankei Shimbun, ul. Sadovaya-Samotechnaya 12/24, kv. 6	299-6667	200-0220	413385
Sannibul JV, Tsvetnoy Bulvar 11	209-2639	200-1095	
Sanofi, see Elf Aquitaine			
Sanoma Publications,			
ul. 26-Bakinskikh-Komissarov 9, kv. 5	434-3685	230-2421	413053
Santa International JV (FRG), ul. Chekhova 8	200-2111	200-4208	
Santa Lucia Bar, Hotel Intourist, 3rd floor	203-1632		
Santi Brokerage Firm, ul. 3rd Parkovaya 33, str. 1	163-7462	163-0033	
Saor JV (Lebanon), Shosse Entuziastov 36	273-4056		207348
SAP JV (US), 1st Vrazhskiy per. 4a	450-9391		
Sappora Restaurant, Prospekt Mira 14	207-8253		
Sarp JV (Austria), ul. Adama Mitskevicha 7	291-5989		
Sarpinservis, ul. Nikolskaya 5/1	923-1739		
SAS, see Scandinavian Airlines			
Satire Theater, Bolshaya Sadovaya 18	299-9915		
Satirikon Theater, Sheremetevskaya ul. 8	289-7844		
Satra Aerospace, Leningradskiy prospekt 45/5	157-3258	157-3616	413129
Satra Corporation, Trekhprudny per. 11/13	299-9169	200-0250	413360

	Phone	Fax	Telex
Saturn Cinema, ul. Snezhnaya 18	180-4352		
Saturn-Comfort JV (Poland), ul. Shchipok 2	230-1088		41653 P
Saturn-Inmet, ul. Panfilova 20	198-4254		
SAV Entertainment JV (Canada), Olympiyskiy prosp. 16	288-1422	975-2003	411030
Savio, Krasnopresnenskaya nab. 12, Office 1302	253-2084	230-2723	413940
Savoy Hotel, ul. Rozhdestvenka 3	929-8555	230-2186	411620
Business Center, ul. Rozhdestvenka 3	928-3780	230-2186	
Dry Cleaning, ul. Rozhdestvenka 3	929-8693		
Restaurant, ul. Rozhdestvenka 3	928-0450		
Savyolovskiy Train Station, Pl. Savyolovskovo Vokzala	266-9007		
Sayani Cinema, ul. Sayanskaya 9	307-1864		
Sayani Hotel, Yaroslavskoye shosse 116, korpus 2	183-1456		
Sayat-Nova cafe, ul. Yasnogorskaya 17, korpus 1	426-8511		
SB EuroGroup JV (FRG), Trubnikovskiy per. 29/31	232-4787		
SB-Engineering JV (Sweden), ul. Adama Mitskevicha 3	204-7090	230-2940	207633
SB-Inquiring JV (FRG), ul. Adama Mitskevicha 3	209-7090		
Sbergatelny Bank, Head Office	928-0094	928-2620	
Anadyrskiy prospekt 21	472-6786		
Aviamotornaya, ul. 51	273-5248		
Chertanovskaya, ul. 32, korpus 1	314-6111		
Gvozdeva, ul. 7/4	272-2110		
Lobachevskovo. ul. 2	432-4874		
Neglinnaya, ul. 12	928-0094		
Nemanskiy prospekt 9	942-3624		
Obrucheva, ul. 28, korpus 5	434-6605		
Olympiyskiy prospekt 10, korpus 2	288-4678		
Sredne-Pervomayskaya ul. 38/7	463-9770		
Stromynka, ul. 19	269-4433		
Svobody, ul. 65	497-6609		
Volgogradskiy prospekt 1	276-3301		
SBF Creative Union JV, ul. Druzhinnikovskaya 15	205-1392	205-2680	411070
SBS Business School	155-0789	155-0168	
Scan-Cargo, Head Office, Institutskiy per. 2/1	200-1522		411310
Butovo	548-7144		411310
Scandinavian Airlines, Kuznetskiy Most 3	925-4747	230-2142	413468
Sheremetevo II	578-2727		413077
Scanflot JV, ul. Kudryavtseva 10	572-4515	572-4907	
Scanflot-Scanior Design, ul. Biryuzovaya 19	194-8811		
Schenck, see Carl Schenck AG			
Schiess AG Lentjes AG, Krasnopresnenskaya nab. 12. Office 1502	253-2460		413646
Schreiber, see Ulrich Schreiber			
Schwing/Stetter Baumaschinen-Fabriken, Hotel Soyuz II, room 243	256-1930	253-9779	143722
Scientific & Tech. Exchange Center JV, ul. Krasikova 32	129-6491	310-7015	
Scientific-Tech. Engineering JV, Sechenovskiy per. 6	229-3937	200-3277	411354
SCOA Groupe, see Olivier S.A.			
Scott-European Co., Krasnopresnenskaya nab. 12, Office 501	253-1094	253-9382	411813
Screen JV, ul. Vasilyevskaya 13	251-3018	251-3641	411939
Scriabin Museum, ul. Vakhtangova 11	241-0303		
Seabeco Group, Mezhdunarodnaya II, room 1647	253-1785	230-2821	413508
SeaLand	926-1733		

	Phone	Fax	Telex
SEBA Spectrum JV, ul. Usacheva 35	245-5480	245-5070	411554
Secondex JV (UK), 2nd Botkinskiy prospekt 5	259-4527	200-2216	
Security Joint Stock Company	265-5258		
Sefameks Soviet Export Film Ameks, Kalashny per. 14	290-6665	200-1256	411143
Segol Ltd., Khoroshevskoye shosse 34	458-7229		
Seibolt-Analit JV (Finland), 2nd Smolenskiy per 2/3	319-1365	310-7076	
Seibu International Trading LTD, Krasnopresnenskaya nab. 12, Office 702a	253-1255	253-1259	413191
Seidel, Mezhdunarodnaya II, room 1142	253-1017		
Seiko Epson Corporation, Krasnopresnenskaya nab. 12, Office 1808	253-1679	230-2720	413057
Sekom JV, ul. Skladochnaya 6			
Selkhozpromexport, Ovchinnikovskaya nab. 18/1	220-1692	921-9364	411933
Selskaya Zhizn, ul. Pravdy 24	257-2963		
Semiramis JV (FRG), Oruzheyny per. 15, str. 1	972-1261	251-1889	
Separs JV, see Moscow Interregional Commercial Bank			
Sept JV, ul. Nametkina 10a	172-9708	331-4777	
SER (Sociedad Espanola de Radiodifusion), Gruzinskiy per. 3, kv. 266	250-4165		413013
Serco JV (FRG), ul. 3rd Kabelnaya 1	200-3510		
Serebryany Slonyonok cafe, Bolotnikovskaya 52	121-2011		
Serpukhovskaya Zastava, see Diana			
Serso JV (FRG), ul. Markhlevskovo 14	928-2381	928-3335	
Serveko JV (Switz.), ul. Marshala Biryuzova 1	252-5266	253-9318	411035
Service Exhibit, ul. Chernyshevskovo 43, str. 1	925-7129	292-6511	411700
Service Globus (US), ul. Planetnaya 29	155-7295	155-7295	
Sheremetevo II	578-7534	578-4650	
Service Station No. 7, 2nd Selskokhozyaystvenny prosp. 6	181-1374		
Service Vang JV (Austria), Komsomolskiy prospekt 1/1	112-3411	112-1380	
Servicenter International (Austria), Novy Arbat 25	203-7407	290-4519	911633
Servoimport, Profsoyuznaya ul. 88/20	335-9866	330-1555	
Setek JV (FRG), Volzhskiy bulvar 19	178-8011	128-9723	411700
Seti JV (UK), ul. Kachalova 27	202-5611	200-1213	411153
Sevastopol Cinema, Bolshaya Cherkizovskaya 93	161-5301		
Sevastopol Hotel, ul. Yushunskaya 1a	119-8182		
Seventh Day Adventists Services	297-5167		
Sever Cinema, ul. Bazhova 9	181-2044		
Severnaya Hotel, ul. Sushchevskiy val 50	289-6413		
Severo-Vostochny Aktsionerny Kommerchesky Bank, see North-Eastern Joint Stock Commercial Bank			
Sezam JV, Shlyuzovaya nab. 8	183-5047	183-4374	
SFAO JV (France), Leningradskoye shosse 61a	459-7444		411968
SFS JV (Finland), Prospekt Andropova 1/2	118-0854		411700
SGS, see Societe Generale De Surveillance			
Shadow Theater, Izmaylovskiy bulvar 60/10	465-6592		
Shaeffer Shop, see Interoko			
Shakovskaya House, ul. Gertsena 19	201-6408		
Shalom Jewish Theater, Varshavskoye shosse 71	110-4853		
Shamrock Pub, Novy Arbat 19			
Sheldon Trading Co., Mezhdunarodnaya II, room 1209	253-1209		411432
Shell International Petroleum Co., Ltd., Koroviy val 7, Office 11	237-7186	230-2885	413930
Sheraton JV (US), Hotel Pekin, room 802	209-3816		

	Phone	Fax	Telex
Sheremetevo Customs Point, Sheremetevo II	578-2120		
Sheremetevo Hotel, Sheremetevo II	578-5753		
Sheremetevo II Airport	578-9101		
Sherman and Sterling, ul. Obrucheva 34/63	333-9070		
Shimadzu Europa GmbH, Hotel Belgrade, room 1805	248-2463		
Shkola Dramaticheskovo Isskustva, ul. Vorovskovo 20	290-5888		
Shuvalova House, ul. Vorovskovo 30/1	201-6408		
SI-Gruppa (India), Universitetskiy prospekt 9	930-6430		
SI-XXI JV (Italy), ul. Prechistenka 35-7	246-9632		
Siberian American Oil Co. JV, Krasnopresnenskaya nab. 12, Office 1026	253-1026		
Sibir Inc., Pekin Hotel, room 502	209-0902		
Sidiamed, see Sidvim Aktiengesellschaft			
Sididmed JV (Switzerland), Michurinskiy prosp. 12, kor. 2	932-5651	420-2016	411829
Sidvim Aktiengesellschaft, Mezhdunarodnaya II, #1734	253-1734	253-1011	411446
Siemens, 1st Donskoy proyezd 2	237-6476		412412
Siemens AG, ul. Mytnaya 1, kv. 25	230-0810	230-2616	413413
Siemens-Sovmedtekhnika JV, Novy Arbat 54	291-9834		
SIF Television, Rublevskoye shosse 26/1, korpus 2, kv. 84	415-4209	415-2940	413638
Sigma-Trade JV (FRG), Hotel Budapest, room 533	928-6665	928-3374	411724
Sigulla JV (FRG), Aviamotornaya 4	362-6210		
Silicon Technology Corporation, Prosp. Vernadskovo 82	433-2575		
Simos JV, Skatertny per. 8	137-8007	137-8007	
Sims & Klein, ul. Tverskaya 36	251-8950	230-2078	413252
Sinergy International JV (US), Lopukhinskiy per. 3	248-8280	201-7444	
Sinion JV (Italy), ul. Ibragimova 15	366-4347	365-1065	
Sinko Light JV (Switz.), Golikovskiy per. 11	233-0686	230-2047	
SIPA Press, ul. Bolshaya Spasskaya 12, kv. 3	975-2000		
Siprom JV, Pugovishnikov per. 11	246-9983	246-9662	
Siren, Novy Arbat 44	291-1225		
Sirin JV (Italy), ul. Vorovskovo 4	202-2419		
Sisan JV, 60-Letiya Oktyabrya prospekt 9	135-4246	938-2209	411237
SISI, see Societa Di Iniziative Sovietico Italianeo			
Sitek JV (Lichtenstein), Pechatnikov per. 13	921-4223	200-4212	
Sitko JV, Starokonyushenny per. 47/27	291-0710		
Skadden, Arps, ul. Solyanka 3, building 3	126-9574	415-7094	
Skandinaviska Enskilda Banken, ul. Pushkinskaya 5/6, kv. 34	292-0338	200-0237	413286
Skantek JV (Canada), Sechenovskiy per. 6	202-5818		
Skazka Cafe, Tovarishcheskiy per. 1	271-0998		
Skazka II Restaurant, Yaroslavskoe shosse, 43rd km	184-3436		
Skif JV (France), Maly Karetny per. 4-8	299-2527	229-1680	411055
Skiy 100.4 FM Stereo/Kathimerini, ul. Marksistskaya 1, korpus 1 kv. 11	270-1426		413536
SKK Space Commerce Corporation JV, ul. Krasnoproletarskaya 9	972-4436	288-9583	411879
Skopbank, Pereulok Sadovskikh 4, kv. 2	209-6836	200-0259	413432
Skotoimport, Skatertny per. 8	291-7406		
Skut Stamp Making, Bezbozhny per. 9	473-4109		
Slastena i Moulen de la Galette JV, ul. Krasnokazarmennaya 3	261-8626	267-9726	
Slastyona Bakery, Krasnokazarmennaya 3	261-8626		
Slava Cinema, Shosse Entuziastov 58	176-0417		
Slavinform JV (FRG), 12th Parkovaya ul. 5	463-0072	463-9872	

	Phone	Fax	Telex
Slavyanskaya-Radisson Hotel, Berezhkovskaya nab. 2	941-8020		
Health Club	941-8027		
Slavyanskiy Bazaar Restaurant, ul. 25 Oktyabrya 13	921-1872		
Sloboda JV, Seleznevskaya ul. 1	973-0719		
Sloveniyales	254-0587		
Slovo JV (UK), ul. Bolshaya Filevskaya 37/1	144-0562	144-0558	411311
Small Business Development International Center JV, MGU, 2nd Gumanitarny korpus, kv. 473	939-3555		
Smena, Bumazhny proyezd 14	212-1507		
Smeshannaya Company TIM JV, ul. Ogareva,17/9	229-9310	229-9315	
Smolenskaya Investment JV (France), ul. Granovskovo 5, kv. 5	229-5510	200-5246	
SNC Radio Station (Stas Namin Center), Krymskiy val 9	191-1026		
SNIA BPD, Krasnopresnenskaya nab. 12, Office 1402	253-2179		413459
Sobesednik, Novoslobodskaya 73	285-4849		
Socialist Countries Insurance Joint Venture, ul. Pyatnitskaya 12	233-2668		
Societa Di Iniziative Sovietico Italiane, Oleny val 24, korpus 2, kv. 146	161-3983	288-9572	413577
Societe Generale, Krasnopresnenskaya nab. 12, Office 1009	253-5145	230-2783	413190
Societe Generale De Surveillance, Krasnopresnenskaya nab. 12, Office 1201	253-8293	253-9174	413481
Socomext, Kutuzovskiy prospekt 7/4, kv. 127	243-7385	253-9011	413960
Sodeco, Kutuzovskiy prospekt 7/4, kv. 149	243-1554	230-2243	413275
Soemtron AG, Leninskiy prospekt 95a	936-2623		
Sofi Courier Services JV (Finland), ul. Myasnitskaya 22, room 404	925-9587	928-6555	411787
Sofia Cinema, Sirenevy bulvar 31	163-8320		
Sofinta JV (Finland), ul. Vesennyaya 14	265-5953	532-0997	
Sofis JV (Finland), Kuznetskiy most 3, str. 2	292-2274		
Sofiteco SRL, Hotel Volga II, room 147-148	280-3779	975-2023	411672
Sofracop, Pokrovskiy bulvar 4/17, korpus 3, kv. 5	208-9714	230-2713	413324
Sofraplast JV (France), 2nd Nagatinskiy proyezd 6	111-7110	111-7392	411711
SoftKomplex JV (Poland), Leninskiy prospekt 63/2, B-296	135-8509		
Sogecred, Krasnopresnenskaya nab. 12, Office 1402	253-2179	253-9092	413459
Soglab JV (FRG), Shubinskiy per. 2/3	241-4870		
Soil Science and Agronomy Museum, Timiryazevskiy ul. 55	216-1619		
Sokhem, see Chimmashexport			
Sokolniki Exhibition Complex, Sokolniki Park	268-7151		
Sokolniki Park	268-5430		
Sokolniki Sports Palace, Sokolnicheskiy val 1b	268-6958		
Sokro JV (FRG), ul. Vavilova 15	135-7525	310-7052	412215
Solidarnost Advertising Firm	222-0961		
Solnechnaya Polyana Resort	592-6064		
Solnechny Customs Clearing Center, Varshavskoye Highway, 21st kilometer	382-8278	385-0272	
Solntsevo Cinema, ul. Bogdanova 19	435-2092		
Solyanka Art Gallery, Solyanka 1/2	921-6332		
Somirko JV, Stolovy per. 6	203-9903	203-0993	412247
Sona Ventures Ltd. JV (Canada), Krasnopresnenskaya nab. 12, Office 1421	253-1421	230-2821	413508

	Phone	Fax	Telex
Soniko JV, Podsosenskiy per. 12	297-0316		
Soniko JV (Japan), 1st Samotechny per. 17a	971-6179	230-2607	413169
Soninfo JV, Gorodok Baumana	367-0772	166-0818	411892
Soreal JV (France), Stupinskiy proyezd 4a	384-0613	384-8670	411179
Sorice, ul. Petrovka 15/31, kv. 21	923-9549	230-2762	413116
Sorok Cheterie (44) cafe, Leningradskoye shosse 44	159-9951		
SOS Assistance S.A., Berezhkovskaya nab. 12, korpus 15	240-9999		212257
SOS Systems JV (Singapore), ul. Akademika Pilyugina 8, korpus 1, podyezd 2	132-2677		
Sosiacline	280-9654		
Sotrudnichestvo, ul. Rozhdestvenka 8, stroenie 2	923-6405		
Sotrudnichestvo Foreign Trade Assoc., ul. Kiyevskaya 2, kv. 106	240-5252	230-2818	411670
Southam News, Kutuzovskiy prosp. 13/3, kv. 103	243-6708	243-3712	413538
Southern River Port, Prospekt Andropova 11, korpus 2	118-7811		
Souvenir Trading JV (US), ul. Miklukho-Maklaya 37	335-1444		
Sov It As JV, Nastasinskiy per. 3, korpus 2	299-8406	299-7990	
SOV KRS JV, Oruzheyny per. 3	250-0630		
Sovagrital JV, Pekin Hotel, room 802	209-3816		
SovAm, see Marine Resources Company International			
SovAm Teleport, ul. Nezhdanovoy 2a	229-9663	229-4121	411809
Sovamer Trading Company, Inc., ul. Koroleva 28, kor. 1	482-2903	482-2910	
Sovaminco, ul. Gertsena 11/4, korpus 2	923-5581	200-2289	411466
Sovamit JV, Kompozitorskaya ul. 25/5	241-7580	244-7234	
Sovampex JV (US), Leningradskoye shosse 8/2, kv. 173	150-4744		
Sovaro JV, ul. Neglinnaya 14	923-0417	921-4986	
Sovaustralteknika, ul. Chekhova 25, kv. 20	299-0680	200-0260	
Sovbunker, Novoslobodskaya 14/19, str. 7	258-9122	288-9569	411134
Sovcruise JV, ul. Rozhdestvenka 1/4	289-0327	926-3038	411197
Soveke JV (Finland), Tovarishcheskiy per. 19	204-8057		
Soveks JV, ul. 1st Karacharovskaya 8	175-9457		
Sovel JV (Cyprus), ul. Yablochkova 29 B/16	979-6319		
Sovelan Aroma JV (US), Rublevskoye sh. 26, kor. 1, kv. 43	415-4039	415-2911	113211
Sovelektro, Sadovaya-Spasskaya ul. 1/2	208-2837		411033
Sovenergo-MDI JV, Hotel Molodyozhnaya, room 2220	298-5844		414713
Sovengo JV (UK), ul. Kachalova 27	202-5611	202-1213	411153
Sovenz New Zealand, Leninskiy prosp. 83, kor. 5, kv. 490	133-5740	230-2644	4131177
Sovetekavtomatika JV, ul. Gazoprovod 4	388-8588		
Sovetskaya Kultura, see Kultura			
Sovetskaya Rossiya Publishers, see Russkaya Kniga			
Sovetskaya Torgovlya Publishers, see Torgovaya Gazeta Publishers			
Sovetskiy Soyuz, see Voskresenie			
Sovetsko-Italyanskoe JV, Dubininskaya ul. 65	235-2251		
Sovexportfilm, Kalashny per. 14	290-5009		411143
Sovfinamtrans JV, ul. Krasnoprudnaya 26/1	262-3603	262-5346	
Sovfinechemie JV (FRG), 4th Likhachevskiy proyezd 6	154-7091	943-0067	417622
Sovfinlift JV (Finland), 2nd Lykovskaya ul. 63	498-7951	200-2265	214151
Sovfintrade, Bolshaya Yushunskaya 1a, korpus 3, 10th floor	318-2807	310-7081	
Sovfintrade Joint Stock Co., ul. B. Yushunskaya 1a, kv. 3	318-5787		
Sovfrakht, ul. Rozhdestvenka 1/4	926-1032	230-2640	411168
Sovhispan S.A., Novinskiy bulvar 7/1	205-2008		413291
Soviet Children's Fund, see Children's Fund			

	Phone	Fax	Telex
Soviet Committee of the Int Council of Museums, see National Committee of the Int Council of Museums			
Soviet Committee of Veterans of War, Gogolevskiy bulv. 4	202-5952		
Soviet Cultural Fund, see Russian International Cultural Fund			
Soviet Culture Guide, ul. Georgu-Dei 3, kv. 34	157-3150		
Soviet Fund of Goodwill and Health, see International Fund of Goodwill and Health			
Soviet Peace Fund, ul. Prechistenka 10	202-4236		
Soviet Travels	248-3607	288-9587	
Soviet Women's Committee, see Union of Women of Russia			
Soviet-American Gas and Oil Energy Resources JV, ul. Mayakovskovo 20	203-9264		411467
Soviet-American Joint Advertising Company, Mozhayskoye shosse 165	447-8761	230-2387	411211
Soviet-British Creative Cooperation JV, see East-West Creative Association			
Soviet-French Activity in Ocean JV (France), Leningradskoye shosse 61a	459-7444	292-6511	411968
Soviet-Polish Informatics & Services Enterprise JV, ul. Yunnatov 18	212-8142		
Soviet-Spanish Foreign Trade Society, Novinskiy bulvar 7/1	205-2008	200-0247	413291
Sovietskaya Hotel, Leningradskiy prospekt 32/2	250-2342		
Sovigco Export-Import JV Filial, Nagatinskaya nab. 16/3	118-3447		
SovImax JV (Canada), Proyezd Serova 4	924-5549	921-5542	411630
Sovincenter, Krasnopresnenskaya nab. 12	256-6303	253-2400	411486
Car Rental	253-2477		
Sovindata JV (India), Kuznetskiy most 21/5	928-4197	200-2234	111115
Sovindtex JV (India), ul. Znamenka 11	246-4230		417227
Sovinfilm, see Soyuzkinoservice			
Sovingra JV, Babaevskaya ul. 1/8	268-4293		413104
Sovinpred JV (India), see Sefameks			
Sovinservice JV (Austria), Skatertny per. 4	290-2471	238-3345	411700
Sovinstandart, Novy Arbat 56	290-8780		
Sovintel JV (US), 25 Dubovaya Rosche	215-6097	215-5787	
Sovinterarkhstroi JV (Italy), ul. 1st Tverskaya-Yamskaya 55	251-5392	253-9172	214525
Sovinteravtoservice, Institutskiy per. 2/1	299-7773	288-9575	411008
Car Sales	288-9535		
Parts Shop	288-9056		
Technical Assistance, ul. Ilovayevskaya 38a	356-0701		
Sovinterluch JV (Bulgaria), ul. 3rd Kabelnaya 1	361-0560	290-3676	
Sovintertrade JV, see Radioexport			
Sovintervest JV (US), ul. Dimitrova 7/8	230-2038	230-2039	
Sovintex, 2nd Tverskaya-Yamskaya 6	251-5304		
Sovintkom Technologies JV (Switz.), Mezhdunarodnaya II, room 933	276-4722	253-9380	411432
Sovintrade Limited JV, Ukrainskiy bulvar 8	443-7732		411386
Sovit-tours JV (Italy), ul. Angarskaya 15a	290-3270		
Sovitem JV (Italy), ul. Chekhova 27, str. 6a	257-1259	257-1588	
Sovitkom JV (Italy), Kuznetskiy most 16	921-8625	928-7262	
SovJord JV (Jordan), Leninskiy prospekt 146	434-9739	420-2208	

	Phone	Fax	Telex
Sovkabel, Shosse Entuziastov 5	277-4028		
Sovkelme JV (Spain), ul. Ostozhenka 37	203-1266	248-0814	411287
Sovkhalidz JV (Kuwait), Leninskiy prospekt 52	137-3191	137-4769	411700
Sovkomflot, Rozhdestvenka 1/4	926-1301		
SovKuwait Engineering JV, Varshavskoye shosse 145	387-7204	310-7033	411006
Sovlaks, Kulakov per. 16	289-3407	344-7965	411664
Sovmara JV (Italy), ul. Initsiativnaya 9, korpus 2	151-7347		
Sovmav JV, ul. Gavrikova, 3/1, kv.98	367-3063	972-6250	411700
Sovmestny Put JV (US), Timiryazevskaya 4/12	485-6266		
Sovmortrans, ul. Petrovka 20/1	925-0803	925-0857	411369
Sovmortrans JV, ul. Rozhdestvenka 1/4	926-1142	230-2640	411168
Sovo & Cie France, Smolenskiy bulvar 22/14, kv. 9	248-7970	230-2211	413357
Sovpak JV (Thailand), ul. 2nd Karacharovskaya 3	170-7110	171-5355	412192
Sovpoles JV, ul. Profsoyuznaya 43, korpus 1	331-1433	332-6542	
Sovpolifin JV (Finland), Perovskoye shosse 7	174-2802		
Sovpolital JV (Italy), ul. Zelenodolskaya 3, korpus 2	378-3356	378-3356	
Sovpoliuplas JV (Yugoslavia), Podkopayevskiy per. 4	297-5018	227-8914	
Sovremennik Publishers, Khoroshevskoye shosse 62	941-2992	941-3544	
Sovremennik Theater, Chistoprudny bulvar 19a	921-6473		
Sovrybflot, Rozhdestvenskiy bulvar 9	926-5828	230-2487	411208
Sovsaderm JV (Switz.), ul. Tatyany Makorovoy 18	239-3306	238-3553	412250
Sovtech Inc., ul. Tekstilshchikov 1, kv. 1007	171-8657		
Sovtech JV (Australia), Leninskiy prospekt 45	137-6619		411784
Sovtrak JV, Zvezdny bulvar 17	287-0752		411008
Sovtransavto, Institutskiy per. 2/1 (Butovo)	971-3663		
Oktybraskaya ul. 2/4, 2/12	292-8965	288-9558	4111251
Sovtransavto-Expeditsia, ul. Bolshaya Ochakovskaya 15a	548-7675		
Sovtransservice JV, ul. Bolshaya Ochakovskaya 15a	430-7867	430-7819	411927
ul. Malogvardeyskaya 58	417-2134		411241
Sovventextile JV (Hungary), Proyezd Serebryankova 4	180-1002	180-0410	
Sovyetskaya Entsiklopedia Publishers, see Bolshaya Rossiyskaya Entsiklopedia Publishers			
Sovyetskaya Rossiya, see Pressa Publishers			
Sovyetskiy Pisatel Publishers, Vorovskovo 11	202-8668		
Sovyetsky Kompozitor Publishers, see Russian Kompozitor Publishing Association			
Soyuz Hotel, ul. Levoberezhnaya 12	457-9004		
Soyuz II Hotel, 1st Krasnogvardeyskiy prospekt 25b	259-3004		
Soyuz International JV, Tankovy prospekt 4, korpus 12	362-3227	230-2408	411662
Soyuz Marine Service JV (US), Gruzinskiy per. 3, kv. 63	254-3162	253-9771	413996
Soyuz Pisateley (Writers' Union) Restaurant, ul. Vorovskovo 52	291-2169		
Soyuz Restaurant, Gospitalny val 22	360-7432		
Soyuzforinvest JV, 5th Monetchikovskiy per. 4/6, str. 1	233-8787	233-3540	411705
Soyuzgasexport, Leninskiy prospekt 20	230-2440		
Soyuzgranpribor, see Elektroprivod			
Soyuzkarta, Volgogradskiy prospekt 45	177-4050		
Soyuzkhimexport, ul. Smolenskaya-Sennaya 32/34	244-2181		
Soyuzkinoservice, Skatertny per. 20	290-1000		
Soyuzkoopvneshtorg, Cherkasskiy per. 15	925-6822		
Soyuzluchpribor, ul. 3-Kabelnaya 1	237-1915		
Soyuzneftexport, ul. Smolenskaya-Sennaya 32/34	244-4048		
Soyuzpatent, ul. Ilyinka 5/2	925-1661		

	Phone	Fax	Telex
Soyuzpechat, Proyezd Kuybysheva 3	206-0709		
Soyuzplodimport, ul. Smolenskaya-Sennaya 32/34	244-2258		
Soyuzprofbank			
Soyuzpromexport, ul. Smolenskaya-Sennaya 32/34	253-9489		
Soyuzpromimporttorg, Prospekt Vernadskovo 25	131-5128		
Soyuzservice JV, Sokolnicheskiy Val, Dom 50, korp.2			
Soyuztransit, ul. Smolenskaya-Sennaya 32/34	244-3951		
Soyuzvneshstroyimport, Tverskoy bulvar 6	290-0684		
Soyuzvneshtrans, Gogolevskiy bulvar 17	203-1179		
Sozheks JV (Switz.), ul. Ilyinka 5/2	253-1913	921-5675	411883
Sozialdemokratische Pressedienste, Kutuzovskiy prospekt 14, kv. 151-152	230-2563		
Space Commerce Corp. JV (US), Krasnoproletarskaya ul. 9	972-4436		
Spanish Bar, Moskva Hotel	292-2893		
Spantek JV (US), Tatarskaya ul. 7, kv. 37	233-5019		411049
Sparta JV (Australia), Tovarishcheskiy per. 25	272-7561	272-7561	
Spate-Moscow JV (US), Ukraine Hotel	243-5448	243-5810	412174
Spectrum HDT JV (Canada), ul. Usacheva 35	261-7405	245-5070	411554
Spekfilm JV, Mosfilmovskaya 1			
Spektrum JV (UK), ul. Karla Marksa 19	267-7529	200-4240	
Spetzavtosentr, Kiyevskaya ul. 8	240-2092		
Sphera Theater, Karetny Ryad 3	299-9645		
Spie Batignolles, ul. Mytnaya 1, kv. 14	230-0776	230-2647	413175
Spiegel (der), Krutitskiy val 3, korpus 2, kv. 33, 36	274-0009	274-0003	413288
Spiro & Associates, see Samuel M. Spiro & Associates, Ltd.			
Sport Cinema, Bolshaya Pirogovskaya 53/55	246-1758		
Sport Hotel, Leninskiy prospekt 90/2	131-1191		
Sport Venture Moscow JV (FRG), Krasnopresnenskaya nab. 14	256-5078	259-7048	
Sportcenter Luzhniki JV (Austria), Luzhnetskaya nab. 24	201-1665		
Sportpromtex JV (FRG), ul. Ostozhenka 37	203-1577	202-0747	411287
Sports Palace, Luzhniki	201-0955		
Sprint JV (Luxembourg), Volgogradskiy prospekt 46B	178-6171	179-0038	
Sprint Networks, ul. Tverskaya 7, entrance 7	201-6890	923-2344	412941
Sprint-Form JV (FRG), ul. Marksistskaya 22	277-0183	270-7602	
SprintTset JV (US), see Sprint Networks			
Spros Hotel JV (Switz.), Leninskiy prospekt 95/15	133-4393		414711
Sputnik, Bolshaya Pochtovaya 7	265-5408		
Sputnik Cinema, Soldatskaya ul. 15	361-4220		
Sputnik Hotel, Leninskiy prospekt 38	938-7096		
Sputnik Tourist Agency, Maly Ivanovskiy per. 6, str. 2	925-9278	230-2787	411253
Ssha-Ekonomika, Politika, Ideologiya (USA), ul. Tverskaya 16/2	229-5041		
St. Andrew's Church, ul. Stankevicha 9	143-3562		
St. Basil's Cathedral, Red Square	298-3304		
St. George's Church, ul. Varvarka 12	298-3872		
St. Vlasiy's Church Concert Hall, ul. Ryleyeva 20	299-5322		
Stamco Trading Company, LTD, ul. Bolshaya Dorogomilovskaya 14, korpus 1, kv. 76	243-3837	230-2010	413669
Stampa (La), Kutuzovskiy prospekt 7/4, kv. 167	243-1751	230-2147	413455
Stanbet JV (US), Krymskiy val 9, Zelyony teatr	237-1089	237-3435	
Sredne-Tishinskiy per. 14, str. 4	253-7011		

	Phone	Fax	Telex
Stanislavskiy & Nemirovich-Danchenko Musical Theater Pushkinskaya ul. 17	229-8388		
Stanislavskiy Drama Theater, ul. Tverskaya 23	299-7224		
Stanislavskiy House Museum, ul. Stanislavskovo 6	229-2855		
Stanislavskovo 2 cafe, ul. Stanislavskovo 26a	291-8689		
Stankinbank, ul. Tverskaya 20	209-2857		
Stanko-Fanuk Service Limited JV (Japan), ul. Kalanchevskaya 31	208-5125		
Stankoimport, ul. Obrucheva 34/63	333-5101	310-7021	411993
Stankovendt JV (FRG), ul. Sushchevskiy val 5	289-2382	289-9541	
Star Progress JV (US), Frunzenskaya nab. 30, pavilion 15	242-8982	230-2601	
Starkar JV (Finland), Bratsevskaya ul. 13	949-0177		
Starlight JV, ul. S. Eisensteina 8	181-1841	181-0451	411841
Start JV (US), ul. Druzhinnikovskaya 15	205-2978	205-2680	411070
Startgroup JV, ul. Mantulinskaya 10	434-2320	200-2216	411700
Stas Namin's, see Victoria Cafe			
State Automobile Inspection (GAI), ul. Sadovaya-Samotechnaya 1	923-5373		
State Bank of India, Pokrovskiy bulvar 4/17, kv. 32	297-2190		413012
State Joint Stock Assoc. for Machinery & Equipt., ul. Tverskaya 20	209-5520		
State Tretyakov Art Gallery, ul. Krymskiy val 10	230-1116		
Statfall, ul. 1905 Goda 10a, 4th floor	252-0803	124-4047	
Statsevich Solicitors, ul. Kostyakova 6/5	216-1611		
Status Credit Bank, ul. Krylatskaya 32, korpus 2	413-7115		
Stavan-Engineering JV, ul. Elektrozavodskaya 1			
Steepler Ltd., Post Box 30, Moscow 103031	245-2194		
Steptoe and Johnson, c/o USCO, Novinskiy bulvar 15	255-4848	230-2101	
Sterch Controls, ul. Lobachika 17/19	264-5311	200-1216	411678
Sterkh-Avtomazatsia JV (US), Trekhprudny per. 11/13	299-2531	230-2600	413255
Stern Magazine, Kutuzovskiy prosp. 7/4, kor. 5, kv. 15	243-3396	230-2950	413339
Stetlan JV (FRG), Lyalin per. 1, str. 2	434-3319		
STF-US JV, ul. Akademika Koroleva 12	217-9034	975-2073	
Stim JV (US)	921-8471		
STN JV, ul. Pisemskovo 8			
Stockmann, see Oy Stockmann AB			
Stoelck Aussenhandel AG, Mezhdunarodnaya II, #438	253-1557	255-0504	411432
Stokmos JV, ul. Terekhova 13	191-61433	248-7291	
Stoleshniki Cafe, Stoleshniki per. 8	229-2050		
Stolichny Bank, ul. Pyatnitskaya 72	233-5892	237-2993	411913
Stolitsa Trade House	924-0243	928-4739	
Storyfirst Communications, Prospekt Vernadskovo 14	133-9620		
Strastnoy 7, Strastnoy bulvar 7	299-0498	200-1243	
Streif AG - Industrieanlagen, ul. Mytnaya 1, kv. 29	230-0754		
Strela Cinema, Smolenskaya-Sennaya ploshchad 23/35	244-0953		
Stroydormashexport, Suvorovskiy bulvar 7	291-4931	202-9056	
Stroymaterialintorg, Kiyevskaya 19	243-7531		411887
Stroyservice JV (Austria), ul. Tverskaya 24/2	229-6590	229-9731	
Stroytekhindustria JV (Bulgaria), Novaya Basmannaya 9	267-7568		
Studio Theater on Spartakovskaya Ploshchad, Spartakovskaya ploshchad 9-1	571-3266		
Studio Theater on Yugo Zapade, Prospekt Vernadskovo 125	434-7483		

	Phone	Fax	Telex
Sub-Scri, Inc. JV (US)	263-6200		
Success JV (USA), Kutuzovskiy prospekt 3	148-9966	200-2217	411700
Sudoexport, ul. Chaikovskovo 11	255-1813	200-2250	411116
Sudoimport, Uspenskiy per. 10	229-6849	209-1313	411287
Sueddeutsche Zeitung, Kutuzovskiy prospekt 7/4, korpus 5, kv. 25	243-1166		413334
Suiproekt JV (Yugoslavia), 3rd Tverskaya-Yamskaya 22	251-8247	241-4707	
Sulzer Brothers LTD, Kursovoy per. 9, Office 4	202-1717	200-1234	413526
Sumitomo Corporation, Krasnopresnenskaya nab. 12, Office 1203	253-2030	230-2664	413134
Summit Systems Computers	265-5813		
Sun World, Kostyanskiy per. 13, room 111	208-9287	200-0238	411294
Sunday Express, Leninskiy prospekt 45, kv. 426	135-1164	230-2010	413199
Sunday News-Journal Union, see Voskresenye News-Journal Union			
Sunday Telegraph, see Daily Telegraph			
Sunday Times, The, Kutuzovskiy prospekt 14, kv. 37	243-0778		413010
Sunday Tribune, ul. Sadovaya-Samotechnaya 12/24, kv. 72	200-2530		
Sunds Defibrator AB, Pereulok Sadovskikh 6/8	209-2817	200-0214	413223
Sunkyong Limited, ul. Profsoyuznaya 23	120-4311	120-4157	411687
Sunrise JV, 3rd Golutvinskiy per. 2	233-2935		
Superkeramika JV (Switz.), ul. Ostrovityanova 23, korpus 5	486-8895		
Supershop, Astrakhanskiy per. 5	280-2545		
Suprimex JV, ul. Polkovaya 3/4	289-0229		
Supriz cafe, Medynskaya 5, korpus 1	384-4400		
Susuman Gold Exchange, see Kolyma Susuman Gold Exchange			
SVAK, see North-Eastern Joint Stock Commercial Bank			
Svatstroy JV (Canada), Pushkinskaya ul. 10	921-4129	921-5059	
Svenska Dagbladet, Kutuzovskiy prospekt 9/2, kv. 119	243-6632		413193
Svenska Handelsbanken, Pokrovskiy bulvar 4/17, kv. 35	207-6018	230-2544	413201
Svetoreklama JV, ul. Polyarnaya 13V	473-9266	473-5051	
Svetozor JV (US), Leninskiy prospekt 70/11	125-8574	938-2158	
Svoboda Cinema, ul. Trofimova 17	279-2524		
Svobodnaya Mysl (Free Thought), ul. Marksa i Engelsa 5	291-6067		
SWAPO, see Embassy of Namibia			
Swatstroy, ul. Karla Marksa 14	921-4129	921-5059	
Swedbank, Pereulok Sadovskikh 4, kv. 2	209-6836	200-0259	413432
Swedish Furniture, Leninskiy prospekt 64	137-0291		
Swedish Radio, Sadovaya Samotechnaya 12/24, kv. 64	200-0770	200-2200	413365
Swedish School, Leninskiy prospekt 78	131-8766		
Swedish TV, Kutuzovskiy prospekt 7/4, kv. 130-131	243-5165	253-9179	413365
Swimming Pool of TsSKA, Leningradskiy prospekt 39	213-2583		
Swiss-Medical Interline, Hotel Intourist, room 2030	203-9496		
Swissair, Krasnopresnenskaya nab. 12, Office 2005	253-8988	253-1852	413417
Sheremetevo II	578-2740		413030
Sydney Morning Herald, ul. Kalyayevskaya 29, kv. 115	258-1940		
Symantec Representation	396-4644		
Synergia JV (Italy), Stremyanny per. 28	237-8481		
Syntez Corporation JV, Kutuzovskiy prospect 30/32			
Syrian Arab Airlines, Koroviy val 7	237-1727		
Syrin Moskovskoe Obshchestvo	199-1015	199-0055	
Sytco, Pereulok Sadovskikh 6, kv. 4	209-6662	200-0262	413911

T

Name / Address	Phone	Fax	Telex
Tabakov's Studio Theater, see O. Tabakov's Studio Theater			
Tabani Corporation, Krasnopresnenskaya nab. 12, Office 1505	253-2462	253-9375	413524
Tadzhikistan Cinema, ul. Katukova 8	499-1511		
Taganka Bar, v. Radishchevskaya 15	272-4351		
Taganka Drama and Comedy Theater, Zemlyanoi val 76	272-6300		
Taganka JV (Austria), ul. Taganskaya 17-21	928-1614	253-9483	
Taganskaya 31/22 Gallery, Taganskaya ul. 31/22	278-5578		
Taiga Cafe, Aerostar Hotel	155-5030		
Taiga JV (Switz.), ul. Gertsena 46	290-5572		
Tairiku Trading Co., LTD, ul. Mytnaya 1, 2nd flr	237-2060	230-2466	413058
Tais Sport JV, Luzhnetskaya nab. 10	201-1129		
Taki-Moskva JV, ul. Mnevniki, 10	191-9471	288-9539	
Takt JV (Australia), ul. Khmeleva 23/15	924-5080		
Talisman cafe, ul. Shchepkina 1	208-9055		
Tallinn Cinema, Sevastopolskiy prospekt 33	127-9003		
Tamada Duty Free Shop, Hotel Moskva	292-2874		
Tamilas Limited, see M J Exports			
Tamko S.A., Kotelnicheskaya nab. 25/8, kv. 40	272-5897	274-0060	413333
Tampella, ul. Lunacharskovo 7, kv. 2	203-1602		413502
Tanako JV, ul. Malaya Lubyanka 16	280-4447	975-2060	
Tangra MS (JV), Kutuzovskiy prospekt 14	243-5805		
Tashkent Cinema, 1st Novokuzminskaya ul. 1	371-6587		
TASS Fotokhronika, ul. Bolshaya Dorogomilovskaya 12	243-3903		411220
TASS News Agency, see ITAR			
Tavi JV, ul. Chaplygina 1a			
Taxi Reservations,			
24 hours a day	927-2108		
24 hours a day	927-0000		
9am - 6 pm	975-5101		
9am - 6pm	457-9005		
9am - 6pm	975-3101		
Tbilisi Cinema, ul. Novocheremushkinskaya 53a	120-9006		
Tchaikovsky Concert Hall, Ploshchad Mayakovskovo 4/31	299-3487		
Teatr Kinoaktyora (Filmactor Theater), ul. Vorovskovo 33	290-5524		
Teatr Yunovo Zritelya, Pereulok Sadovskikh 10	299-5360		
Tebost JV (FRG), ul. Ostozhenka 30, str. 2	203-1434		
Tebowa, Mezhdunarodnaya II, room 1509	253-1509	253-9192	413624
Tech Trade JV (Sweden), Prospekt Mira 186	283-5952	187-5847	48484 T
Techimex JV (Austria), Rybny per. 2	298-3485		
Technik und Technologie, Krutitskiy val 3, kv. 105	276-9520		413440
Technip, see Tecnologie Progretti Lavori SpA			
Technische Beratung Schittko GmbH, Mezhdunarodnaya II, room 1226	253-1226	253-9170	411486
Technobridge JV, ul. Lukhovitskaya 5	180-3239	189-4555	411280
Technofarm Engineering JV (Sweden), ul. Novaya Basmannaya 23	291-3856	434-1020	111438
Technointorg, Pyatnitskaya ul. 24	231-2600	230-2642	411200

	Phone	Fax	Telex
Technological & Marketing Centre JV,			
ul. Seleznevskaya 1/3, str. 1	972-4482		411013
Technopark Business Center, VDNKh	181-9926	181-6231	411043
Technopolis Innovation Bank, Novopeschanaya ul. 20	943-4102		
Technosoft JV (Italy), ul. Zverinetskaya 34/38	238-9679	230-2093	413507
Technotherm GmbH & Co., KG	253-1765		
Tecnologie Progetti Lavori, Per. Sadovskikh 4, kv. 10	209-2839	200-0288	413235
Teda JV (Yugoslavia), ul. Marksa-Engelsa 15	290-5061	290-5061	411614
TEK Trade JV, Prospekt Mira 186	283-5952	187-5847	
Tekhmashexport, ul. Mosfilmovskaya 35	143-8660		411068
Tekhmashimport, Trubnikovskiy per. 19	202-4800	291-5808	411194
Tekhnoexport, Ovchinnikovskaya nab. 18/1	220-1782	230-2080	411228
Tekhnointorg, Pyatnitskaya ul. 64	233-0032	230-2642	
Tekhnokultura JV, ul. Arbat 35	248-2410		
Tekhnopromimport, Ovchinnikovskaya nab. 18/1	220-1218		411233
Tekhnoservice JV, ul. Pervomayskaya 126	461-3514	461-3514	
Tekhnostroyexport, Ovchinnikovskaya nab. 18/1	220-1448		
Tekhpromexport, Ovchinnikovskaya nab. 18/1	220-1523	233-3373	411158
Tekhpromimport, Ovchinnikovskaya nab. 18/1	220-1505		
Tekhsnabexport, Staromonetny per. 26	233-4846	230-2638	411328
Tekhvneshreklama, ul. Bolshaya Ordynka 7/2	231-8428		
Tekhvneshtrans, see Technoexport			
Tekom JV (US), 1st Smolenskiy per. 9	241-0109	299-9576	
Tekotex JV (FRG), ul. Novo-Basmannaya 23, str. 1	265-3663	292-6511	
Tekstil Universal Exchange, ul. Profsoyuznaya 3	124-7900		
Tekur JV (Australia), Prospekt Vernadskovo 95	433-1507	230-2844	
Teldico Communications, see Capricone International S.P.R.L.			
Telefonica Internacional,			
Rublevskoye shosse 36, korpus 2, kv. 241, 243	415-5109	415-2956	
Teleset Service	166-9763	362-8070	
Temp Cinema, ul. Begovaya 5	946-0165		
Tempbank Commercial Bank, Krutitskiy val 26	276-3502		
Tereza JV, Strastnoy Bulvar 10	924-5496	230-2258	
Termolik JV, 1st Institutskiy proyezd 1	371-0125		
Terra Blok Sovetskiy Soyuz JV (Holland),			
ul. Zoi i Aleksandra Kosmodemyanskikh 26/21	150-9885	943-0079	411085
Terrace Bar, Aerostar Hotel	155-5030		
Tetra Pak, Krasnopresnenskaya nab. 12, Office 502	253-1086	253-9898	411813
Textil Commerz, Leninskiy prospekt 95a	132-4110	936-2659	
Theater cafe, ul. Tverskaya 5			
Theater Salon Gallery, Tverskoy bulvar 11	290-0215		
Theater Tickets, see Box Office Theater Tickets			
Theodor Votteler, Mezhdunarodnaya II, room 1050	253-1711		
Thermax Limited, ul. Mytnaya 1, Office 13	230-0276	230-2531	413011
Thomesto, ul. Mytnaya 1, kv. 19-20	230-0378	230-2366	413047
Thomson Holidays	203-4025		
Thomson S.A., Pokrovskiy bulvar 4/17, korpus 3, kv. 6	208-9716	230-2355	413287
THY, Turkish Airlines, Kuznetskiy Most 1/8	292-5121		
Sheremetevo II	578-2728		
Thyssen Vertretung Moskau, ul. Lunacharskovo 7, kv. 15	203-1938	230-2264	413306
Tiana Brokerage Firm	169-9171	230-2467	
Tiedonantaya, ul. Dostoyevskovo 1/21, kv. 9	288-9511		413569
Tifla JV, Petroverigskiy per. 4	921-3622	924-5021	112781

	Phone	Fax	Telex
TIM Ltd. JV (Austria), Petroverigskiy per. 4	928-9798	924-5021	112781
Time Magazine, Kutuzovskiy prospekt 14, kv. 3-4	243-1511	243-3752	413433
Times of India, The, Frunzenskaya nab. 12, kv. 7	242-4440		413318
Times, The, ul. Bolshaya Dorogomilovskaya 14, kv. 78	230-2457		413010
Tino Fontana			
Restaurant, Hotel Mezhdunarodnaya, 3rd floor	253-2241		
Store, Hotel Mezhdunarodnaya II	253-1787		
Tissa JV (Hungary), Prospekt Vernadskovo 33	131-5746	138-3743	414511
Tissa-Ogilvy and Mathers JV, Prospekt Vernadskovo 33	131-5749		414511
Titan JV (Austria), ul. Volodarskovo 16	438-2557		
TM-Elektronika JV, ul. Kosmonavta Volkova ,12	150-4640		417603
TMG in Moscow JV, ul. Vavilova 81	132-0055	938-2285	
TMS JV, ul. Seleznevskaya 1/3, str. 1	972-4482		411013
TNT Express Worldwide, 3rd Baltiyskiy per. 3	156-5771	151-2277	
Tokobank, ul. Mashi Poryvayevoy 15	972-9496	237-2993	411817
Tokyo Boeki LTD, Pokrovskiy bulvar 4/17, kv. 24-5	298-3591	230-2855	413397
Tokyo Broadcasting System,			
Kutuzovskiy prospekt 9, kv. 20	243-9980	230-2528	413132
Tokyo Maruichi Shoji Co., LTD, ul. Mytnaya 1, 2nd flr.	237-3050	230-2037	413061
Tolstoy House, ul. Lva Tolstovo 21	246-6112		
Tolstoy Museum, ul. Prechistenka 11	202-3091		
Toma JV (Belgium), Grokholskiy per. 32, korpus 2	138-4969	938-2136	
Tomen Corporation,			
Krasnopresnenskaya 12, Office 1309	253-2154	253-9905	413170
Tomo JV (Canada), ul. Karetny ryad 5/10, str. 6	429-1377	404-1767	411661
Torgovlya Gazeta Publishers, ul. Varvarka 14	298-4901		
Toronto Star, ul. Vavilova 83, kv. 62	132-4856		413513
Torrent-Lendaria-Transworld JV,			
ul. Bolshaya Polyanka,63	137-0882	137-0882	
Tourist Hotel, ul. Selskokhozyaystvennaya 17/2	187-6018		
Tourist's Clinic, Gruzinskiy proyezd 2	254-4396		
Toyota Tshusho Corporation, ul. Mytnaya 1	230-0943		413596
TPL, see Tecnologie Progetti Lavori SpA			
Tracosa S.A., 4th Dobryninskaya per. 6/9	237-6065	230-2128	413470
Trademetinvest JV (FRG), Ovchinnikovskaya nab. 18/1	220-1585	233-9317	411931
Train Information Service (24 hrs),			
Komsomolskaya Ploschad 5	266-9000		
Train Ticket Delivery Service	262-8684		
Alternative number	266-8333		
Traktoroexport, ul. Lesnaya 41	258-5934	288-9559	411273
Trans World Airlines,			
Slavyanskaya-Radisson Hotel, room 5028	941-8146		
Transbirzha, ul. Krasnoprudnaya 20	266-0957		
Transcargo, Putevoy proyezd 3	253-1182	230-2104	414851
Transcom JV (Austria), ul. Geroev Panifilovtsev 24	250-0434		
Transimage JV (US), ul. Podolskikh Kursantov 3a	921-0955		
Transnautic Uberseeschiffahrtsagentur GmbH & Co. KG,			
Pereulok Sadovskikh 6, kv. 3	200-0292	200-0292	413925
TransSuper	177-1274	288-7781	
Transtrade, ul. Myasnitskaya 26	287-6741	292-6511	
Travelco, TBA JV (US),			
Izmailovo Hotel, Bldg. B, room 1733	166-2882		

	Phone	Fax	Telex
TrekKingtour JV (FRG), ul. Malaya Yakimanka 2/1	230-7426		
Tremo JV (Italy), Taganskaya ploshchad 88, str. 1	272-0657		
TrenMos Restaurant, Komsomolskiy prospekt 21	245-1216		
Tretyakov Gallery (New), State Tretyakov Art Gallery			
Tretyakov Gallery (Old), Lavrushinskiy per. 10	231-1362		
Tribuna de Actualidad,			
ul. Akad. Koroleva 4, korpus 2, kv. 69-70	215-2492	283-0657	
Trio International, Krasnopresnenskaya nab. 12, #609	253-1182		413375
Trio JV (UK), ul. Vyborgskaya 16	150-9934	150-9934	
Troika JV, Krasnopresnenskaya nab. 12, Office 1603	253-2255		
Troika-Press JV, 1st Yamskaya ul. 8	289-1313	289-9287	411160
Tropinin Museum, Shchetininskiy per. 10	231-1799		
TROS, KRO (Radio & TV), Het Parool,			
ul. Marksistskaya 1, kv. 1	270-1539		413544
Trud Publishers, Nastasinskiy per. 4	299-3906		
Tsakhkadzor cafe, ul. Lesnaya 15	251-0257		
Tsaritsyno JV, Shipilovskiy prospekt 43, korpus 1	392-0665	391-6862	
Tsentr-100 JV, Proyezd Zagorskovo 23	443-4764		
Tsentralnaya Hotel, ul. Tverskaya 10	229-8589		
Tsentralny Detskiy Kinoteatr, ul. Bakhrushina 25	233-4206		
Tsentralny Dom Sovetskoy Armii, Pl. Kommuni 2	281-5550		
Tsentralny Dom Turista (Central House of Tourism),			
Leninskiy prospekt 146	434-2756		
Concert Hall	434-9492		
Tsentralny Restaurant, ul. Tverskaya 10	229-0241		
Tsentrosoyuz Bank, Bolshoy Cherkasskiy per. 15	928-7683		
Tsitotrans JV, Komsomolskaya ploshchad 5	266-67879	928-6389	
Tsvetmetpromexport, Ovchinnikovskaya nab. 18/1	220-1610		
Tudor S.A., ul. Konyushkovskaya 28, Office 4	253-9601		413572
Tumba Golf Course JV (Sweden), see Golf Club Tumba			
Turbotest JV (India), Aviamotornaya 2	267-1350		411686
Turkish Airlines, see THY, Turkish Airlines			
Turun Sanomat, Frunzenskaya nab. 12, kv. 7	242-4440		413318
TV de Espana, Krutitskiy val 3, korpus 2, kv. 130	276-4768	274-0053	413994
TV-AM, ul. Akademika Koroleva 4, korpus 2, kv. 10-11	215-2292	975-2036	
TV-Asahi, ul. Mytnaya 3, kv. 53		938-2094	413107
Tverskaya 25 Gallery, ul. Tverskaya 25	299-1844		
TVK JV (Lichtenshtein), ul. Nezhdanovoy 7, kv. 70/71	299-2176		
TWA, see Trans World Airlines			
Twenty-First Century Development Commercial Bank,			
1st Krasnogvardeyskiy prospekt 12/2	205-3900		
TXS Ltd. JV (India), ul. Kalanchevskaya 11, str. 3	975-4367		114529
Tyazhpromexport, Ovchinnikovskaya nab. 18/1	220-1610	230-2203	411931
Tyson Products	229-8290		
Tyumen Commodity and Stock Exchange	261-1590		

U

	Phone	Fax	Telex
U Kamina cafe, Chernyshevskovo 32	297-0840		
U Nikitskikh Vorot Studio Theater, ul. Gertsena 23/9	291-8419		
Lebed Hall, Leningradskoye shosse 35	159-7844		
U Petra, see Peter's Place			
U Pirosmani cafe, Novodevichy proyezd 4	247-1926		
U Yosefa cafe, Dubininskaya 11/17	238-4646		
U.G.T., see Union, Gas & Technic GmbH			
U.K. Paints, Ltd, ul. Akademika Koroleva 4, kor. 2, kv. 1-2	286-0790		
UAB Technologies JV, ul. Verkhnyaya Pervomayskaya 2a	163-1261		
Udarnik Cinema, ul. Serafimovicha 2	238-7664		
Ukraine Cinema, ul. Barklaya 9/2	145-6255		
Ukraine Hotel, Kutuzovskiy prospekt 2/1	243-3020		
Ulan-Bator Cinema, ul. Grimau 12	126-2012		
Ulrich Schreiber	253-2704		
Umitec Exchange, ul. Profsoyuznaya 113, korpus 3	248-7643	248-7645	
UN Information Center, ul. Lunacharskovo 4/16	241-2894		413595
Underground Press Museum, Lesnaya ul. 55	251-2593		
UNESCO, ul. Vozdvizhenka 9	290-0853	202-1083	411587
Uni-Export Instruments Ltd, Mezhdunarodnaya II, room 1417	255-6609	253-1415	413338
Unibor JV (Cyprus), ul. Skladochnaya 6	289-1187	289-0016	412271
Unicom JV (Yugoslavia), ul. Skladochnaya,6	289-1025		
Unicoop Japan, Bolshoy Gnezdnikovskiy per. 7, 2nd flr	200-2520	973-2024	413517
UNIDO, ul. Kuusinena 21b	198-9902	943-0018	411925
Unifarm JV (UK), Skatertny per. 13	202-5071		
Uniko JV (France), ul. Krzhizhanovskovo 15, kv. 1	941-4587	124-8056	
Unikom JV (Austria), ul. Maksimova 6	196-4758		411594
Unikombank, Khrustalny per. 1	925-3462	921-7754	
Unimas JV, Leningradskiy Prospekt 80	158-9546	158-5671	
Union Bank of Finland LTD, ul. Pushkinskaya 5/6, kv. 34	292-0338	200-0237	413286
Union Bank of Switzerland, Pokrovskiy bulvar 4/17, kv. 4	207-3429	230-2456	413188
Union JV (UK), ul. Chasovaya 24/1	151-1501	943-0075	
Union of Architects of the CIS, ul. Shchuseva 3	290-3047	290-4384	
Union of Architects of the RFSFR, ul. Shchuseva 22	291-5578		
Union of Cinematographers, Vasilyevskaya ul. 13	250-4114	200-4284	411939
Union of Composers, ul. Nezhdanovoy 8/10	229-5218	200-4273	411702
Union of Designers, Arbatskaya ploshchad 1/2, str. 3	202-4648		
Union of Joint Stock Companies, Balakirevskiy per. 23	261-8293	292-6511	
Union of Journalists, Zubovskiy bulvar 4	201-4891		
Union of Theater Workers, ul. Tverskaya 12, str. 7, kv. 228	209-2436		
Union of Women of Russia, ul. Nemirovicha-Danchenko 6	209-7433		
Union of Writers, Komsomolskiy prospekt 13	246-4350		
ul. Vorovskovo 52	291-6307	230-2716	
Union, Gas & Technic GmbH	248-2341		
Unionchimstroy JV, Elokhovskiy pereulok 3	261-86865	261-8686	
Uniset JV (Switz.), 2nd Smolenskiy per. 2/3	291-6966	292-6511	
Unison JV (US), ul. Maroseika 7/8	206-8524	206-8274	411855
Unistone JV (Austria), ul. Vakhtangova 13	254-5129		
United News of India, ul. Pelshe 11, kv. 85	437-4360		413007

	Phone	Fax	Telex
United Parcel Service, see UPS Express Mail JV			
United Press International, Kutuzovskiy prosp. 7/4, kv. 67	243-6829		413424
United Stone JV, ul. Pyatnitskaya 22, str.2	231-4888		
Unitek JV (Sweden), ul. Miklukho-Maklaya 18	330-7829	336-0993	
Unitex JV, MGU	939-5069	938-2136	
Universitetskaya Hotel, Michurinskiy prospekt 8/29	939-9731		
Univolt JV (Sweden), ul. Lobninskaya 21	483-4422		207080
Unona JV (Yugoslavia), ul. Dimitrova 39	244-1022	230-2117	411160
Unsere Zeit, ul. Ivana Babushkina 3, kv. 284	310-7013		413414
UPDK, see GlavUPDK			
Upjohn Company, Chistoprudny bulvar 2, kv. 45	928-6678	975-2242	
UPS Express Mail JV (Finland), B. Ochakovskaya ul. 15a	430-6373		411927
UPS-Sovtransavto JV, see UPS Express Mail JV			
Ural Cinema, Ploshchad Bela Kuna 1	462-5337		
Ural Hotel, ul. Chernyshevskovo 40	297-4258		
Urals JV (Holland), Gruzinskiy per. 3, kv. 255	254-6969	253-9387	413256
US News & World Report, Leninskiy prospekt 36, kv. 53	938-2051	137-2593	413216
US Sprint, see Sprint Networks			
US-USSR Trade & Economic Council, Inc., Nab. Shevchenko 3	243-4028	230-2467	413212
USSR Independent Theater Union, see Arlekin, Inc.			
USSR Trade Union Confederation, Leninskiy prosp. 42	938-7428		
UTS Testesysteme	253-2422		
Uts-Umi-Test JV (FRG), Maly Ivanovskiy per. 11/6, str. 1	924-8984		411767
UUSI Suomi & MTV, ul. Narodnaya 13, kv. 34	272-7930	274-0007	413130
UVIR, see Visa Registration Office for Foreigners			

V

	Phone	Fax	Telex
V. Spesivtsev's Experimental Studio Theater, ul. Rustaveli 19	218-2332		
VAAP, see All Union Copyright Agency			
Vakhtangov Theater, Arbat 26	241-0728		
Valentin Yudashkin Salon, Passage Department Store			
Valio, Koroviy val 7, Office 14	230-2810		413040
Valmet Oy, Pokrovskiy bulvar 4/17, kv. 8 & 11	207-3318	230-2631	413257
Valtex International Corporation	137-5197	137-1374	
Vanguardia (La), Leninskiy prospekt 93, korpus 2, kv. 66	938-2154	938-2167	413658
Varioline Handelsgesellschaft mbH, Frezer shosse 17	170-3101	274-0057	413600
Varshava Cinema, Ploshchad Ganetskovo 1	156-8001		
Varshava I Hotel, Leninskiy prospekt 2	238-1970		
Varshava II Hotel, Kotelnicheskaya nab. 1/15	227-4078		
Vartecon, Krasnobogatyrskaya 79	963-9077		
Varus Video JV, Skatertny per. 20	290-4258	200-1286	411114
Varust JV, Khrustalny per. 1, kv. 84	298-5800		
Vasinkraft JV, ul. Nikolskaya 19	924-7505		
Vasnetsov House (A.M. Vasnetsov) Museum, Furmanny per. 6	208-9045		
Vasnetsov House (V.M. Vasnetsov) Museum, Pereulok Vasnetsova 13	281-1329		
VDNKh see All Russian Exhibition Center			
Vecherny Siluet Restaurant, Taganskaya ploshchad 88	272-1503		

	Phone	Fax	Telex
Vedomosti S'ezda Narodnikh Deputatov Ross. Fed. & Verkh. Sov. RSFSR, Krasnopresnenskaya nab. 2	205-6210		
VEEK JV, ul. Kirova 8	928-5560	975-2008	
VEK, LTD, Krasnopresnenskaya nab. 12, Office 1701	253-2842	253-2845	413968
Vektor JV (FRG), ul. Shenogina 4	256-7064		
Vektor SP Brokerage Firm, ul. Safonovskaya 17/43	415-7734	415-7635	
Velikaya Stena JV, Profsoyuznaya ul. , 5/9	125-1252		
Velyus JV (FRG), ul. Perovskaya 28	306-7817		
Vemo JV (Austria), 3rd Lyusinovskiy per. 3	236-4467		
Vensta JV (Austria), ul. Vorontsovskaya 15/10	272-1848		411802
Vent-Inter JV (Finland), Nikolo-Yamskoi tupik 3	227-3537		
Vera Moda, ul. Chekhova 8	209-7553		
Vernadskiy Museum, ul. A.N. Kosygina 47a	137-0011		
Vernisage Theater, Begovaya ul. 5	946-0165		
Veronica TV, NOS TV & De Telegraaf, Rublevskoye shosse 26, kv. 102-103	415-4064	415-2905	
Veslek JV, ul. Myasnitskaya 18	928-5560	975-2008	
Vespek JV, ul. Gilyarovskovo 31	284-8054	281-3904	
Vesta Car Rental, Leningradskaya Hotel, room 61	248-2657		
Vesti, Kosmos Hotel	217-1194		
Slavyansky-Radisson Hotel	941-8080		
Vestnik JV (Austria), ul. Arbat 54/2	241-8704	244-4160	411584
Veterinarian, ul. Yunnatov 16a	212-8076		
VG Enterprises Inc., Bobrov per. 4/2	928-0637		
Video Informatics Service Trade JV (US), Trekhprudny per., 4	200-3568		
Videocomputer JV (FRG), Chistoprudny bulvar 12	928-7883		
VideoForce, Krasnopresnenskaya nab. 12	253-7708		
Videoline JV (Switz.), 2nd Frunzenskaya ul. 10, korpus 1	242-2035		
Vienna Cafe, Olympic Penta Hotel	971-6101		
Viking JV, ul. Bolshaya Pochtovaya 26	234-2265	229-0775	411325
Viktoria (Hard Rock Cafe) cafe, Zelyoni Theater, Kymskiy val 9	237-0709		
Viktoria JV (FRG), Leninskiy prospekt 90/2	202-9501		
Viktoria Restaurant, Prospect Mira 78	971-0721		
Villa Peredelkino JV (Italy), Solntsevskiy Rayon, 2nd Chobotovskaya alleya 2	435-1578		
Vima JV (Sweden), ul. Ostozhenka 6	201-1051		
VIP Center JV (Finland), ul. Osipenko 77	230-5973	230-2202	412950
VIP JV (FRG), ul. Marksa-Engelsa 8	202-8535	202-6075	411135
Visa Registration Office for Foreigners (UVIR), ul. Chernyshevskovo 42	924-9349		
Visit-Dialogue JV (US), ul. Malaya Bronnaya 23	209-4185		122205
Visnews Television, Gruzinskiy per. 3, kv. 219-220	253-9296	253-9295	413428
VIST JV (US), Trekhprudny per. 4	200-3568		
Vista JV (US), ul. Bakhrushina 28	258-2920	220-2211	
VITA, ul. Poklonnaya 6	249-9667	249-7818	
Vita-Commerce U.B. JV, Avtomobilny proyezd 10	124-5305	274-0027	
Vitas Corporation, Trekhprudny per. 11/13	299-6723	200-0250	413129
Vityaz Cinema, ul. Miklukho-Maklaya 27a	335-7192		
VIZA Bank, Gogolevskiy bulvar 3/2	291-9514		
Vladivostok Cinema, ul. Lazo 3	309-1195		
Vltava cafe, Vasilyevskaya 15/24	251-6898		

	Phone	Fax	Telex
Vmeste-Interoko JV (FRG), Pivchenkova 1, korpus 3	144-7577	938-2033	411432
Vneshagro JV, Bobrov Pereulok 4, str. 2	928-6974		
Vneshconsult JV (Finland), VDNKh, Pavilion 4	181-4294	181-4133	411418
Vnesheconombank, Krasnopresnenskaya nab. 12	253-1799		
Plyushchikha, ul. 37	246-6788		
Serpukhovskiy val 8	292-8292		
Vnesheconomservis, ul. Kuybysheva 6	259-3753		
Vneshiberika JV (Spain), ul. Fadeyeva 1	200-5205	200-5205	411238
Vneshmaltigraf JV, ul. Fadeyeva 1	299-3663		
Vneshnaya Torgovlya (Foreign Trade) Magazine, Minskaya ul. 11	145-6894		
Vneshposyltorg, Marksistskaya ul. 5	272-7222	274-0102	411250
Vneshpromtekhobmen, Pereulok Vasnetsova 9	284-7241	284-7395	441135
Vneshsigma JV (Belgium), ul. Fadeyeva 1	181-9139	253-9794	411238
Vneshtekhnika, Starokonyushenny per. 6	201-7260	201-7357	411418
Vneshterminalkomplex, ul. Zenlyachkiy 3. str. 2	275-8879		412190
Vneshtorgbank, Kuznetskiy Most 16	928-7116		
Vneshtorgizdat Publishers, ul. Fadeyeva 1	250-5162		
Vneshtorgreklama, ul. Kakhovka 31	331-8311	310-7005	411265
Vneshtradeinvest JV (Austria), ul. Dimitrova 7/8	238-9316	230-2039	207557
Vnukovo Airport	234-8656		
Voaysh JV, Gorodok Baumana 3, korpus 4			
Voest-Alpine Aktiengesellschaft, Krasnopresnenskaya nab. 12, Office 1107	253-1478	230-2830	413234
Voice of America, Rublevskoye shosse 26, kv. 134	415-4236	415-2950	413682
Voith, ul. Kalyayevskaya 19	200-1265	200-4290	
Vokrug Sveta (Around the World) Magazine, Novodmitrovskaya ul. 5a	285-8883		
Volga Cinema, Dmitrovskoye shosse 133	485-5111		
Volga Hotel, Dokuchayev per. 10	280-7729		
Volga II Hotel, ul. Bolshaya Spasskaya 4			
Volgograd Cinema, Ferganskaya ul. 17	371-6496		
Volkskrant (De), ul. Vishnevskovo 4, kv. 75	253-9796		413562
Volksstimme, Prospekt Mira 68, kv. 24	971-3496		413999
Voloknor Company	397-6265	395-2602	411700
Voltek JV, Kotelnicheskaya nab. 1/15, kor. BV, pod. 6, 357	227-4649	227-4685	414530
Volyfagroles JV (Austria), ul. Volkhonka 5/6, str. 11	203-4294	213-4747	
Voprosy Economiki (Problems of Economics), ul. Krasikova 27	129-0454		
Vorlaufer, ul. Akad. Pilyugina 14, korpus 3, kv. 958-959	936-2604	936-2160	
Voskhod Cinema, ul. Mikhailova 29, korp. 1	171-9983		
Voskhod Hotel, Altufyevskoye shosse 2	401-9822		
Voskresenie, ul. Moskvina 8	229-1419		
Voskresenye News-Journal Union	206-2936		
Vostochno-Evropeisky Investistionny Bank, see East European Investment Bank			
Vostok Bank, ul. Yaroslavskaya 8, korpus 3	217-6165		
Vostok Cinema, Ploshchad Akademika Kurchatova 1/1	196-4949		
Vostok Ltd.	536-1281		
Vostokintorg, ul. Smolenskaya-Sennaya 32/34	205-6055		
Votteler, see Theodor Votteler			
Voyenno-Promyshlennaya Investitsionnaya Kompaniya, see Military-Industrial Investment Company			

	Phone	Fax	Telex
Vozrozhdenie Bank, Khrustalny per. 1	921-6172	975-2349	
Vozrozhdenie Foundation, Novy Arbat 56	290-8977		
VPIK, see Military-Industrial Investment Company			
Vremex, ul. Chasovaya 24/1	151-5511	943-0075	411720
Vremya, Pyatnitskaya ul. 62	233-5081	229-3511	
Vstrecha cafe, ul. Gilyarovskovo 3	208-4597		
Vstrecha Cinema, Sadovaya-Chernogryazskaya 5/9	975-4389		
Vsya Moskva JV (FRG), Chistoprudny bulvar 8	921-0735	928-4274	
Vsye Rossiyskiy Birzhevoy Bank, see All Russian Exchange Bank			
VTsION and Public Onpinion Fund, ul. Nikolskaya 17	921-8079	928-2980	
Vympel Cinema, ul. Kominterna 8	472-3240		
Vympel Fatex JV (UK), Stary Petrovsko-Razumovskiy proyezd 1/23	213-6613	213-6111	411797
Vysota Cinema, ul. Yunykh Lenintsev 52	178-5880		

W

	Phone	Fax	Telex
Wako Koeki Co., LTD, Mezhdunarodnaya II, room 1121	253-1676	253-9500	413347
Wall Street Journal, ul. Bolshaya Spasskaya 12, kv. 134	280-5049		413299
Wang -- Service, Kolomenskiy proyezd 1/1	112-3324		
Wang Computer Systems, VDNKh, building 1, unit 17	188-4071		414822
Wartsila, ul. Lunacharskovo 7, kv. 13-14	203-1502	230-2584	413371
Washington Film Associates, Leningradskoye sh. 8/170	150-5682		
Washington Post, Kutuzovskiy prospekt 7/4, kv. 2-3	243-1848		413430
Wasinkraft JV (Switz.), Zagarodnoye shosse 2	126-8801		
Wega Aussenhandels GmbH, Hotel Budapest, room 401	921-4461		411662
Weimos JV, ul. Kalanchevskaya 21/40, k. 201	975-4012		
Welt (Die), Kutuzovskiy prospekt 7/4, kv. 169	243-5286		413230
Wesorta, ul. Lunacharskovo 7, kv. 6	203-5730	200-1248	413282
West International, Lavochkina ul. 19	451-5364	455-8470	
Westdeutsche Landesbank Europa AG, Krasnopresnenskaya nab. 12, Office 1207-1208	255-6464	253-9093	413098
Westdeutscher Rundfunk (ARD & ARD TV), Kutuzovskiy prospekt 7/4, kv. 121-124	243-4355	243-0795	413124
Westdeutscher Rundfunk (ARD), Kutuzovskiy prospekt 7/4, kv. 125	243-9744	243-6068	413551
Western Atlas International, Inc., Leninskiy prospekt 2, kv. 26	239-1788		
WestLB, see Westdeutsche Landesbank Girozentrale			
Westlink JV, Varshavskoye shosse 8	276-6507		
WestOst JV (UK), ul. Malaya Kommunisticheskaya 25	272-4503		
What and Where in Moscow Journal, Frunzenskaya nab. 46	151-1168	245-6473	
White & Case, ul. Tverskaya 7, entrance 7	201-9292	201-9284	
Wilma Sanatorium	496-9810		
Winebrant Life JV (US), Platovskaya ul. 4			
Wise Marketing and Management JV (UK), ul. Spartakovskaya 6a	261-2232		
Wogen Resources Ltd., Mezhdunarodnaya II, room 1623	253-1623	230-2173	
Wolff Aktiengesellschaft, see Otto Wolff Aktiengesellschaft			
World Bible Translation Center, Krylatskiye Kholmy 34	413-8294		

	Phone	Fax	Telex
World Monitor TV, ul. Vorovskovo 23A, kv. 3	291-6064	230-2298	
World Trade Consultants Corporation, Koroviy val 7, Office 64	238-9146	230-2035	413932
Worldwide Television News, Presnenskiy val 19, kv. 513	254-4758		412305
WTCC, see World Trade Consultants Corporation			

X

	Phone	Fax	Telex
Xerox, see Rank Xerox Limited			
Xinhau News Agency, ul. Druzhby 6	143-1951	938-2007	413983

Y

	Phone	Fax	Telex
Yak Air Service JV, ul. Timiryazevskaya, 10/12	211-3074		
Yakimanka cafe, Bolshaya Polyanka 2/10, Str. 1	238-8888		
YAM International Trading Ltd., ul. Profsoyuznaya 57, room 905	332-6420		
Yamskoy Dvor, Leninskiy prospekt 30	135-8255		
Yantar Cinema, Otkrytoye shosse 4	168-6228		
Yanusles JV (FRG), ul. Volkhonka 5/6, str. 11	203-4294	213-4747	
Yapi Ve Kredi Bankasi A.S., Krasnopresnenskaya nab. 12, Office 1206a	253-1947	253-1647	413705
Yaroslavskaya Hotel, Yaroslavskaya ul. 8	283-1733		
Yaroslavskiy Train Station, Komsomolskiy ploshchad 5	266-0218		
Yatig Engineering JV (Lichtenschtein), Prospekt Mira 52	288-3212	288-9566	
Yeiwa Trading Co., LTD, ul. Mytnaya 1, 2nd flr	237-2040	230-2323	
Yelbimbank, 2nd Tverskaya-Yamskaya 15	251-0334		
Sheremetevo II, Office 646	578-2708		413973
Yenisey Cinema, 3rd Parkovaya ul. 53	164-4896		
Yerevan Cinema, Dmitrovskoye shosse 82	489-9464		
Yermolova Drama Theater, ul. Tverskaya 5	203-9063		
Yermolova Museum, Tverskoy bulvar 11	290-0215		
Yeruslan Coop, Sheremetevo II	578-8879	578-6539	
Yit-Yhtyma, ul. Mytnaya 1, kv. 21	230-0465		413049
Yokohama Trading Corp., LTD, ul. Mytnaya 1, 2nd flr	237-1628		
Yomiuri, Kutuzovskiy prospekt 14, kv. 70	243-0776	230-2140	413143
Young and Rubicam/Sovero JV (US), ul. Druzhinnikovskaya 11a	253-1357		
Young Millionaires Club, see Russian Club of Young Millionaires			
Yunona JV (Yugoslavia), Merzlyakovskiy per. 7/2	290-6223	230-2117	411160
Yunost Cinema, ul. Marshala Rybalko 1/4	194-0275		
Yunost Hotel, ul. Khamovnicheskiy val 34	242-4861		
Yuridicheskaya Literatura, ul. Kachalova 14	202-8384		
Yuridicheskyie Uslugi, VDNKh, Metallurgy Pavilion	181-2517		
Yustas JV, ul. Kasatkina 3a	187-8185		
Yuzhnaya Hotel, Leninskiy prospekt 87	134-3065		

	Phone	Fax	Telex

Z

	Phone	Fax	Telex
ZA Art Action Agency JV, ul. Studencheskaya 22			
Za Rubezhom, ul. Pravdy 24	257-2387		
Zagorye Hotel, ul. Yagodnaya 15	329-3011		
Zagranreklama, see Interdepartmental Council for Foreign Advertising			
Zahnradfabrik Friedrichshafen AG, Penta Hotel, 4th Flr	971-6101		411061
Zaidi Poprobui cafe, Prospect Mira 124, korpus 11	286-7503		
Zamoskvorechie cafe, Bolshaya Polyanka 54	230-7333		
Zapchastexport, 2nd Skotoprogonnaya 35	278-6305		
Zapsibinvest JV (FRG), Staraya Basmannaya ul. 4-405	925-0327		
Zarital JV (Italy), Kashirskoye shosse 65	398-8066	393-1635	412241
Zarubezhgeologia, Kaloshin per. 10	241-1515		
Zarya Vostoka cafe, ul. 26 Bakinskikh Komissarov 4, kor. 2	433-2201		
Zaryadye Cinema, Moskvoretskaya nab. 1	298-5687		
Zavidovo Dacha	203-1033		
Zeit (Die), ul. Sr. Pereyaslavskaya 14, kv. 19, 200-201	280-0385	288-9550	
Zeitung vum Letzbuerger Vollek, Leninskiy prospekt 68/100, kv. 33	938-2170		413303
Zenit Cinema, Taganskaya ul. 40/42	271-1440		
Zenit Interior JV Filial (Switz.), Nikolskaya ul. 19	199-9706		
Zheldorbank, ul. Krasnoprudnaya 26/1	262-8880		
Zhen Shen, Petrovskiy Passage	921-6460		
Zhilsotsbank of the USSR, see Mosbiznesbank			
Zhukovskiy Museum, ul. Radio 17	267-5054		
Zigzag Venture Group, Krasnopresnenskaya nab. 12, Office 504	253-1365	253-9383	411636
Zil and Stahl JV (FRG), ul. Avtozavodskaya 23	275-3328	253-9800	411006
Znamenskiy Monastery Concert Hall, ul. Varvarka 8	298-3398		
Znaniye Publishers, Proyezd Serova 4	928-1531		
Zolotaya Roza, Moskva Hotel	292-1194		
Zolotoe Koltso (Belgrade II) Hotel, Smolenskaya ul. 15	248-6734		
Zolotoy Kolos Hotel, Yaroslavskaya 15, korpus 3	286-2703		
Zoo, Bolshaya Gruzinskaya ul. 1	255-5327		
Zoo Beauty Salon	252-2088		
Zoology Museum, ul. Gertsena 6	203-8923		
ZPA C Akovice	250-1982	250-1592	
Zvezda Cinema, Zemlyanoi val 18/22	297-6209		
Zvezdnaya Hotel, Zvezdny bulvar 42	215-4292		
Zvyozdny Cinema, Prospekt Vernadskovo 14	133-9778		
Zweites Deutsches Fernsehen, ul. Bolshaya Dorogomilovskaya 14, kv. 46-47	243-4078	230-2054	413106

Moscow City Street Map

MOSCOW
Scale 1:35,000
Cafe
Restaurant
Metro Station
Ring Line Metro Station
Park or Cemetery
Railroad & Station
Boat Stop
Cinema
Embassy
Gas Station
Market
Theater
Christian Church
Russian Orthodox
Synagogue
Mosque
Kilometers
Miles
Krasny Severyanin
Vorobyevskiy
Saburovo
Khimki-Khovrino
Novokhovrino
Degunino
Beskudnikovo
Slobodka
Kozeyevo
Khovrino
Krasno-Oktyabrskiy
Otradnoye
Babushkin
Verkhniye Likhobory
Vladykino
Golovino
Sviblovo
Novomedvedkovo
Nizhniye Likhobory
Mikhalkovo
Petrovsko-Razumovskoye
Academy of Sciences Botanical Garden
Rostokino
All Russia Exhibition Center
Gorodok Mossoveta
Ivankovo
Pokrovsko-Streshnevo
Kashenkin Lug
Ipatovka
Podbelskovo
Vsekhsvyatskoye
Koptevo
Dubovaya Roshcha
Marina Roshcha
Sokolniki
Bogorodskoye
Sokol
Central Airfield
Khoroshevo
See Central Moscow Map for Detail
Vekhniye

9
10
11
12
13
14
15
16
17
18
19
20
21
22
23
24
Shelepikha
Fili
Sloboda Kutuzova
Mazilovo
Davydkovo
Kamennaya Plotina
Volynskoye
Leninskiye Gory
Luzhniki
Gorky Park
Matveyev-skoye
Ramenki
Nikolskoye
Cheremushki
Semenovskoye
Shabolovo
Vorontsovo
Volkhonka
Kotly
Nizhniye Kotly
Verkhniye Kotly
Novinki
Sadovniki
Kolomenskoye
Nagatino
Dyakovskoye
Batyunino
Pererva
Lyublino
Pechatnikovo
Tekstilshchiki
Gravornovo
Karacharovo
Chukhlinka
Lyublinskiy

J
K
L
M
Saburovo
Molodtsova
Polyarny
Polyarnaya
Shokalskovo proyezd
Sukhonskaya
Yasny proyezd
Kozeyevo
Commission Store
Dezhneva
Dezhneva pr.
Kolskaya
Babushkinskaya
Menzhinskovo
Babush-kinskiy
Severny
bulvar
Yurlovskiy proyezd
Otradnoye
Baykonur
Lenskaya
Yeniseyskaya
Pechorskaya
Iskry
Protection of Our Lady
Otradnoye
Dekabristov
Ivovaya
Vereskovaya
Kolskaya
Raduzhnaya
Verkhoyanskaya
3
Otradnoye Station
Institute Puti Station
Igarskiy proyezd
Dzerzhinskaya Station
Rusanova pr.
Beringov pr.
Otradnaya
Otradny pr.
Selskokhozyaystvennaya
Sviblovo
Snezhnaya
Malygina
Amundsena
Zheleznodorozhnaya
Urzhumskaya
4
Berezovaya alleya
Olonetskaya
Sedova
Sviblovo
Saturn
Nansena
Lazorevy pr.
4
Novomedvedkovo
proyezd Serebryakova
Academy of Sciences Botanical Garden
Botanicheskiy Sad
Rostokino Station
Zolotoy Kolos
Okhotnichiy
Deposition of the Robe
5
Rostokino
Iskra Sports Club
Tourist Hotel
Baykal Hotel
Vilgelma Pika
Dokukina
Sever
Selskokhozyaystven.
All Russia Exhibition Center
Rostokinskaya
Sergeya Eyzenshteyna
proyezd Kadomtseva
Budayskaya
6
Sviblovskaya B.
Praskovina
prospekt Mira
St. Trinity
Ostankinskaya 1.
Bus Terminal
Kasatkina
Borisa Galushkina
Television Center
VDNKh
Kosmos Hotel
Yaroslavskaya
Akademika Koroleva
International Television Center
Ostankino Television Tower
Zolotoy Kolos Hotel
Kosmonavtov
Konstantinova
Kosmos
Tikhvin Icon of Our Lady
Raketny bulvar
Hotel
Yaroslavskaya
Tsandera
Ostankino Station

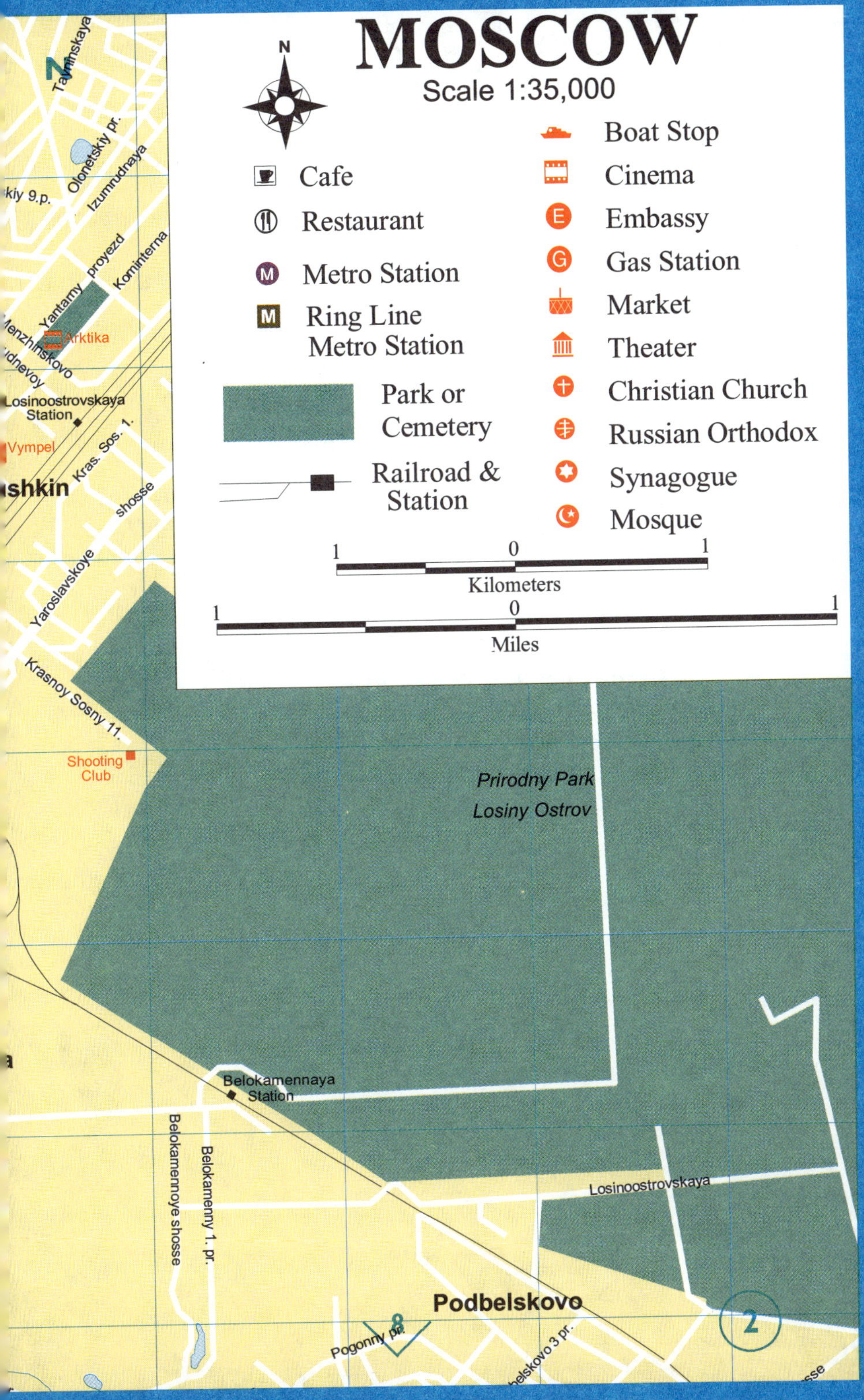
MOSCOW
Scale 1:35,000
N
Cafe
Restaurant
Metro Station
Ring Line Metro Station
Park or Cemetery
Railroad & Station
Boat Stop
Cinema
Embassy
Gas Station
Market
Theater
Christian Church
Russian Orthodox
Synagogue
Mosque
1 0 1
Kilometers
1 0 1
Miles
Taininskaya
Olonetskiy pr.
Izumrudnaya
kiy 9.p.
Yantarny proyezd
Kominterna
Arktika
Menzhinskovo
Losinoostrovskaya Station
Vympel
Kras. Sos. 1.
shkin
shosse
Yaroslavskoye
Krasnoy Sosny 11.
Shooting Club
Prirodny Park Losiny Ostrov
Belokamennaya Station
Belokamennoye shosse
Belokamenny 1. pr.
Losinoostrovskaya
Podbelskovo
Pogonny pr.
2

Hotel-1
A
B
C
D
E
Krasny Severyanin
Zelenogradskaya
Basovskaya
Levoberezhnaya
Dybenko
Angarskaya
Taldomskaya
Beskudnikovskiy
cemetery
Fyodorov Eye
Pullman Hotel
Korovinskoye
Susanina
Ivana
himki-Khovrino
Lenin.
Khovrino Station
Belomorskaya
Klinskaya
Petrozavodskaya
Novokhovrino
Degunino
St. Boris and Gleb
2
Neva
Khovrino
Mosselmash Station
Solnechnogorskaya
Onezhskaya
Festivalnaya
Lavochkina
Pr. No. 5455
Icon of Our Lady
3
Rechnoy Vokzal
Universal Sports Hall
Flotskaya
Voyk.
Krasno-Oktyabrskiy
Geodesy, Aerial Photography and Cartography Institute
Friendship Park
Likhoborskaya nab.
Smolnaya
Konakovskiy pr.
Lavochkina
Leningradskoye
Likhachevskiy 3 p.
Avtomotornaya
Golovino
Avangardnaya
Onezhskaya
4
Likha. 1 p.
Pulkovskaya
Likhachevskiy 2. pereulok
Likhobory Station
Kronshtadtskiy bulvar
Pakgauz. sh.
Cherepanovykh
proyezd
shosse
Vodny Stadion
Golovinskoye Cemetery
Narvskaya
G. Rychagova
Dom Okhotnika i Rybolova Hotel
Golovinskoye
shosse
Mikhalkovskaya
Mikhalkovskaya
Mikhalkovo
Baykal
Koptevskaya
5
Valkh.
(Reservoir)
Star. p.
Dolina
Admirala
Vyborgsk.
Sport Science Training Center
Koptevskiy
Sobolev. pr.
Makarova
Klary Tsetkin
Koptevskiy bulvar
Ivankovskiy pr.
TSSK VMF (Swimming)
6
nkovo
Brattsevo Station
Novopetrovskaya
Novopod.6.p.
Rassvet
Pokrovsko-Streshnevo
Staropetrovskiy pr.
Zoi i Aleksandra Kosmodemyanskikh
Akademicheskaya B.
Voykov.4.pr.
Varshava
No.5.p.
No.4.p.
Priorova
Ipatovka N.
7
Rad.1.
Voykovskaya
Sorok Tehetyri
Ganetskovo Pl.
Nov.2.p.
Nov.3.p.
3
5
Ipatovka
Vokzal.2.p.
Novo 1.p.
Voykovskiy 1 pr.
Kosmonavta Volkova
Leningradskaya

Inzhenernaya
Mars
Bibirevskaya
F
G
H
I
Vorobyevskiy
800 Let Moskvy
ramicheskiy pr.
Putevoy
proyezd
shosse
Rimskovo-Korsakova
Slobodka
Bestuzhevykh
Slobodka Station
Severny
Dekabristov
Otradnoye
Baykonur
Beskudnikovskiy
Dubninskaya
Seligerskaya
Yerevan
Beskudnikovo
bulvar
Degunino Station
Altufyevskoye
Tumanyana Pl.
Dmitrovskoye
Pomorskaya
Kargopolskaya
Sanikova
shosse
Likhoborka
Otradny pr.
Vladykino
Verkhniye Likhobory
Berezovaya alleya
NATI Station
Nativity of Our Lady
Voskhod Hotel
Signalny pr.
Vladykino
Vladykino Station
Okruzhnaya Station
Nizhnelikhoborskiy 3 pr.
Loko pr.
Gostin. pr.
Vostok Hotel
Altay Hotel
Vladykinskoye Cemetery
Oktyabr Zhelez.
Nizhniye Likhobory
Zarya Hotel
Riga
Komdiva Orlova
Academy of Sciences Botanical Garden
Likhobor. Bug.
Lineyny pr.
Komsomolets
Botanicheskaya
Petrovsko-Razumovskoye Station
Petrovsko-Razumovskaya
Petrovsko-Razumovskoye
Kostyakov
Listvenichnaya alleya
Timiryazev. pr.
Pasechnaya
Ostankino Hotel
Marfinskaya B.
Botanichesk. M.
Akademica
Komarova
Molodezhnaya Hotel
Kashenkin Lug
Botanicheskaya
Krasnostudenchskiy pr.
Timiryazevskaya
Nemchinova
Milashenkova
St. Trinity
Akademika Korol.
Television Center
Timiryazevskaya
Dubki
Ivanovskaya
Dmitrovskoye shosse
Fonvizina
Kash. lug
International Television Center
Ostankino Television
4
6
Astradam.2.pr.
Ostankino Station

Dom Okhotnika i Rybolova Hotel
Golovinskoye shosse
Mikhalkovskaya
Mikhalkov
Baykal
A
B
C
D
E
3
6
Vdkhr. (Reservoir)
Admirala
Vyborgsk.
Makarova
Koptevskaya
Star. p.
Dolina
Sobolev. pr.
Koptevskiy
Sport Science Training Center
Klary Tsetkin
Koptevskiy bulvar
Ivankovskiy pr.
TSSK VMF (Swimming)
nkovo
Brattsevo Station
Novopetrovskaya
Rassvet
Novopod.6.p.
Zoi i Aleksandra Kosmodemyanskikh
Staropetrovskiy pr.
Pokrovsko-Streshnevo
Voykov.4.pr.
Rad.1.
Varshava
No.4.p.
No.5.p.
Nov.3.p.
Nov.2.p.
Priorova
Akademicheskaya B.
Ipatovka N.
Ipatovka
Sorok Tehetyri
Voykovskaya
Ganetskovo Pl.
Novo 1.p.
Vokzal.2.p.
Pokrovskoye-Streshnevo Station
Voykovskiy 1 pr.
Leningradskaya Station
Kosmonavta Volkova
Krasny Baltiyets Station
Volokolamskoye shosse
Leningradskoye shosse
Vsekhsvyatskoye
Experimental Biology Institute
Aviatsionnaya
Zagorodny
Shchukinskaya
Koptevo
Hydro-Projects Institute
Akadem. Kurchatova
Pekhot. 1.p.
Volokol.Bolpr.
Ordzhonikidze Aviation Institute
Baltiyskaya
Leningradskiy
Chasovaya
9
Sosnovaya
Usiyevicha
Sokol
Baku
Vrubelya
Kontinent
Bone Hospital
Pekhotnaya
Mar.Koneva
Shishkina
Leningradskiy prosp.
Raskovoy Pl.
Sokol
All Saints
Chamber Music Theater
Chernyakhovskovo
Kurchatova Akademika Pl.
Levitana
Peschanaya
Aeroport
Sokol
Ernsta Telmana Pl.
Molodost
cem.
park
Panfilova
Alabyana
Chapayevskiy p.
Central Bureau of Interpreters
Marshala Rybalko
Leningrad
Lazov.
10
Marshala Biryuzova
Yunost
Raspletina
Novopeschanaya
Central Army Sports Complex
Oktyabrskoye Pole
Peschanaya Pl.
Aeroflot Hotel
Iriny Lev.
Mar. Vershinina
Peschanaya 3.
Bus Shuttle
Serebryany Bor Station
Berzarina
11
Berzarina
oroshevo
Central Airfield
Kuusinena
Zorge
Khoroshevskaya 3.
Narodnovo Opolcheniya
12
5
9
Polezhayevskaya
Marshala Babadzhanyana Pl.
Serebryany
4.

Razumovskoye Station
Petrovsko-Razumovskoye
Petrovsko-Razumovskaya
G
H
I
4
Kostyakov
Timiryazev. pr.
Listvenichnaya alleya
Pasechnaya
Botanicheskaya
Ostankino Hotel
Marfinskaya B.
Botanichesk. M.
Akademica
Komarova
Molodezhnaya Hotel
Kashenkin Lug
Botanicheskaya
St. Trinity
Krasnostudenchskiy pr.
Timiryazevskaya
Nemchinova
Timiryazerskaya
Milashenkova
Television Center
Akademika Korol.
Kash. Lug
International Television Center
Dubki
Ivanovskaya
Dmitrovskoye shosse
Fonvizina
Yablochkova
Dobrolyubova
Astradam.2.pr.
Ostankino Station
Ogorodny pr.
Vuchehticha
Goncharova
Rustaveli
7
Astradamskiy 1 pr.
Estafeta
Iskra
Dubovaya Roshcha
Solomennoy Stor.pr.
Kostyak
Dobrol.
Dmitrovskaya
Chuksin t.
Dmitrovskiy 1.pr.
Dmitrovskaya Station
Khutorskaya 2.
Marina Roshcha
Icon of Our Lady
St. Metrophanius
Grazhdanskaya Station
Khutorskaya 1.
Marta
Petrovsko-Razumovskiy
Novodmitrovskaya Bolshaya
Butyrskaya
Skladochnaya
Annenskaya
Staromar insk. sh.
Vyatskiy 4. pereutok
Petrovsko-Razumov.St.pr.
Mishina
Poltavskaya
Stankolit Station
Polkovaya
Sheremetevskaya
Bashilov.
proyezd
Kolenchataya
Savelovskiy Station
Streletskaya
Yamskaya 1.
Petrovskiy Palace (Zhukovskiy Academy)
Butyrskiy
Sts. Vera, Nadezhka, Lyubov
Dvintsev
Novotikh. 2.
Miusskoye cem.
Synagogue of Marina Roshcha
Kvesisskaya 1.
Praga
Savelovskaya
Teatral. al.
Maslovka Nizhnyaya
Minayevskiy
Dinamo Stadium
Butyrskoy Zastavy Pl.
Dinamo
Turkey
Vadkovskiy p.
Tikhvinskaya
Novosushchevskaya
Oktyabrskiy p.
Oktyabrskaya
Pravda Sports Center
Yamskovo Polya 5.
Bumazhny pr.
Val
Uglovoy p.
Novoslobodskaya
Obraztsova
Institutskiy p.
Raskovoy
Pravdy
Sovetskaya Hotel
Romen Gypsy Theater
Young Pioneers
Botkinskiy 1. pr.
Palikha
Bor. Dostoyevskovo
Novolesnaya
Kryla Sovetov (Sports Club)
Botkin Hospital
Begovaya
Bega Hotel
Botkinskiy 2.pr.
Skakovaya
Leningradskiy prospekt
Butyrskiy
Lesnaya
Mendeleevskaya
Seleznevskaya
Icon of Our Lady
Tzakhkadzor
Lesnoy 2.p.
6
Novoslobodskaya
Verkhnyaya
10
Samotech.1.p.
Belorussia
Tverskaya Zastava Pl.
Hippodrome
St. Pimen

Rostokino
Iskra Sports Club
Tourist Hotel
Baykal Hotel
Vil'gelma Pika
J
K
L
M
Dokukina
Sever
Rostokinskaya
Budayskaya
proyezd Kadomtseva
All Russia Exhibition Center
Selskokhozyaystven.
Sergeya Eyzenshteyna
prospekt Mira
Sviblovskaya B.
Praskovina
St. Trinity
Ostankinskaya 1.
Bus Terminal
Television Center
Kasatkina
Borisa Galushkina
Kosmos Hotel
Yaroslavskaya
VDNKh
Akademika Koroleva
Kosmonavtov
International Television Center
Ostankino Television Tower
Kash. Lug
Zolotoy Kolos Hotel
Kosmos
Tsandera
Ostankino Station
Tikhvin Icon of Our Lady
Raketny bulvar
Konstantinova
Hotel VDNKh
Yaroslavskaya Hotel
Kibalchicha
Pavla Korchagina
Rizhskiy pr.
Ros
Novomoskovskaya
Argunovskaya
Zvezdnaya Hotel
Zvezdny bulvar
Zaidi-Poprobuy
Moskovskaya Malaya
Malenkovskaya Station
Dubovaya Roshcha
Ogonek
Yaroslavskiy
Commission Store
Staroalekseyev.
Kalibrovsk.
Godovikova
Marinskaya Bolshaya
Mira
Novo-Alekseevskaya
Icon of Our Lady
Murmanskiy proyezd
Annenskaya
Staromar insk. sh.
Vetkina
prospekt
Kulakov pereulok
Grafskiy p.
Poperechny prosek
Sokolniki Park
St. Trinity
Pyatnitskoye Cemetery
Mytishchinsk.1.
Moskva 3. Station
Luchevoy 3 prosek
Drobolitey.p.
Polkovaya
Tadzhikistan
Sheremetevskaya
Mar.Ro.2.pr.
Mar.Ro.3.pr.
Mar.Ro.4.pr.
Rizhskaya Station
Yamskaya 1.
Riga Station
Rzhevskaya Station
Mytishch.2.
Luchevoy 1. prosek
Synagogue of Marina Roshcha
Satirkon
Rizhskiy
Fialka
Severnaya Hotel
Rizhskaya
Sokolniki Sports Palace
Festivalny Detskiy Park
Verzemneka
Viktoria
Icon of Our Lady
Sokolnicheskiy Va
Oktyabrskiy p.
Oktyabrskaya
Armii
Trifonovskaya
Gilyarovskovo
Perey.Sr.
Rybinsk.3.
Lobachika
Shumkina
Staroslobodsk.
Obraztsova
St. Tryphon
Orlovskiy p.
Banny p.
Pereyaslavskaya Bolshaya
Panteleyevskaya
Institutskiy p.
Sovetskoy
Armed Forces Museum
Olympic Penta
Bor. Dostoyevskovo
Frunze Central Army Park
Olympiskiy Sports Club
Krasnoselsk V.
cem.
Russian Army Theater
St. Philip
Mira
Ethiopia
Mos.-Kaz. Pl.
Seleznevskaya
All Saints
Moscow Moslem Mosque
Durov Animal Theater
Durova
Novoslobodskaya
Krasnoselskaya
Samotech.1.p.
Samotechn
Burkino Faso
Prospekt Mira
Portugal
Moscow City Court
Leningrad Station
Yaroslavl Station
Krasnoprudnaya
St. Pimen
Sri Lanka
Ireland
Kalanchevskaya
Bolshaya Station
Beriozka
Komsomolskaya
Troitskaya
7
8
9
10
12

N
O
P
Q
R
2
Belokamennaya Station
Belokamennoye shosse
Belokamenny 1. pr.
Losinoostrovskaya
Podbelskovo
Pogonny pr.
Podbelskovo 3 pr.
bul. Rokossovskovo Marsh
Podbelskovo
Rubin
shosse
Ulitsa Podbelskovo
Bogatyrsk. 3
Transfiguration
Krasnobogatyrskaya
Grazhdanskaya 3.
Glebovskaya
Detskaya
Otkrytoye
Bogorod-skoye
Yantar
Olenya Bolshaya
Shiryayevskaya B.
Tikhonovskaya B.
Spartak Center
Boytsovaya
Otkrytaya
Alymova
Cherkizovskaya M.
Prostornaya
Khalturin.pr.
Lokomotiv Hotel
Lokomotiv Stadium
Znamenskaya
Sevastopol
Cherkizovskaya
St. Prophet Elijah
kolniki
Praga
Bogorodskiy Val
Poteshnaya
Bukhvostova 1
Krasnobogatyrskaya
Nekrasovskaya
Khromova
Buntarskaya 1.
Khalturinskaya
Cherkizovskaya Bolshaya
Pugach. 1.
Sokolov.
Bogorodskoye sh.
Korolenko
Kolodeznaya
Orion
Preobrazhenskaya Pl.
Preobrazhenskaya
Pugachev. 2.
Mossoveta
Ograd. p.
Preobrazhenskiy
Yegersk.
Ostroumovsk. Bol.
Stromynka
Skin-Venereal Hospital
Babayevskaya
Tishina
Exhaltation of the Holy Cross
Exhaltation of the Holy Cross
Izmaylovo Hotel
Znamenskiy Brothers Training Center
Sokolniki
Sokolnichesk. 4.
Matrosskaya
Rusakov. nab.
Preobrazhenskaya nab.
Elektrozavodskaya
Suvorovskaya
Preobrazhenskoye Cemetery
Izmaylovskiy Val.
Dormition
Neptun Hotel
Ibragimova
Mironovskaya
Lechebnaya
Borisovskaya
Fortunatovskaya
Izmaylovskiy Park
Izmaylovo Water Sports Palace
Tkatskaya
Gastello
Sokolnicheskaya 2.
Semenov. M.
Semenovskaya
Zverinetskaya
Shcherbakovskaya
Elektrozavodskaya
Zhuravleva Pl.
Izmaylovskovo Zverintsa 1.
Narodny prospekt
Elektrozavodskaya Station
Semenovskaya
Auto Mechanics Institute
12
Bol. Izmaylovskoye
Blagusha shosse
8
Perevedenovskiy 1.p.
Semenovskoye Cemetery
Kirpichnaya
Volnaya

A
B
C
D
E
Serebryany Bor
Marshala Babadzhanyana Pl.
Khoroshevskoye shosse
Mnevniki
Demyana Bednovo
Silikatny 3. proyezd
Magistralnaya 4.
5
13
Serebryany Bor Beach
Magistralnaya 1.
Moskva
Presnya-Tovarnaya Station
Magistralny 1.pr.
Shenogina
Silikatny 1.pr.
Magistralnaya 3.
Zvenig
Magistralnaya 2.
14
Podvoyskovo
Krasnogvar. bul.
Zarech.
Beregovoy proyezd
Shelep. 1.
Shelep. 5.
Antonova-Ovsey.
Shelepikha
Shmitov. pr.
Testovskaya Station
Novozavodskaya
15
Fizkulturny proyezd
Mukomolny pr.
Shele. sh.
Krasno. 2.pr.
Krasnogvardeys
Krasno. 4.pr.
Soyuz-2 Hotel
Barklaya
Slobo.2
Fili
Bagrationovskiy proyezd
Fili Station
Bagrationovskaya
Alyabyeva
Seslavinskaya
Minskaya
Bolshaya
Promyshlenny pr.
Ukraina
Beriozka
Oleko Dundicha
Filevskiy Park
Generala Yermolova
1812 Goda
Borodino Battle Museum
Kiyev
prospekt
Kutuzovskaya
Kastanayevskaya
Oleko Dundi.
Romena RollanaPl.
Kutuzovskiy
Pobedy Pl.
Poklonn. 1.
Vasilisy Kozhinoy
Victory Over Napolean
17
Gerasima Kurina
Marshala Grechko
Staromozhayskoye shosse
Sloboda Kutuzova
Victory Park
Brat. Fonch.
Setun
Setunskiy 4.pr.
Moskva-Sortirovochnaya Station
shosse
Pudovkina
Vorobyev. shosse
18
Minskaya
St. Trinity
Tumba Golf Club
Costa Rica
Rublev. shosse
Chad
Dovzhenko
Mosfilmovskaya
Mosfilm Studio
United Arab Emerates
Nicaragua
Malaysia
Kosygina
Cuba
Angola
Libya
Ochakovskoye
Liberia
Yugoslavia
Kamennaya Plotina
Sweden
Institute of Military History
Hungary
9
13
Romania
Central Hotel Defense Ministry
Bulgaria
North Korea

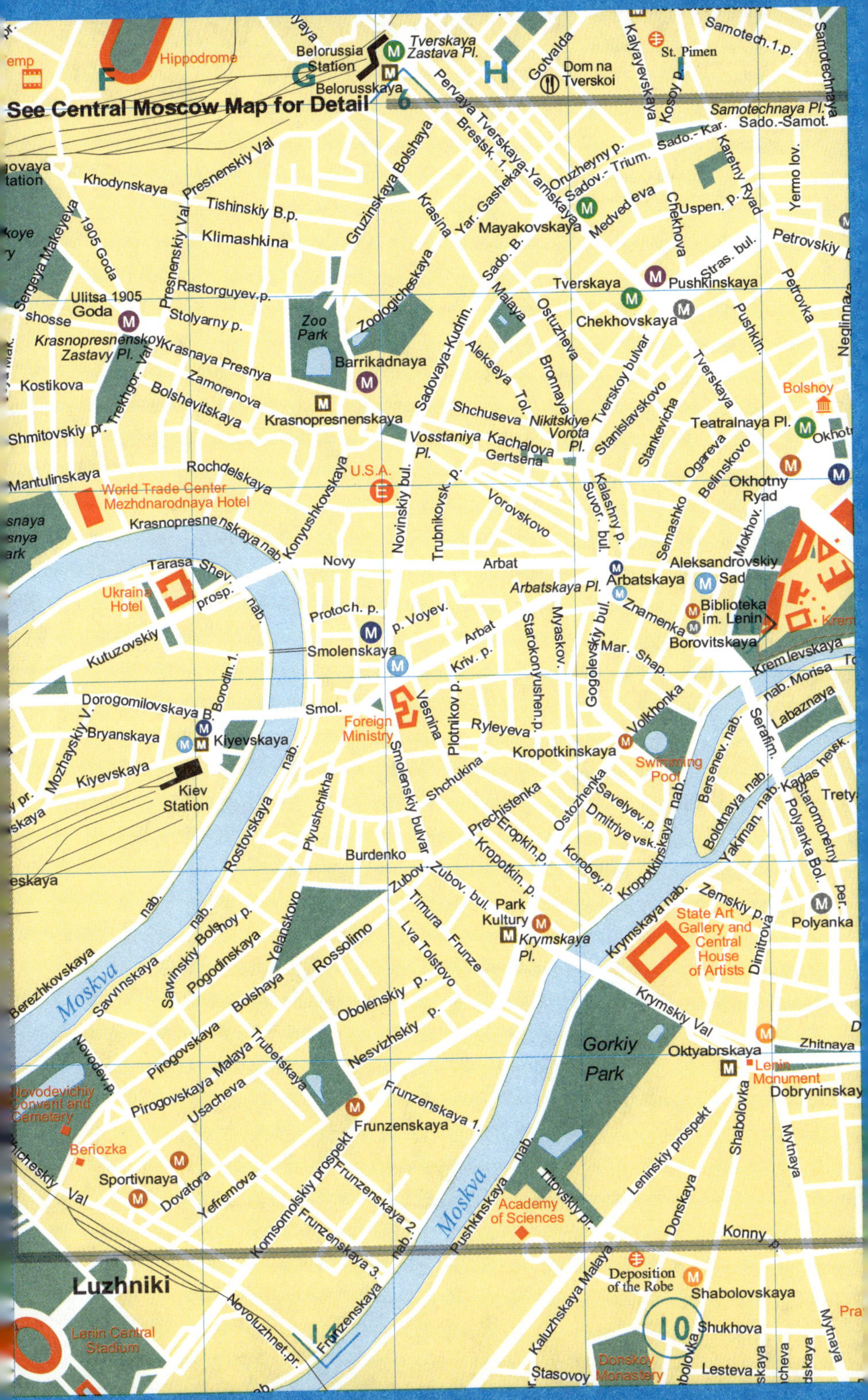
See Central Moscow Map for Detail
Hippodrome
Belorussia Station
Belorusskaya
Tverskaya Zastava Pl.
St. Pimen
Dom na Tverskoi
Samotechnaya Pl.
Khodynskaya
Presnenskiy Val
Tishinskiy B.p.
Klimashkina
1905 Goda
Ulitsa 1905 Goda
Rastorguyev.p.
Stolyarny p.
Krasnopresnenskoy Zastavy Pl.
Krasnaya Presnya
Zoo Park
Zoologicheskaya
Barrikadnaya
Gruzinskaya Bolshaya
Krasina
Mayakovskaya
Sadovaya-Kudrin.
Tverskaya
Pushkinskaya
Chekhovskaya
Chekhova
Petrovskiy
Petrovka
Neglinnaya
Bolshoy
Teatralnaya Pl.
Okhotny Ryad
Kostikova
Zamorenova
Bolshevitskaya
Shmitovskiy pr.
Krasnopresnenskaya
Vosstaniya Pl.
Kachalova
Gertsena
Nikitskiye Vorota Pl.
Tverskoy bulvar
Mantulinskaya
Rochdelskaya
U.S.A.
World Trade Center
Mezhdnarodnaya Hotel
Krasnopresnenskaya nab.
Konyushkovskaya
Novinskiy bul.
Vorovskovo
Novy
Arbat
Arbatskaya Pl.
Arbatskaya
Biblioteka im. Lenin
Borovitskaya
Aleksandrovskiy Sad
Kreml
Ukraina Hotel
Tarasa Shev.
Kutuzovskiy prosp.
Smolenskaya
Protoch. p.
Dorogomilovskaya
Bryanskaya
Kiyevskaya
Kiev Station
Smol.
Foreign Ministry
Vesnina
Plotnikov p.
Ryleyeva
Starokonyushen.p.
Gogolevskiy bul.
Kropotkinskaya
Volkhonka
Swimming Pool
Kremlevskaya
Serafim.
Bersenev. nab.
Bolotnaya nab.
Yakiman. nab.
Tretyakovskaya
Polyanka
Smolenskiy bulvar
Shchukina
Prechistenka
Ostozhenka
Plyushchikha
Rostovskaya
Burdenko
Zubov. bul.
Park Kultury
Krymskaya Pl.
Krymskaya nab.
State Art Gallery and Central House of Artists
Dimitrova
Krymskiy Val
Oktyabrskaya
Lenin Monument
Dobryninskaya
Zhitnaya
Gorkiy Park
Moskva
Berezhkovskaya
Savvinskaya
Pogodinskaya
Yelanskovo
Rossolimo
Timura Frunze
Lva Tolstovo
Obolenskiy p.
Nesvizhskiy p.
Pirogovskaya Bolshaya
Pirogovskaya Malaya
Trubetskaya
Usacheva
Frunzenskaya
Frunzenskaya nab.
Novodevichiy Convent and Cemetery
Beriozka
Sportivnaya
Dovatora
Yefremova
Komsomolskiy prospekt
Academy of Sciences
Leninskiy prospekt
Shabolovka
Donskaya
Mytnaya
Konny p.
Deposition of the Robe
Shabolovskaya
Shukhova
Lesteva
Donskoy Monastery
Kaluzhskaya Malaya
Luzhniki
Lenin Central Stadium
Novoluzhnet.pr.
Stasovoy

Sri Lanka
Ireland
prospekt
Bolshaya
Station
Krasno
Troitskaya
Samotechnaya Pl.
Sado.-Kar.
Sado.-Samot.
Sado.-Sukh.
Beriozka
Komsomolskaya
K
7
L
M
Kazan Station
Sadovaya - Spasskaya
Spasskaya
Novokirovskaya
Orlikov p.
Kalanchevskaya
Olkhovskaya
Cathedral of the Epiphany
Razgulyay
Novoryazanskaya
Baumanskaya Pl.
Sukharevskaya
Trubnaya
Tsvetnoy bul.
Yermo lov.
Karetny Ryad
13
Uspen. p.
Chekhova
Tsvetnoy Bulvar
Trubnaya Pl.
Petrovskiy bul.
Rozh. bul.
Sret. bul.
Sretenka
Kostyan. p.
Ulanskiy p.
Myasnitskaya
Griboyed.
Krasny Vorota
Sad. Cher.
Novaya Basmannaya
Razgulyay Pl.
Bauman Park
Tokmakov p.
Stras. bul.
Pushkinskaya
Petrovka
Pushkin.
Neglinnaya
Turgenevskaya
Chistiye Prudy
Christoprud. bul.
Chaplygina
Mashkova
Gorokhovskiy p.
Engineer's Institute of Geodesy, etc.
Ecuador
Kazakova
Tverskaya
14
Kuznetskiy Most
B. Lubyanka
Lubyan. M.
Markhlev.
Myasnitskaya
Krivoko. p.
Armyan. p.
Zemlyanoi Val
Saltykovs.
Bolshoy
Teatralnaya Pl.
Okhotny Ryad
Lubyanka
Chernyshevsk ovo
Kurskaya
Kurskaya
Akademika
Krasn
Ogareva
Belinskovo
Okhotny Ryad
Pl. Revolyutsii
Maroseika
Pokrovskiy bul.
Podso. p.
Yelizarov.
Kurskovo Vokz. Pl.
Kursk Station
Syromyatn ichesk.
Zolotorozhsk nab.
Mokhov.
GUM
Ilyinka
pr. Serova
Arkhipova
Staraya Pl.
Vu.B.p.
Obukha
Syrom. Ver.
Aleksandrovskiy Sad
St. Basil's
Varvarka
Kitay-Gorod
Podkolokolny p.
Syrom.N.
Biblioteka im. Lenin
Red Square
Rossia Hotel
Yauz. bul.
Kost.p.
Yauza
Kremlin
Borovitskaya
Mos kvoretskaya nab.
Ustin. pr.
Kost. nab.
And. nab.
Ancient Russia Museum
Kremlevskaya nab.
Tor.
Raushskaya nab.
Serebryaniches. nab
Bernikovsk. nab.
10
nab. Morisa
Balch.
Osipenko
Ulyanovskaya
Cathedral of Our Saviour
Tulinskaya
Labaznaya
Ovchinn ikov nab.
Zemlyanoi Val
Pryamikovo Pl.
Ulyanovskaya
Serafim.
Kotelnicheskaya Apartments
Kotelnichesk. nab.
Volo dar.
Bersenev. nab.
16
Pyatnitskaya
Kommunistichesk. Bol'.
Andronyevskaya Bol.
Bibliotec
nab. Maksima
Osipenko
Taganskaya Pl.
Vekovaya
Bolotnaya nab.
Kadashevsk. nab.
Tretyakovskaya
Taganskaya
Marksistskaya
Yakiman. nab.
Staromonetny
Polyanka Bol.
Novokuznetskaya
Gorkovo
Fakelny
B.p.
Taganskaya
Zemlyachki
Ozerovskaya nab.
Gonch. pr.
Narodnaya
Kamenshchi.M.
Mayakov. p.
Abelm
Zasta
Zemskiy p.
per.
A.N. Ostrovskovo
Ordynka Bolshaya
Zenit
Abelman.
State Art Gallery and Central House of Artists
Polyanka
Dimitrova
Novokuznetskaya
Bakhrushina
Tatarskaya
Kras. Ni.
Voron
Marksistskaya
Pobeda
Stroy.
Val
Paveletskaya
Zatsep. Val
Shlyuzov. nab.
Novospasskiy Monastery
Krestyanskoy Zastavy Pl.
Oktyabrskaya
Zhitnaya
Dobryninskaya Pl.
Valovaya
Paveletskaya
Kozhevnicheskaya
Krestyanskaya Pl.
Sar.pr.
Krut.3.p.
Proletarskaya
Volgogra
Lenin Monument
Dobryninskaya
Serpukhovskaya
Paveletskiy Station
Sosinskaya
U Yuzefa
Novo dubrovskaya
Svirskaya
Dobrovskaya 1.
Shabolovka
18
Mytnaya
Lyusinovskaya
Serpukhovsk. Bol.
Shch ipok
Dubininskaya
Letnikovskaya
Krutitskaya nab.
Melnikova
Melnikova
Volg
Mayak
Derbenevskaya
Zhukov pr.
Konny p.
Simonovskiy Val
Sharikopodshipnikov.
Der benevskaya nab.
Shabolovskaya
Pavlov.3.p.
Moskva-Tov. Station
Moskva
Sharikopodshipnikovskaya
Shukhova
Pravda
Mytnaya
19
11
Podolskaya
AZLK Sport Center
Lesteva
Khavskaya
Tatishcheva
Gorodskaya
Danilovskaya Pl.
Transport Book Store
15
Simonov Monastery
Velozavodskaya
Pamir
Mashinostroyeniya 1.
Serpukhovskoy
Dubininskaya
Paveletskiy3.pr.
Nativity of
Lipki

N
O
P
Q
R
8
16
12
Bauman Technical School
Baumanskaya
Lefortovskaya Pl.
Bauman Technical School
Vvedenskoye Cemetery
Gospitalnaya Pl.
Sts. Peter and Paul
Yekaterinskiy Palace
Sputnik
Lefortova Prison
Sortirovochnaya Station
Agdam
Lefortovo Station
Stomach Hospital
Kalininskiy
Prolomnoy Zastavy Pl.
Aviamotornaya
Fakel
Entuziastov shosse
Novaya Station
Pl. Ilicha
bulvar Entuziastov
Moskva 2. Station
Rogozhskiy
Perovskiy pr.
Rogozhskoye Cemetery
St. Nicholas
St. Nicholas
Cathedral of the Intercession of the Virgin
Frezer Station
Andronovka Station
Basovskaya
Kalitnikovskiy
Joy of All Sorrowful Icon
Kalitnikovskoye Cemetery
4. Kilometer Station
Rubin
Karacharovo Station
Chukhlink
Karacharovo
Nizhegorodskaya
Ryazanskiy prospekt
2. Grayvoronovskaya pr.
Grayvoronovskaya
Gravornovo
"Moskvich" Auto Plant
Ugreshskaya Station
Ostapovskiy proyezd
Volgogradskiy pr.
Saratovskaya

A
B
C
D
E
9
20
21
22
23
24
25
26
13
China
Uruguay
Druzhby
Michurinskiy prosp.
St. Trinity
Leninskiye Gory
Ski Jump
Litva
Universitetskaya Hotel
Indira Gandi Pl.
Stolet.
Akademika
Universitetskiy prospekt
Mendeleyevskaya
Matveyevskaya Station
Ramenka
Moscow State University
Khokhlova
Lebedeva
Lomonosovskiy prospekt
Ramenki
Michurinskiy prospekt
prospekt Vernadskogo
Children's Musical Theater
(New) Circus
Nik. Kopernika
Molodezh.
Universitet
Commission Store
Fotiyevoy
Progress
60-letiya SSSR
Lomonosovskiy prospekt
Ramenki 2.
50 Let Oktyabrya Lesopark
Stroiteley 8.
Stroiteley
Anglo-American School
Cheremushkinskiy
Krupskoy
Panferova
prospekt Vernadskovo
Marii Ulyanovoy
Nikolskoye
Prospekt Vernadskovo
Koshtoyan tsa
Borovskoye shosse
Zvezdny
Kravchenko
Havana
Leninskiy prospekt
Yuzhnaya Hotel
Vavilova
Garibaldi
Semen
Druzhba Hotel
Sport Hotel
Spros Hotel
International Relations Institute
Chere
Lobachevskovo
St. Trinity
Novatorov
Kaluzhskoye shosse
Bre.
Problems of Physics Institute
Kazakhstan
Yugo-Zapadnaya
Vorontsovo
26. Bakinskikh Komissarov
Tsentralny Dom Turista
Profsoyuznaya
Akademika Keldysha Pl.
Kaluzhskaya
Space Research Institute
Miklukho-Maklaya
Russian Language Institute
Salyut Hotel
Lumumba University
Moscow Intercity Telephone Exchange
Obrucheva
Geological Prospecting Institute
Akademika Volgina
Vilnyus
Univermag
Butlerova
Pirogov Medical Institute
Vityaz
Derevlevo

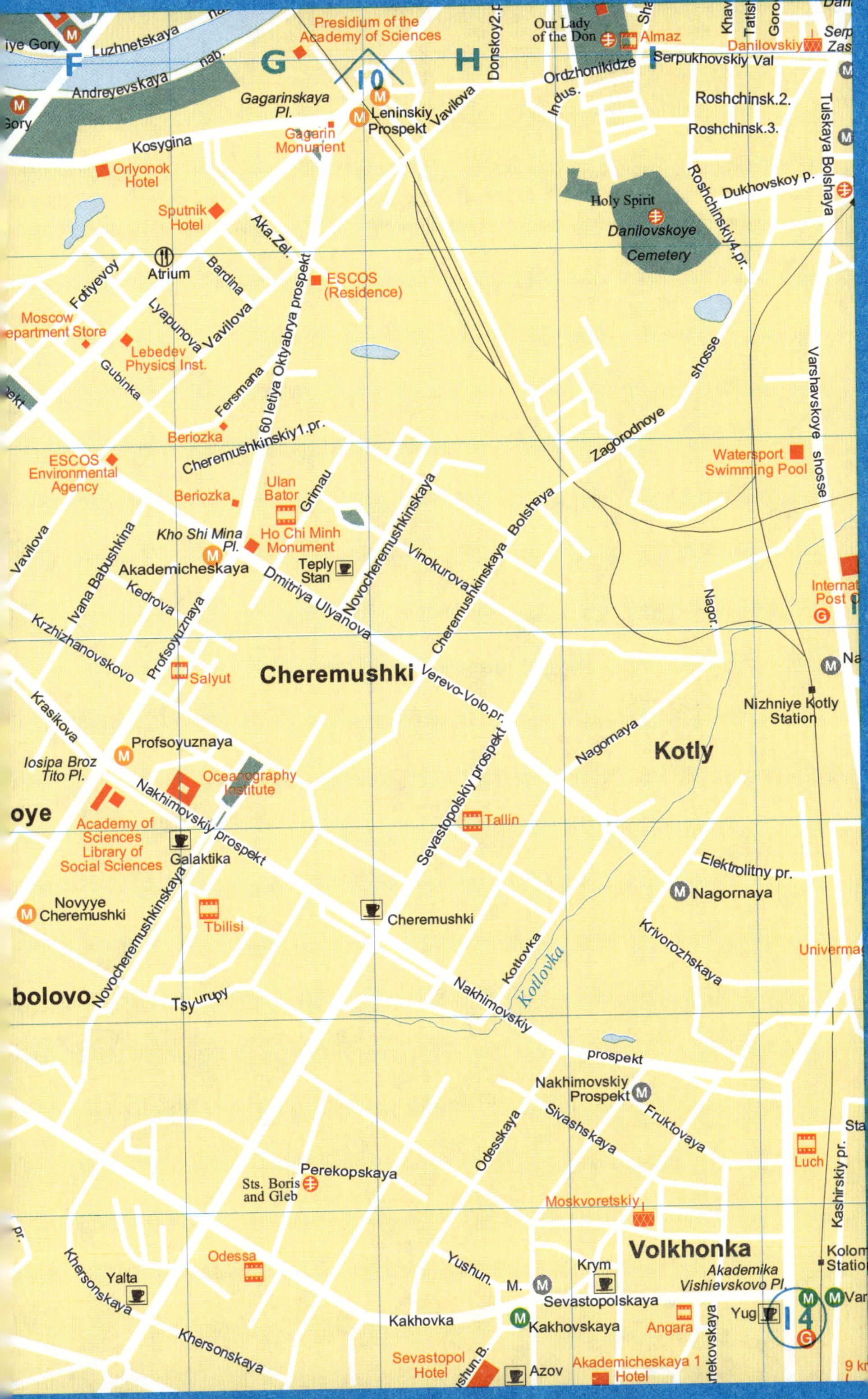
Presidium of the Academy of Sciences
Luzhnetskaya
Andreyevskaya
nab.
F
G
H
Donskoy2.p
Our Lady of the Don
Almaz
Danilovskiy
Serpukhovskiy Val
Ordzhonikidze
Indus.
Gagarinskaya Pl.
Leninskiy Prospekt
Vavilova
Gagarin Monument
Kosygina
Roshchinsk.2.
Roshchinsk.3.
Tulskaya Bolshaya
Orlyonok Hotel
Sputnik Hotel
Holy Spirit
Danilovskoye Cemetery
Dukhovskoy p.
Roshchinskiy4.pr.
Aka.Zel.
Atrium
Bardina
ESCOS (Residence)
Fotiyevoy
Moscow Department Store
Lyapunova
Vavilova
Lebedev Physics Inst.
Gubinka
60 letiya Oktyabrya prospekt
Fersmana
Beriozka
Cheremushkinskiy1.pr.
Zagorodnoye
shosse
Varshavskoye shosse
Watersport Swimming Pool
ESCOS Environmental Agency
Beriozka
Ulan Bator
Grimau
Novocheremushkinskaya
Bolshaya
Vavilova
Ivana Babushkina
Kho Shi Mina Pl.
Ho Chi Minh Monument
Akademicheskaya
Teply Stan
Vinokurova
Cheremushkinskaya
Kedrova
Dmitriya Ulyanova
Krzhizhanovskovo
Profsoyuznaya
Salyut
Cheremushki
Verevo-Volo.pr.
Nagor.
Nizhniye Kotly Station
Krasikova
Profsoyuznaya
Nagornaya
Kotly
Iosipa Broz Tito Pl.
Oceanography Institute
Nakhimovskiy prospekt
Sevastopolskiy prospekt
Tallin
Academy of Sciences Library of Social Sciences
Galaktika
Elektrolitny pr.
Nagornaya
Novyye Cheremushki
Tbilisi
Novocheremushkinskaya
Cheremushki
Krivorozhskaya
Kotlovka
Kotlovka
Nakhimovskiy
Tsyurupy
prospekt
Nakhimovskiy Prospekt
Sivashskaya
Fruktovaya
Odesskaya
Luch
Kashirskiy pr.
Perekopskaya
Sts. Boris and Gleb
Moskvoretskiy
Volkhonka
Kolom Statio
Khersonskaya
Odessa
Yushun.
M.
Krym
Akademika Vishievskovo Pl.
Yalta
Sevastopolskaya
Yug
Kakhovka
Kakhovskaya
Angara
Khersonskaya
Sevastopol Hotel
Azov
Akademicheskaya 1 Hotel
9 km

Lesteva
Shabolo
Khavskay
Tatishchev
Gorodska
Danilovskaya Pl.
Dubininskaya
Book Store
Simonov Monastery
Mashinostroyeniya
Almaz
Danilovskiy
Serpukhovskoy Zastavy Pl.
Paveletskiy3.pr.
Paveletskiy2.pr.
Nativity of Our Lady
Lipki
Vostochnaya
Serpukhovskiy Val
Tulskaya
Zhelezno.pr.
Velozavodskiy
Roshchinsk.2.
Roshchinsk.3.
Tulskaya Bolshaya
Danilovskaya nab.
Kozhukhovsk
Dukhovskoy p.
St. Daniel Monastery
Simonovskaya nab.
Masterkova
Kozhukhovskiy1.pr.
Kozhukhovskiy2.pr.
Kozhuk. 6.
Commission Store
Avtozavodskaya Pl.
Avtozavodskaya
Kozhuk. 5.
Rechnoy Station
Roshchinskiy4.pr.
Novoye Vremya Hotel
Saykina
Trofimova
Torpedo (Swimming)
Lobanova
Likhachev Auto Plant
Kozhukovo Station
shosse
Varshavskoye shosse
Novodanilovskaya nab.
Andropova
Watersport Swimming Pool
Park im.60-l
Belikovo Okty
Nagatinskaya
prospekt
International Post Office
Southe Passeng Termina
Nagor.
nab.
Nagatinskaya
Klenovy
Nizhniye Kotly Station
Kotly
Nizhniye Kotly
Srednyaya
Sude
bulvar
Kolomenskaya
Sadovniki
Novinki
Orbita
Novinki
Elektrolitny pr.
Nagornaya
Nagatinskaya 2.
Nizhnyaya
Bolshaya
Verkhnyaya
Zhuzha
Kazan Icon of Our Lady
Univermag
Verkhniye Kotly
Sadovniki
Kolomenskoye Museum Reserve
Kolomenskiy pr.
Shtatnaya Sloboda
prospekt Andropova
Sokolinskaya Tower
Moskva
Starokashirskoye shosse
Kashirskoye shosse
Luch
Kashirskiy pr.
Oncology Center
Dachny
Dyakovskoye
Akademika Vishievskovo Pl.
Kolomenskoye Station
Oncology Center
Kashirskaya
Varshavskaya
Yug
20
21
22
23
24
25
26
J
K
L
M
14
15

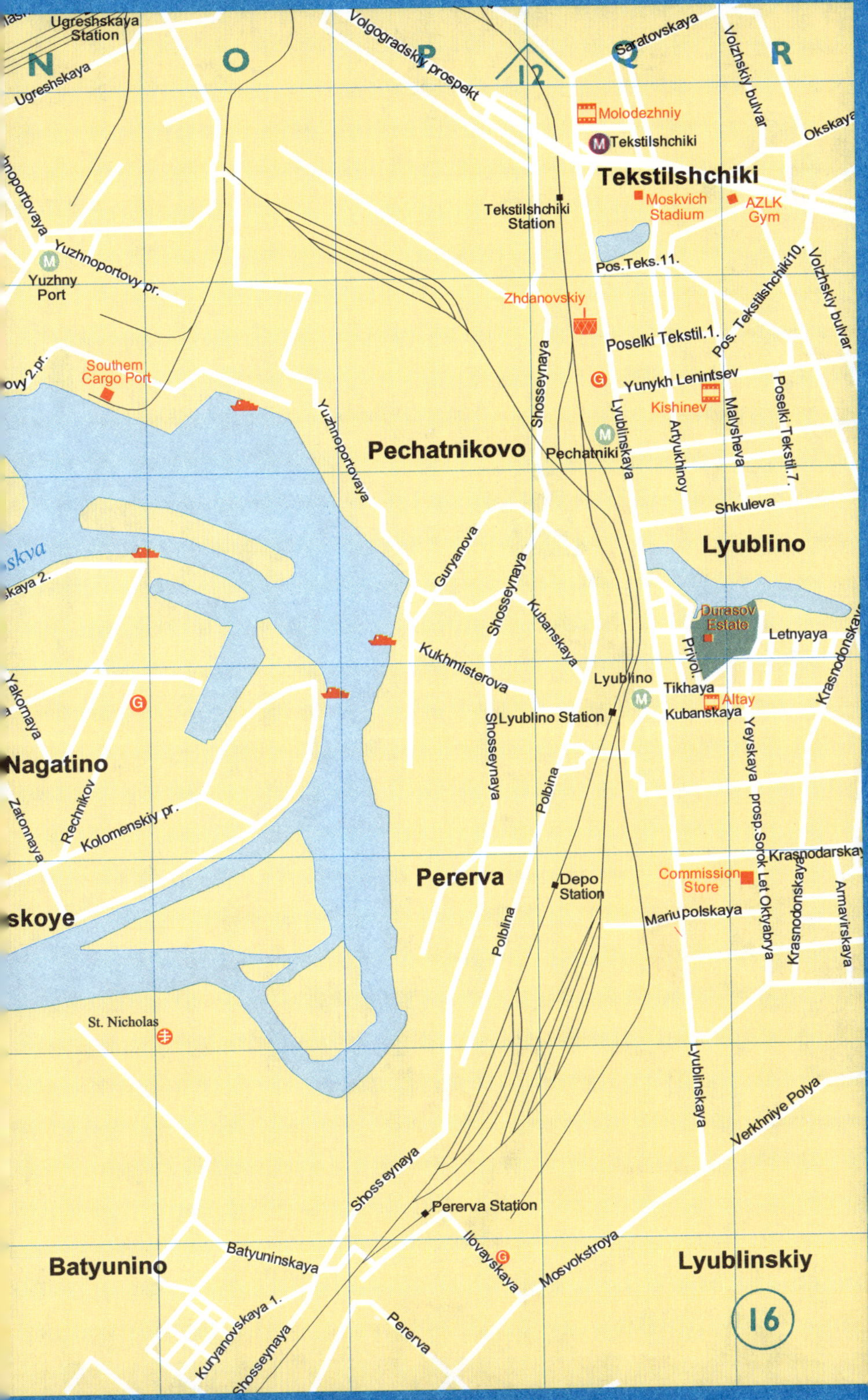

N
O
P
Q
R
12
Ugreshskaya Station
Ugreshskaya
Volgogradskiy prospekt
Saratovskaya
Volzhskiy bulvar
Okskaya
Molodezhniy
Tekstilshchiki
Tekstilshchiki
Tekstilshchiki Station
Moskvich Stadium
AZLK Gym
Pos.Teks.11.
Yuzhnoportovy pr.
Yuzhny Port
Zhdanovskiy
Poselki Tekstil.1.
Pos. Tekstilshchiki10.
Volzhskiy bulvar
Southern Cargo Port
Yunykh Lenintsev
Kishinev
Shosseynaya
Lyublinskaya
Artyukhinoy
Malysheva
Poselki Tekstil.7.
Yuzhnoportovaya
Pechatnikovo
Pechatniki
Shkuleva
Lyublino
Guryanova
Shosseynaya
Kubanskaya
Durasov Estate
Letnyaya
Krasnodonskaya
Privol.
Kukhmisterova
Lyublino
Tikhaya
Altay
Kubanskaya
Lyublino Station
Yeyskaya
Yakornaya
Nagatino
Shosseynaya
Polbina
Rechnikov
Kolomenskiy pr.
Zatonnaya
prosp.Sorok Let Oktyabrya
Krasnodarskaya
Pererva
Depo Station
Commission Store
Krasnodonskaya
Armavirskaya
Mariupolskaya
Polbina
St. Nicholas
Lyublinskaya
Verkhniye Polya
Shosseynaya
Pererva Station
Batyunino
Batyuninskaya
Ilovayskaya
Mosvokstroya
Lyublinskiy
Kuryanovskaya 1.
Shosseynaya
Pererva
16

F
G
6
Gruzinskiy
Polyclinic #6
Kon. Sr. p.
Elektricheskiy p.
Presnenskiy Val
Tishin. M. p.
Khodynskaya
Tishinskiy
Sredniy pere
Vagankovskoye Cemetery
13
Bolshoy
Tishinskiy
pereulok
Resurrection
Malaya
Vagankovskiy
Makeyeva Sergeya
Klimashkina
Presnenskiy Val
Poland
1905 Goda
Dekabrskaya Bolshaya
St. Andrew
Malaya Gruzinskaya
Germany
Novopre. p.
Armenian
Foreign Mission
Bulgaria
Rastorguyevskiy p.
Gruzinskaya
Zoologicheskiy p.
Zoo. t.
Zvenigorodskoye
shosse
Ulitsa 1905 Goda
Biological Museum
9
Stolyarny pereulok
Krasnopresnenskoy Zastavy Pl.
Makeyeva Sergeya
Moscow Pravda
Volkov pereulok
Zoo Park
Krasnaya Presnya
Trekhgorny Val
Olimp
Delhi
1905 Goda
Kostikova
Bolshoy pereulok
14
Zvenigor. 2.
Zamorenova
Krasnopresneskaya
Anatoliya Zhiv.
Bolshevitskaya
Barrikady
Anny Severyanovoy
Weather Center
Predt. M. p.
St. John the Baptist
Shmitovskiy pr.
Pavlika Moro. p.
Arlecchino
Plamya
1905 Goda
Studenet. p.
Trekhgorny
V. Pred. p.
Trekh. M. p.
Druzhinnikovskaya
Kony.
Kap. p.
Rochdelskaya
Metrostroy Stadium
Mantulinskaya
Krasnaya Presnya
World Trade Center and Mezhdunarodnaya (Intercontinental) Hotel
Glubokiy p.
Konyushkovskaya
Devyatinskiy
Krasnaya Presnya Park
naberezhnaya
Mir Hotel
Krasnoprenenskaya
Russian Government Offices
Moskva
Inflotel (Aboard the Alexander Blok)
Boat Stop
Moscow Mayoral Office (Former CEMA Building)
Tarasa
Kalininskiy Most
Shevchenko
15
naberezhnaya
Pryamoy p.
Panfil. p.
Nov. B. p.
Brewery
Dor. Val
Ukrainskiy bulvar
Ukraina Hotel
Protochny
Magazin Malysh
Our Lady of Hope
21
Smolenskaya
Kutuzovskiy prospekt
Russian Souvenirs
Metro Most
Smolenskiy 1. p.
17
Dom Igrushki
Beriozka
Borodinskaya 2.
Pizza Hut
Equatorial Guinea
naberezhnaya
US Trade and Economic Council
Borodinskaya 1.
Beriozka (Groceries)
Sadko
Voskhod
Dorogomilovskaya
Borodinskiy
Shu. p.
Smole
Belgrad Hotel #2

Diplomatic Gastronom
Commission Store
Pervaya Tverskaya-Yamskaya
Tverskoy-Yamskoy 1.
Decorative, Applied, and Folk Art
Delegats
H
Okhotnik
6
pereulok
Sadovaya-Karetnaya
Kinematografistov
Brestskaya 1.
Brestskaya 2.
Oruzheyny
Triumfalnaya
Ermitazh
Karetny Ryad
Vasilyevskaya
Tishinskaya Pl.
Yuliusa Fuchika
Czechoslovakia
Sadovaya-
Argentina
Vorotnik. p.
Sfera
Miniatures (skits)
Hermitage Gardens
Moskva
Mayakovskovo Pl.
Sofiya
Sovetskaya Muzika
Chekhova
Burundi
Gasheka
Yaroslava
Mayakovskaya
Baku
Uspenskiy p.
Benin
Diplomatic Gas Station
Krasina p.
Chaykovskiy
Medvedeva
Pekin Hotel
Satire
Mossovet
Intercar Supermarket
Aquarium Gardens
Degtyarny p.
Krasina
Minsk Hotel
Blagov. p.
Lenkom
pr. Skvortsova-St
ITA
Zoologicheskaya
Ring
Sadovaya Bolshaya
Stanislavskiy
Nastasin. p.
Nativity of Our Lady
First Gallery
Strastnoy
Uganda
p. Sadovskikh
Tverskaya
Jordan
Young Viewers
Museum of Russian Revolutions
Izvestia
Strasnoi 7
Zholt ovsk ovo
Pushkinskaya
Rossiya
American Express
Trekh. p.
Chekovskaya
Cafe Margarita
Tverskaya
Lakomka
Pakistan
Pushkinsaya Pl.
Kozitskiy p.
Fu
Patriarshie Prudy
Kozikhin. M. p.
Yuzhinskiy p.
McDonald's
Sytinskiy p.
19
Stan. and Nem.-Dan. Musical Theater
Pushkin
Children's Clinic
M. Patri. p.
Ostuzheva
Bogoslavskiy
Ring
Tsentranaya Hotel
Tsentralny
Nemirovicha-D.
Adama Mits.
Intermarket
Spiridonyev. p.
Marco Polo Presnya Hotel
Bolshaya
Pushkin
Art
Africa Inst.
Malaya Bronnaya
St. John the Theologian
Gnezd. B. p.
Gnezd. Maly p.
Moscow Drama Theater
Bat Cabaret
Pizza Hut
Sovetskaya Pl.
Garden
Sadovaya - Kudrinskaya
Vspolny pereulok
Bronnaya
Aragvi
Aist
Boulevard
Tverskoy bulvar
MKhAT (new building)
Moscow City Government
Planetarium
Alekseya Tolstovo
P.D.R.Y. (S. Yemen)
Azerbaydzhan
Commission Store
Tunisia
Shchuseva
Resurrection of Christ in Jerusalem
Sever
Ukraine
Stanislavskovo
Malaya Bronnaya
Togo
Communications Ministry and Ctr. Telegram
Vosstaniya Pl.
Brazil
Kachalova
Stankevicha
Nezhdanovoy
Nigeria
Nikitskiye Vorota Pl.
ITAR
Stanis. 2
Spain
Writers' Union
Cyprus
Gertsena
Myanmar
Big Ascension
Greece
Moscow Bar Assoc.
Kinoakter
Egypt
Paliashvili
Mayakovskiy
Ogareva
Intouri Hot
New Zeland
Skaterny p.
Stol. p.
Georgia
Merzlyakov. p.
U Nikitskikh Vorot
Chaykovskiy Conservatory
Old US Embassy
Cameroon
Iceland
Ghana
Suvor. bul.
Kalash. p.
Sobin.
Belinskovo
National H
Intourist Of
Gnesiny Music Institute-Concert Hall
Tadzhikistan
Belgium
Gertsena
Moscow State University
Kislov. Sr. p.
Estonia
Sierra Leone
Khlebny p.
USA & Canada Institute
Japan
Netherlands
Semashko
Mongolia
Trubnikovskiy p.
(Former) Supreme Court
Granovskovo
Pisemskovo
Sudan
Ni. p.
Moscow State University
Lithuania
Molchan. M.
Norway
Vorovskovo
Kislovskiy
Friendship House
Melodia
Ivushka
Arbatskaya Pl.
Voentorg
Oktyabr
Petchora
Dom Knigi
Manezhnaya
Irish Arbat
Khudozhestvenny
Arbat
VESNA
Biryusa
Angara
Valday
Zhiguli Bar
Arbatskaya
Vozdvizhenka
Aleksandrovsky Sad
Praga
Komp.
Arbat Passport Photo
Arbat. p.
Arbatskaya
Russian State Library
Mokhovaya
Tzentralniy Baths
The Residence (US Amb.)
Fed.
Serebrya. p.
(no thru traffic)
Yanysheva
Vakh.
Afan. M. p.
Foreign Mission Jerusalem
Somalia
Znamenka
Engelsa
p. Voyevodina
Vakhtangov
Buratino
22
Biblioteka im. Lenina
Singapore
Spasopeskov. Pl.
Turkmenia
Borovitskaya
Karmanits. p.
Biskvit
Starokonyushenny
Myaskovskovo
Boulevard Ring
Gogolevskiy bulvar
18
Pasakov House
Staroye Russkiye Pelmeni
Commission Store
Today Gallery
Kaloshin p.
Gritsevets
Marksa i
Borovitskaya Pl.
Troil. p.
Arbat pedestrian mall
Krivoarb. p.
p. Aksakova
Mar. Shaposh.
Nauka i Znaniye
Central Chess Club
p. Sivtsev Vrazhek
Lenivka
Foreign Affairs
Canada
Kampuchea
Pushkin Museum

Decorative, Applied, and Folk Art
GAI
Central Puppet
Samotechnaya Pl.
Samotechnaya Estakada
pereulok
Sadovaya-Samotech.
Sadovaya-Karetnaya
Karetny Ryad
Kolkhida
Lebanon
Narva
Sadovaya-
Oruzheyny
Triumfalnaya
Ermitazh
Venezuela
Yermolovoy
Tzvetnoy Bulvar Sport Club
Tsvetnoy
Sadovaya-
Vorotnik. p.
Sfera
Miniatures (skits)
Karetny M. p.
Argentina
Hermitage Gardens
Karetny Sr. p.
Militsiya Headquarters
Tsentralny
Sovetskaya Muzika
Mayakovskaya
Chekhova
Burundi
Circus (old)
Sukhar. M. p.
Baku
Medvedeva
Uspenskiy p.
Kolob. 2. p.
Espace Mir
bulvar
Benin
Kolobov
Kol. 3. p.
1. p.
Ser. M. p.
Trubnaya
Mossovet
Degtyarny p.
Tsvetnoy Bulvar
Minsk Hotel
Blagov. p.
pr. Skvortsova-St.
ITAR
Petrovka
Petrovskiy bulvar
Boulevard
Ring
Stanislavskiy
Nastasin. p.
Lenkom
Strastnoy bulvar
Algeria
Krapiven. p.
Trubnaya Pl.
Rozhdestvenskiy
Sadovskikh
Young Viewers
Nativity of Our Lady
First Gallery
Strasnoi 7
MkhAT (Annex)
Uzbekistan
Cathedral of the Nativity of Our Lady
Tverskaya
Museum of Russian Revolutions
Izvestia
Pushkinskaya
Rossiya
Chekovskaya
Moskvina
Marika
Tverskaya
Lakomka
Pushkinsaya Pl.
Kozitskiy p.
Fur Kommissioni
Health Ministry
Neglin. 3. p.
Rakh. p.
Neglin 2. p.
Kiselny B.
Trekh. p.
Yuzhinskiy p.
McDonald's
Sytinskiy p.
Stan. and Nem.-Dan. Musical Theater
Pushkinskaya
Petrovka
Budapesht Hotel
Neglinnaya
Rozhdestvenka
Bogoslavskiy
Tsentranaya Hotel
Tsentralny
Moscow Academic Musical Theater
Neglin. 1. p.
Ring
Bolshaya
Nemirovicha-D.
Razdan
Sanduniy Baths
Varsonofyev.
Polo Hotel
Pushkin
Gnezd. Maly p.
Bat Cabaret
Arfa
Stoleshnikov
Petrovskiy Passage
Goskontsert
Automotive Industry Ministry
St. John the Theologian
Moscow Drama Theater
Pizza Hut
Sovetskaya Pl.
pereulok
Shokoladnoye
Kuznetskiy Most
Moldova
Bronnaya
Gnezd. B. p.
Dmitrovskiy p.
Druzhba
Most
Aragvi
3 KzM
Kuznetskiy
Higher and Special Education Ministry
Boulevard
Tverskoy bulvar
MKhAT (new building)
Moscow City Government
Sadko
TsUM
Alitalia
Former KGB Headquarters
Azerbaydzhan
MKhAT
Pushechnaya
Bolshoy
Tverskaya
Khudozh. T. pr.
Armenia Hotel
Savoy Hotel
Lubyanka
Resurrection of Christ in Jerusalem
Sever
Ukraine
Finnair
Malev
Operetta
Maly
Stanislavskovo
Moskovskoe
Central Children's
Detskiy Mir
Lubyans
Communications Ministry and Ctr. Telegram
Georgiye. p.
Teatralny proyezd
Alpha Shop
Dzerzh.
Stankevicha
Nezhdanovoi
Children's
Metropol Hotel and Cinema
Stanis. 2
Pl. Sverdlova
Ogni Moskvy
History Reconstr. of Mosc. Museum
ITAR
Ogareva
Kosmos
House of Unions
Teatralnaya Pl.
Greece
Moscow Bar Assoc.
Yer. Dr.
Gosplan
Okhotny ryad
Nikolskaya
Mayakovskiy
Intourist Hotel
Moskva Hotel
Pl. Revolyutsii
Slavinskiy Bazar
Cherkasskiy B. p.
U Nikitskikh Vorot
Chaykovskiy Conservatory
Belinskovo
National Hotel
Pl. Revolyutsii
Pl. Revolyutsii
Suvor. bul.
Kalash. p.
Sobin.
Intourist Office
Okhotny ryad
Lenin Cent. Museum
Kuybysh. pr.
Gertsena
Moscow State University
Manezhnaya Pl.
1st. pr.
Supreme Court RSFSR
Kislov. Sr. p.
Estonia
Cathedral of the Epiphany
pr. Sapunova
Canada
Japan
Semashko
Netherlands
Granovskovo
Tomb of the Unknown Soldier
Historical Museum
Ni. p.
Moscow State University
Ilyinka
Chamber of Commerce
Kislovskiy
Lenin Mausoleum
Friendship House
Central Exhibition Hall
Arsenal
GUM
Arbatskaya Pl.
Voentorg
Council of Ministers
Khrustal. p.
Rybny
Khudozhestvenny
Manezhnaya
Krasnaya Pl. (Red Square)
Praga
Arbatskaya
Vozdvizhenka
Alexander Gardens
Varvar.
Aleksandrovsky Sad
Palace of Congresses
Kremlin Theater
Arbatskaya
Russian State Library
Yanysheva
Mokhovaya
Tzentralniye Baths
St. Basil's
Moskvoretskaya
M. p.
Foreign Mission Jerusalem
Armory
Znamenka
Great Kremlin Palace
KREMLIN
Engelsa
Biblioteka im. Lenina
Borovitskaya
Boulevard Ring
Gogolevskiy bulvar
Gritsevets
Marksa i
Pasakov House
Zaryad.
naberezhnaya
Moskvoretskiy Bolshoy Most
Borovitskaya Pl.
Mar. Shaposh.
Kremlevskaya
Raus.
Morisa Toreza
Ministry of Oil and Gas
Defense Ministry Reception Office
Bukhar. Hotel
Central Chess Club
Lenivka
B. Kamenny Most
naberezhnaya
Faleyevs.
Balchug
Pushkin Museum
United
Bukhare.

K
L
Komsomolskaya Pl.
International Banking Center
Leningradskaya Hotel
Kazan Station
Cape Verde
Bolshay
Spasskaya
Kopetskiy
prospekt Mir
Dochuchayev p.
#2
#1
Volga Hotels
Sukharevskaya Pl.
Trinity
Kolkhoznaya
Pankrat. p.
Emergency Medical Service
Sadovaya - Spasskaya
Ring
Sretenskiy tupik
Novokirovskaya
Orlikov
Kalanchevskaya
Ryazanskiy pr.
pereulok
Yuz. pr.
Novoryazansk
Ryazan. p.
Basma
Beriozka (jewelry)
Uran
pereulok
Seliverstov p.
Dayev
State Bank for Foreign Trade
Agriculture Ministry
Kras. pr.
Novaya Basmannaya
Sretenka
Golovin M. p.
Prosvirin p.
Lukov p.
Ashcheulov p.
Rybnikov p.
Ulanskiy
pereulok
Novokirovskaya
Kirovskiy pr.
Railway Ministry
Lermontovskaya Pl.
Krasny Vorota
Vstrecha
Sadovaya
Urozhay Book Store
Dubrovnik
Khom. t.
Basmany Tupik
Stret. Vor. Pl.
Sret. bul.
Myasnitskaya
Griboyedova
Kozlovskiy B. p.
INSET
Kirov. Vor. Pl.
Turg. pr.
Bobrov p.
Turgenevskaya Pl.
Chistiye Prudy
Bolshevistskiy p.
pereulok Stopani
Switzerland
Hydromet Center
Kazakhstan
Bolshoy
Koz. M. p.
pereulok
Eye Hospital
Chernogryazskaya
Commission Store
Staraya Basm
Turgenevskaya
Moscow Post Office
Kharitonyevskiy
Latvia
Furmanny pereulok
Novorossiysk
Tsen. Kun. Pl.
Chistoprudny bulvar
Boulevard
Zhukovskovo
Chaplygina
Mashkova
UVIR
Kazakova
Gogo Dram Theatre
Malaya
Markhlevskovo
St. Louis
Myasnitskaya
St. Michael the Archangel
Ural Hotel
Chernyshevskovo
Zemlyanoi Val
Russkiy Tchay
Moscow Palette Assoc.
Krivokolenny p.
Telegrafny
Potapovskiy
Procurement Ministry
Sovremenik
Makarenko
Afghanistan
Sverchkov
pereulok
Belo. pr.
Lyalina Pl.
Mechnikova
p. Arkadiya Gaydara
Zvezda
Komsom. B. p.
Armyanskiy pereulok
Heart Hospital
Pokrovskikh Vorot Pl.
Barash. p.
Kurska
Armenia
Khokhlovskaya Pl.
Lyalin pereulok
Kurskaya
Kurskovo Vokz. Pl.
Luch. p.
St. Nicholas
Belorussia
Chernyshevskovo
Ring
Yelizarovoy
Komsomol
St. Prince Vladimir
Maroseika
Petrov. p.
Starosadskiy p.
Kolpachny p.
Khokhlovskiy p.
Pokrovskiy bulvar
Podsosenskiy p.
Kazarmen. p.
pr. Serova
Arkhipova
Choral Synagogue
Central Committee Communist Party (closed)
Ivanov.
Zabelina
Vuzovskiy B. p.
Iran
Syrom.
Baptist and Seventh Day Adventist
Maly p.
Vuzovskiy
Durasov. p.
Pl. Nogina
XVII Century Arts Museum
Kitay-gorod
Solyan. t.
Podkopayev. p.
St. Nicholas
Justice Ministry
India
Obukha
Museum of Oriental Art
Obukha
Kamenskiy Cathedral Concert Hall
Kitayskiy proyezd
Podkolokolny p.
Solyanka
Nikolovor. B. p.
Power and Electrification Ministry
Sts. Peter and Paul
Yauzskiy bulvar
Ring
Yauzskikh Vorot Pl.
Yauzskaya
Serebryanicheskiy p.
Central Concert Hall
Former Foundling Hospital
Poluyar.
Serebryanicheskaya
naberezhnaya
Vysoko-Yauzskiy Most
Nikol.
Yauza
naberezhnaya
20
Astakhovskiy Most
Bernikovskaya
naberezhnaya
Boat Stop
Ustinskiy proyezd
Ustinskaya nab.
Podgorskaya nab.
Illyuzion
Foreign Literature Library
Veil of the Virgin
Garden
Siyakov
naberezhnaya
Ustinskiy Bolshoy Most
Ustinskiy
Kotelnicheskaya
Ulyanovskaya

Igrushki
Kutuzovs
Beriozka
Equatorial Guinea
Pizza Hut
F
17
G
US Trade and Economic Council
Beriozka (Groceries)
Dorogomilovskaya Bolshaya
Sadko
Voskhod
Borodinskaya 1.
Borodinskiy Most
Beriozka
Smolenskaya
Belgrad Hotel #2
Belgrad Hotel #1
Shu. p.
Rayevskovo
16
Bolshoy Kolkhozny
Bryanskaya
Bryanskiy 2. p.
Kiyevskaya
Kiyevskovo Vokz. Pl.
Kiyevskaya Hotel
Kiyevskaya
Kiev Station
Slavianskaya Hotel
Boat Stop
Platovskiy pr.
Khukhrikov p.
Mozhayskiy
Val
Rezervny pr.
Kiyevskaya
naberezhnaya
Ros. 4. p.
Ros. 6. p.
Ruzheyn
Plyushchikha
Zemledelcheskiy p.
Exhibition of Moscow Architecture
Moskva
Rostovskaya
Vra. 1. p.
Bangladesh
Colombia
9
Frunze Academy
proyezd
Devichyego
Vrazh. 2. p.
Truzhenikov 1. p.
Truzhe. 2. p.
Zolotoi Drakon
Skver Devichye Pole
St. Michael
Yelanskovo
17
Berezhkovskaya
naberezhnaya
Bolshoy pereulok
Savvinskiy
Savvinskaya
Vietnam
Rossolimo
Iraq
Pogodinskaya
Olsufyevskiy p.
Ar. 1. p.
pereulok
Savvinskiy Maly p.
Klin. 1. p.
Bolshaya
U Pirosmani
Novodevichya nab.
Abrik. p.
St. Demetrius
Pirogovskaya
Malaya
Trubetskaya
Kholzunova
Novodevichiy p.
Sport
Pirogovskaya
Shibayevskiy 1. p.
Trubetskovo Park
Novodevichiy Convent
Dormition
18
Rynok Hotel
Usacheva
Arena Hotel
Frunzenskaya
proyezd
10 letiya
Novodevichiy Cemetery
Khamovnicheskiy
Luzhnetskiy
Uchebny p.
Sportivnaya
Oktyabrya
14
Kooperativnaya
Yefremova
Beriozka
21
Usacheva
Savelyeva
Komsomolskiy prospekt
Frunzenskaya
Val
Sportivnaya
Dovatora
Yunost Hotel
Frunzenskaya

Staroye
Russkiye Pelmeni
Commission Store
Gallery
Arbat pedestrian mall
Krivoarb. p.
H
Kaloshin p.
Kovskovo
p. Aksakov
18
Boulevard Ri
Gogolevskiy
Gritsev.
Mar. Shaposh.
I
Borovitskaya Pl.
House
Nauka i Znaniye
p. Sivtsev Vrazhek
Taneyevykh
pereulok
Canada
Kampuchea
Furmanova
Central Chess Club
Pushkin Museum of Fine Arts
Lenivka
Foreign Affairs and Trade Ministries
Plotnikov p.
Vlasyev. B. p.
Ryleyeva-9
Kropotkinskaya
Volkhonka
Moscow Outdoor Swimming Pool
naberezhnaya
Boat Stop
Estrada (Variety)
Vesnina
Gabon
Ryleyeva
Adriatika
U Margarity
Kropotkinskaya Pl.
Soymonovskiy pr.
Zaire
Morocco
Luxembourg
Lunachar.
Mog. B. p.
p. Ostrovskovo
Ostozhenka
Austria
Mexico
Denmark
Italy
A.N. Tolstoy Museum
Krylenko
Kropotkinskaya
Bersenevskaya nab.
Udamik
Chisty p.
Vsev. p.
Obyden. 2. p.
St. Prophet Elijah
Bersen. p.
Peru
Shchukina
Levshin M. p.
Chancellery of Patriarch
UPDK
Prechistenka
Lopukh. p.
Barykov. p.
Bolivia
Savelyevskiy p.
bulvar
Glazur
Serbskiy Institute
Sechenov. p.
Dmitriyevskovo
Madagascar
Niger
Kursovoy p.
Burg (float
nab.
Bolotnaya
Kuwait
Beriozka
Erop. p.
Mansurovskiy p.
Zach. 3. p.
Za chat. 2. p.
(N. Yemen)
P.L.O.
Syria
Ostozhenka
Kropotkinskaya-36
Thailand
Ivory Coast
23
Yakimanskaya
Kropotkinskiy pereulok
Guinea
Molo. p.
Butikovskiy p.
Sholokhom Pl.
Pomerantsev p.
Khilkov p.
Korobeynikov p.
Golut.
Golutvinskiy
Finland
Congo
naberezhnaya
Dash. p.
ITAR (Information Telegraph Agency of Russia)
Australia
Oktyabrskaya Hotel
Zemskiy pereulok
Turchaninov p.
Kropotkinskaya
Babyegorodskiy 1. p.
Zubov. pr.
Tchayok
Zubovskiy bulvar
Viru
Chayka Swimming Pool
Novokrym. pr.
Krymskaya naberezhnaya
Krymskaya Pl.
Park Kultury
Maronovskiy p.
Dimitrova
Timura Frunze
Krymskiy pr.
Krymskiy Most
Krymskaya Estakada
State Art Gallery and Central House of Artists
Babyegorodskiy 2. p.
Zamosk
Lva Tolstovo
Boat Stop
Aeroflot
Garden Ring
Yakimanskiy p.
St. John the Warrior
pereulok
Pugovishnik. p.
naberezhnaya
Krymskiy Val
Youth Art School
St. Nicholas
Timura Frunze
Fitil
Commission Store
Fun. 4. p.
pereulok
Ksen. p.
Guria
Kavkaz
Shokoladnitza
Moskva
Okty
Oktyabrs Pl.
Gorkiy
Komsomolskiy prospekt
Frunzenskaya
Oktyabrskaya
Park
Varshava Hotel-1
Children Library
Tren-Mos
Gorizont
(no thru traffic)
Hard Rock Cafe
Akadem
Frunzenskaya 1.
Tro Bus Te
Leninskiy prospekt
Donskaya
14
naberezhnaya
City Clinical Hospital No. 1
22
Shabolovka
Senegal
Pushkinskaya
Titovskiy proyezd
St. Prince Demetrius
Amphitheater
Education Ministry

Boulevard
Gogolevski
Grits
Mar. Shaposh.
Borovitskaya Pl.
Kremlevskaya
Bolshoy Mos
Central Chess Club
Pushkin Museum of Fine Arts
Lenivka
B. Kamenny Most
naberezhnaya
Morisa Toreza
Ministry of Oil and Gas
Defense Ministry Reception Office
Bukha Hot
Bukha Hote
Balchug
United Kingdom
Falejevskiy p.
Volkhonka
Moscow Outdoor Swimming Pool
naberezhnaya
Boat Stop
Serafimovichicha
Estrada (Variety)
Labaznaya
Repina Pl.
Makar. Tatya.
Chugu Mos
Moskvoretskiy M. Most
Kropotkinskaya
Kropotkinskaya Pl.
Ostozhenka
Soymonovskiy pr.
Kropotkinskaya
Bersenevskaya nab.
Vodootvodny Kanal
Kadashevskaya nab.
Ordynka
Pyatnitskaya
Krylenko
Obyden. 2. p.
St. Prophet Elijah
Udarnik
M. Kamenny Most
Tolmachev. M. p.
Lavrushinskiy p.
Kadashev. 1. p.
Kada. 2. p.
Chern.
Bolshaya
Savelyevskiy p.
Bersen. p.
Staromonetny
Laos
Ingos
Dmitriyevskovo
Kursovoy p.
Madagascar
Niger
Burgas (floating)
Tretyakovskaya
Icon of Our Lady
Klimentovski
Tretyakovs
Bolotnaya nab.
Yakimanka M.
Polyanka Bolshaya
Tretyakov Gallery
Ordyn. t.
Tolmach. B. p.
St. Nicholas
Za chat. 2. p.
Ivory Coast
Molo. p.
Butikovskiy p.
Yakimanskaya nab.
Golut. 1. p.
Yakimanka
pereulok
Golikov. p.
naberezhnaya
Golutvinskiy 3. p.
Polyan. p.
Pyzhevskiy p.
Geography Institute
Guinea Bissau
Kropotkinskaya
Oktyabrskaya 1 Hotel
Zemskiy pereulok
Brodnikov p.
Polyanka
Lasagne
Toy House
Polyanka
Babyegorodskiy 1. p.
Khvo. 2. p.
Malaya
Krymskaya naberezhnaya
Maronovskiy p.
Dimitrova
Khvostov 1. p.
Kazachiy 1. p.
Ordynka Bolshaya
Ostrovskovo A.N.
Pyatnitskaya
Krymskiy Most
State Art Gallery and Central House of Artists
Babyegorodskiy 2. p.
Zamoskveetchye
Polyanka
Guyana
Kazachiy 2. p.
Shchetin. p.
Marat. B. p.
Kirgizia
Garden Ring
Krymskiy Val
Yakimanskiy p.
St. John the Warrior
France
Spasonalivkovskiy 1. p.
Polyanka
Pogorelskiy p.
Uzbekistan
Youth Art School
Kazanskiy p.
Spasonaliv. 2.p.
Bolshaya
Mauritania
Commission Store
Monet. 2.
Kavkaz
Shokoladnitza
Gosbank
Kenya
Maly (annex)
Rwanda
Gorkiy Park
Oktyabrskaya
Oktyabrskaya Pl.
Zhitnaya
Dobryninskaya Pl.
Oktyabrskaya
Varshava Hotel-1
Dobryninskaya
Serpukhovs
Koroviy Val
Burevestnik
Children's Library
Air France
Air India
Oman
Malta
Jamaica
Moskovsko-Leninskiy Dept. Store
Hard Rock Cafe
Akademicheskaya 2. Hotel
Lyu. 1. p.
Dobrynin. 4. p.
Diplomatic Polyclinic
Lyu. 2. p.
Dobryninskiy 1. p.
Serpukhovskaya
Trolley Bus Terminal
Ascension
Leninskiy prospekt
Donskaya
Mytnaya
Shabolovka
City Clinical Hospital No. 1
Senegal
Lyusinovskiy 3. p.
Lyusinovskaya
Bolshaya
Surge Institu
St. Prince Demetrius
Education Ministry
Krasny Proletariy Stadium
16
17
18
22
23
15

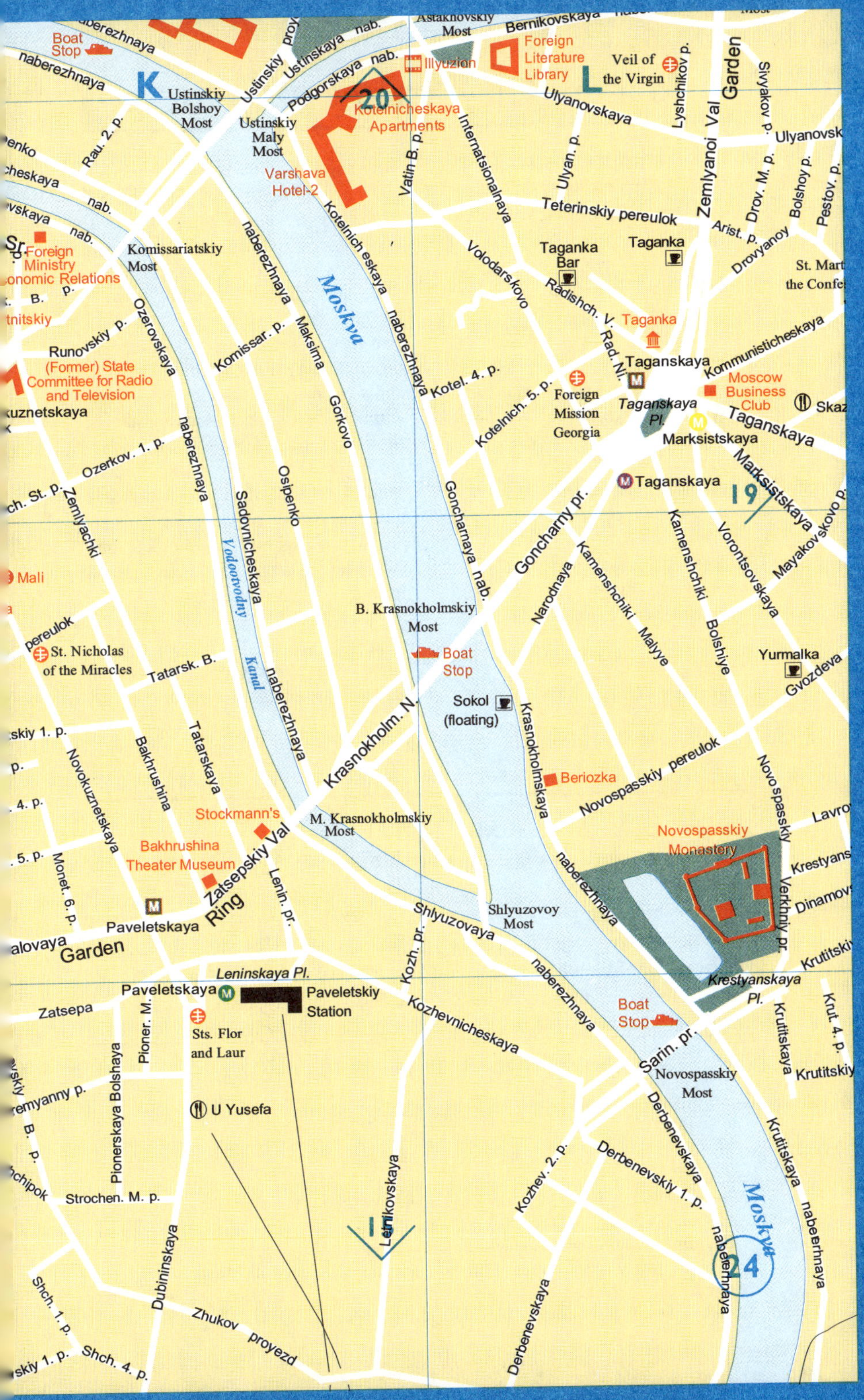

Boat Stop
naberezhnaya
K
Ustinskiy Bolshoy Most
Ustinskiy proyezd
Ustinskaya nab.
Podgorskaya nab.
Astakhovskiy Most
Bernikovskaya
Illyuzion
Foreign Literature Library
Veil of the Virgin
L
Lyshchikov p.
Garden
Zemlyanoi Val
Sivyakov p.
Ulyanovskaya
Ulyanovsk
20
Kotelnicheskaya Apartments
Ustinskiy Maly Most
Varshava Hotel-2
Vatin B. p.
Internatsionalnaya
Ulyan. p.
Teterinskiy pereulok
Bolshoy p.
Pestov. p.
Drov. M. p.
Arist. p.
Drovyanoy
Rau. 2. p.
nab.
Komissariatskiy Most
Foreign Ministry
Economic Relations
Taganka Bar
Taganka
Radishch. V.
Rad. N.
Volodarskovo
St. Mart the Confe
Moskva
Kotelnicheskaya
naberezhnaya
Runovskiy p.
Ozerovskaya
(Former) State Committee for Radio and Television
Kuznetskaya
Komissar. p.
Maksima
Gorkovo
Kotel. 4. p.
Kotelnich. 5. p.
Foreign Mission Georgia
Taganskaya
Taganskaya Pl.
Kommunisticheskaya
Moscow Business Club
Skaz
Marksistskaya
Ozerkov. 1. p.
Zemlyachki
Osipenko
Goncharnaya nab.
Goncharny pr.
Taganskaya
19
Marksistskaya
Kamenshchiki
Vorontsovskaya
Mayakovskovo p.
Mali
Sadovnicheskaya
Vodootvodny Kanal
B. Krasnokholmskiy Most
Narodnaya
Kamenshchiki Malyye
Bolshiye
pereulok
St. Nicholas of the Miracles
Tatarsk. B.
Boat Stop
Sokol (floating)
Yurmalka
Gvozdeva
Krasnokholm. N.
Krasnokholmskaya
Tatarskaya
Bakhrushina
Novokuznetskaya
Beriozka
Novospasskiy pereulok
Novospasskiy
Lavro
Stockmann's
M. Krasnokholmskiy Most
Novospasskiy Monastery
Krestyans
Bakhrushina Theater Museum
Zatsepskiy Val
Ring
Lenin. pr.
Monet. 6. p.
Dinamovs
Verkhniy pr.
Paveletskaya
Garden
Shlyuzovaya
Shlyuzovoy Most
Kozh. pr.
naberezhnaya
Krutitski
Leninskaya Pl.
Paveletskaya
Paveletskiy Station
Krestyanskaya Pl.
Zatsepa
Pioner. M.
Kozhevnicheskaya
Boat Stop
Krut. 4. p.
Sts. Flor and Laur
Sarin. pr.
Novospasskiy Most
Krutitskaya
Krutitskiy
Pionerskaya Bolshaya
U Yusefa
Derbenevskaya
Derbenevskiy 1. p.
Kozhev. 2. p.
Strochen. M. p.
Moskva
naberezhnaya
Letnikovskaya
24
Dubininskaya
Derbenevskaya
Zhukov proyezd
Shch. 1. p.
Shch. 4. p.

Moscow City Street Map Index

ABBREVIATIONS AND GLOSSARY

B. Bolshoy, -aya, -oye: big, great
bul. bulvar: boulevard
estakada: overpass
M. Maly, -aya, -oye: small, little
most: bridge
nab. naberezhnaya: embankment
Nizhniy, -yaya, -oye: lower
Novy, -aya, -oye: new
p. pereulok: side street
pl. ploshchad: square
pr. proyezd: passage
prosek: lane
prosp. prospekt: avenue
sh. shosse: highway
Sr. Sredniy, -yaya, -oye: middle
St. Stary, -aya, -oye: old
tupik: blind alley
ul. ulitsa: street, avenue
V. Verkhniy, -yaya, -oye: upper
val: rampart, embankment

This map utilizes the most current "official" names of streets, squares and metrostations, as designated by Moscow City Soviet. There have been at least fifty name changesin recent history. These include re-naming some of the most prominent streets in the city center.Prospekt Marksa, Ulitsa Dzerzhinskovo, Ulitsa Kirova, Kalinina Prospekt and sections of UlitsaGorkovo, for example, are among those with new names. (In fact, most are returning to their previous names.) In many cases, outdated street signs are left in place until they require repair or replacement. This index which lists both the previous and currentstreet names. The maps label all features with current names only.

This index includes the Russian generic terms (abbreviated) for all the streets listed. Please notethat the generic "ulitsa" (street) has been omitted from the street names on the map.

FINDING STREETS

Alphanumeric grid coordinates printed in brackets ([A1], [B2], etc.) refer to the "Central Moscow" map. Numbers in bold refer to the map page number (those in brackets refer to the central Moscow map page number). For example, the reference to Alekseya Tolstovo ul., H14, [H14], **10 [18]** indicates that the street is at map coordinates H14 and can be found on map page 10 or on the more detailed Central Moscow map, page 18.

STREETS

BRIDGES

LOCALITIES

SQUARES

Order Form

☐ **Yes!**

I would like to order the Russian Information Services publications which I have indicated below. I have included my delivery and payment information on the reverse side of this form.

☐ **No.**

I am not currently interested in purchasing any more publications, but please put me on your mailing list of future publications. I have included the requisite information on the reverse side of this form.

Russian Information Services publications:

☐ **Russia Business Survival Guide:** The third edition of this popular guide has been wholly updated and hugely expanded. Includes business travel information, summaries and analyses of business legislation, tips on doing business in Russia, a telephone directory with over 4000 entries, an unequaled yellow pages directory of essential goods and services, a full-color city street map of Moscow, and new reference sections on Western resources for doing business in Russia. (ISBN 1-880100-06-1) **$24.50 plus $3 shipping/handling.**

☐ **Russian Business Reports:** The only business weekly on Russia and the Commonwealth published in North America. Features insightful reporting and analysis direct from Moscow by a highly-experienced group of Russian and Western editors and writers. (ISSN 1060-569X) **$495 per year**

☐ **Where in Moscow:** Ideal for the independent traveler. Includes a 24 page color city street map of Moscow, a yellow pages directory of essential goods and services and a concise white pages phone directory, with over 4000 listings. (ISBN 1-880100-08-8) **$13.50 plus $3 shipping/handling**

☐ **Where in St. Petersburg:** Following the model of ***Where in Moscow***, this is the first publication to provide a yellow and white pages phone book of essential St. Petersburg companies and businesses, plus a full color city street map. (ISBN 1-880100-03-7) **$13.50 plus $3 shipping/handling**

☐ **The New Moscow: City Map and Guide:** an unprecedented map with the most current information, including changes brought on by the recent collapse of the USSR. Created by Northern Cartographic of Burlington, VT. **$7.50 (includes shipping/handling)**

Order Form

Delivery and Payment Information

☐ Please charge the items indicated on the reverse side of this form to my credit card. I have included the requisite information below.

☐ Please find enclosed a check for the full amount of the order.

☐ Please find enclosed a company purchase order for the full amount of the order.

Please deliver to:

Name ______________________________

Company ______________________________

Address ______________________________

City ______________ State ________ Zip ________

Phone ______________________________

Fax ______________________________

Credit card information

Credit Card (circle one): VISA MC AMEX

Credit Card Number ______________________________

Exp. date ______________

Name on card ______________________________

Amount of purchase: $ ______________

Signature ______________________________

Mail or fax this form to (or call):

RUSSIAN INFORMATION SERVICES

89 Main Street, #2
Montpelier, VT 05602 USA
phone (802) 223-4955
fax (802) 223-6105

Bolshoy Kondratyevskiy per. 4
korpus 2, kv. 168
Moscow 123056, Russia
phone/fax (095) 254-9275